D1615653

CICERO

XI

THE SPEECHES

CICERO

IN TWENTY-EIGHT VOLUMES

XI

PRO ARCHIA POETA—POST REDITUM IN
SENATU—POST REDITUM AD QUIRITES—
DE DOMO SUA—DE HARUSPICUM
RESPONSIS—PRO PLANCIO

WITH AN ENGLISH TRANSLATION BY

N. H. WATTS

SOMETIME SCHOLAR OF PETERHOUSE, CAMBRIDGE

CAMBRIDGE, MASSACHUSETTS
HARVARD UNIVERSITY PRESS
LONDON
WILLIAM HEINEMANN LTD
MCMLXXIX

American
ISBN 0-674-99174-5

British
ISBN 0 434 99158 9

First printed 1923
Reprinted 1935, 1955, 1961, 1965, 1979

Printed in Great Britain

CONTENTS

EDITORIAL NOTE (1979)

THE following editions require mention:

Pro Archia, ed. A. Eberhard, rev. H. Nohl, 1926.
De Domo Sua, ed. R. G. Nisbet, Oxford, 1939.

Further information relevant to the speeches contained in this volume will be found in David Stockton's *Cicero, A Political Biography*, Oxford, 1971, and D. R. Shackleton Bailey's edition of Cicero's Correspondence (Cambridge: *Ad Atticum*, 1965–1968; *Ad Familiares*, 1977), both of which works contain full bibliographies.

PREFATORY NOTE

In translating the speech *Pro Archia* and the four *Post Reditum* I have based my text upon that of Klotz in the Teubner Edition (1866). In the *Pro Plancio* I have used Garatoni (Leipzig, 1824). I have occasionally adopted emendations of Sir W. Peterson in his Oxford Text, and have duly acknowledged such adoptions in the critical notes *passim*. I owe much to Reid's edition of the *Pro Archia*, and to Holden's of the *Pro Plancio*. Long's edition of the speeches *Post Reditum* in the Bibliotheca Classica has been of occasional use.

The following MSS. are referred to in the critical notes :—

P = Codex Parisinus 7794, 9th cent.
G = Cod. Bruxellensis (Gemblacensis), 12th cent.
H = Cod. Harleianus, 12th cent.
B = Cod. Bernensis, 12th to 13th cent.
Er. = Cod. Erlangensis, 1466.

Pet. refers to Peterson's text in Script. Class. Bibl. Oxon.

† in the text denotes that the MSS. are untranslatable; in the translation that a rendering is doubtful.

Dates are B.C. except where otherwise stated.

LIST OF CICERO'S WORKS

SHOWING THEIR DIVISION INTO VOLUMES IN THIS EDITION

LIST OF CICERO'S WORKS

LIST OF CICERO'S WORKS

LIST OF CICERO'S WORKS

THE SPEECHES OF CICERO

THE SPEECH ON BEHALF OF
ARCHIAS THE POET

INTRODUCTION

This speech, slight and unimportant in its occasion and its subject, has attained, by reason of an irrelevant digression artificially, yet withal most artistically, grafted upon it, to a fame and popularity which few of its author's weightier and profounder efforts have gained. For it contains what is perhaps the finest panegyric of literature that the ancient world offers us : a panegyric which has been quoted and admired by a long series of writers from Quintilian, through Petrarch, until to-day, when it has lost none of its lustre ; and which perhaps inspired a great Elizabethan scholar and gentleman to write of poetry that it " holdeth children from play and old men from the chimney-corner ; and, pretending no more, doth intend the winning of the mind from wickedness to virtue " :—" *haec studia adolescentiam acuunt, senectutem oblectant, secundas res ornant, adversis perfugium ac solacium praebent, delectant domi, non impediunt foris, pernoctant nobiscum, peregrinantur, rusticantur.*" [a]

Cicero undertook his defence of Archias' impugned

---

[a] Chap. VII.

citizenship in 62. As an orator he was at the zenith of his powers, and as a statesman, by triumphantly baffling Catiline's conspiracy in the previous year, he had been lifted to the height of his prestige, and had been definitely marked out as the supporter of order and senatorial tradition as against the forces of anarchy and innovation. It was in Pompey, whose triumphs over the pirates and Mithridates had made him the most powerful figure in the state, that the hopes of these were centred. Cicero had given them a handle against himself by his violation of the letter of the constitution in having had the conspirators executed without trial; and their aim was to establish Pompey as dictator, and then, by applying their handle, to bring down Cicero, and with him the whole fabric of senatorial government of which he was the avowed protector.

Prominent among Pompey's senatorial opponents was L. Licinius Lucullus, who had returned to Rome in 64, after a series of brilliant victories in the East. The fact that he had been supplanted in his command by Pompey exacerbated the mutual antipathy between them. The senatorial party looked to Lucullus to protect them against the encroachments of one who threatened to make himself a despot, and a sort of political guerilla broke out between the partisans of each.

The prosecution of Archias was an episode in this campaign of petty vexation carried on by the Pompeians against the Luculli. It was the fashion among the Roman aristocracy to adopt and patronize a tame poet or philosopher, usually a Greek, and this was the relation in which Archias stood

3

to the family of the great general. Beyond what this speech tells us, and two slight references in Cicero's letters to Atticus,[a] we know nothing of him. The enactment invoked against him was the Lex Papia, which expelled foreigners from Rome, and the prosecution endeavoured to bring Archias within its range by claiming that he had no title to citizenship. Now there were two laws, under either of which Archias might have become a Roman citizen. These were (1) the Lex Julia (90), which gave the franchise to all corporate communities (*municipia*) in Italy who desired it, provided that they had not taken up arms against Rome in the Social War (90); (2) the Lex Plautia Papiria (89),[b] which gave the franchise to any *individual* who (a) belonged to a city of Italy having treaty relations with Rome, (b) was permanently resident in Italy, and (c) reported himself to a praetor within sixty days of the passing of the law.

The prosecutor based his case on two purely technical flaws : (1) that there was no documentary evidence of Archias being a citizen of Heraclea, (2) that his name did not appear in the Roman census-rolls. Cicero counters (1) by producing eye-witnesses of Archias' enrolment in lieu of documentary evidence which could not, owing to circumstances, be forthcoming, and invalidates (2) by pointing out that on the only two recent occasions when a careful registration had been carried out Archias had been absent from the city.[c]

    [a] *Ad Att.* i. 16. 15 ; i. 20. 6.
        [b] Chap. IV.
        [c] Chaps. IV. and V.

INTRODUCTION

" Cicero's speech for Archias," says Brougham " which is exquisitely composed, but of which not more than one-sixth is to the purpose, could not have been delivered in a British Court of Justice." But, to the ancient orator, all was to the purpose which might conceivably influence a jury in his client's favour.[a] Archias the Greek made no appeal to Roman exclusiveness and contempt, but Archias the poet had done much, and might do yet more, to spread Roman fame and heighten Roman self-satisfaction. Cicero knew his jury, and skilfully weaves into his client's cause an appeal to that patriotism which was the weakness (and the strength) of the Roman character.[b]

[a] See Jebb, *Attic Orators*, vol. i. Introd. p. lxxviii. ff.
[b] Chaps. IX. and X.

PRO A. LICINIO ARCHIA POETA
ORATIO

1 I. Si quid est in me ingenii, iudices, quod sentio quam sit exiguum, aut si qua exercitatio dicendi, in qua me non infitior mediocriter esse versatum, aut si huiusce rei ratio aliqua ab optimarum artium studiis ac disciplina profecta, a qua ego nullum confiteor aetatis meae tempus abhorruisse, earum rerum omnium vel in primis hic A. Licinius fructum a me repetere prope suo iure debet. Nam quoad longissime potest mens mea respicere spatium praeteriti temporis et pueritiae memoriam recordari ultimam, inde usque repetens hunc video mihi principem et ad suscipiendam et ad ingrediendam rationem horum studiorum exstitisse. Quod si haec vox, huius hortatu praeceptisque conformata, non nullis aliquando saluti fuit, a quo id accepimus quo ceteris opitulari et alios servare possemus, huic profecto ipsi, quantum est situm in nobis, et opem et

---

ᵃ Cic. uses his client's Roman name, to produce a favourable effect. Why A. adopted the praenomen Aulus is uncertain ; Licinius was the name of the clan (*gens*) to which the Luculli belonged.

THE SPEECH ON BEHALF OF
ARCHIAS THE POET

[DELIVERED BEFORE A COURT OF INQUIRY, 62]

1   I. GENTLEMEN OF THE JURY: Whatever talent I possess (and I realize its limitations), whatever be my oratorical experience (and I do not deny that my practice herein has been not inconsiderable), whatever knowledge of the theoretical side of my profession I may have derived from a devoted literary apprenticeship (and I admit that at no period of my life has the acquisition of such knowledge been repellent to me),—to any advantage that may be derived from all these my friend Aulus Licinius [a] has a pre-eminent claim, which belongs to him almost of right.   For if I strain my mental vision far into the past, and strive to recall the most remote memories of my boyhood, the impression which such a survey leaves with me is that it was he who first fitted my back for its burden and my feet for their destined path.   If this voice of mine, trained by his precepts and his exhortation, has on some few occasions proved of service, it is my client who has put into my hands the means of succouring others and perhaps saving some, and it is to his cause, therefore, that any power of help or protection, which it lies with me to exert, should be

2 salutem ferre debemus. Ac ne quis a nobis hoc ita dici forte miretur, quod alia quaedam in hoc facultas sit ingenii neque haec dicendi ratio aut disciplina, ne nos quidem huic uni studio penitus umquam dediti fuimus. Etenim omnes artes, quae ad humanitatem pertinent, habent quoddam commune vinculum et quasi cognatione quadam inter se continentur.

3 II. Sed ne cui vestrum mirum esse videatur me in quaestione legitima et in iudicio publico, cum res agatur apud praetorem populi Romani, lectissimum virum, et apud severissimos iudices, tanto conventu hominum ac frequentia, hoc uti genere dicendi, quod non modo a consuetudine iudiciorum, verum etiam a forensi sermone abhorreat, quaeso a vobis, ut in hac causa mihi detis hanc veniam, accommodatam huic reo, vobis, quem ad modum spero, non molestam, ut me pro summo poëta atque eruditissimo homine dicentem, hoc concursu hominum litteratissimorum, hac vestra humanitate, hoc denique praetore exercente iudicium patiamini de studiis humanitatis ac litterarum paullo loqui liberius et in eius modi persona, quae propter otium ac studium minime in iudiciis periculisque tractata est, uti prope 4 novo quodam et inusitato genere dicendi. Quod si mihi a vobis tribui concedique sentiam, perficiam profecto ut hunc A. Licinium non modo non segre-

2 applied. My remarks may cause surprise; for it may be urged that the genius of the defendant is exercised in a sphere which bears no connexion with my own study and practice of oratory. But I would point out in reply that I myself have never concentrated my energies upon my professional interests to the exclusion of all others. Indeed, the subtle bond of a mutual relationship links together all arts which have any bearing upon the common life of mankind.

3 II. It may, however, be a matter for surprise in some quarters that in an inquiry dealing with statute law, in a public trial held before a specially selected praetor of the Roman people and a jury of high dignity, in the presence of a crowded audience of citizens, my speech should be made in a style out of keeping not merely with the conventions of the bar, but also with forensic language. But I crave your indulgence, an indulgence which will, I trust, cause you no inconvenience, and which is peculiarly applicable to the nature of my client's case; and I would ask you to allow me, speaking as I am on behalf of a distinguished poet and a consummate scholar, before a cultivated audience, an enlightened jury, and the praetor whom we see occupying the tribunal, to enlarge somewhat upon enlightened and cultivated pursuits, and to employ what is perhaps a novel and unconventional line of defence to suit the character of one whose studious seclusion has made him a stranger to the anxious perils of the

4 courts. Let me but assure myself that you grant me this kind concession, and I will engage to convince you of the propriety, not only of refusing to exclude my client from the civic roll, since he is a

gandum, cum sit civis, a numero civium, verum
etiam, si non esset, putetis asciscendum fuisse.

III. Nam ut primum ex pueris excessit Archias
atque ab iis artibus, quibus aetas puerilis ad
humanitatem informari solet, se ad scribendi studium
contulit, primum Antiochiae—nam ibi natus est loco
nobili, — celebri quondam urbe et copiosa atque
eruditissimis hominibus liberalissimisque studiis ad-
fluenti, celeriter antecellere omnibus ingenii gloria
coepit.[1] Post in ceteris Asiae partibus cunctaeque
Graeciae sic eius adventus celebrabantur, ut famam
ingenii exspectatio hominis, exspectationem ipsius
5 adventus admiratioque superaret. Erat Italia tum
plena Graecarum artium ac disciplinarum studiaque
haec et in Latio vehementius tum colebantur quam
nunc iisdem in oppidis et hic Romae propter tran-
quillitatem rei publicae non negligebantur. Itaque
hunc et Tarentini et Regini et Neapolitani civitate
ceterisque praemiis donarunt, et omnes, qui aliquid
de ingeniis poterant iudicare, cognitione atque
hospitio dignum existimarunt. Hac tanta celebritate
famae quum esset iam absentibus notus, Romam venit
Mario consule et Catulo. Nactus est primum
consules eos, quorum alter res ad scribendum
maximas, alter quum res gestas tum etiam studium
atque aures adhibere posset. Statim Luculli, cum

---

[1] coepit *Ernesti* : contigit MSS. : condidicit *conj. Reid.*

---

[a] The capital of Syria. [b] 102.

citizen, but even of adding his name to that roll,
supposing that he were not.

III. As soon as Archias had left behind him his
boyhood, and those influences which mould and
elevate the boyish mind, he applied himself to the
pursuit of a literary career. First at Antioch,[a] where
he had been born of gentle parents, a place which in
those days was a renowned and populous city, the
seat of brilliant scholarship and artistic refinement,
his intellectual pre-eminence rapidly gained for him
a commanding position among his contemporaries.
During his subsequent travels through Greece and
the rest of Asia, his arrival created such a stir
that the hope of seeing him went beyond the
rumour of his genius, and the hope was continually
surpassed by the wonder of his actual presence.
5 In Southern Italy at that time the arts and studies
of Greece had great vogue, and excited more ardent
interest in the towns of Latium also than even
to-day ; while here at Rome, too, owing to the
rest from civil strife, they were not neglected.
Accordingly, at Tarentum, at Rhegium, at Neapolis,
he was presented with civic rights and other distinctions, and all that could discern true genius elected
him to the circle of their acquaintance and hospitality.
So, when the voice of fame had made him well
known to men whom he had never met, he came
to Rome, where Marius and Catulus were consuls.[b]
He was fortunate to find in the occupation of that
office two men, one of whom could provide him with
a magnificent theme for his pen, and another whose
achievements could supply him with a theme, and
who could also lend him an appreciative hearing.
Immediately upon his arrival, and even before he

11

praetextatus etiam tum Archias esset, eum in domum suam receperunt. Sed etiam hoc non solum ingenii ac litterarum, verum etiam naturae atque virtutis est, domum, quae huius adolescentiae prima favit,[1] eandem esse familiarissimam senectuti.

6 Erat temporibus illis iucundus Metello illi Numidico et eius Pio filio, audiebatur a M. Aemilio, vivebat cum Q. Catulo et patre et filio, a L. Crasso colebatur, Lucullos vero et Drusum et Octavios et Catonem et totam Hortensiorum domum devinctam consuetudine cum teneret, adficiebatur summo honore, quod eum non solum colebant qui aliquid percipere atque audire studebant, verum etiam si qui forte simulabant.

IV. Interim satis longo intervallo, cum esset cum M. Lucullo in Siciliam profectus et cum ex ea provincia cum eodem Lucullo decederet, venit Heracliam : quae cum esset civitas aequissimo iure ac foedere, ascribi se in eam civitatem voluit, idque, cum ipse per se dignus putaretur, tum auctoritate et gratia Luculli ab Heracliensibus

7 impetravit. Data est civitas Silvani lege et Carbonis, SI QUI FOEDERATIS CIVITATIBUS ASCRIPTI FUISSENT : SI TUM, CUM LEX FEREBATUR, IN ITALIA DOMICILIUM HABUISSENT ET SI SEXAGINTA DIEBUS APUD PRAETOREM

---

[1] favit *Madvig* : fuerit (*some* fuit) MSS.

---

[a] The *toga praetexta* was worn until the age of seventeen by Roman youths; the terms of Roman life are applied to Archias for effect. See note on Chap. I.

[b] A Greek city in Lucania.

[c] *Lex Plautia Papiria* ; see Introduction to this Speech.

had assumed the garb of manhood,[a] the Luculli
welcomed Archias to their home. Moreover, it
speaks well for my client's inborn goodness, as well
as for his genius as a poet, that the home, which
was the earliest resort of his youth, has given an
6 affectionate shelter to his declining years. He
enjoyed at this time the warm friendship of Metellus,
the hero of Numidia, and of his son Pius ; he read
his works to Marcus Aemilius ; the doors of Quintus
Catulus and his son were ever open to him ; Lucius
Crassus cultivated his acquaintance ; he was bound
by ties of close intimacy to the Luculli, Drusus, the
Octavii, Cato, and the whole family of Hortensius ;
in a word, so honoured a position did he hold, that
he was courted not only by those who wished to
enjoy the elevating influences of hearing his poems,
but also by those who perhaps feigned a desire for
such enjoyment.

IV. After a lapse of some few years he went
to Sicily with Marcus Lucullus, and, returning
with him from that province, came to Heraclea.[b]
Full civic privileges had been accorded to this
town by the terms of its treaty with Rome, and
Archias expressed a wish to be enrolled among its
burgesses. His personal qualities would have been
sufficient recommendation, even had Lucullus not
thrown the influence of his own popularity into the
scale, and his wish was readily gratified by the
7 inhabitants. He was granted the franchise by the
terms of the law of Silvanus and Carbo,[c] which
enacts "that all who have been admitted to citizenship in federate townships must have been resident
in Italy at the time of the passing of the law, and
must have reported themselves to the praetor within

ESSENT PROFESSI. Cum hic domicilium Romae multos iam annos haberet, professus est apud praetorem Q. Metellum familiarissimum suum.

8 Si nihil aliud nisi de civitate ac lege dicimus, nihil dico amplius, causa dicta est. Quid enim horum infirmari, Grati, potest ? Heracliaene esse tum ascriptum negabis ? Adest vir summa auctoritate et religione et fide, M. Lucullus, qui se non opinari, sed scire, non audisse, sed vidisse, non interfuisse, sed egisse dicit. Adsunt Heraclienses legati, nobilissimi homines, huius iudicii causa cum mandatis et cum publico testimonio venerunt, qui hunc ascriptum Heracliensem dicunt. Hic tu tabulas desideras Heracliensium publicas, quas Italico bello incenso tabulario interisse scimus omnes. Est ridiculum ad ea, quae habemus, nihil dicere, quaerere quae habere non possumus, et de hominum memoria tacere, litterarum memoriam flagitare, et, cum habeas amplissimi viri religionem, integerrimi municipii ius iurandum fidemque, ea, quae depravari nullo modo possunt, repudiare, tabulas, quas idem dicis 9 solere corrumpi, desiderare. An domicilium Romae non habuit ? Is, qui tot annis ante civitatem datam

---

a The prosecutor, otherwise unknown.
b Social War, 90–88.

sixty days." My client had for many years resided
at Rome, and reported himself duly to the praetor
Quintus Metellus, who was his personal friend.

8   If the validity of Archias' enfranchisement and
his compliance with the law are the only points at
issue, I now close the case for the defence. For
can you, Gratius,*a* disprove either of these facts?
Will you deny the enrolment at Heraclea at the
time in question? We have here in court an
influential witness of incorruptible honour, Marcus
Lucullus, who is ready to state not that he thinks
but that he knows, not that he heard but that he
saw, not that he merely was present at the event
but that he was the agent of it. We have here a
distinguished body of representatives from Heraclea,
who have come to Rome expressly for this trial to
present their city's official evidence of my client's
enrolment. And after all this my opponent asks
that the archives of Heraclea should be brought into
court, when it is a matter of universal knowledge
that those archives were destroyed in the burning
of the record-office during the Italian war.*b* It
is absurd to ignore the evidence which lies to
our hand, and to demand evidence which cannot
possibly be produced; to shut the ears to the
record of living men, and to insist that a written
record should be forthcoming. You have the statement of a noble gentleman, whose word is his bond.
You have the sworn asseveration of an incorruptible
corporation. There can be no tampering with these;
yet you wave them aside, and demand documentary
evidence, though in the same breath you admit its
9 corruptibility. Or do you deny that my client resided
at Rome, when for so many years before he was

sedem omnium rerum ac fortunarum suarum Romae
collocavit? An non est professus? Immo vero
iis tabulis professus, quae solae ex illa professione
collegioque praetorum obtinent publicarum tabu-
larum auctoritatem.

V. Nam cum Appii tabulae negligentius ad-
servatae dicerentur, Gabinii, quamdiu incolumis fuit,
levitas, post damnationem calamitas omnem tabu-
larum fidem resignasset, Metellus, homo sanctissimus
modestissimusque omnium, tanta diligentia fuit, ut
ad L. Lentulum praetorem et ad iudices venerit et
unius nominis litura se commotum esse dixerit.
His igitur tabulis nullam lituram in nomine A.
10 Licinii videtis. Quae cum ita sint, quid est quod
de eius civitate dubitetis, praesertim cum aliis
quoque in civitatibus fuerit ascriptus? Etenim
cum mediocribus multis et aut nulla aut humili
aliqua arte praeditis gratuito civitatem in Graecia
homines impertiebant, Reginos credo aut Locrenses
aut Neapolitanos aut Tarentinos, quod scaenicis
artificibus largiri solebant, id huic summa ingenii
praedito gloria noluisse! Quid? cum ceteri non
modo post civitatem datam, sed etiam post legem

---

[a] Probably the father of P. Clodius, who was later Cicero's
enemy.
[b] *i.e.* of Magna Graecia, as is clear from the context.
[c] In Republican times the actor's profession was considered beneath Roman dignity.

16

admitted to the franchise he had made Rome the
depositary of all his possessions and all his hopes?
Or did he fail to report himself? No; he did report
himself; and, what is more, out of all the declarations made at that time before the board of praetors,
his alone was supported by documents which possess
all the weight of official sanction.

V. For though the burgess-rolls of Appius,[a] so it
was alleged, had been carelessly kept, and though
the authenticity of all such documents had been
impaired by the frivolity of Gabinius, so long
as his reputation survived, and by his downfall,
after his conviction, yet Metellus, that most
conscientious and discreet of men, displayed in
regard to them such scrupulous accuracy that he
came to Lucius Lentulus the praetor, and a jury,
and professed himself deeply embarrassed by the
erasure of a single entry. These, then, are the
rolls; and here no erasure is to be seen in the entry
10 of Aulus Licinius' name. This being so, what
grounds have you for questioning his enfranchisement, especially as his name is to be found on
the rolls of other cities as well as Heraclea?
Citizens of the ancient Greek states[b] often went
out of their way to associate with themselves in
their civic privileges undistinguished men, of
unimportant attainments, or of no attainments
at all; and you would have me believe that
the citizens of Rhegium or Locri, Neapolis or
Tarentum, withheld from a brilliant genius like my
client an honour which was commonly bestowed
by them on play-actors.[c] Others have found some
way of creeping into the rolls of the cities I
have mentioned, not merely after they had received

17

Papiam aliquo modo in eorum municipiorum tabulas irrepserunt, hic, qui ne utitur quidem illis, in quibus est scriptus, quod semper se Heracliensem esse

11 voluit, reiicietur? Census nostros requiris. Scilicet; est enim obscurum proximis censoribus hunc cum clarissimo imperatore L. Lucullo apud exercitum fuisse, superioribus cum eodem quaestore fuisse in Asia, primis Iulio et Crasso nullam populi partem esse censam. Sed quoniam census non ius civitatis confirmat ac tantum modo indicat eum, qui sit census, ita se iam tum gessisse pro cive, iis temporibus, quem tu criminaris ne ipsius quidem iudicio in civium Romanorum iure esse versatum, et testamentum saepe fecit nostris legibus et adiit hereditates civium Romanorum et in beneficiis ad aerarium delatus est a L. Lucullo pro consule. VI. Quaere argumenta, si quae potes : numquam enim hic neque suo neque amicorum iudicio revincetur.

12 Quaeres a nobis, Grati, cur tanto opere hoc homine delectemur. Quia suppeditat nobis ubi et animus ex hoc forensi strepitu reficiatur et aures

---

[a] An act for the expulsion of aliens, passed about 65; see Introduction to this Speech.
[b] 89.

the citizenship, but even after the passing of the
law of Papius[a]; my client does not even avail
himself of the presence of his name on these lists
in which he is enrolled, because he has always
desired to belong to Heraclea; and shall he there-
11 fore be rejected? You say you look in vain for his
name upon our census-rolls. Yes; it is, I suppose,
a close secret that at the time of the last census
he was with the army on the staff of the gallant
general Lucius Lucullus; at the time of the census
before that he was again with Lucullus, who was
quaestor in Asia, while in the first year[b] when
censors, in the persons of Julius and Crassus, were
appointed after his admission to the franchise, no
census of any section of the people was held. But,
since the census-roll is no proof of a man's civil
status, and since the appearance of his name there
does but indicate that when the census was taken
he lived as a citizen, let me further point out
that at that time my client, whom you assert to
have had, even in his own view, no rights as a
Roman citizen, had frequently made his will according to Roman law, had entered upon legacies left
to him by Roman citizens, and had been recommended to the treasury for reward by Lucius
Lucullus as proconsul. VI. Upon you lies the
burden of proof, if proof you can offer; for my
client will never be refuted by an appeal to any
judgement which either he himself or his friends
have passed upon him.

12   You will no doubt ask me, Gratius, to account
for the deep interest I feel in my friend. It is
because he provides refreshment for my spirit after
the clamour of the courts, and repose for senses

convitio defessae conquiescant. An tu existimas
aut suppetere nobis posse quod cotidie dicamus in
tanta varietate rerum, nisi animos nostros doctrina
excolamus, aut ferre animos tantam posse contentionem, nisi eos doctrina eadem relaxemus ? Ego
vero fateor me his studiis esse deditum : ceteros
pudeat, si qui se ita litteris abdiderunt, ut nihil
possint ex his neque ad communem adferre fructum
neque in aspectum lucemque proferre : me autem
quid pudeat, qui tot annos ita vivo, iudices, ut a
nullius umquam me tempore aut commodo aut
otium meum abstraxerit aut voluptas avocarit aut
13 denique somnus retardarit ? Qua re quis tandem me
reprehendat aut quis mihi iure suscenseat, si, quantum ceteris ad suas res obeundas, quantum ad festos
dies ludorum celebrandos, quantum ad alias voluptates et ad ipsam requiem animi et corporis
conceditur temporum, quantum alii tribuunt tempes-
tivis conviviis, quantum denique alveolo, quantum
pilae, tantum mihi egomet ad haec studia recolenda
sumpsero ? Atque hoc adeo mihi concedendum est
magis, quod ex his studiis haec quoque crescit oratio
et facultas, quae quantacumque in me est, numquam
amicorum periculis defuit. Quae si cui levior
videtur, illa quidem certe, quae summa sunt, ex
14 quo fonte hauriam sentio. Nam nisi multorum
praeceptis multisque litteris mihi ab adolescentia
suasissem nihil esse in vita magno opere expetendum
nisi laudem atque honestatem, in ea autem per-
sequenda omnes cruciatus corporis, omnia pericula

---

a Lit. "that begin early."   b Dicing was disreputable,
and forbidden by law ; cp. Hor. *Od.* iii. 24. 58.

jaded by their vulgar wrangling. Do you think
that I could find inspiration for my daily speeches
on so manifold a variety of topics, did I not cultivate
my mind with study, or that my mind could endure
so great a strain, did not study too provide it with
relaxation? I am a votary of literature, and make
the confession unashamed; shame belongs rather
to the bookish recluse, who knows not how to apply
his reading to the good of his fellows, or to manifest
its fruits to the eyes of all. But what shame should
be mine, gentlemen, who have made it a rule of
my life for all these years never to allow the sweets
of a cloistered ease or the seductions of pleasure or
the enticements of repose to prevent me from
13 aiding any man in the hour of his need? How
then can I justly be blamed or censured, if it shall
be found that I have devoted to literature a portion
of my leisure hours no longer than others without
blame devote to the pursuit of material gain, to
the celebration of festivals or games, to pleasure
and the repose of mind and body, to protracted ^a
banqueting, or perhaps to the gaming-board ^b
or to ball-playing? I have the better right to
indulgence herein, because my devotion to letters
strengthens my oratorical powers, and these, such
as they are, have never failed my friends in their
hour of peril. Yet insignificant though these powers
may seem to be, I fully realize from what source
14 I draw all that is highest in them. Had I not
persuaded myself from my youth up, thanks to
the moral lessons derived from a wide reading,
that nothing is to be greatly sought after in this
life save glory and honour, and that in their
quest all bodily pains and all dangers of death or

21

mortis atque exsilii parvi esse ducenda, numquam
me pro salute vestra in tot ac tantas dimicationes
atque in hos profligatorum hominum cotidianos
impetus obiecissem. Sed pleni sunt omnes libri,
plenae sapientium voces, plena exemplorum vetustas :
quae iacerent in tenebris omnia, nisi litterarum lumen
accederet. Quam multas nobis imagines non solum
ad intuendum, verum etiam ad imitandum fortissimorum virorum expressas scriptores et Graeci et
Latini reliquerunt, quas ego mihi semper in admini-
stranda re publica proponens animum et mentem
meam ipsa cogitatione hominum excellentium
conformabam.

15 VII. Quaeret quispiam : quid ? illi ipsi summi
viri, quorum virtutes litteris proditae sunt, istane
doctrina, quam tu effers laudibus, eruditi fuerunt ?
Difficile est hoc de omnibus confirmare, sed tamen
est certum quod respondeam. Ego multos homines
excellenti animo ac virtute fuisse et sine doctrina
naturae ipsius habitu prope divino per se ipsos et
moderatos et graves exstitisse fateor : etiam illud
adiungo, saepius ad laudem atque virtutem naturam
sine doctrina quam sine natura valuisse doctrinam.
Atque idem ego hoc contendo, cum ad naturam
eximiam et illustrem accesserit ratio quaedam
conformatioque doctrinae, tum illud nescio quid
16 praeclarum ac singulare solere exsistere. Ex hoc
esse hunc numero, quem patres nostri viderunt,

exile should be lightly accounted, I should never have borne for the safety of you all the brunt of many a bitter encounter, or bared my breast to the daily onsets of abandoned persons. All literature, all philosophy, all history, abounds with incentives to noble action, incentives which would be buried in black darkness were the light of the written word not flashed upon them. How many pictures of high endeavour the great authors of Greece and Rome have drawn for our use, and bequeathed to us, not only for our contemplation, but for our emulation! These I have held ever before my vision throughout my public career, and have guided the workings of my brain and my soul by meditating upon patterns of excellence.

15   VII. "But," an objector may ask, "were these great men, whose virtues are perpetuated in literature, themselves adepts in the learning which you describe in such fulsome terms?" It would be difficult to make a sweeping and categorical reply, but at the same time I have my answer ready. Many there have been, no doubt, exceptionally endowed in temperament and character, who, without any aid from culture, but only by a heaven-born light within their own souls, have been self-schooled in restraint and fortitude; I would even go so far as to say that natural gifts without education have more often attained to glory and virtue than education without natural gifts. Yet I do at the same time assert that when to a lofty and brilliant character is applied the moulding influence of abstract studies, the result is often inscrutably and 16 unapproachably noble. Such a character our fathers were privileged to behold in the divine figure of

divinum hominem Africanum, ex hoc C. Laelium,
L. Furium, moderatissimos homines et continentis-
simos, ex hoc fortissimum virum et illis temporibus
doctissimum, M. Catonem illum senem : qui profecto
si nihil ad percipiendam colendamque virtutem
litteris adiuvarentur, numquam se ad earum studium
contulissent.   Quod si non hic tantus fructus osten-
deretur et si ex his studiis delectatio sola peteretur,
tamen, ut opinor, hanc animi adversionem humanis-
simam ac liberalissimam iudicaretis.   Nam ceterae
neque temporum sunt neque aetatum omnium
neque locorum : haec studia adolescentiam acuunt,[1]
senectutem oblectant, secundas res ornant, adversis
perfugium ac solacium praebent, delectant domi,
non impediunt foris, pernoctant nobiscum, peregrinantur, rusticantur.

17   Quod si ipsi haec neque attingere neque sensu
nostro gustare possemus, tamen ea mirari debere-
mus, etiam quum in aliis videremus.   VIII. Quis
nostrum tam animo agresti ac duro fuit, ut Roscii
morte nuper non commoveretur ? qui cum esset
senex mortuus, tamen propter excellentem artem
ac venustatem videbatur omnino mori non debuisse.
Ergo ille corporis motu tantum amorem sibi con-
ciliarat a nobis omnibus : nos animorum incredibiles
motus celeritatemque ingeniorum negligemus ?

18 Quotiens ego hunc Archiam vidi, iudices,—utar

----

[1] acuunt *Gulielmius* : alunt *Halm* : agunt MSS.

----

a *i.e.* Minor ; the leader of the famous Scipionic circle,
and the chief promoter of Greek culture at Rome in the
latter half of the second century B.C.

b Or, reading *alunt,* " strength " ; or, reading *agunt,*
" employment."

Scipio Africanus [a] ; such were those patterns o continence and self-control, Gaius Laelius and Lucius Furius ; such was the brave and venerable Marcus Cato, the most accomplished man of his day. These surely would never have devoted themselves to literary pursuits, had they not been aided thereby in the appreciation and pursuit of merit. But let us for the moment waive these solid advantages ; let us assume that entertainment is the sole end of reading ; even so, I think you would hold that no mental employment is so broadening to the sympathies or so enlightening to the understanding. Other pursuits belong not to all times, all ages, all conditions ; but this gives stimulus [b] to our youth and diversion to our old age ; this adds a charm to success, and offers a haven of consolation to failure. In the home it delights, in the world it hampers not. Through the night-watches, on all our journeying, and in our hours of country ease, it is our unfailing companion.

17   But it might happen that we ourselves were without literary tastes or attainments ; yet even so, it would be incumbent upon us to reverence their manifestation in others. VIII. Was there a man among us so boorish or so insensible that the recent death of Roscius [c] did not stir his deepest emotions ? He died full of years, and yet we all felt that an artist of such grace and brilliance deserved immunity from our mortal lot. Merely by the motions of his body he had won all our hearts ; and shall those hearts be insensible to the inscrutable motions of 18 the soul and the agile play of genius ? How often, gentlemen, have I seen my friend Archias,—I shall

[c] The great comedian of the Roman stage.

enim vestra benignitate, quoniam me in hoc novo
genere dicendi tam diligenter attenditis,—quotiens
ego hunc vidi, cum litteram scripsisset nullam,
magnum numerum optimorum versuum de iis ipsis
rebus, quae tum agerentur, dicere ex tempore!
quotiens revocatum eamdem rem dicere commutatis
verbis atque sententiis! Quae vero accurate cogi-
tateque scripsisset, ea sic vidi probari, ut ad
veterum scriptorum laudem perveniret. Hunc ego
non diligam, non admirer, non omni ratione defendendum putem? Atqui sic a summis hominibus eruditissimisque accepimus, ceterarum rerum
studia et doctrina et praeceptis et arte constare,
poëtam natura ipsa valere et mentis viribus excitari
et quasi divino quodam spiritu inflari. Qua re suo
iure noster ille Ennius sanctos appellat poëtas,[a]
quod quasi deorum aliquo dono atque munere
19 commendati nobis esse videantur. Sit igitur, iudices,
sanctum apud vos, humanissimos homines, hoc poëtae
nomen, quod nulla umquam barbaria violavit. Saxa
et solitudines voci respondent, bestiae saepe immanes
cantu flectuntur atque consistunt: nos instituti
rebus optimis non poëtarum voce moveamur?[b]
Homerum Colophonii civem esse dicunt suum, Chii
suum vindicant, Salaminii repetunt, Smyrnaei vero
suum esse confirmant, itaque etiam delubrum eius
in oppido dedicaverunt: permulti alii praeterea[c]

---

[a] The father of Roman poetry; born at Rudiae in
Calabria, 239.

[b] The references are to Amphion, to the sound of whose
lyre the walls of Thebes arose, and to Orpheus.

[c] A rivalry expressed in the well-known epigram:

ἑπτὰ πόλεις διερίζουσιν περὶ ῥίζαν Ὁμήρου,
Σμύρνα Ῥόδος Κολοφῶν Σαλαμὶς Χίος Ἄργος Ἀθῆναι.

presume upon your kindness, since I see you give
so careful a hearing to my unconventional digression,—how often, I say, have I seen him, without
writing a single letter, extemporizing quantities of
excellent verse dealing with current topics ! How
often have I seen him, when recalled, repeat his
original matter with an entire change of word and
phrase ! To his finished and studied work I have
known such approval accorded that his glory
rivalled that of the great writers of antiquity. Does
not such a man deserve my affection and admiration ?
Should I not count it my duty to strain every nerve
in his defence ? And yet we have it on the highest
and most learned authority that while other arts
are matters of science and formula and technique,
poetry depends solely upon an inborn faculty, is
evoked by a purely mental activity, and is in-
fused with a strange supernal inspiration Rightly,
then, did our great Ennius [a] call poets " holy,"
for they seem recommended to us by the
19 benign bestowal of God. Holy then, gentlemen,
in your enlightened eyes let the name of poet
be, inviolate hitherto by the most benighted of
races ! The very rocks of the wilderness give
back a sympathetic echo to the voice ; savage
beasts have sometimes been charmed into still-
ness by song ; [b] and shall we, who are nurtured
upon all that is highest, be deaf to the appeal of
poetry ? Colophon asserts that Homer [c] is her
citizen, Chios claims him for her own, Salamis
appropriates him, while Smyrna is so confident that
he belongs to her that she has even dedicated a
shrine to him in her town ; and many other cities
besides engage in mutual strife for his possession.

pugnant inter se atque contendunt. IX. Ergo illi
alienum, quia poëta fuit, post mortem etiam ex-
petunt : nos hunc vivum, qui et voluntate et legibus
noster est, repudiabimus ? praesertim cum omne
olim studium atque omne ingenium contulerit
Archias ad populi Romani gloriam laudemque
celebrandam ? Nam et Cimbricas res adolescens
attigit et ipsi illi C. Mario, qui durior ad haec studia
20 videbatur, iucundus fuit. Neque enim quisquam est
tam aversus a Musis qui non mandari versibus
aeternum suorum laborum facile praeconium patiatur.
Themistoclem illum, summum Athenis virum, dixisse
aiunt, cum ex eo quaereretur, quod acroama aut
cuius vocem libentissime audiret, eius, a quo sua
virtus optime praedicaretur. Itaque ille Marius
item eximie L. Plotium dilexit, cuius ingenio putabat
21 ea, quae gesserat, posse celebrari. Mithridaticum
vero bellum, magnum atque difficile et in multa
varietate terra marique versatum, totum ab hoc
expressum est : qui libri non modo L. Lucullum,
fortissimum et clarissimum virum, verum etiam populi
Romani nomen illustrant. Populus enim Romanus
aperuit Lucullo imperante Pontum et regiis quondam
opibus et ipsa natura et regione vallatum : populi
Romani exercitus eodem duce non maxima manu
innumerabiles Armeniorum copias fudit : populi

---

[a] Marius defeated the Cimbri at Vercellae, 102.
[b] The first Roman to teach rhetoric at Rome.

IX. These peoples, then, are ambitious to claim, even after his death, one who was an alien, merely because he was a poet; and shall a living poet be repudiated by us, though he is ours both by inclination and by the laws? Shall we do so, in spite of the fact that a short while ago he bent all the energies of his genius to celebrating the fame and glory of the Roman people? For in his youth he wrote on the Cimbrian[a] campaign, thereby winning the approbation of the great Gaius Marius himself, who was generally considered to be in-
20 sensible to such refinements. For indeed there is no man to whom the Muses are so distasteful that he will not be glad to entrust to poetry the eternal emblazonment of his achievements. It is related that the great Athenian hero, Themistocles, when asked what recital or what voice he loved best to hear, replied, " That which bears most eloquent testimony to my prowess." On a like foundation rested the deep attachment felt by Marius towards Lucius Plotius,[b] whose genius he thought well quali-
21 fied to perpetuate his exploits. Again, my client has treated in its entirety the great and difficult theme of the war with Mithridates, pursuing all its diverse operations by land and sea, and his work sheds lustre not only on the gallant and renowned Lucius Lucullus, but also upon the fame of the Roman people. For it was the Roman people who, with Lucullus at their head, opened up the Pontus, fortified as it was not only by the resources of its monarch, but also by an advantageous situation. It was an army of the Roman people, which, under the same commander, routed with a moderate force the innumerable hordes of Armenia. And it

CICERO

Romani laus est urbem amicissimam Cyzicenorum eiusdem consilio ex omni impetu regio atque totius belli ore ac faucibus ereptam esse atque servatam : nostra semper feretur et praedicabitur L. Lucullo dimicante cum interfectis ducibus depressa hostium classis et incredibilis apud Tenedum pugna illa navalis : nostra sunt tropaea, nostra monumenta, nostri triumphi. Quae quorum ingeniis efferuntur, ab iis populi Romani fama celebratur.

22 Carus fuit Africano superiori noster Ennius, itaque etiam in sepulcro Scipionum putatur is esse constitutus ex marmore. At iis laudibus certe non solum ipse qui laudatur, sed etiam populi Romani nomen ornatur. In caelum huius proavus Cato tollitur : magnus honos populi Romani rebus adiungitur. Omnes denique illi Maximi, Marcelli, Fulvii non sine communi omnium nostrum laude decorantur. X. Ergo illum, qui haec fecerat, Rudinum hominem, maiores nostri in civitatem receperunt: nos hunc Heracliensem, multis civitatibus expetitum, in hac autem legibus constitutum, de nostra civitate eiiciemus ?

23 Nam si quis minorem gloriae fructum putat ex Graecis versibus percipi quam ex Latinis, vehementer

---

a 73, against Mithridates.
b See Livy xxxviii. 56 ; remains of the tomb are still to be seen on the Via Appia.
c Q. Fabius Maximus (Cunctator).
d See note on Chap. VIII.

is to the Roman people, still under the directing
skill of Lucullus, that the credit belongs of having
torn away and saved the friendly city of Cyzicus
from all the assaults of the king, and from being
swallowed up in the ravaging jaws of war. To us
shall it ever be imputed with praise that under
Lucullus again we crushed a hostile fleet, slew its
admirals, and fought that astonishing naval battle
at Tenedos.[a] Ours, inalienably ours, are the
trophies, memorials, and triumphs of that campaign ;
and it is the glories of the Roman people which are
sounded abroad by the genius of those who laud
exploits such as these.

22 Our great Ennius enjoyed the close affection of
the elder Africanus, and so a marble statue of him
is reputed to have been placed even in the tomb of
the Scipios.[b] Yet we may be sure that the panegyric he bestowed upon his patron lends adornment
not only to its theme, but also to the name of the
Roman people. He exalted to heaven the Cato
whose great-grandson is now with us ; and great
glory is added thereby to the name of the Roman
people. The rule holds good in every case ; the
glory of universal Rome borrows an added lustre
from those works which distinguish the bearers of
the great names of Maximus,[c] Marcellus, or Fulvius.
X. For this reason our ancestors admitted their
author, a citizen of Rudiae,[d] to the franchise ; and
shall we eject from our franchise one for whom many
states have striven, and whom Heraclea has gained,
and constituted her citizen by due process of law ?

23 For if anyone thinks that the glory won by the
writing of Greek verse is naturally less than that
accorded to the poet who writes in Latin, he is

errat, propterea quod Graeca leguntur in omnibus
fere gentibus, Latina suis finibus, exiguis sane,
continentur. Qua re si res eae, quas gessimus,
orbis terrae regionibus definiuntur, cupere debemus,
quo manuum nostrarum tela pervenerint, eodem
gloriam famamque penetrare, quod quum ipsis
populis, de quorum rebus scribitur, haec ampla
sunt, tum iis certe, qui de vita gloriae causa dimicant,
hoc maximum et periculorum incitamentum est et
24 laborum. Quam multos scriptores rerum suarum
magnus ille Alexander secum habuisse dicitur !
Atque is tamen, quum in Sigeo ad Achillis tumulum
astitisset : " O fortunate, inquit, adolescens, qui tuae
virtutis Homerum praeconem inveneris ! " Et vere.
Nam nisi Ilias illa exstitisset, idem tumulus, qui
corpus eius contexerat, nomen etiam obruisset.
Quid ? noster hic Magnus, qui cum virtute fortunam
adaequavit, nonne Theophanem Mitylenaeum, scrip-
torem rerum suarum, in contione militum civitate
donavit, et nostri illi fortes viri, sed rustici ac milites,
dulcedine quadam gloriae commoti, quasi participes
eiusdem laudis, magno illud clamore approbaverunt ?
25 Itaque, credo, si civis Romanus Archias legibus non
esset, ut ab aliquo imperatore civitate donaretur,
perficere non potuit. Sulla quum Hispanos donaret

---

* At W. entrance of Hellespont, S. shore.
♭ Pompey.

entirely in the wrong. Greek literature is read in nearly every nation under heaven, while the vogue of Latin is confined to its own boundaries, and they are, we must grant, narrow. Seeing, therefore, that the activities of our race know no barrier save the limits of the round earth, we ought to be ambitious that whithersoever our arms have penetrated there also our fame and glory should extend ; for the reason that literature exalts the nation whose high deeds it sings, and at the same time there can be no doubt that those who stake their lives to fight in honour's cause find therein a lofty incentive to
24 peril and endeavour. We read that Alexander the Great carried in his train numbers of epic poets and historians. And yet, standing before the tomb of Achilles at Sigeum,[a] he exclaimed,—" Fortunate youth, to have found in Homer an herald of thy valour ! " Well might he so exclaim, for had the *Iliad* never existed, the same mound which covered Achilles' bones would also have overwhelmed his memory. Again, did not he to whom our own age has accorded the title of Great,[b] whose successes have been commensurate with his high qualities, present with the citizenship before a mass meeting of his troops Theophanes of Mytilene, the historian of his campaigns ? Were not our brave fellows, soldiers and peasants though they were, so smitten with the glamour of renown that they loudly applauded the act, feeling that they too had a share in the glory that had been shed upon their
25 leader ? Accordingly, if Archias were not legally a Roman citizen already, it would have been beyond his power, presumably, to win the gift of citizenship from some military commander. Sulla, no doubt,

et Gallos, credo hunc petentem repudiasset : quem
nos in contione vidimus, cum ei libellum malus
poëta de populo subiecisset, quod epigramma in
eum fecisset tantummodo alternis versibus longius-
culis, statim ex iis rebus, quas tum vendebat, iubere
ei praemium tribui sub ea condicione, ne quid postea
scriberet. Qui sedulitatem mali poëtae duxerit
aliquo tamen praemio dignam, huius ingenium et
virtutem in scribendo et copiam non expetisset ?
26 Quid ? a Q. Metello Pio, familiarissimo suo, qui
civitate multos donavit, neque per se neque per
Lucullos impetravisset ? qui praesertim usque eo
de suis rebus scribi cuperet, ut etiam Cordubae
natis poëtis, pingue quiddam sonantibus atque
peregrinum, tamen aures suas dederet.

XI. Neque enim est hoc dissimulandum, quod
obscurari non potest, sed prae nobis ferendum,
trahimur omnes studio laudis et optimus quisque
maxime gloria ducitur. Ipsi illi philosophi etiam
illis libellis, quos de contemnenda gloria scribunt,
nomen suum inscribunt : in eo ipso, in quo praedi-
cationem nobilitatemque despiciunt, praedicari de
27 se ac nominari volunt. Decimus quidem Brutus,
summus vir et imperator, Accii, amicissimi sui,

---

^a Centre of Roman culture ; mod. Cordova.

who gave it so freely to Spaniards and Gauls, would have refused it to the request of my client. It will be remembered that once at a public meeting some poetaster from the crowd handed up to that great man a paper containing an epigram upon him, improvised in somewhat unmetrical elegiacs. Sulla immediately ordered a reward to be paid him out of the proceeds of the sale which he was then holding, but added the stipulation that he should never write again. He accounted the diligent efforts of a poet worthy of some reward, bad though that poet was ; and think you he would not have eagerly sought out my client, whose literary powers were so magnificent, and whose 26 pen was so ready ? Again, could not his own credit or the influence of the Luculli have gained him his desire from Quintus Metellus Pius, who was his intimate friend, and who had presented the citizenship to not a few ? And it must be remembered that so ambitious was Metellus to have his deeds immortalized that he even deigned to lend a hearing to poets from Corduba,[a] overladen and exotic though their style might be.

XI. Ambition is an universal factor in life, and the nobler a man is, the more susceptible is he to the sweets of fame. We should not disclaim this human weakness, which indeed is patent to all ; we should rather admit it unabashed. Why, upon the very books in which they bid us scorn ambition philosophers inscribe their names ! They seek advertisement and publicity for themselves on the very page whereon they pour contempt upon advertisement 27 and publicity. That gallant officer and gentleman, Decimus Brutus, adorned the vestibules of the

carminibus templorum ac monumentorum aditus
exornavit suorum. Iam vero ille, qui cum Aetolis
Ennio comite bellavit, Fulvius, non dubitavit Martis
manubias Musis consecrare. Qua re in qua urbe
imperatores prope armati poëtarum nomen et
Musarum delubra coluerunt, in ea non debent
togati iudices a Musarum honore et a poëtarum
salute abhorrere.

28   Atque ut id libentius faciatis, iam me vobis,
iudices, indicabo et de meo quodam amore gloriae
nimis acri fortasse, verum tamen honesto vobis
confitebor. Nam quas res nos in consulatu nostro
vobiscum simul pro salute huius urbis atque imperii
et pro vita civium proque universa re publica
gessimus, attigit hic versibus atque inchoavit:
quibus auditis, quod mihi magna res et iucunda
visa est, hunc ad perficiendum adhortatus[1] sum.
Nullam enim virtus aliam mercedem laborum
periculorumque desiderat praeter hanc laudis et
gloriae: qua quidem detracta, iudices, quid est
quod in hoc tam exiguo vitae curriculo et tam brevi
29 tantis nos in laboribus exerceamus? Certe, si nihil
animus praesentiret in posterum et si quibus
regionibus vitae spatium circumscriptum est, eisdem
omnes cogitationes terminaret suas, nec tantis se
laboribus frangeret neque tot curis vigiliisque
angeretur nec totiens de ipsa vita dimicaret. Nunc
insidet quaedam in optimo quoque virtus, quae

---

[1] adornavi *Klotz and Halm* (*foll. G* adortavi).

---

[a] See note on *Pro Plancio*, Chap. XXIV.

temples and monuments which he raised with the poems of his friend Accius [a]; more, the great Fulvius, who took Ennius with him upon his Aetolian campaign, had no misgivings in dedicating to the Muses the spoils of the god of war. Surely, then, in a city where honour has been paid to the name of poet and the shrines of the Muses by generals who have scarce doffed the panoply of battle, it would ill befit a jury of peaceful citizens to disdain to pay respect to the Muses by extending protection to their bard.

28 And the more to incline you so to do, gentlemen of the jury, I will now proceed to open to you my heart, and confess to you my own passion, if I may so describe it, for fame, a passion over-keen perhaps, but assuredly honourable. The measures which I, jointly with you, undertook in my consulship for the safety of the empire, the lives of our citizens, and the common weal of the state, have been taken by my client as the subject of a poem which he has begun; he read this to me, and the work struck me as at once so forcible and so interesting, that I encouraged him to complete it. For magnanimity looks for no other recognition of its toils and dangers save praise and glory; once rob it of that, gentlemen, and in this brief and transitory pilgrimage of life what further incentive have we to 29 high endeavour? If the soul were haunted by no presage of futurity, if the scope of her imaginings were bounded by the limits set to human existence, surely never then would she break herself by bitter toil, rack herself by sleepless solicitude, or struggle so often for very life itself. But deep in every noble heart dwells a power which plies night

37

noctes ac dies animum gloriae stimulis concitat atque admonet non cum vitae tempore esse dimetiendam commemorationem nominis nostri, sed cum omni posteritate adaequandam.

30   XII. An vero tam parvi animi videamur esse omnes, qui in re publica atque in his vitae periculis laboribusque versamur, ut, cum usque ad extremum spatium nullum tranquillum atque otiosum spiritum duxerimus, nobiscum simul moritura omnia arbitremur ? An statuas et imagines, non animorum simulacra, sed corporum, studiose multi summi homines reliquerunt, consiliorum relinquere ac virtutum nostrarum effigiem nonne multo malle debemus, summis ingeniis expressam et politam ? Ego vero omnia, quae gerebam, iam tum in gerendo spargere me ac disseminare arbitrabar in orbis terrae memoriam sempiternam. Haec vero sive a meo sensu post mortem afutura est, sive, ut sapientissimi homines putaverunt, ad aliquam mei partem pertinebit, nunc quidem certe cogitatione quadam speque delector.

31   Qua re conservate, iudices, hominem pudore eo, quem amicorum videtis comprobari cum dignitate tum etiam vetustate, ingenio autem tanto, quantum id convenit existimari, quod summorum hominum ingeniis expetitum esse videatis, causa vero eius modi, quae beneficio legis, auctoritate municipii, testimonio Luculli, tabulis Metelli comprobetur. Quae cum ita sint, petimus a vobis, iudices, si qua non modo humana, verum etiam divina in tantis ingeniis commendatio debet esse, ut eum, qui vos,

and day the goad of glory, and bids us see to it that the remembrance of our names should not pass away with life, but should endure coeval with all the ages of the future.

XII. Are we to show so poor a spirit to the world, we, who are exposed to all the perils and toils that beset a public career, as to think that, after having lived out our allotted span without ever drawing the breath of peace and repose, all is to die along with us? Many great men have been studious to leave behind them statues and portraits, likenesses not of the soul, but of the body; and how much more anxious should we be to bequeath an effigy of our minds and characters, wrought and elaborated by supreme talent? For my part, in the very enactment of my exploits, I felt that I was sowing broadcast to reap an undying memory throughout the whole world. It may be that after death I shall be insensible to it. It may be that, as philosophers have held, some part of my being shall yet be conscious of it. Be that as it may, now at any rate I find satisfaction in the thought and in the hope.

Wherefore, gentlemen, protect, I beg of you, a man whose honour you see to be attested both by the high position of his friends, and the durability of their friendship, whose genius you can estimate at its true worth by the fact that genius itself has set a premium upon it, and the righteousness of whose cause is established by the support of the law, the authority of a municipality, the evidence of Lucullus, and the burgess-rolls of Metellus. Throughout his career he has shed glory upon you, upon your generals, and upon the history of the Roman people; he is engaged upon a work which

qui vestros imperatores, qui populi Romani res gestas semper ornavit, qui etiam his recentibus nostris vestrisque domesticis periculis aeternum se testimonium laudis daturum esse profitetur, estque ex eo numero, qui semper apud omnes sancti sunt habiti itaque dicti, sic in vestram accipiatis fidem, ut humanitate vestra levatus potius quam acerbitate violatus esse videatur.

32 Quae de causa pro mea consuetudine breviter simpliciterque dixi, iudices, ea confido probata esse omnibus : quae a foro aliena iudicialique consuetudine et de hominis ingenio et communiter de ipsius studio locutus sum, ea, iudices, a vobis spero esse in bonam partem accepta, ab eo, qui iudicium exercet, certo scio.

---

a Tradition says that this was Cicero's brother Quintus.

promises to be a glorious and undying testimony to those public perils which we have recently faced together ; and he belongs to a profession which has been universally held inviolable, both in act and word. I implore you therefore, gentlemen, if such high talent deserves any commendation from men, nay more, from heaven, let him rest in the assurance of your protection, and let it be seen that so far from being assailed by your displeasure, he has been assisted by your humanity.

2   I am sure that my statement of the case, brief and straightforward as I, true to my practice, have made it, has appealed to every one of you ; and I hope that my departure from the practice and the conventions of the courts, and my digression upon the subject of my client's genius, and, in general terms, upon the art which he follows, has been welcomed by you in as generous a spirit as I am assured it has been welcomed by him who presides over this tribunal.ᵃ

THE SPEECHES DELIVERED BY CICERO AFTER HIS RETURN FROM EXILE

Including (1) Before the Senate, (2) Before the People, (3) Concerning his House, (4) Concerning the Response of the Soothsayers

INTRODUCTION

Sketch of Events leading up to Cicero's Exile and Return.—In 62, the year following Cicero's consulship, Pompey returned from the East, and in 61 celebrated his triumph. Treated coldly by a suspicious senate, and disdaining to ally himself with the popular party which had been discredited by Catiline's revolutionary schemes, he retired into inactivity. In the year following Caesar returned from Spain, and, renouncing the triumph which was his due, was elected consul for 59, the recognized leader of the democrats. With a view to the humiliation of the senate, an informal coalition —generally known as the " First Triumvirate "— was formed by Caesar, Pompey, and Crassus ; Cicero was sounded as to his attitude, but refused to be detached from the conservative cause. Caesar, having passed measures for the satisfaction of Pompey's veterans, according to compact, and for his own tenure of command in Gaul for five years,

43

left Rome for his legions in 58, leaving his tool, the dissolute and anarchical Clodius, to watch over his interests in the city. Clodius' first object was to remove Cicero, whose uncompromising attitude was a standing menace to the " Triumvirate." He carried a decree pronouncing sentence of banishment against anyone who had put a Roman citizen to death without a trial. The reference to the execution of Catiline's fellow - conspirators was obvious ; Cicero bowed to the storm and left Rome. A further decree was then carried, in which Cicero's name was introduced,[a] banishing him four hundred miles from Rome, and ordering that his house on the Palatine should be destroyed. Cicero retired to Thessalonica in Macedonia.

Meanwhile the arrogance and turbulence of Clodius was alienating Pompey and exasperating the senate. Efforts were made by his fellow-tribunes to pass measures for Cicero's recall, but Clodius' gangs of ruffians frustrated all attempts at legislation. Finally, in the middle of 57, the senate called on the country voters to attend the assembly in force, and on August 4 a bill for his restoration was passed. He entered Rome in triumph on September 4. On the following day he returned thanks to the senate for his restoration in the speech which is most probably (for it has been doubted) that which has come down to us. Two days later he thanked the people at a mass meeting.[b]

---

[a] This was the *privilegium* or law directed against a specified individual which so aroused Cicero's wrath ; see *In senatu*, Chap. II. ; *De domo*, Chap. XVII.

[b] The events of these days are most vividly narrated by Cicero in a letter to Atticus (iv. 1).

INTRODUCTION

But as yet Cicero did not look upon his restoration as complete. In his absence Clodius had pulled down his house on the Palatine, consecrated the site, and erected thereon a monument to Liberty, hoping thereby to place it beyond recovery by its owner. At the end of September Cicero appealed to the senate to declare the consecration null and void, and on the question being referred by the senate to the College of Pontiffs, the body with whom lay the decision in matters of public religion, the orator stated his case before them " elaborately " (*Ad Att.* iv. 2) in the speech which is the third of this series. The pontiffs gave a ruling in Cicero's favour, the senate passed a decree for restitution accordingly, and the house was re-built, in spite of Clodius' efforts to intimidate the workmen.

The irrepressible agitator, foiled for the time being, lost no opportunity of harassing Cicero. Early in 56 strange sounds were reported to have been heard in the outskirts of the city, and the senate decreed that soothsayers should be summoned from Etruria to interpret the prodigy. The soothsayers replied that the sounds were an intimation of the anger of the gods at the lax celebration of games, the desecration of sacred places, the murder of politicians, and the violation of oaths. Clodius, who was aedile in this year, asserted that the desecration alleged to have been committed consisted in Cicero's reoccupation of his house. Cicero, in the speech which we possess, delivered before the senate, retorted the charge upon his assailant, visiting upon Clodius the responsibility for all the offences which were said to have occasioned the prodigy.

45

INTRODUCTION

Genuineness of the Speeches.—For a century and a half a fierce controversy, comparatively recently laid to rest, raged around these speeches. The critics of Antiquity, of the Middle Ages, and of the Renascence accepted them without question as genuine works of Cicero, and it was not until 1745 that doubt was cast upon them by Markland. At an interval of a few years Gesner, a professor of Göttingen, delivered what was held to be a conclusive reply to Markland, and the struggle was dormant until reawakened by the great iconoclast of criticism, Wolf. In 1795 Wolf's famous Prolegomena had appeared, impugning the unity of the Homeric poems, and the scalpel which had been thus fleshed was in 1801 applied to the speeches *Post reditum.* Wolf's strictures were accepted by that sceptical age, and fifty years were to pass before any voice was heard on the other side. Long, who edited the speeches in the *Bibliotheca Classica,* did so with the avowed object of " proving them to be spurious " ; and if sarcasm and contempt could have effected such a proof, his would have effected it. The last sixty years, which have witnessed the rehabilitation of so many hastily discredited doctrines, have been kinder to the speeches. Madvig led the van of the reaction by characterizing Wolf's objections as " superficial and misleading," and the genuineness of the speeches was later defended by Hoffman (1878), Ruck (1881), and Jordan (1886). To-day they are almost universally accepted to be those which Cicero in his letters states himself to have delivered.

It is beyond denial that in all these speeches there are passages which are turgid, declamatory, and

vapid ; that inaccuracies, forced antitheses, and wearisome repetitions are common ; and that the tone is often one of puerile swagger and malignity. But to admit this is only to admit that those weaknesses which were always latent in Cicero were sometimes unamiably displayed, when circumstances were such as to undermine self-restraint and moderation. Bearing these weaknesses in mind, and remembering what Cicero had suffered, and the burst of applause in which those sufferings had ended, we shall surely have no difficulty in accounting for, and excusing, what strikes us as offensive. Add to this that the first two were probably dictated hurriedly upon the journey from Greece, and that they may have received no careful revision, and we shall have the more reason to deprecate the uncritical and temerarious ingenuity of those who would have rejected them. Madvig (*Adversaria Critica*, ii. 211) speaks in wiser tones :

" Sunt hae orationes tumidae . . . sed Ciceronis sunt, de statu deiecti, pristinum dignitatis et auctoritatis fastigium neque firmis viribus neque constanti et gravi animo repetentis, maiores quidem duae certissimae." [a]

[a] " These speeches are bombastic . . . but Cicero is their author, a Cicero cast down from his pedestal, striving with unsteady effort and with wavering and irresolute mind to regain his ancient eminence of dignity and influence; with regard to the two longest there is not the least doubt."

POST REDITUM IN SENATU

1 I. Si, patres conscripti, pro vestris immortalibus
in me fratremque meum liberosque nostros meritis
parum vobis cumulate gratias egero, quaeso obtestorque, ne meae naturae potius quam magnitudini
vestrorum beneficiorum id tribuendum putetis.
Quae tanta enim potest exsistere ubertas ingenii,
quae tanta dicendi copia, quod tam divinum atque
incredibile genus orationis quo quisquam possit
vestra in nos universa promerita non dicam complecti
orando, sed percensere numerando ? qui mihi fratrem
optatissimum, me fratri amantissimo, liberis nostris
parentes, nobis liberos, qui dignitatem, qui ordinem,
qui fortunas, qui amplissimam rem publicam, qui
patriam, qua nihil potest esse iucundius, qui denique
2 nosmet ipsos nobis reddidistis. Quod si parentes
carissimos habere debemus, quod ab iis nobis vita,

THE SPEECH DELIVERED BEFORE THE SENATE AFTER HIS RETURN FROM EXILE

[57]

1   I. CONSCRIPT FATHERS : Should the expression of my gratitude prove to be inadequate to the unforgettable services performed by you to my brother, to myself, and to our children, I earnestly beg that you will impute such inadequacy rather to the multitude of your own kindnesses than to any lack of feeling in myself. For where shall we find such fecundity of mind, where such exuberance of language, where an eloquence of so miraculous an inspiration, as to be able, I will not say fully to express all the benefits you have conferred upon us, but even to enumerate them in a cursory review ? My brother was the apple of my eye, and you have restored him to me ; he loved me dearly, and you have given me back to him. You have reunited parents with children and children with parents ; you have given back to us honour, position, wealth, a broad field of public activity. You have given back to us that sweetest of all human possessions, our country ; last and greatest, you have given back 2 to us ourselves. But if we owe the deepest affection of our hearts to our parents, since it is from them

49

patrimonium, libertas, civitas tradita est, si deos
immortales, quorum beneficio et haec tenuimus et
ceteris rebus aucti sumus, si populum Romanum,
cuius honoribus in amplissimo consilio et in altissimo
gradu dignitatis atque in hac omnium terrarum arce
collocati sumus, si hunc ipsum ordinem, a quo
saepe magnificentissimis decretis sumus honestati,
immensum quiddam et infinitum est, quod vobis
debemus, qui vestro singulari studio atque consensu
parentum beneficia, deorum immortalium munera,
populi Romani honores, vestra de me multa iudicia
nobis uno tempore omnia reddidistis, ut, cum
multa vobis, magna populo Romano, innumerabilia
parentibus, omnia dis immortalibus debeamus, haec
antea singula per illos habuerimus, nunc universa
per vos recuperarimus.

3   II. Itaque, patres conscripti, quod ne optandum
quidem est homini, immortalitatem quamdam per
vos esse adepti videmur. Quod enim tempus erit
umquam quum vestrorum in nos beneficiorum
memoria ac fama moriatur, qui illo ipso tempore
quum vi, ferro, metu, minis obsessi teneremini,

---

a There is some confusion in this sentence, and the text,
"Hunc ipsum ordinem, . . vobis," and "vobis . . . per
vos" should refer to different people, but they all refer
to the Senate. Possibly Cicero distinguishes between the
Senate generally and individual senators.

that we have received our lives, our heritage, our
liberty, and our citizenship ; to the immortal gods,
since it is by their grace that we enjoy these
blessings and others with which they have endowed
us ; to the people of Rome, since it is to their promotion that we owe our place in their most august
assembly, on the loftiest stage of dignity, and in that
chamber which is the bulwark of the whole world ;
to this body whom I have the honour of addressing,[a]
since they have often complimented us by their
most generous decrees : surely, then, incalculable
and immeasurable must be our debt to you, who
by an unique and united display of devotion have,
by one single act and at one single moment, restored
to us the affection of our parents and the gifts
of the gods, the distinctions conferred upon me
by the Roman people, and the many testimonials
bestowed upon me by you. So it comes about that,
while our debt to you is considerable, to the Roman
people great, and to our parents infinite, while to the
immortal gods we owe everything, whereas hitherto
we have been debtors to each of these in regard
to what each has given us, to you it is that we owe
it to-day that we find ourselves once more in possession of the whole.

3   II. For these reasons, conscript fathers, we feel
that, in a sense, you have procured for us immortality, a boon to which it is unlawful for mortal
men even to aspire. For when shall a time ever
come, when the glorious memory of the benefits
which you have conferred upon us shall die ? In
the very midst of the incidents to which I refer,
you were hedged about and straitly beset by the
threats and terrors of armed violence ; yet, not-

non multo post discessum meum me universi revocavistis, referente L. Ninnio, fortissimo atque optimo viro ? quem habuit ille pestifer annus et maxime fidelem et minime timidum, si dimicare placuisset, defensorem salutis meae : postea quam vobis decernendi potestas facta non est per eum tribunum plebis, qui cum per se rem publicam lacerare non posset, sub alieno scelere delituit,[1] numquam de me siluistis, numquam meam salutem non ab iis con-
4 sulibus, qui vendiderant, flagitavistis. Itaque vestro studio atque auctoritate perfectum est, ut ipse ille annus, quem ego mihi quam patriae malueram esse fatalem, octo tribunos haberet, qui et promulgarent de salute mea et ad vos saepe numero referrent. Nam consules modesti legumque metuentes impediebantur lege, non ea, quae de me, sed ea, quae de ipsis lata erat, cum meus inimicus promulgavit, ut, si revixissent ii, qui haec paene delerunt, tum ego redirem : quo facto utrumque confessus est, et se illorum vitam desiderare et magno in periculo rem publicam futuram, si, cum hostes atque interfectores rei publicae revixissent, ego non revertissem. Atque illo ipso tamen anno, cum ego cessissem, princeps autem civitatis non legum

---

[1] delituit *Er.* : deluit *P* : diruit *H.*

---

[a] P. Clodius.　　　　　　[b] Piso and Gabinius.
[c] The Catilinarian conspirators, executed by Cicero.
[d] Pompey.

withstanding, I had not been long an exile before your unanimous voice recalled me, on the motion of the gallant and upright Lucius Ninnius, than whom that baleful year found no trustier champion of my safety, and none that would have shown himself more dauntless, had it been determined to have resort to arms. Hindered from passing a measure for my recall by a tribune of the plebs [a] who, being unable of himself to mutilate the constitution, skulked behind the effrontery of another, you were never silent in my cause, but without intermission importuned for my preserva-

4 tion the consuls [b] who had bargained it away. To your interest and to your influence, therefore, was it due that the very year which I would rather have seen prove fatal to myself than to my country, found among its tribunes eight men who were ready to initiate a measure for my recall, and to bring that measure repeatedly before you. For the consuls, scrupulous in their observance of the letter of the constitution, were prevented from doing so, not by the law which had been passed in reference to me, but by that law which affected themselves. This measure was moved by an opponent of mine,[a] and it enacted that I should not return to Rome until those who had so nearly annihilated our world should have returned to life.[c] This proposal of his involved him in a twofold admission : first, that he regretted their death, and second, that the state would be in great peril, if the resurrection of her enemies and assassins should not synchronize with the recall of myself. In the very year that followed my retirement, when the leading citizen [d] of the state betook himself for safety to the shelter of

53

praesidio, sed parietum vitam suam tueretur, res
publica sine consulibus esset, neque solum parentibus
perpetuis, verum etiam tutoribus annuis esset orbata,
sententias dicere prohiberemini, caput meae proscriptionis recitaretur, numquam dubitastis meam salu-
5 tem cum communi salute coniungere. III. Postea
vero quam singulari virtute et praestantissima
P. Lentuli consulis ex superioris anni caligine et
tenebris lucem in re publica Kalendis Ianuariis
dispicere coepistis, cum Q. Metelli, nobilissimi
hominis atque optimi viri, summa dignitas, cum
praetorum, tribunorum plebis paene omnium virtus
et fides rei publicae subvenisset, cum virtute,
gloria, rebus gestis Cn. Pompeius, omnium gentium,
omnium saeculorum, omnis memoriae facile princeps.
tuto se venire in senatum arbitraretur, tantus vester
consensus de salute mea fuit, ut corpus abesset
6 meum, dignitas iam in patriam revertisset. Quo
quidem mense quid inter me et meos inimicos
interesset existimare potuistis. Ego meam salutem
deserui, ne propter me civium vulneribus res publica
cruentaretur : illi meum reditum non populi Romani
suffragiis, sed flumine sanguinis intercludendum
putaverunt. Itaque postea nihil vos civibus, nihil
sociis, nihil regibus respondistis : nihil iudices
sententiis, nihil populus suffragiis, nihil hic ordo

---

a Probably the Senate is meant.
b For 57, with Q. Metellus Nepos.

his house rather than to that afforded by the laws, when the state was without consuls, and was bereaved not only of her permanent parents *a* but also of her annual guardians, when you were prohibited from expressing your opinions, and when the leading clause of the bill of outlawry against me was being publicly read ; at such a time you never wavered in your determination to identify my safety with

5 that of the state at large. III. But when, thanks to the unsurpassed and unexampled courage of Publius Lentulus, our consul,*b* you caught on the Kalends of January the first faint gleam of dawn after the mists and gloom which had enwrapt the state throughout the previous year ; when the noble and upright Quintus Metellus had put his unbounded prestige, and nearly all the tribunes their valour and loyalty, at the service of the state ; when Gnaeus Pompeius, whose courage, fame, and achievements are unapproached in the records of any nation or any age, thought that he could safely venture into the senate ; with such unanimity did you support my restoration that, though I was absent in body, my influence had already gained

6 full restitution. In this month at last you were enabled to judge of the contrast between myself and my opponents. *I* resigned my safety that the state might not on my account be ensanguined with the blood of its citizens ; *they* considered that my return should be barred, not by the votes of the Roman people, but by rivers of blood. Hence it was that from that time citizens, allies, even kings, waited upon you in vain ; your juries pronounced no verdicts, your assemblies recorded no votes, your House lent the weight of its authority to no

auctoritate declaravit : mutum forum, elinguem curiam, tacitam et fractam civitatem videbatis. 7 Quo quidem tempore cum is excessisset, qui caedi et flammae vobis auctoribus restiterat, cum ferro et facibus homines tota urbe volitantes, magistratuum tecta impugnata, deorum templa inflammata, summi viri et clarissimi consulis fasces fractos, fortissimi atque optimi tribuni plebis sanctissimum corpus non tactum ac violatum manu, sed vulneratum ferro confectumque vidistis. Qua strage non nulli permoti magistratus, partim metu mortis, partim desperatione rei publicae, paullulum a mea causa recesserunt : reliqui fuerunt quos neque terror nec vis nec spes nec metus nec promissa nec minae nec tela nec faces a vestra auctoritate, a populi Romani dignitate, a mea salute depellerent.

8 IV. Princeps P. Lentulus, parens ac deus nostrae vitae, fortunae, memoriae, nominis, hoc specimen virtutis, hoc indicium animi, hoc lumen consulatus sui fore putavit, si me mihi, si meis, si vobis, si rei publicae reddidisset : qui ut est designatus, numquam dubitavit sententiam de salute mea se et re publica dignam dicere. Cum a tribuno plebis vetaretur, cum praeclarum caput recitaretur, NE

_____

ᵃ It is uncertain to whom this refers.
ᵇ Sestius, see note p. 74.

measures; you beheld a forum that was dumb, a senate-house that had lost its tongue, a state that was 7 voiceless and humbled to the dust. At such a time as this, when the man who, backed by your authority, had withstood fire and slaughter, had departed from you, you saw men flitting hither and thither about the city with swords and brands, you saw the houses of magistrates beset, the temples of the gods set on fire, the rods of a great man and a renowned consul *a* broken, and the inviolable person of a gallant and honourable tribune *b* of the plebs not merely defiled by the violation of a touch, but wounded with the sword and done to death. In the consternation which this bloodshed aroused, some of the magistrates, either through fear of death or despair of the state, abated somewhat of their zeal for my cause ; but the remainder were men whom neither threats nor violence, neither hopes nor fears, neither promises nor menaces nor weapons nor brands, could wean from their adherence to the authority of your order, the honour of the Roman people, or the restoration of my fortunes.

8 IV. First and foremost, Publius Lentulus, parent and guardian deity of my life, my fortunes, my memory, and my good name, realized that, could he but succeed in giving me back to myself, to my dear ones, to you, and to the state, his courage would be thereby exemplified, his affection demonstrated, and his consulship made illustrious. From the day of his election to that office, he unflinchingly expressed himself on the subject of my restoration in a manner worthy of himself and of the republic. When a tribune of the plebs imposed his veto upon him, and when that·astounding clause of the law was

57

QUIS AD VOS REFERRET, NE QUIS DECERNERET, NE
DISPUTARET, NE LOQUERETUR, NE PEDIBUS IRET, NE
SCRIBENDO ADESSET, totam illam, ut ante dixi,
proscriptionem non legem putavit, qua civis optime
de re publica meritus nominatim sine iudicio una
cum senatu rei publicae esset ereptus. Ut vero
iniit magistratum, non dicam quid prius, sed quid
omnino egit aliud nisi ut me conservato vestram in
9 posterum dignitatem auctoritatemque sanciret? Di
immortales, quantum mihi beneficium dedisse vide-
mini, quod hoc anno P. Lentulus consul populi Romani[1]
fuit, quo quanto maius dedissetis, si superiore
anno fuisset! Nec enim eguissem medicina consulari, nisi consulari vulnere concidissem. Audieram
ex sapientissimo homine atque optimo civi et viro,
Q. Catulo, non saepe unum consulem improbum,
duo vero numquam excepto illo Cinnano tempore
fuisse : qua re meam causam semper fore firmissimam
dicere solebat, dum vel unus in re publica consul
esset. Quod vere dixerat, si illud de duobus consulibus, quod ante in re publica non fuerat, perenne
ac proprium manere potuisset. Quod si Q. Metellus
illo tempore consul fuisset, dubitatis quo animo in me
conservando fuerit futurus, quum in restituendo

---

[1] populi Romani (= p. R.) *Pet.* : prefuit (*sic*) MSS.

[a] Consul 87–84.

being publicly read, forbidding anyone " to move, decree, discuss, allude to, vote upon, or witness the drafting of, a measure to this end," he treated the whole document not as a law, but (as I have already called it) as a proscription ; since according to its terms a citizen whose services to the state had been pre-eminent, and whom it mentioned by name, had been torn without trial from that state, and the senate with him. But after entering upon his term of office, he made it his first, nay, his one and only object to preserve me, and so to render inviolate to future generations your prestige and your
9 authority. Immortal gods ! how beneficently did you ordain that in that year Publius Lentulus should be consul of the Roman people ! How yet more beneficently, had he been consul in the previous year ! I should not then have needed the healing hand of a consul, for I should not have been stricken down by the wound a consul dealt. Quintus Catulus, who was not only a man of great wisdom, but an excellent patriot and gentleman, once remarked to me that rarely had there been one wicked consul, but never two, save in the dark days of Cinna^a ; and he often asserted that, for that reason, my position would be unassailable, so long as the state had even a single consul. The truth of his words would have been unimpaired to this day, if only his statement that the coincidence of two wicked consuls was an unparalleled phenomenon could have remained for ever unrefuted by experience. Can you doubt what the attitude of Quintus Metellus, had he been consul at that time, would have been, as regards the preservation of my safety, seeing, as you do, that he was a prime

10 auctorem fuisse ascriptoremque videatis ? Sed fuerunt ii consules, quorum mentes angustae, humiles, pravae, oppletae tenebris ac sordibus, nomen ipsum consulatus, splendorem illius honoris, magnitudinem tanti imperii nec intueri nec sustinere nec capere potuerunt, non consules, sed mercatores provinciarum ac venditores vestrae dignitatis, quorum alter a me Catilinam, amatorem suum, multis audientibus, alter Cethegum consobrinum reposcebat : qui me duo sceleratissimi post hominum memoriam non consules, sed latrones non modo deseruerunt in causa praesertim publica et consulari, sed prodiderunt, oppugnarunt, omni auxilio, non solum suo, sed etiam vestro ceterorumque ordinum spoliatum esse voluerunt. Quorum alter tamen neque me neque 11 quemquam fefellit : V. Quis enim ullam ullius boni spem haberet in eo, cuius primum tempus aetatis palam fuisset ad omnes libidines divulgatum, qui ne a sanctissima quidem parte corporis potuisset hominum impuram intemperantiam propulsare, qui cum suam rem non minus strenue quam postea publicam confecisset, egestatem et luxuriem domestico lenocinio sustentavit, qui nisi in aram tribunatus confugisset, neque vim praetoris nec multitudinem creditorum nec bonorum proscriptionem effugere potuisset : quo in magistratu nisi

---

^a Gabinius.

10 mover and supporter of my restoration ? But the consuls then in office were men whose minds, narrow, cringing, and depraved, were so choked and darkened with refuse that they could not endure the sight, nor elevate themselves to the burden, or even the comprehension, of the bare name of consul, its splendid distinction, and the magnificence of its sway. Consuls do I call them ? Nay, rather traffickers of the provinces, hucksters of your good name. One of them, before many witnesses, begged of me the life of Catiline, whose minion he was ; the other that of Cethegus, his cousin. History shows us no such abandoned wretches ; they were brigands rather than consuls ; for though my cause was the cause of the state and of an ex-consul, not merely did they desert me, but betrayed and attacked me, and used their best endeavours to deprive me of all assistance I might have obtained from themselves, from you, and from all other classes of the community. As regards one *a* of the two, however, neither I nor anyone else was under any 11 illusion. V. For who could hope for any good thing from one who, in his earliest youth, had degraded himself to pander openly and indiscriminately to the lowest of human passions ; who had been unable to protect his chastity from the licentious assaults of impurity ; who, having applied himself as busily to the exhaustion of his private resources as later to that of the state's, supported his destitution and extravagance by turning his house into a brothel, and who, had he not flown for refuge to the sanctuary of the tribunate, would have been unable to escape either the multitude of his creditors or the proscription of his fortunes ? Had he not,

rogationem de piratico bello tulisset, profecto egestate et improbitate coactus piraticam ipse fecisset, ac minore quidem cum rei publicae detrimento quam quod intra moenia nefarius hostis praedoque versatus est : quo inspectante ac sedente legem tribunus plebis tulit, NE AUSPICIIS OPTEMPERARETUR, NE OBNUNTIARE CONCILIO AUT COMITIIS, NE LEGI INTERCEDERE LICERET : UT LEX AELIA ET FUFIA NE VALERET : quae nostri maiores certissima subsidia rei publicae contra tribunicios furores esse voluerunt.

12 Idemque postea, cum innumerabilis multitudo bonorum de Capitolio supplex ad eum sordidata venisset cumque adolescentes nobilissimi cunctique equites Romani se ad lenonis impudicissimi pedes abiecissent, quo vultu cincinnatus ganeo non solum civium lacrimas, verum etiam patriae preces repudiavit ! Neque eo contentus fuit, sed etiam in contionem escendit[1] eaque dixit, quae, si eius vir Catilina revixisset, dicere non esset ausus : se Nonarum Decembrium, quae me consule fuissent, clivique Capitolini poenas ab equitibus Romanis esse repetiturum, neque solum id dixit, sed quos ei

---

[1] escendit P : descendit B : ascendit H.

---

[a] 67, in which year the *lex Gabinia* was passed, giving Pompey the command of this war.

[b] Clodius.

[c] Giving to a magistrate the power of suspending business in the assembly by declaring that the omens were adverse (*obnuntiatio*).

[d] When Catiline's conspirators were executed in the Tullianum, the prison on the " slopes of the Capitol," 63.

as tribune, succeeded in carrying through his bill dealing with the war against the pirates,[a] there can be no doubt that the stress of his own poverty and profligacy would have compelled him to turn pirate himself, a calling which he would have pursued with less damage to the state than he inflicted upon it when he moved, a vile traitor and robber, within the city walls. He sat and looked calmly on when a tribune[b] of the plebs enacted a law "that the auspices should be ignored, that no augural declaration should prevent the assembly or the elections, that none might lay his veto upon the measure," and, finally, "that the law of Aelius and Fufius,"[c] designed by our ancestors to be a sure shield for the constitution against tribunician assaults, "should be 12 held a dead letter." He it was, too, who not long afterwards, when a countless throng of patriots from the Capitol approached him with humble deference and in the guise of mourning, and when young men of the highest rank and the whole body of Roman knights flung themselves before the feet of a shameless procurer, brazenly, like the curled debauchee he was, treated with contempt not merely the tears of his fellow-citizens, but even the prayers of his country. And, not content with this, he actually went up to a mass meeting, and expressed himself in terms which his favourite Catiline, could he have returned to life, would not have dared to employ. He swore that he would wreak vengeance upon the Roman knights for the events of the fifth of December[d] in the year of my consulship, and for that punishment that was exacted upon the slopes of the Capitol. Nor did he stop short at words, but actually arraigned some, when he could serve

63

commodum fuit compellavit, L. vero **Lamiam,** equitem Romanum, praestanti dignitate hominem et saluti meae pro familiaritate, rei publicae pro fortunis suis amicissimum, consul imperiosus exire ex urbe iussit : et cum vos vestem mutandam censuissetis cunctique mutassetis atque idem omnes boni iam ante fecissent, ille unguentis oblitus, cum toga praetexta, quam omnes praetores aedilesque tum abiecerant, irrisit squalorem vestrum et luctum gratissimae civitatis, fecitque, quod nemo umquam tyrannus, ut quo minus occulte vestrum malum gemeretis nihil diceret, ne aperte incommoda patriae lugeretis ediceret.

13   VI. Cum vero in circo Flaminio, non a tribuno plebis consul in contionem, sed a latrone archipirata productus esset, primum processit qua auctoritate vir ! vini, somni, stupri plenus, madenti coma, composito capillo, gravibus oculis, fluentibus buccis, pressa voce et temulenta : quod in cives indemnatos esset animadversum, id sibi dixit gravis auctor vehementissime displicere.   Ubi nobis haec auctoritas tam diu tanta latuit ?   cur in lustris et helluationibus huius calamistrati saltatoris tam eximia virtus tam diu cessavit ?   Nam ille alter Caesoninus Calventius ab adolescentia versatus est in foro, cum eum praeter

---

a See *Pro Plancio,* Chap. XII. *n.*

b See *ibid.* Chap. XXIII. *n.*

c Cicero here alludes to Piso by the name of his Gallic maternal grandfather, in order to discredit him. Cp. "Transalpini sanguinis," Chap. VII.

his ends by so doing, and peremptorily ordered Lucius Lamia, a universally respected Roman knight, whose friendship with me made him a staunch adherent of my safety, and whose consideration for his own fortunes made him an ardent supporter of the state, to leave the city. When you had decreed that mourning should be worn, and had to a man acted upon that decree, as all good patriots had already done, then he, reeking with unguents, and wearing the robe of office,[a] which all the praetors and aediles had by then discarded, mocked at your garb, which testified to the grief of a grateful country. Also he did a thing which no despot has ever dared to do; he had not a word to say against your lamenting your calamity in private, but he published an edict that you should not openly bewail the misfortunes of your fatherland.

13 VI. Dignified, indeed, was the figure he presented when, in the Circus of Flaminius,[b] he was first introduced as consul to a meeting of the people, not by a tribune of the plebs, but by a past master in piracy and brigandage; when, heavy with wine, somnolence, and debauchery, with hair well-oiled and neatly braided, with drooping eyes and slobbering mouth, he announced with tipsy mutterings, and an air of sage sententiousness, that he was gravely displeased at the punishment of uncondemned citizens. Under what bushel has this mouthpiece of wisdom so long been hiding his light? Why has this curled dancer suffered his sublime virtues to lie for so long eclipsed by a life of junketings and brothelry? The other, Caesoninus Calventius,[c] has been engaged from his youth in public affairs, though he has had nothing, save an hypocritical assumption

65

simulatam versutamque[1] tristitiam nulla res commendaret, non consilium, non dicendi facultas, non rei militaris, non cognoscendorum hominum studium, non liberalitas : quem praeteriens cum incultum, horridum maestumque vidisses, etiam si agrestem et inhumanum existimares, tamen libidinosum et
14 perditum non putares. Cum hoc homine an cum stipite[2] in foro constitisses, nihil crederes interesse : sine sensu, sine sapore, elinguem, tardum, inhumanum negotium, Cappadocem modo abreptum de grege venalium diceres. Idem domi quam libidinosus, quam impurus, quam intemperans non ianua receptis, sed pseudothyro intromissis voluptatibus ! Cum vero etiam litteris studere incipit et belua immanis cum Graeculis philosophari, tum est Epicureus, non penitus illi disciplinae quaecumque est deditus, sed captus uno verbo voluptatis. Habet autem magistros non ex istis ineptis, qui dies totos de officio ac de virtute disserunt, qui ad laborem, ad industriam, ad pericula pro patria subeunda adhortantur, sed eos, qui disputent horam nullam vacuam voluptate esse debere : in omni parte corporis semper oportere aliquod
15 gaudium delectationemque versari. His utitur quasi praefectis libidinum suarum : hi voluptates omnes vestigant atque odorantur : hi sunt conditores instructoresque convivii : iidem expendunt atque aestimant voluptates sententiamque dicunt et iudi-

---

[1] versutamque *PB* : irritamque *H*.
[2] stipite *Er.* : ethiope *B*.

---

[a] The meanest slaves were commonly Cappadocians.
[b] The E. held that pleasure was the end of life.

of austerity, to recommend him, neither mental vigour, nor eloquence, nor military skill, nor an interest in the study of mankind, nor liberal culture. Had you chanced to see in passing that unkempt, boorish, sullen figure, you might have judged him to be uncouth and churlish, but scarcely a libertine 14 or a renegade. To hold converse with such a man as this, or with a post in the forum, would be all one in your eyes ; you would call him stockish, insipid, tongue-tied, a dull and brutish clod, a Cappadocian *a* plucked from some slave-dealer's stock-in-trade. But now see our friend at home ! see him profligate, filthy, and intemperate ! the ministers to his lust not admitted by the front door, but skulking in by a secret postern ! But when he developed an enthusiasm for the humanities, when this monster of animalism turned philosopher by the aid of miserable Greeks, then he became an Epicurean *b* ; not that he became a whole-hearted votary of that rule of life, whatever it is ; no, the one word pleasure was quite enough to convert him. He chooses for his mentors not those dull dotards who devote entire days to discussions upon duty or virtue, who preach industry and toil and the glory of risking life for one's country ; he chooses rather those who argue that no hour should be devoid of its pleasure, and that every physical member should ever be partaking of some delightful 15 form of indulgence. These he employs as his superintendents of carnality ; these are his detectives and sleuth-hounds in every form of licentiousness ; these are the stewards and caterers of his banquet ; these are the dispensers and assessors of his pleasures, who lay down the law for him, and

cant quantum cuique libidini tribuendum esse
videatur. Horum ille artibus eruditus ita contempsit
hanc prudentissimam civitatem, ut omnes suas
libidines, omnia flagitia latere posse arbitraretur,
si modo vultum importunum in forum detulisset.
VII. Is nequaquam me quidem—cognoram enim
propter Pisonum adfinitatem quam longe hunc ab
hoc genere cognatio materna Transalpini sanguinis
abstulisset —, sed vos populumque Romanum non
consilio neque eloquentia, quod in multis saepe
16 accidit, sed rugis superciliique decepit. L. Piso,
tune ausus es isto oculo, non dicam isto animo, ista
fronte, non vita, tanto supercilio, non enim possum
dicere, tantis rebus gestis, cum A. Gabinio consociare
consilia pestis meae? Non te illius unguentorum
odor, non vini anhelitus, non frons calamistri notata
vestigiis, in eam cogitationem adducebat, ut, cum
illius re similis fuisses, frontis tibi integimento ad
occultanda tanta flagitia diutius uti non liceret?
Cum hoc tu coire ausus es, ut consularem dignitatem,
ut rei publicae statum, ut senatus auctoritatem, ut
civis optime meriti fortunas provinciarum foedere
addiceres? Te consule, tuis edictis et imperiis,
senatui populi Romani non est licitum non modo

ᵃ C.'s daughter married C. Piso Frugi.
ᵇ Some light may be thrown on this difficult expression
by Mart. ii. 29, where we hear of a senator who wore patches
on his forehead to conceal the brands (FVR or FVG) that
betrayed his servile origin.

pass judgement upon the allotment that must be made to each several vice. Fortified by this mental equipment, he has held this sage commonwealth in such disdain as to think that all his wicked profligacy can pass unnoticed, if only he brings that brazen countenance into the forum. VII. He succeeded in hoodwinking you and the Roman people, not by those well-worn instruments of deception, wisdom, and eloquence, but by a knitted forehead and a disdainful air ; but me he could not hoodwink ; for I was connected by marriage *a* with the Pisos, and knew how far the Transalpine strain which he inherited from his mother had distinguished
16 him from the family type. Did you dare, Lucius Piso, bold of eye rather than of mind, fortified by insolence rather than innocence, relying on high disdain rather than high deeds (for I cannot accuse you of such), to unite your ingenuity with Aulus Gabinius for my downfall ? Did the perfume of his unguents, the vinous reeking of his breath, the brand of the curling-iron upon his brow, never suggest to you the thought that your actual resemblance to him in character would make it impossible for you any longer to avail yourself of any covering for your own brow *b* in order to dissemble your heinous wickedness ? Did you dare to co-operate with him to barter away, by means of an agreement concerning the assignation of provinces, the dignity of a consul, the security of the state, the authority of the senate, and the property of a benefactor of his country ? It was in your consulship, by your edicts, and in virtue of the powers which reposed in you, that the senate of the Roman people was forbidden to aid the

sententiis atque auctoritate sua, sed ne luctu quidem
17 ac vestitu rei publicae subvenire. Capuaene te putabas, in qua urbe domicilium quondam superbiae fuit,
consulem esse, sicut eras eo tempore, an Romae:
in qua civitate omnes ante vos consules senatui
paruerunt ? Tu es ausus in circo Flaminio, productus
cum tuo illo pare, dicere te semper misericordem
fuisse ? quo verbo senatum atque omnes bonos tum,
quum a patria pestem depellerent, crudeles demon-
strabas fuisse. Tu misericors me adfinem tuum,
quem comitiis tuis praerogativae primum custodem
praefeceras, quem Kalendis Ianuariis tertio loco
sententiam rogaras, constrictum inimicis rei publicae
tradidisti : tu meum generum, propinquum tuum,
tu adfinem tuam, filiam meam, superbissimis et
crudelissimis verbis a genibus tuis reppulisti :
idemque tu, clementia ac misericordia singulari,
cum ego una cum re publica non tribunicio, sed
consulari ictu concidissem, tanto scelere tantaque
intemperantia fuisti, ut ne unam quidem horam
interesse paterere inter meam pestem et tuam
praedam, saltem dum conticisceret illa lamentatio
18 et gemitus urbis. Nondum palam factum erat
occidisse rem publicam, cum tibi arbitria funeris
solvebantur : uno eodemque tempore domus mea

ᵃ P. was duovir at Capua.
ᵇ Catiline and his fellow-conspirators.
ᶜ Officials who looked after the voting-tablets.
ᵈ " Arbitria funeris," so called because fixed by assessors
(*arbitri*) according to the rank and wealth of the deceased.
C. here means that the expenses of the state's "funeral"
were refunded to Piso in the form of plunder from his house.

commonwealth even by the garb of mourning, let alone by their moral influence and the expression 17 of their opinion. Did you think you were consul of Capua (as indeed you were *a* at this time), a city wherein arrogance had once her dwelling, or of Rome, a state wherein all consuls before you have bowed to the will of the senate ? When you were introduced in the Circus of Flaminius with your noble partner, did you dare to assert that you had always been of a compassionate nature ? —an expression wherein you clearly intimated that the senate and all good patriots had been hard-hearted men when they cleansed their country of a plague-spot.*b* You compassionate ! I was your connexion by marriage ; at your election you had appointed me to be first overseer *c* of the tribe which opened the voting ; on the Kalends of January you called upon me to speak third in the senate ; and yet you handed me over bound to the enemies of the republic ; with arrogant and heartless words you drove from my feet my son-in-law, your own flesh and blood, and my daughter, who was bound to you by ties of marriage ; and it was you, too, paragon of tenderness and compassion, who, when I, and the state with me, had been struck down by the blow, not of a tribune, but of a consul, were so flown with insolence and sin that you allowed not a single hour to elapse between my ruin and your rapine, not even waiting for the sighs and lamentations of the city to die down into silence. 18 The decease of the state had not yet been noised abroad, when the funeral expenses *d* were already being paid out to you. At one and the same moment my house was being plundered, was ablaze ;

71

diripiebatur, ardebat, bona ad vicinum consulem[a] de Palatio, de Tusculano ad item vicinum alterum consulem[b] deferebantur ; cum iisdem operis suffragium ferentibus, eodem gladiatore latore, vacuo non modo a bonis, sed etiam a liberis atque inani foro, ignaro populo Romano quid ageretur, senatu vero oppresso et adflicto, duobus impiis nefariisque consulibus aerarium, provinciae, legiones, imperia donabantur.

VIII. Horum consulum ruinas vos consules[c] vestra virtute fulsistis, summa tribunorum plebis praetorumque fide et diligentia sublevati. Quid ego de praestantissimo viro, T. Annio,[d] dicam ? aut quis de tali cive satis digne umquam loquetur ? qui cum videret sceleratum civem aut domesticum potius hostem, si legibus uti liceret, iudicio esse frangendum, sin ipsa iudicia vis impediret ac tolleret, audaciam virtute, furorem fortitudine, temeritatem consilio, manum copiis, vim vi esse superandam, primo de vi postulavit : postea quam ab eodem iudicia sublata esse vidit, ne ille omnia vi posset

---

^a Piso, who received the plunder in his mother-in-law's house on the Palatine.
^b Gabinius, who had a villa at Tusculum.
^c P. Lentulus and Q. Metellus Nepos.
^d T. A. Milo, who was defended by Cic. on a charge of killing Clodius, 52.

the contents of that on the Palatine were being made over to the consul,[a] my neighbour, and those of my villa at Tusculum to the other consul,[b] also my neighbour ; while, by a measure which was voted upon by the same gangs that had served you before, and introduced by the same gladiator, when the forum was empty and deserted not merely by men of sound views but even by free men, and when the Roman people were in the dark as to what was going forward, and when the senate was crushed and humiliated, two abominable and lawless consuls were being presented with the treasury, the provinces, the legions, and the posts of supreme command.

VIII. It was you, the consuls [c] of to-day, who by your courage propped the edifice of the state which our consuls of yesterday had so nearly brought tumbling about our ears ; and it was the unflinching and unflagging loyalty of the praetors and the tribunes of the plebs that supported you in those

19 efforts. What can I say of that splendid gentleman, Titus Annius [d] ? Who could ever adequately describe so admirable a patriot ? Realizing that that unprincipled citizen, whom it would be truer to call that foe whom the state nourished in her own house, must be broken by process of law, if legal action could be taken ; but that otherwise, if legal processes themselves should be blocked and rendered unavailing by turbulence, effrontery must be overcome by courage, recklessness by resolution, desperation by circumspection, violence by armed resistance, and, in a word, force by force ; he first impeached him on a charge of assault. When he saw that the object of his impeachment had abolished all judicial proceedings, he used all his efforts to prevent

efficere curavit, qui docuit neque **tecta** neque
templa neque forum neque curiam sine summa
virtute ac maximis opibus et copiis ab intestino
latrocinio posse defendi, qui primus post meum
discessum metum bonis, spem audacibus, timorem
20 huic ordini, servitutem depulit civitati. Quam
rationem pari virtute, animo, fide P. Sestius secutus,
pro mea salute, pro vestra auctoritate, pro statu
civitatis nullas sibi inimicitias, nullam vim, nullos
impetus, nullum vitae discrimen vitandum umquam
putavit : qui causam senatus exagitatam contionibus
improborum sic sua diligentia multitudini **commen-**
davit, ut nihil tam populare quam vestrum **nomen,**
nihil **tam** omnibus carum aliquando quam **vestra**
auctoritas videretur : qui me quum omnibus rebus,
quibus tribunus plebis potuit, defendit, tum reliquis
officiis, iuxta ac si meus frater esset, sustentavit :
cuius ego clientibus, libertis, familia, copiis, litteris
ita sum sustentatus, ut meae calamitatis non adiutor
21 solum, verum etiam socius videretur. Iam ceterorum
officia ac[1] studia vidistis : quam cupidus mei C.
Cestilius, quam studiosus vestri, quam non varius
fuerit in causa. Quid M. Cispius ? cui ego ipsi,

---

[1] ac *supplied by Halm.*

---

a *Trib. plebis* 57 ; nearly killed in the forum by adherents
of Clodius
b See *Pro Plancio*, Chap. XXXI. *n.*

violence becoming a means to omnipotence. He demonstrated that neither temples nor forum nor senate-house could be protected against intestine brigandage without the highest courage and plentiful resources of men and money ; and he was the first who, after my departure, relieved patriots of their apprehensions, rascals of their hopes, this order 20 of its fears, and the state from despotism. This policy found an adherent of no less courage, spirit, and loyalty in Publius Sestius,[a] who, in the cause of my safety, your authority, and the security of the commonwealth, thought it his duty to shirk no unpopularity, no violence, no assaults, and no peril of life. When the cause of the senate was being attacked in meetings held by inflammatory demagogues, he pleaded in its behalf before the populace with characteristic earnestness, and with such success, as to produce the conviction that nothing was so beloved of the people as your name, nothing ever so universally cherished as your authority. He not only employed in my defence every weapon which the tribunate of the plebs put into his hand, but he also supported me with an unofficial devotion as though he had been my brother ; his clients, his freedmen, his household, his material resources, and his letters, were devoted so generously to this end, that he seemed to be not merely the alleviator, but even the sharer, of 21 my disasters. You have witnessed the unselfish devotion of my other friends ; you know how ardent Gaius Cestilius was for me, and how zealous for you ; you know his unflinching adherence to the good cause. Need I allude to Marcus Cispius,[b] to whom I fully realize the extent of my indebted-

75

parenti fratrique eius sentio quantum debeam:
qui, cum a me voluntas eorum in privato iudicio
esset offensa, publici mei beneficii memoria privatam
offensionem oblitteraverunt. Iam T. Fadius, qui
mihi quaestor fuit, M. Curtius, cuius ego - patri
quaestor fui, studio, amore, animo huic necessitudini
non defuerunt. Multa de me C. Messius et
amicitiae et rei publicae causa dixit: legem sepa-
22 ratim initio de salute mea promulgavit. Q. Fabricius si quae de me agere conatus est, ea contra
vim et ferrum perficere potuisset, mense Ianuario
nostrum statum recuperassemus: quem ad salutem
meam voluntas impulit, vis retardavit, auctoritas
vestra revocavit. IX. Iam vero praetores quo animo
in me fuerint vos existimare potuistis, cum L.
Caecilius privatim me suis omnibus copiis studuerit
sustentare, publice promulgarit de mea salute cum
collegis paene omnibus, direptoribus autem bonorum
meorum in ius adeundi potestatem non fecerit. M.
autem Calidius statim designatus sententia sua quam
23 esset cara sibi mea salus declaravit. Omnia officia
C. Septimii, Q. Valerii, P. Crassi, Sex. Quinctilii,
C. Cornuti summa et in me et in rem publicam
constiterunt.

ness, as well as to his father and his brother ? They, though in a certain private action their interests ran counter to my own, effaced this unofficial estrangement by adverting to the benefits I had conferred upon the state. Again, Titus Fadius, who was my quaestor, and Marcus Curtius, under whose father I myself had served as quaestor, failed not to meet, by their zeal, affection, and energy, the claims which these relations laid upon them. Gaius Messius, actuated both by private friendship and political sympathy, constantly raised his voice on my behalf, and immediately upon my retirement he individually promulgated a measure 22 for my restitution. Had Quintus Fabricius been able, in spite of armed violence, to carry out the plans he had framed to help me, I should in January have regained the position I had lost ; his efforts for my restoration were prompted by goodwill, checked by lawlessness, and revived by your authority. IX. Finally, you were enabled to judge of the feelings of the praetors towards me by the fact that unofficially Lucius Caecilius was at pains to devote his personal wealth to my succour, and that officially in conjunction with nearly all his colleagues he initiated public measures for my return, while he refused to allow to the despoilers of my property access to the praetorian court. Marcus Calidius, too, was no sooner elected praetor than he intimated by a clear declaration how high 23 a value he set upon my restitution ; while the undivided services of Gaius Septimius, Quintus Valerius, Publius Crassus, Sextus Quintilius, and Gaius Cornutus were most generously applied to myself and to the public cause.

Quae cum libenter commemoro, tum non invitus non nullorum in me nefarie commissa praetereo. Non est mei temporis iniurias meminisse, quas ego etiam si ulcisci possem, tamen oblivisci mallem : alio transferenda mea tota vita est, ut bene de me meritis referam gratiam, amicitias igni perspectas tuear, cum apertis hostibus bellum geram, timidis amicis ignoscam, proditores non indicem, dolorem
24 profectionis meae reditus dignitate consoler. Quod si mihi nullum aliud esset officium in omni vita reliquum, nisi ut erga duces ipsos et principes atque auctores salutis meae satis gratus iudicarer, tamen exiguum reliquae vitae tempus non modo ad referendam, verum etiam ad commemorandam gratiam mihi relictum putarem. Quando enim ego huic homini ac liberis eius, quando omnes mei gratiam referent ? Quae memoria, quae vis ingenii, quae magnitudo observantiae tot tantisque beneficiis respondere poterit ? qui mihi primus adflicto et iacenti consularem fidem dextramque porrexit : qui me a morte ad vitam, a desperatione ad spem, ab exitio ad salutem revocavit : qui tanto amore in me, studio in rem publicam fuit, ut excogitaret quem ad modum calamitatem meam non modo levaret, sed etiam honestaret. Quid enin magnificentius, quid praeclarius mihi accidere potuit, quam quod

---

^a Lentulus.

It is a pleasure to put such acts on record. On the other hand, I am little loath to pass over the scandalous crimes committed against me by certain persons. To call to mind my wrongs would sort ill with my present position ; I should prefer to forget them, even were it in my power to avenge them. My whole life should be lifted to a different plane ; I should show gratitude for services received, I should cherish the friendships that have been proved sterling in the fire, I should wage war against our avowed foes, pardon my timorous partisans, forbear to expose traitors, and mollify the resentment roused by my departure by the magnanimity 24 of my return. Were I for the rest of my life permitted to discharge no other duty save that of giving proof of adequate gratitude towards merely the chief promoters and foremost champions of my restoration, I should nevertheless count the years that yet remain to me all too scanty a span even for the mere verbal expression of my gratitude, far more for its translation into deeds. For when shall I, or when shall the united efforts of all my dear ones, requite my friend and his children here [a] ? What memory so retentive, what intellect so powerful, what regard so deep, as to be able to cope with the task of repaying benefits so numerous and so great ? When I lay prostrate in the dust, he was the first to extend to me the right hand of his consular protection ; he recalled me from death to life, from despair to hope, from destruction to salvation ; so devoted was his affection, and so ardent his patriotism, that he devised a means not merely of alleviating, but actually of lending a dignity to my downfall. For what could have brought me greater pride or honour

illo referente vos decrevistis, ut cuncti ex omni
Italia, qui rem publicam salvam vellent, ad me
unum, hominem fractum et prope dissipatum,
restituendum et defendendum venirent ? ut qua
voce ter omnino post Romam conditam consul usus
esset pro universa re publica apud eos solum, qui
eius vocem exaudire possent, eadem voce senatus
omnes ex omnibus agris atque oppidis cives totamque
Italiam ad unius salutem defendendam excitaret ?

25   X. Quid ego gloriosius meis posteris potui relinquere quam hoc, senatum iudicasse, qui civis me non
defendisset, eum rem publicam salvam noluisse ?
Itaque tantum vestra auctoritas, tantum eximia
consulis dignitas valuit, ut dedecus et flagitium se
committere putaret, si qui non veniret. Idemque
consul, cum illa incredibilis multitudo Romam et
paene Italia ipsa venisset, vos frequentissimos in
Capitolium convocavit. Quo tempore quantam vim
naturae bonitas haberet et vera nobilitas intelligere
potuistis. Nam Q. Metellus et inimicus et frater
inimici perspecta vestra voluntate omnia privata
odia deposuit : quem P. Servilius, vir quum clarissimus tum vero optimus mihique amicissimus, et
auctoritatis et orationis suae divina quadam gravitate
ad sui generis communisque sanguinis facta virtutes-

---

    a Cic. elsewhere (*Pro Sestio*, 60) says that this was the
only occasion ; the command as expressed there was :
" ut . . . omnes qui rem publicam salvam esse vellent
convocarentur."
    b Consul 57.
    c P. S. Isauricus, grandson of Q. Metellus Macedonicus ;
see *De har. resp.* Chap. I. *n.*

than the decree which you enacted at his request, that all men to the length and breadth of Italy, who had the safety of the state at heart, should concentrate their whole resources upon the restitution and defence of a broken and all but shattered man like myself ? Or that the same command [a] which had been but thrice uttered by a consul in the cause of the state since the foundation of Rome, and then had merely been addressed to those who could catch the sound of his voice, might be uttered by the senate in order to rally from their fields and their townships all the citizens of all Italy for the protection of a single life ?

25   X. What prouder boast could I have handed on to posterity than that the senate had pronounced that the citizen who had not helped me had shown his unwillingness to preserve the state ? So irresistible, then, was the authority of your order and the unsurpassed qualities of the consul, that any who failed to rally at that call felt that he was incurring a criminal disgrace. It was that consul, too, who, when that incredible multitude (Italy personified, we might call it) had flocked to Rome, convoked to the Capitol the full muster of your assembly. That event enabled you to realize the force of natural goodness of heart and true nobility. For Quintus Metellus,[b] my opponent and the cousin of my opponent, no sooner gauged your inclinations than he waived all private grudges ; for Publius Servilius,[c] a man whose renown was equalled by his moral excellence and his affection for myself, by the impressive inspiration of his personality and his eloquence so called upon him to act in a manner worthy of the heroic deeds of his kindred whose blood

81

que revocavit, ut haberet in consilio et fratrem ab
inferis, socium rerum mearum, et omnes Metellos,
praestantissimos cives, paene ex Acheronte excitatos :
in quibus Numidicum illum, cuius quondam de patria
discessus honestus omnibus, sed luctuosus tamen
26 visus est.   Itaque divinitus exstitit non modo salutis
defensor, qui ante hoc suum beneficium fuerat
inimicus, verum etiam ascriptor dignitatis meae.
Quo quidem die cum vos ccccxvii senatores essetis,
magistratus autem omnes adessent, dissensit unus,
is qui sua lege coniuratos etiam ab inferis excitandos
putarat.   Atque illo die cum rem publicam meis
consiliis conservatam gravissimis verbis et plurimis
iudicassetis, idem consul curavit, ut eadem a principibus civitatis in contione postero die dicerentur :
cum quidem ipse egit ornatissime meam causam
perfecitque astante atque audiente Italia tota, ut
nemo cuiusquam conducti aut perditi vocem acerbam
27 atque inimicam bonis posset audire.   XI. Ad haec
non modo adiumenta salutis, sed etiam ornamenta
dignitatis meae reliqua vos iidem addidistis :
decrevistis, ne qui ulla ratione rem impediret : qui
id impedisset, vos graviter molesteque laturos :
illum contra rem publicam salutemque bonorum

---

was the same as his, that he had as his councillors
his brother, returned from the dead to share my lot,
and all the Metelli, those noble citizens, who were
almost roused from Acheron, and among them the
hero of Numidia, whose retirement from his country
was once looked upon as a disaster to the community,
though the actual victim faced it without even a
26 sigh. So, by the grace of heaven, he who before this
act of kindness had been my enemy now stood forth
not merely as the defender of my safety, but as the
attestor of my merits. Yes, on that day, though you
four hundred and seventeen senators were assembled,
though all the magistrates were there, one voice alone
was raised in dissent, the voice of him [a] who by the
measure he proposed signified his opinion that
the conspirators should be resuscitated even from
the dead. On that day, too, when in weighty and
lengthy terms you had declared that the state had
been preserved by my measures, the same consul
saw to it that an announcement to the same effect
should be made at a mass meeting on the following
day by the leading men of the state ; and at this
meeting he pleaded my cause with consummate
eloquence, and effected, in the presence and in
the hearing of all Italy, that no ears should be
affronted by the voice of any hireling or scoundrel
raised in bitterness or enmity against patriots.
27 XI. These efforts, the result of which was not
merely to further my restoration, but also to enhance
my reputation, were supplemented by yourselves ;
you decreed that no contrivance should be employed by any to impede your end ; that any who
should impede it should be visited with your deep
resentment ; that such impediment would constitute

concordiamque civium facturum, et ut ad vos de eo
statim referretur, meque, etiam si diutius calum-
niarentur, redire iussistis. Quid ? ut agerentur
gratiae iis, qui e municipiis venissent ? quid ? ut ad
illam diem, res cum redissent, rogarentur, ut pari
studio convenirent ? Quid denique illo die, quem P.
Lentulus mihi fratrique meo liberisque nostris nata-
lem constituit non modo ad nostram, verum etiam
ad sempiterni memoriam temporis ? quo die nos
comitiis centuriatis, quae maxime maiores comitia
iusta dici haberique voluerunt, arcessivit in patriam,
ut eaedem centuriae, quae me consulem fecerant, con-
28 sulatum meum comprobarent. Eo [1] die quis civis fuit
qui fas esse putaret, quacumque aut aetate aut
valetudine esset, non se de salute mea sententiam
ferre ? Quando tantam frequentiam in campo, tantum
splendorem Italiae totius ordinumque omnium,
quando illa dignitate rogatores, diribitores custodes-
que vidistis ? Itaque P. Lentuli beneficio excellenti
atque divino non reducti sumus in patriam ita, ut
non nulli clarissimi cives, sed equis insignibus et
curru aurato reportati.

---

[1] eo *Madvig* : quo MSS.

[a] *i.e.* of the voting-tablets.

an act of hostility to the commonwealth, the safety of patriots, and the unity of citizens, and that the man responsible for it would be made the subject of an immediate motion to your body ; furthermore, you ordered me to return forthwith, even though their misrepresentations should continue. What of the fact that you decreed that thanks should be accorded to those who had gathered from the corporate townships ? And that a request should be made to them to assemble with undiminished fervour on the day appointed for the resumption of public business ? Finally, what of the fact that upon the day which Lentulus made a day of new birth for myself, my brother, and my children, a day destined not to die with the present age, but to be held on record for all eternity,—the day, I mean, whereon he, in the assembly of the Centuries, which above all other assemblies our ancestors wished to be called and considered most authoritative, summoned me back to my country,—what of the fact that the same Centuries which had made me consul now expressed their approval of my consulship ? On that day what citizen was there who, whatever might be his age or the state of his health, did not think that a failure to register his vote for my safety would have been a violation of his duty ? When have you seen the Campus packed as it was then, with so brilliant a gathering of every order in all Italy ? When have you seen canvassers, distributors,[a] overseers, of such high position ? So it came about that by the surpassing and superhuman service of Publius Lentulus we were not merely, as several distinguished citizens have been, permitted to return to our country, but we were conveyed thither in a gilded car drawn by caparisoned steeds

29 Possum ego satis in Cn. Pompeium umquam gratus videri ? qui non solum apud vos, qui omnes idem sentiebatis, sed etiam apud universum populum salûtem populi Romani et conservatam per me et coniunctam esse cum mea dixerit : qui causam meam prudentibus commendarit, imperitos edocuerit eodemque tempore improbos auctoritate sua compresserit, bonos excitarit : qui populum Romanum pro me, tamquam pro fratre aut pro parente, non solum hortatus sit, verum etiam obsecrarit : qui cum ipse propter metum dimicationis et sanguinis domo se teneret, iam a superioribus tribunis petierit, ut de salute mea et promulgarent et referrent : qui in colonia nuper constituta, cum ipse gereret magistratum, in qua nemo erat emptus intercessor, vim et crudelitatem privilegii auctoritate honestissimorum hominum et publicis litteris consignarit princepsque Italiae totius praesidium ad meam salutem implorandum putarit : qui cum ipse mihi semper amicissimus fuisset, etiam ut suos necessarios

30 mihi amicos redderet elaborarit. XII. Quibus autem officiis T. Annii beneficia remunerabor ? cuius omnis ratio, cogitatio, totus denique tribunatus nihil aliud fuit nisi constans, perpetua, fortis, invicta defensio salutis meae ? Quid de P. Sestio loquar ? qui suam erga me benevolentiam et fidem non solum animi dolore, sed etiam corporis vulneribus ostendit.

---

a Capua, where Caesar had established a colony, 59.
b See note p. 72.   *c* See note p. 74.

9 Can I ever adequately manifest my gratitude towards Gnaeus Pompeius for having stated not merely in the presence of you, who were united in sentiment, but also before the whole people, that the safety of the Roman people had been secured by me, and stood or fell with my own ; who recommended my cause to the instructed, who enlightened the ignorant, and who employed the weight of his personality at once to crush traitors and to rouse patriots ; who not only harangued but supplicated the Roman people on my behalf, as though on that of his brother or parent ; who, though in his apprehension of sanguinary encounters he shut himself in his own house, had even then requested the tribunes of the year before to promulgate and introduce a measure for my restoration ; who, during his own tenure of office, in a recently established colony,[a] where none had been bribed to interpose his veto, attested by the authority of honourable men and by official documents the arbitrary and cruel nature of a law directed against an individual, and was the chief supporter of the view that the resources of all Italy should be solicited on behalf of my safety ; and who, though he himself had always been my close friend, even exerted himself to make 30 his own intimates my friends. XII. And by what services shall I recompense Titus Annius[b] for his kindnesses to me ? All his conduct, policy, and deliberations, in a word his whole tribunate, was nothing but a firm, unceasing, brave, and undaunted championship of my well-being. What am I to say of Publius Sestius,[c] who displayed the kindness and loyalty of his feelings towards me not merely by mental grief, but even by physical wounds ?

Vobis vero, patres conscripti, singulis et egi et
agam gratias. Universis egi initio quantum potui :
satis ornate agere nullo modo possum. Et quamquam sunt in me praecipua merita multorum, quae
sileri nullo modo possunt, tamen huius temporis ac
timoris mei non est conari commemorare beneficia
in me singulorum : nam difficile est non aliquem,
nefas quemquam praeterire. Ego vos universos,
patres conscripti, deorum numero colere debeo. Sed
ut in ipsis dis immortalibus non semper eosdem atque
alias alios solemus et venerari et precari, sic in
hominibus de me divinitus meritis ; omnis erit aetas
mihi ad eorum erga me merita praedicanda atque
31 recolenda. Hodierno autem die nominatim a me
magistratibus statui gratias esse agendas et de
privatis uni, qui pro salute mea municipia coloniasque
adisset, populum Romanum supplex obsecrasset,
sententiam dixisset eam, quam vos secuti mihi
dignitatem meam reddidistis. Vos me florentem
semper ornastis, laborantem mutatione vestis et
prope luctu vestro quoad licuit defendistis. Nostra
memoria senatores ne in suis quidem periculis mutare
vestem solebant : in meo periculo senatus veste
mutata fuit quoad licuit per eorum edicta, qui mea

---

a Pompey   b See *Pro Plancio*, Chap. XII. *n.*

88

And to each one of you, conscript fathers, I have already expressed, and shall continue to express, my gratitude. At the outset I thanked you collectively to the best of my ability ; to thank you with eloquence adequate to the occasion is beyond me. And although many have laid me under deep obligations, which it is impossible to pass over in silence, nevertheless both my situation and my scruples forbid me to attempt to particularize individual instances of kindness. It would be difficult not to omit some one, yet iniquitous to omit any one. It is but right, conscript fathers, that collectively I should accord you the veneration due to the gods. But, as in our dealings even with the powers of heaven it is our custom not to address our worship and our supplication to the same deities at all times, but rather to special deities on special occasions, so shall be my dealings with my fellow-creatures. While I shall hold no time unseasonable for proclaiming and 31 dwelling upon their services to me, I have determined on this day to thank the magistrates by name, and with them one private citizen,[a] who interceded on my behalf with the municipalities and the colonies, who humbly supplicated the Roman people, and who gave utterance to sentiments in compliance with which you restored me to the proud position which was once mine. In the hour of my glory you honoured me ; and in the hour of my trial you defended me by your change of garments and, as far as you were allowed, almost by your lamentations. Within my recollection it was never customary with senators to change their garments[b] even in their own perils ; but in the hour of my peril the whole senate changed their garments, in so far as they were not prevented

89

pericula non modo suo praesidio, sed etiam vestra deprecatione nudarunt.

32 Quibus ego rebus obiectis, cum mihi privato confligendum viderem cum eodem exercitu, quem consul non armis, sed vestra auctoritate superaram, multa mecum ipse reputavi. XIII. Dixerat in contione consul se clivi Capitolini poenas ab equitibus Romanis repetiturum : nominatim alii compellabantur, alii citabantur, alii relegabantur : aditus templorum erant non solum praesidiis et manu, verum etiam demolitione sublati. Alter consul, ut me et rem publicam non modo desereret, sed etiam hostibus rei publicae proderet, pactionibus se suorum praemiorum obligarat. Erat alius ad portas cum imperio in multos annos magnoque exercitu, quem ego inimicum mihi fuisse non dico, tacuisse, cum

33 diceretur esse inimicus, scio. Duae partes esse in re publica cum putarentur, altera me deposcere propter inimicitias, altera timide defendere propter suspitionem caedis putabatur. Qui autem me deposcere videbantur, ii hoc auxerunt dimicationis metum, quod numquam infitiando suspitionem hominum curamque minuerunt. Qua re cum viderem senatum ducibus orbatum, me a magistratibus partim oppugnatum, partim proditum, partim

---

^a See note on Chap. V.   ^b Caesar.

from doing so by the edicts of those who robbed me in my perilous situation not only of their own protection but of your intercession.

2   Faced by these difficulties, and seeing that in my private capacity I was called upon to sustain the onset of the same forces which, when consul, I had mastered not by arms but by your moral support, many reflections occurred to me. XIII. The consul had said at a mass meeting that he would exact from Roman knights satisfaction for the deed wrought upon the slope of the Capitol.^a By express nomination some were arraigned, others cited to appear in court, others banished. Access to the temples was barred, not merely by armed guards, but even by destruction of the steps. The other consul had engaged himself by bargaining for his rewards not only to desert me and the state, but also to betray us to the state's enemies. There was another ^b who hovered at the city gates with a large army and with a command which was prolonged to him for many years. He I do not say was my enemy ; but I do know that when he was stated to be my enemy

33 he never uttered a word of denial. Two parties were held to exist in the state, one of which, it was supposed, was led by hostility towards me to demand my surrender, while the other was backward in my defence, because of the taint of murder which they thought clung to me. Those who were supposed to demand my surrender increased the apprehension of an armed struggle, because they never by any disclaimer allayed the general suspicion and anxiety. Consequently, realizing, as I did, that the senate was bereft of leaders, that the magistrates had either attacked me, betrayed me, or deserted me,

derelictum, servos simulatione collegiorum nominatim esse conscriptos, copias omnes Catilinae paene iisdem ducibus ad spem caedis et incendiorum esse revocatas, equites Romanos proscriptionis, municipia vastitatis, omnes caedis metu esse permotos, potui, potui, patres conscripti, multis auctoribus fortissimis viris me vi armisque defendere, nec mihi ipsi ille animus idem meus vobis non incognitus defuit. Sed videbam, si vicissem praesentem adversarium, nimium multos mihi alios esse vincendos : si victus essem, multis bonis et pro me et mecum etiam post me esse pereundum, tribuniciique sanguinis ultores esse praesentes, meae mortis poenas iudicio et posteritati 34 reservari. XIV. Nolui, cum consul communem salutem sine ferro defendissem, meam privatus armis defendere, bonosque viros lugere malui meas fortunas quam suis desperare : ac si solus essem interfectus, mihi turpe, si cum multis, rei publicae funestum fore videbatur. Quod si mihi aeternam esse aerumnam propositam arbitrarer, morte me ipse potius quam sempiterno dolore multassem. Sed cum viderem me non diutius quam ipsam rem

---

* Sestius ; see Chap. VIII. *n.*

and that slaves had been enrolled by name under plea of being formed into clubs, that all Catiline's forces with scarcely any change of leaders had been led to renew their hopes for opportunities of slaughter and incendiarism, that Roman knights were stirred by apprehension of a proscription, the municipalities of devastation, and all men by dread of a violent death, then I might, conscript fathers, I say I *might*, have defended myself by armed force, and have been supported in that policy by many gallant gentlemen ; and indeed that same courage, of which I have afforded you proof in the past, was still with me then. But I saw that, if I proved victorious over my immediate foe, there would still be others, too many others, whom I should have to vanquish ; and if, on the other hand, I were defeated, many good patriots would shortly have to meet their doom with me, for me, even after me, and while the blood of a tribune*a* might find immediate avengers, retribution for my own death was reserved for 34 the verdict of later generations. XIV. Since, as consul, I had looked for no assistance from the sword in my championship of the universal welfare, I shrank from employing arms in the defence of my own ; and I preferred that the patriotic party should lament my condition rather than despair for their own. Should I prove the sole victim, disgrace was in prospect for myself ; but should others fall along with me, ruin was in prospect for the state. But if I had thought that an eternity of mortification was in store for me, I should rather have inflicted death upon myself than unending sorrow. But realizing that my absence from this city would not outlast the absence from it of the

publicam ex hac urbe afuturum, neque ego illa
exterminata mihi remanendum putavi et illa, simul
atque revocata est, me secum pariter reportavit.
Mecum leges, mecum quaestiones, mecum iura
magistratuum, mecum senatus auctoritas, mecum
libertas, mecum etiam frugum ubertas, mecum
deorum et hominum sanctitates omnes et religiones
afuerunt. Quae si semper abessent, magis vestras
fortunas lugerem quam desiderarem meas : sin
aliquando revocarentur, intelligebam mihi cum illis
35 una esse redeundum. Cuius mei sensus certissimus
testis est hic idem, qui custos capitis fuit, Cn.
Plancius, qui omnibus provincialibus ornamentis
commodisque depositis totam suam quaesturam in
me sustentando et conservando collocavit. Qui si
mihi quaestor imperatori fuisset, in filii loco fuisset :
nunc certe erit in parentis, cum fuerit consors [1]
non imperii, sed doloris mei.

36 Quapropter, patres conscripti, quoniam in rem
publicam sum pariter cum re publica restitutus,
non modo in ea defendenda nihil imminuam de
libertate mea pristina, sed etiam adaugebo. XV.
Etenim si eam tum defendebam, cum mihi aliquid
illa debebat, quid nunc me facere oportet, cum
ego illi plurimum debeo ? Nam quid est quod
animum meum frangere aut debilitare possit, cuius
ipsam calamitatem non modo nullius delicti, sed
etiam binorum in rem publicam beneficiorum testem

---

[1] consors *Pet.* : quaestor MSS.

---

[a] "The 'res publica' was . . . sent out of the limits of
the city, when C. was, or rather it was sent out before he
went, and he would not stay after it was gone " (Long).

republic itself, I did not think it my duty to remain there after its extinction, and, what is more, no sooner was it recalled than it brought me back in its company.[a] My absence synchronized with the absence of laws, courts of justice, magisterial jurisdiction, the authority of the senate, freedom, a plentiful corn-supply, all reverence and all compunction in matters human or divine. Were these things to be lost to us for ever, I should rather bewail your misfortune than regret my own ; but I recognized that, should a day come when they should be recalled, it would be my duty to return with

35 them. Here again infallible testimony is borne to these convictions of mine by Gnaeus Plancius,[b] who acted as the guardian of my person, and who laid aside all the distinctions and material advantages of his provincial command that he might devote his whole quaestorship to my support and preservation. Had I been a general, and he my quaestor, I should have viewed him as a son ; now, since he has been associated with me not in command but in calamity, I shall at all events view him as a parent.

36 Wherefore, conscript fathers, since I have been restored to the state along with the state, so far from abating in her defence aught of my old freedom of speech, I shall even add to it. XV. And indeed, if I defended her then, when she was somewhat in debt to me, what does my duty bid me do now, when I am deeply in debt to her ? For what is there that could avail to cow or enfeeble my courage, since, as you see, my very disasters bear witness, not alone to the irreproachable nature of my conduct,

[b] Quaestor in Macedonia 58; see *Pro Plancio*, Chap. XXX. *n.*

esse videatis ? Nam importata est, quia defenderam
civitatem, et mea voluntate suscepta est, ne a me
defensa res publica per eumdem me extremum in
37 discrimen vocaretur. Pro me non, ut pro P. Popilio,
nobilissimo homine, adolescentes filii, non propinquorum multitudo populum Romanum est deprecata,
non, ut pro Q. Metello, summo et clarissimo viro,
spectata iam adolescentia filius, non L. et C. Metelli,
consulares, non eorum liberi, non Q. Metellus Nepos,
qui tum consulatum petebat, non Luculli, Servilii,
Scipiones, Metellarum filii, flentes ac sordidati
populo Romano supplicaverunt, sed unus frater, qui
in me pietate filius, consiliis parens, amore, ut erat,
frater inventus est, squalore et lacrimis et cotidianis
precibus desiderium mei nominis renovari et rerum
gestarum memoriam usurpari coëgit. Qui cum
statuisset, nisi me per vos recuperasset, eamdem
subire fortunam atque idem sibi domicilium et vitae
et mortis deposcere, tamen numquam nec magnitudinem negotii nec solitudinem suam nec vim inimi-
38 corum ac tela pertimuit. Alter fuit propugnator
mearum fortunarum et defensor adsiduus, summa
virtute et pietate, C. Piso, gener, qui minas inimicorum meorum, qui inimicitias adfinis mei, propinqui

---

[a] See *Ad Quir.*, Chap. III. *n.*
[b] See *Pro Plancio*, Chap. XXVIII. *n.*

but even to my superhuman benefits to the state?
Why, the very occasion of those disasters was my
defence of the community, and they were faced by
me with cheerful readiness, in order that the state
which I had defended might not on my account
37 be brought into the extremest peril. I had not, to
plead for me, as had Publius Popilius,[a] young sons
of my own, or a crowd of kinsfolk; I had not, as
had that great and famous gentleman Quintus
Metellus,[b] a son whose qualities had won him respect
in spite of his youth; not for me did the ex-consuls
Lucius and Gaius Metellus, nor their children, nor
Quintus Metellus Nepos, who was at that time a
candidate for the consulship, nor the Luculli, the
Servii, the Scipios, whose mothers were of the family
of Metellus, intercede before the Roman people in
tears and dishevelled garb. I had none of these;
but one alone I had, a brother, who, in proving
himself a son in dutifulness, a father in guidance,
and in affection the true brother that he was, by his
guise of mourning, by his tears, and by his daily-
renewed prayers, gave a fresh lease of life to the
enthusiasm my name aroused, and a fresh familiarity
to the report of my achievements. He had made
up his mind that, should he fail, through you, to win
me back to himself, he would ask permission to meet
the same fate and to share the same dwelling with
me in life and in death; and yet, in spite of this,
no toil however formidable, no loneliness, no threat
38 nor weapons of foes, could daunt him. There was
another, too, who with the highest courage and
loyalty was untiring in his championship and defence
of my well-being; I refer to my son-in-law, Gaius
Piso, who held as of no account beside my safety

sui, consulis, qui Pontum et Bithyniam quaestor prae mea salute neglexit. Nihil umquam senatus de P. Popilio decrevit, numquam in hoc ordine de Q. Metello mentio facta est. Tribuniciis sunt illi rogationibus interfectis inimicis denique restituti, cum alter eorum senatui paruisset, alter vim caedemque fugisset. Nam C. quidem Marius, qui hac hominum memoria tertius ante me consularis tempestate civili expulsus est, non modo ab senatu non est restitutus, sed reditu suo senatum cunctum paene delevit. Nulla de illis magistratuum consensio, nulla ad rem publicam defendendam populi Romani convocatio, nullus Italiae motus, nulla decreta municipiorum et coloniarum exstiterunt.

39 Qua re cum me vestra auctoritas arcessierit, populus Romanus vocarit, res publica implorarit, Italia cuncta paene suis humeris reportarit, non committam, patres conscripti, ut, cum ea mihi sint restituta, quae in potestate mea non fuerunt, ea non habeam, quae ipse praestare possim, praesertim cum illa amissa recuperarim, virtutem et fidem numquam amiserim.

---

^a See p. 106 *n*.　　^b See p. 498 *n*.

the threats of my enemies, the hostility of the consul, who was my relative by marriage and his own by blood, and his duties as quaestor in Pontus and Bithynia. No decree was ever passed by the senate in the matter of Publius Popilius ;[a] never in this house was a word uttered concerning Quintus Metellus.[b] No ; but it was on the motion of the tribunes that they were in the end restored, after their enemies had been put to death ; and this was not until the former had complied with the senate's wishes, and the latter had escaped a violent and bloody end. Gaius Marius, indeed, the third ex-consul who, in the memory of men yet living, was banished from the state through civil disturbance, so far from being restored by the senate, even all but abolished the senate after his return. In the cases of these, there was no unity of action among the magistrates, no rallying of the Roman people to the defence of their constitution, no outbreak in Italy, no decrees passed by municipalities and colonies.

39 Wherefore, since it is your authoritative voice which has summoned me, the Roman people which has called out for me, the state who has become my suppliant, and united Italy that has brought me back, I might almost say, upon her shoulders, I shall not be so careless, now that those things have been restored to me which lay outside my own power, as to fail to hold that which my own efforts can secure, above all since, while *they* were recovered after having been lost, my virtue and my honour were never lost at all.

ORATIO
POST REDITUM AD QUIRITES

1   I. Quod precatus a Iove optimo maximo ceterisque
dis immortalibus sum, Quirites, eo tempore, quum
me fortunasque meas pro vestra incolumitate, otio
concordiaque devovi, ut, si meas rationes umquam
vestrae saluti anteposuissem, sempiternam poenam
sustinerem mea voluntate susceptam, sin et ea, quae
ante gesseram, conservandae civitatis causa gessissem
et illam miseram profectionem vestrae salutis gratia
suscepissem, ut, quod odium scelerati homines et
audaces in rem publicam et in omnes bonos conceptum
iam diu continerent, id in me uno potius quam
in optimo quoque et universa civitate defigerent,[1]
hoc si animo in vos liberosque vestros fuissem,
ut aliquando vos patresque conscriptos Italiamque
universam memoria mei, misericordia desideriumque
teneret, eius devotionis me esse convictum iudicio

---

[1] defigerent *Pet. foll. Hotoman* : deficeret MSS.

THE SPEECH DELIVERED BEFORE THE PEOPLE AFTER HIS RETURN FROM EXILE

[57]

1   I. FELLOW-CITIZENS : On the day when I vowed to sacrifice myself and my fortunes in the cause of your safety, tranquillity, and union, I prayed of Jupiter Best and Greatest, and of the other immortal gods, that if ever I had placed considerations of my own interest before those of your welfare, I might be visited with eternal retribution, which I should deliberately have brought upon myself ; but that if my earlier achievements had had the preservation of the community as their object, and if your welfare also had been the motive that led me to submit to the unhappy necessity of retirement, they should make me, and not the state at large and its patriotic citizens, the exclusive mark of the long-pent-up hatred conceived by wicked and unscrupulous men against the republic and its loyal adherents ; and that, had this been my spirit towards you and your children, a day might come when you, when our conscript fathers, and the whole of Italy, might be moved by the recollection of me to compassion and regretful desire.   And now I rejoice exceedingly that I have been held to the conditions of my

101

deorum immortalium, testimonio senatus, consensu
Italiae, confessione inimicorum, beneficio divino
2 immortalique vestro, maxime laetor.   Namque,
Quirites, etsi nihil est homini magis optandum quam
prospera, aequabilis perpetuaque fortuna secundo
vitae sine ulla offensione cursu, tamen, si mihi
tranquilla et placata omnia fuissent, incredibili
quadam et paene divina, qua nunc vestro beneficio
fruor, laetitiae voluptate caruissem.   Quid dulcius
hominum generi ab natura datum est quam sui
cuique liberi ?   Mihi vero et propter indulgentiam
meam et propter excellens eorum ingenium vita sunt
mea cariores : tamen non tanta voluptate erant
3 suscepti quantae nunc sunt restituti   Nihil cuiquam
fuit umquam iucundius quam mihi meus frater : non
tam id sentiebam, quum fruebar, quam tum, quum
carebam, et postea quam vos me illi et mihi eum
reddidistis.   Res familiaris sua quemque delectat :
reliquae meae fortunae recuperatae plus mihi nunc
voluptatis adferunt quam tum incolumes adferebant.
Amicitiae, consuetudines, vicinitates, clientelae, ludi
denique et dies festi quid haberent voluptatis
4 carendo magis intellexi quam fruendo.   Iam vero
honos, dignitas, locus, ordo, beneficia vestra, quamquam mihi semper clarissima visa sunt, tamen ea
nunc renovata illustriora videntur, quam si obscurata

---

a The Scholiast explains "devotionis convictus" as one
who has had his prayer answered, and is therefore bound to
fulfil what he promised, in that event, to do.

sacrifice [a] by the will of the immortal gods, the testimony of the senate, the united voice of Italy, the admission of my opponents, and your own marvellous and imperishable expressions of goodwill. For, fellow-citizens, although there is nothing for which a man should so earnestly pray as for the even tenor of an uninterrupted prosperity with no hidden reefs to mar his calm passage through life, yet, had I experienced nothing but an unruffled tranquillity, I should have missed the incredible and well-nigh super-human transports of delight which your kindness now permits me to enjoy. Of all nature's gifts to the human race, what is sweeter to a man than his children? Mine, indeed, by reason not only of my natural tenderness, but also of their excellence of disposition, are dearer to me than my life; yet my original acceptance of the responsibilities they brought to me was attended with less joy than their present restoration to me. No man ever had a dearer possession than I have in my brother; I was less sensible of this when I enjoyed that possession than when I was deprived of it, and than I have been since you restored me to him and him to me. Every man takes pleasure in his private possessions; but the recovery of the remnant of my fortunes to-day brings me more delight than I had in the secure enjoyment of them. Friends, companions, neighbours, and dependants, and the delights of high days and holidays,—the loss of all these has taught me a truer appreciation of them than their use. Again, though office, reputation, position, rank, and promotions bestowed by you have always been accounted by me the brightest of ornaments, yet in their renewed effulgence they seem more radiant

non essent. Ipsa autem patria, di immortales! dici
vix potest quid caritatis, quid voluptatis habeat!
quae species Italiae! quae celebritas oppidorum!
quae forma regionum! qui agri! quae fruges! quae
pulcritudo urbis! quae humanitas civium! quae rei
publicae dignitas! quae vestra maiestas! Quibus ego
omnibus antea rebus sic fruebar ut nemo magis:
sed tamquam bona valetudo iucundior est iis, qui e
gravi morbo recreati sunt, quam qui numquam aegro
corpore fuerunt, sic haec omnia desiderata magis
quam adsidue percepta delectant.

5 II. Quorsum igitur haec disputo? Quorsum? ut
intelligere possitis neminem umquam tanta eloquentia
fuisse neque tam divino atque incredibili genere
dicendi qui vestrorum magnitudinem multitudinem-
que beneficiorum, quae in me fratremque meum
et liberos nostros contulistis, non modo augere aut
ornare oratione, sed enumerare aut consequi possit.
A parentibus, id quod necesse erat, parvus sum
procreatus: a vobis natus sum consularis. Illi mihi
fratrem incognitum qualis futurus esset dederunt:
vos spectatum et incredibili pietate cognitum
reddidistis. Rem publicam illis accepi temporibus
eam, quae paene amissa est: a vobis eam recuperavi,
quam aliquando omnes unius opera servatam iudi-

than had their light been never dimmed. And what of our country herself? Heaven knows that words can scarce express the love and joy which she inspires! How beauteous is Italy, how renowned are her cities, how fair her landscapes, her fields, and her crops! How splendid is her metropolis, how enlightened her citizens, how majestic her commonwealth, and how great the dignity of you her children! In time past I yielded to none in my enjoyment of all these; but as good health is sweeter to those who have recovered from grievous sickness than to those who have never known physical infirmity, so these are all more keenly appreciated in their loss than in their continued enjoyment.

5   II. Why, then, do I speak of them at this length? It is that you may be able to realize that there has never existed anyone so eloquent, or endowed with so superhuman and miraculous a gift of expression, as to have the power, I will not say of heightening or rhetorically embellishing, but even of presenting a satisfactory catalogue of the great and manifold benefits which you have conferred upon my brother, my children, and myself. As a babe, it was to my parents, in the course of nature, that I owed my being; but now it is to you that I owe my veritable birth as a consular. When those parents gave to me a brother, it was all unknown what manner of man that brother was destined to be; the brother whom you have restored to me is a brother who has been tested and found sterling with a loyalty that passes belief. In those days I took in charge a republic which was all but lost; it is through you that I have regained a republic which, in the universal judgement, on one occasion owed its preservation

caverunt. Di immortales mihi liberos dederunt : vos reddidistis. Multa praeterea a dis immortalibus optata consecuti sumus : nisi vestra voluntas fuisset, omnibus divinis muneribus careremus. Vestros denique honores, quos eramus gradatim singulos adsecuti, nunc a vobis universos habemus, ut quantum antea parentibus, quantum dis immortalibus, quantum vobismet ipsis, tantum hoc tempore universum cuncto populo Romano debeamus.

6 Nam cum in ipso beneficio vestro tanta magnitudo est, ut eam complecti oratione non possim, tum in studiis vestris tanta animorum declarata est voluntas, ut non solum calamitatem mihi detraxisse, sed etiam dignitatem auxisse videamini. III. Non enim pro meo reditu, ut pro P. Popilii, nobilissimi hominis, adolescentes filii et multi praeterea cognati atque adfines deprecati sunt : non, ut pro Q. Metello, clarissimo viro, iam spectata aetate filius, non L. Diadematus consularis, summa auctoritate vir, non C. Metellus censorius, non eorum liberi, non Q. Metellus Nepos, qui tum consulatum petebat, non sororum filii, Luculli, Servilii, Scipiones : permulti enim tum Metelli aut Metellarum[1] liberi pro Q. Metelli reditu vobis ac patribus vestris supplicaverunt. Quod si ipsius summa dignitas maxi-

---

[1] Metellarum *PB* : -orum *other MSS.*

---

[a] Consul, 132 ; presided over court of inquiry which condemned the adherents of Tib. Gracchus ; exiled by C. Gracchus, 123 ; recalled after his death, 121 ; P. and Q. Metellus are C.'s stock parallels to his own case. See *In senatu*, Chap. XV. ; *Pro Cluentio*, Chap. XXXV.

[b] See *Pro Plancio*, Chap. XXVIII. *n.*

to the efforts of a single man. The immortal gods gave me children; you have given them back to me. There is much besides for which I have prayed heaven, and which heaven has bestowed upon me; but had it not been for your goodwill, I should now be denuded of all heaven's gifts. Finally, the distinctions at your disposal, which I had won severally and progressively, I now, of your generosity, hold in the mass; so that the early debt I owe to my parents, to the immortal gods, and to your own selves, is no greater than the sum total of the debt I owe to-day to the Roman people at large.

6   For apart from the fact that the extent of your generosity to me is itself so great that my oratorical powers are not equal to dealing with it, so striking is the expression of goodwill conveyed by your warm interest in me that I feel that not merely have you averted disaster from me, but have actually added to my reputation. III. For my restoration was not interceded for, as was that of the noble Publius Popilius,[a] by young sons and many relatives and kinsmen by marriage besides, nor, as was that of Quintus Metellus,[b] by a son whose years did not detract from the respect he inspired, by the influential Lucullus Diadematus, an ex-consul, by the ex-censor Gaius Metellus, by the children of all these, by Quintus Metellus Nepos, who was at that time a candidate for the consulship, or by bearers of the names of Lucullus, Servilius, and Scipio, nephews of the man for whom they pleaded; for large numbers who bore the name of Metellus, or who were children of ladies of that family, appealed to you and to your fathers for the restoration of Quintus Metellus. Though his own supreme merits and magnificent

maeque res gestae non satis valerent, tamen filii
pietas, propinquorum preces, adolescentium squalor,
maiorum natu lacrimae populum Romanum movere
7 potuerunt. Nam C. Marii, qui post illos veteres
clarissimos consulares, hac vestra patrumque memoria,
tertius ante me consularis subiit indignissimam
fortunam praestantissima sua gloria dissimilis fuit
ratio. Non enim ille deprecatione rediit, sed in
discessu civium exercitu se armisque revocavit : at
me nudum a propinquis, nulla cognatione munitum,
nullo armorum ac tumultus metu, C. Pisonis, generi
mei, divina quaedam et inaudita auctoritas atque
virtus fratrisque miserrimi atque optimi cotidianae
lacrimae sordesque lugubres a vobis deprecatae sunt.
8 Frater erat unus, qui suo squalore vestros oculos
inflecteret, qui suo fletu desiderium mei memoriam-
que renovaret : qui statuerat, Quirites, si vos me sibi
non reddidissetis, eamdem subire fortunam : tanto in
me amore exstitit, ut negaret fas esse non modo
domicilio, sed ne sepulcro quidem se a me esse
seiunctum. Pro me praesente senatus hominumque
praeterea viginti milia vestem mutaverunt : pro
eodem me absente unius squalorem sordesque vidistis.
Unus, qui quidem in foro posset esse, mihi pietate
filius inventus est, beneficio parens, amore idem, qui

---

^a Sulla and his adherents.

achievements had not sufficient weight, still the affection of his son, the prayers of his kinsfolk, the dishevelled robes of his young, and the tears of his elder, adherents, availed to move the Roman people. 7 After these renowned ex-consuls of old time, the third instance, before myself, of an ex-consul who, though standing on a pinnacle of fame, submitted to a totally undeserved calamity, is Gaius Marius. The circumstances of his case, however, are entirely different ; his recall was not the result of intercession, but upon the departure of certain citizens *a* he recalled himself with the aid of armed forces. I, on the other hand, was bereft of my kinsfolk ; I had no influential connexions, no menace of armed rising to back my cause ; and it was only the divine and unparalleled influence wielded by my son-in-law Gaius Piso, and his lofty qualities, together with the assiduous tears and sorrowful guise of my heart-broken and affectionate brother, that 8 interceded to you for me. There was but one— my brother—whose stricken aspect could arrest your gaze, and whose tears could reawaken wistful recollections of myself. He had made up his mind, fellow-citizens, to share my fortunes, should you refuse to restore me to himself ; and so deep was his love towards me, that he said he could not bear the thought of separation from me, not merely in our earthly dwelling, but even in the tomb. When I was in your midst, the senate with twenty thousand more of my fellow-creatures put on mourning for me : but, when I was far away, you saw but one man whose disarray expressed his grief for me. He alone of all who could appear before the public eye showed himself a son in dutifulness a father in

semper fuit, frater. Nam coniugis miserae squalor
et luctus atque optimae filiae maeror adsiduus filiique
parvi desiderium mei lacrimaeque pueriles aut itineri-
bus necessariis aut magnam partem tectis ac tenebris
continebantur. IV. Qua re hoc maius est vestrum
in nos promeritum, quod non multitudini propinquorum, sed nobismet ipsis nos reddidistis.

9　Sed quem ad modum propinqui, quos ego parare
non potui, mihi ad deprecandam calamitatem meam
non fuerunt, sic illud, quod mea virtus praestare
debuit, adiutores, auctores hortatoresque ad me
restituendum ita multi fuerunt, ut longe superiores
omnes hac dignitate copiaque superarem. Numquam
de P. Popilio, clarissimo ac fortissimo viro, numquam
de Q. Metello, nobilissimo et constantissimo cive,
numquam de C. Mario, custode civitatis atque
10 imperii vestri, in senatu mentio facta est. Tribuniciis
superiores illi rogationibus, nulla auctoritate senatus
sunt restituti : Marius vero non modo non a senatu,
sed etiam oppresso senatu est restitutus, nec rerum
gestarum memoria in reditu C. Marii, sed exercitus
atque arma valuerunt. At de me ut valeret, semper
senatus flagitavit : ut aliquando proficeret, cum

tenderness, and in love the true brother that he always was. For the weeds and dejection of my unhappy wife, the inconsolable sorrow of my sweet daughter, and the yearning and infantile tears of my little son were lost upon you by reason of journeys that they were compelled to make, or concealed from your gaze to a great extent by darkness or by the walls of their dwelling. IV. This makes your services to me all the greater, in that you have restored me out of consideration, not for the large numbers of my relatives, but for my very self.

9 But while I was unable to produce my relatives, or to reap the benefit of their appeals against my downfall, yet at the same time—and indeed it was no more than a man of my qualities had a right to be assured of—the number of those who assisted, promoted, or urged my restoration was so great, that, in respect of the prestige and backing I gained thereby, I held a considerable advantage over all the historical characters I have named. The cases of the renowned and gallant Publius Popilius, of that high-born and resolute citizen Quintus Metellus, and of Gaius Marius, the protector of the state and of your empire, were never discussed in the senate.

10 It was by bills of the tribunes, and by no pronouncement of the senate, that the two first were recalled ; while the restoration of Marius, so far from being due to the senate, was only rendered possible by the prostration of that body. Nor was it the memory of his achievements that prevailed to procure the return of Gaius Marius, but rather arms and an army ; but the senate always demanded that the memory of mine should prevail, and at the first opportunity enabled me, by its authoritative

111

primum licuit, frequentia atque auctoritate perfecit. Nullus in eorum reditu motus municipiorum et coloniarum factus est : at me in patriam ter suis decretis Italia cuncta revocavit. Illi, inimicis interfectis, magna civium caede facta, reducti sunt : ego iis, a quibus eiectus sum, provincias obtinentibus, inimico autem, optimo viro et mitissimo consule, altero consule referente reductus sum : cum is inimicus, qui ad meam perniciem vocem suam communibus hostibus praebuisset, spiritu dumtaxat viveret, re quidem infra omnes mortuos amandatus

11 esset.   V. Numquam de P. Popilio L. Opimius, fortissimus consul, numquam de Q. Metello non modo C. Marius, qui erat inimicus, sed ne is quidem, qui secutus est, M. Antonius, homo eloquentissimus, cum A. Albino collega senatum aut populum est cohortatus : at pro me superiores consules semper ut referrent flagitati sunt : sed veriti sunt, ne gratiae causa facere viderentur, quod alter mihi adfinis erat, alterius causam capitis receperam : qui provinciarum foedere irretiti,[1] totum illum annum querelas senatus, luctum bonorum, Italiae gemitum pertulerunt.

---

[1] irretiti *Halm* : infrenati *Pet.* : irinati *most MSS.*

---

[a] Q. Metellus Nepos.
[b] Lentulus.
[f] Probably Clodius.

pronouncement in full concourse, to reap the benefit thereof. The restoration of the men I have just mentioned was supported by no demonstration on the part of the colonies and the corporate towns ; but I was thrice recalled to my country by the resolutions of an united Italy. Their return was rendered possible by the murder of their opponents and by an extensive massacre of their fellow-citizens ; mine coincided with the tenure of provincial governorships by those who had banished me, and with the consulship of an opponent,[a] who was an upright and humane gentleman, and was effected by the motion of the other consul[b] ; while that enemy[c] of mine who had lent his voice to the foes of the state to work my downfall lived indeed, in the sense that breath was yet in his body but in truth he had been removed to a lower depth 11 than all the dead. V. That gallant consul, Lucius Opimius, never urged the senate or the people to interest themselves in the case of Publius Popilius ; nor was this done for Quintus Metellus, I will not say by Gaius Marius, who was his opponent, but even by Marius' successor, the eloquent Marcus Antonius, and Aulus Albinus his colleague. But in my case the consuls of the year previous to my return were constantly appealed to to promote a measure that should effect it. They, however, feared the imputation of favouritism, since one was connected with me by marriage, while I had taken up the other's brief in a capital charge : tied hand and foot by the compact they had entered into with regard to the provinces, they endured for the whole of that year the protests of the senate, the distress of patriots, and the grief of Italy. But on the first

CICERO

Kalendis vero Ianuariis postea quam orba **res publica**
consulis fidem tamquam legitimi tutoris imploravit,
P. Lentulus consul, parens, deus, salus nostrae vitae,
fortunae, memoriae, nominis, simul **ac de** sollemni
deorum **religione** rettulit, nihil humanarum rerum
12 sibi prius quam de **me agendum** iudicavit. Atque
eo die **confecta res esset**, nisi is tribunus plebis,
quem **ego** maximis beneficiis quaestorem consul
ornaveram, cum et cunctus ordo et multi eum
summi viri orarent et Cn. Oppius socer, optimus
vir, ad pedes eius flens iaceret, noctem sibi ad de-
liberandum postulasset : quae deliberatio non in
reddenda, quem ad modum non nulli arbitrabantur,
sed, ut patefactum est, in augenda mercede con-
sumpta est. Postea res acta est in senatu alia
nulla : cum variis rationibus impediretur, voluntate
tamen perspecta senatus causa ad vos mense Ianuario
13 deferebatur. Hic tantum interfuit inter me et
inimicos meos. Ego, cum homines in tribunali
Aurelio palam conscribi centuriarique vidissem, cum
intelligerem veteres ad spem caedis Catilinae copias
esse revocatas, cum viderem ex ea parte homines,
cuius partis nos vel principes numerabamur, partim
quod mihi inviderent, partim quod sibi timerent,
aut proditores esse aut desertores salutis meae,
cum duo consules empti pactione provinciarum

---

^a The first official act of the consuls was to announce
the date of the Latin Festival.

^b Clodius.

^c A stone edifice south-east of the Forum, surrounded by
steps which made it a convenient place for mass meetings ;
see *De domo*, Chap. XXI.

day of January, when the widowed republic had appealed for succour as to its legal protector to the new consul, Publius Lentulus, the parent and divine restorer of my life, my fortunes, my remembrance, and my name, had no sooner made the customary religious proposal,[a] than he carried out his conviction that all other human measures should be 12 postponed to one dealing with myself. And on that very day the business would have been executed, had not the tribune of the plebs,[b] whom, as quaestor, I had in my consulship honoured with extraordinary kindness, demanded a single night for deliberation, though the whole senatorial body and many eminent men begged him to withdraw his veto, and though his father-in-law, the excellent Gnaeus Oppius, prostrated himself in tears at his feet ; and this respite for deliberation he devoted, not, as many thought, to repaying, but, as has since been demonstrated, to increasing, the bribes he had received. From this date discussion in the senate was exclusively confined to this topic ; progress was obstructed by various methods, but when the senate had given a clear expression of their feelings the matter was 13 laid before you in January. Herein lay all the difference between my opponents and myself. I had realized that men were openly being enrolled and told off to their companies at the tribunal of Aurelius[c] ; I realized that Catiline's veteran bands had been reconstituted with a view to bloodshed ; I saw that members of the party of which I was held to be the leading figure were deserting, if not betraying, my cause, either from envy of me or fears for themselves ; the two consuls had been bought over by promises of provinces, and had laid their powers at the dis-

auctores se inimicis rei publicae tradidissent, cum
egestatem, avaritiam, libidines suas viderent expleri
non posse nisi me constrictum domesticis hostibus
dedidissent, cum senatus equitesque Romani flere
pro me ac mutata veste vobis supplicare edictis
atque imperiis vetarentur, cum omnium provinciarum pactiones, cum omnia cum omnibus foedera
ac reconciliationes gratiarum sanguine meo sanci-
rentur, cum omnes boni non recusarent quin vel
pro me vel mecum perirent, armis decertare pro mea
salute nolui, quod et vincere et vinci luctuosum rei
14 publicae fore putavi. At inimici mei mense Ianuario
cum de me ageretur corporibus civium trucidatis
flumine sanguinis meum reditum intercludendum
putaverunt. VI. Itaque dum ego absum, eam rem
publicam habuistis, ut aeque me atque illam re-
stituendam putaretis. Ego autem, in qua civitate nihil
valeret senatus, omnis esset impunitas, nulla iudicia,
vis et ferrum in foro versaretur, cum privati parietum
se praesidio, non legum tuerentur, tribuni plebis
vobis inspectantibus vulnerarentur, ad magistratuum
domos cum ferro et facibus iretur, consulis fasces
frangerentur, deorum immortalium templa in-
cenderentur, rem publicam esse nullam putavi.
Itaque neque re publica exterminata mihi locum

posal of the enemies of the republic, seeing that their lack of resources, their greed, and their lust could only be sated if they gave me up in fetters to foes bred in the state's own household; the senate and the knights of Rome were forbidden by peremptory edicts to weep for me and to appeal to you with their robes of office laid aside; all compacts with regard to the provinces, all private engagements, all renewals of interrupted friendship, were being sealed by my blood; all patriots were expressing their readiness to perish either for me or with me; but I, in spite of all this, refused to win my safety by an armed encounter, thinking that both my victory and my defeat would be calamitous to the 14 republic. My opponents, on the other hand, while my case was under discussion in January, butchered their fellow-citizens, and thought it their duty to bar the way for my return with rivers of blood. VI. The result was, that such was the condition of the state during the period of my absence, that you thought yourselves called upon to restore me, and, by so doing, the state as well. But in a state where the senate was ineffective, crime everywhere unpunished, justice at a standstill, and armed violence at large in the forum, at a time when private persons found protection not in the laws but in the walls of their houses, when tribunes of the plebs were wounded in full view of you all, when swords and torches were carried to the houses of the magistrates, when the rods of the consul were broken, and the temples of the immortal gods set on fire, I could not but hold the republic to be non-existent. I thought, therefore, that, with the republic banished, there could be no place for me in this city, and yet

in hac urbe esse duxi nec, si illa restitueretur, dubitavi
15 quin me secum ipsa reduceret. An ego, cum mihi
esset exploratissimum P. Lentulum proximo anno
consulem futurum, qui illis ipsis rei publicae periculosissimis temporibus aedilis curulis, me consule,
omnium meorum consiliorum particeps periculorumque socius fuisset, dubitarem quin is me confectum
consularibus vulneribus consulari medicina ad salutem
reduceret ? Hoc duce, collega autem eius, clemen-
tissimo atque optimo viro, primo non adversante,
post etiam adiuvante, reliqui magistratus paene
omnes fuerunt defensores salutis meae : ex quibus
excellenti animo, virtute, auctoritate, praesidio,
copiis T. Annius et P. Sestius praestanti in me
benevolentia et divino studio exstiterunt : eodemque
P. Lentulo auctore et pariter referente collega
frequentissimus senatus, uno dissentiente, nullo
intercedente, dignitatem meam quibus potuit verbis
amplissimis ornavit, salutem vobis, municipiis, coloniis
16 omnibus commendavit. Ita me nudum a propinquis,
nulla cognatione munitum consules, praetores,
tribuni plebis, senatus, Italia cuncta semper a vobis
deprecata est : denique omnes, qui vestris maximis
beneficiis honoribusque sunt ornati, producti ad vos
[ab eodem] non solum ad me conservandum vos
cohortati sunt, sed etiam rerum mearum gestarum
auctores, testes, laudatores fuerunt.

VII. Quorum princeps ad cohortandos vos et ad

---

[a] See *In senatu*, Chap. VIII. *n*

I did not doubt that, if she were restored, she herself would bring me back with her. Or, having
ascertained, as I had, that the consul for the forthcoming year would undoubtedly be Publius Lentulus,
who, as curule aedile, had in the very midst of the
state's most hazardous crisis when I was consul been
the sharer in all my counsels and the companion of
all my perils, had I any ground for doubt that he
would bring me back to health by applying a consul's
remedies to a frame stricken by wounds that a
consul had dealt ?   Led by him, and with his humane
and upright colleague at first neutral and later assist-
ing, the remaining magistrates almost to a man came
forward as the champions of my cause.   In their
number, Titus Annius [a] and Publius Sestius, [a] gentlemen of great magnanimity, uprightness, influence,
and helpful resource, behaved towards me with extraordinary kindness and amazing unselfishness ; and
on the motion of Publius Lentulus, who was seconded
by his colleague, a full senate, with but one dissentient voice and none raised in opposition, dwelt
upon my merits in terms of the highest possible
compliment, and recommended my cause to you, to
the corporate towns, and to the colonies.   So it came
about that, bereft of my kinsfolk, and with no influential connexions, I was constantly interceded for
by consuls, praetors, tribunes of the plebs, senate,
all Italy, and by all whom you had honoured with
your distinguished bounties and offices ;   with
Lentulus at their head they came before you, and
not merely urged upon you the necessity of pre-
serving me, but appeared to confirm, to attest,
and to extol my actions.

VII. In the forefront of your appellants and sup-

rogandos fuit Cn. Pompeius, vir omnium, qui sunt,
fuerunt, erunt, virtute, sapientia, gloria princeps :
qui mihi unus uni privato amico eadem omnia dedit,
quae universae rei publicae, salutem, otium, dignitatem. Cuius oratio fuit, quem ad modum accepi,
tripertita : primum vos docuit meis consiliis rem
publicam esse servatam causamque meam cum
communi salute coniunxit hortatusque est, ut
auctoritatem senatus, statum civitatis, fortunas
civis bene meriti defenderetis : tum me in per-
orando posuit vos rogari a senatu, rogari ab equitibus
Romanis, rogari ab Italia cuncta : denique ipse ad
extremum pro mea vos salute non rogavit solum,
17 verum etiam obsecravit. Huic ego homini, Quirites,
tantum debeo, quantum hominem homini debere vix
fas est. Huius consilia, P. Lentuli sententiam,
senatus auctoritatem vos secuti in eo me loco, in
quo vestris beneficiis fueram, iisdem centuriis, quibus
collocaratis, reposuistis. Eodem tempore audistis
eodem ex loco summos viros, ornatissimos atque
amplissimos homines, principes civitatis, omnes consulares, omnes praetorios eadem dicere, ut omnium
testimonio per me unum rem publicam conservatam
esse constaret. Itaque cum P. Servilius, gravissimus vir et ornatissimus civis, dixisset opera mea
rem publicam incolumem magistratibus deinceps

---

a *i.e.* the Comitia centuriata, which had voted for Cic.'s recall.

pliants was Gnaeus Pompeius, a man who has had, has, and will have, no rival in virtue, sagacity, and renown; he gave to me all that he had given to the state at large, what no other has ever given to a private friend,—safety, security, dignity. His speech, as I have been told, was under three heads: first, he demonstrated to you that it had been by my measures that the republic had been preserved, showed that my cause stood or fell with the welfare of all, and urged you to uphold the authority of the senate, the constitution of the commonwealth, and the fortunes of a meritorious citizen; secondly, he asserted in his peroration that the senate, the Roman knights, and the whole of Italy were appealing to you for me; and, finally, he closed by not merely asking, but even imploring, your interest on my behalf. To him, fellow-citizens, I owe a debt such 17 as it is scarce lawful for one human being to owe to another. It was his advice, Lentulus' opinions, and the senate's authority that induced you to restore me to the position which your kindness had once permitted me to occupy, by the vote of the same Centuries [a] which had promoted me to that position. At the same time and in the same place you heard the same statements made by our greatest men, by persons of high renown and influence, by leaders of public life, and by all of consular and praetorian rank, so that it was a fact substantiated by universal testimony that the preservation of the republic was due solely to myself. Consequently, when Publius Servilius, a gentleman of lofty character and a citizen of high distinction, said that by my efforts the republic had been handed down unimpaired to the uninterrupted administration of her future magis-

traditam, dixerunt in eamdem sententiam ceteri. Sed audístis eo tempore clarissimi viri non solum auctoritatem, sed etiam testimonium, L. Gellii, qui, quia suam classem attemptatam magno cum suo periculo paene sensit, dixit in contione vestrum, si ego consul, cum fui, non fuissem, rem publicam funditus interituram fuisse.

18   VIII. En ego tot testimoniis, Quirites, hac auctoritate senatus, tanta consensione Italiae, tanto studio bonorum omnium, causam agente P. Lentulo, consentientibus ceteris magistratibus, deprecante Cn. Pompeio, omnibus hominibus faventibus, dis denique immortalibus frugum ubertate, copia, vilitate reditum meum comprobantibus, mihi, meis, rei publicae restitutus, tantum vobis, quantum facere possum, Quirites, pollicebor : primum, qua sanctissimi homines pietate erga deos immortales esse soleant, eadem me erga populum Romanum semper fore numenque vestrum aeque mihi grave et sanctum ac deorum immortalium in omni vita futurum : deinde, quoniam me in civitatem res publica ipsa reduxit,
19 nullo me loco rei publicae defuturum.   Quod si quis existimat, me aut voluntate esse mutata aut debilitata virtute aut animo fracto, vehementer errat.   Mihi quod potuit vis et iniuria et sceleratorum hominum

---

^a G. was naval legate of Pompey in war against pirates ; Manutius says that " classis " refers to the class of which he was " custos " (see *In senatu*, Chap. VII. *n.*) in the Comitia.

trates, all succeeding speakers echoed his sentiments. Moreover you heard at the same time the illustrious Lucius Gellius give not only his considered opinion, but also his evidence. He had almost positive proof that his fleet *a* had been tampered with to his own great danger, and he asserted at one of your mass meetings that if I had not been consul at the time when I was, the republic would have been utterly destroyed.

18   VIII. Behold me then, fellow-citizens, restored to myself, to my own, and to the republic, by witnesses so manifold, by this exercise of the senate's authority, by so striking an agreement of Italy, and so zealous a co-operation of true men, with Publius Lentulus as my advocate, with all the other magistrates in agreement with him, with Gnaeus Pompeius to intercede for me, with all mankind to give me their countenance, and, finally, with the immortal gods to manifest their approval of my restoration by plentiful supplies and by the low prices of corn. I will make to you the richest promise which it is in my power to fulfil : first, that the dutiful devotion displayed towards the immortal gods by the greatest models of piety shall always mark my dealings with the Roman people, and that in my judgement your majesty shall be as venerable and as inviolable throughout all my life as that of the immortal gods ; and secondly, that, since I have been restored to citizenship by the state herself, the state shall on 19 no occasion find me to fail in my duty to her. But if anyone thinks that my sentiments have changed, or that my resolution has been weakened, or that my spirit has been broken, he is grievously in error. Violence **and** injustice **and** criminal fury have

furor detrahere, eripuit, abstulit, dissipavit : quod
viro forti adimi non potest, id omne [1] manet et per-
manebit. Vidi ego fortissimum virum, municipem
meum, C. Marium—quoniam nobis quasi aliqua
fatali necessitate non solum cum his, qui haec delere
voluissent, sed etiam cum fortuna belligerandum fuit,
—eum tamen vidi, cum esset summa senectute, non
modo non infracto animo propter magnitudinem
20 calamitatis, sed confirmato atque renovato. Quem
egomet dicere audivi, tum se fuisse miserum, cum
careret patria, quam obsidione liberavisset, cum sua
bona possideri ab inimicis ac diripi audiret, cum
adolescentem filium videret eiusdem socium calamitatis, cum in paludibus demersus concursu ac
misericordia Minturnensium corpus ac vitam suam
conservaret, cum parva navicula pervectus in
Africam, quibus regna ipse dederat, ad eos inops
supplexque venisset : recuperata vero sua dignitate
se non commissurum, ut, cum ea, quae amiserat,
sibi restituta essent, virtutem animi non haberet,
quam numquam perdidisset. Sed hoc inter me atque
illum interest, quod ille, qua re plurimum potuit, ea
ipsa re inimicos suos ultus est, armis : ego qua
consuevi utar oratione,[2] quoniam illi arti in bello ac

---

[1] id omne *Pet.* : ideo *MSS.*
[2] oratione *Pet.* : facultate *Klotz.*

---

[a] See *Pro Plancio*, Chap. X. *n.*

snatched from me, carried off, and squandered all that was separable from myself ; but that of which a brave man can never be deprived remains and will remain inviolate for ever. I saw that bravest of men, my fellow-townsman, Gaius Marius,—for he, like myself, was doomed by some irresistible fatality to wage war not only against those who had conceived the ambition of exterminating society, but also with destiny itself,—I saw him, I say, in spite of his extreme old age, not shattered in spirit by reason of his appalling catastrophe, but rather reanimated by a fresh access of courage. I myself heard him say that then he had indeed been unhappy, when he was deprived of his country, which he had freed from a state of siege, when he heard that his property was occupied and plundered by his enemies, when he saw his young son involved in the same calamity with himself, when his person and his life were saved from drowning in the marshes by the folk of Minturnae,[a] who compassionately hastened to his rescue, and when he crossed to Africa in a small boat, there to throw himself, a defenceless suppliant, upon the mercy of those to whom he had once given kingdoms ; but that, when he had won back his ancient position, he would never be so poor-spirited as to resign the steadfastness of mind, which he had never lost, when what he had really lost had been restored to him. But herein lies the contrast between him and me : *he* took vengeance upon his enemies by that wherein lay his chief power, by force of arms ; whereas *I* shall achieve this end by the power of speech, a weapon with which I am more familiar ; *his* method finds its proper exercise in time of war and feud, *mine* in

21 seditione locus est, huic in pace atque otio. Quamquam ille animo irato nihil nisi de inimicis ulciscendis
agebat, ego de ipsis amicis [1] tantum, quantum mihi
res publica permittet, cogitabo.

IX. Denique, Quirites, quoniam me quattuor
omnino hominum genera violarunt, unum eorum, qui
odio rei publicae, quod eam ipsis invitis conservaram,
inimicissimi mihi fuerunt : alterum, qui per simulationem amicitiae me nefarie prodiderunt : tertium,
qui cum propter inertiam suam eadem adsequi non
possent, inviderunt laudi et dignitati meae : quartum,
qui cum custodes rei publicae esse deberent, salutem meam, statum civitatis, dignitatem eius imperii,
quod erat penes ipsos, vendiderunt : sic ulciscar
facinora singula, quem ad modum a quibusque sum
provocatus : malos cives rem publicam bene gerendo,
perfidos amicos nihil credendo atque omnia cavendo,
invidos virtuti et gloriae serviendo, mercatores provinciarum revocando domum atque ab iis provinciarum
22 rationem repetendo. Quamquam mihi, Quirites,
maiori curae est quem ad modum vobis, qui de me
estis optime meriti, gratiam referam quam quem ad
modum inimicorum iniurias crudelitatemque perse-
quar. Etenim ulciscendae iniuriae facilior ratio est
quam beneficii remunerandi, propterea quod supe-

21 time of peace and tranquillity. He, however, incensed as he was, had no thought save to take vengeance upon his foes ; while I shall bestow even upon my friends only such consideration as the public weal shall allow.

IX. Finally, fellow-citizens, my assailants may be comprehensively divided into four classes. There are, first, those who have become my bitter enemies owing to their hatred of the republic, because its preservation by me was contrary to their wishes ; there are, secondly, those who outrageously betrayed me by assuming the mask of friendship ; third comes the class of those who were envious of my credit and reputation, which they were prevented by their own lack of energy from attaining ; while the fourth consists of those who, though their position constituted them the guardians of the republic, bartered away my prosperity, the security of the community, and the prestige of the empire which was committed to their care. This being so, the requital I shall exact for their several crimes shall be accommodated to the provocation I have received from each class ; unpatriotic citizens I shall punish by a wise administration of the state ; my treacherous friends by crediting nothing and suspecting everything ; the envious by a devotion to glory and virtue ; and the traffickers in provinces by recalling them home, and holding them responsible for their provincial govern-

22 ment. Not but what, fellow-citizens, I set greater store by showing my gratitude to you, to whom I am so deeply indebted, than by visiting upon my enemies requital for the cruel wrong I have suffered at their hands. And indeed it is an easier matter to avenge a wrong than to repay a kindness ; for the

127

riorem esse contra improbos minus est negotii quam
bonis exaequari : tum etiam ne tam necessarium
quidem est male meritis quam optime meritis referre
23 quod debeas. Odium vel precibus mitigari potest vel
temporibus rei publicae communique utilitate deponi
vel difficultate ulciscendi contineri [1] vel vetustate
sedari : bene meritos ne colas nec exorari fas est,
neque id rei publicae remittere utique necesse est
neque est excusatio difficultatis neque aequum est
tempore et die memoriam beneficii definire. Postremo qui in ulciscendo remissior fuit, in eo consilium
aperte laudatur [2] : at gravissime vituperatur, qui in
tantis beneficiis, quanta vos in me contulistis, re-
munerandis est tardior, neque solum ingratus, quod
ipsum grave est, verum etiam impius appelletur
necesse est. Atque in officio persolvendo dissimilis
est ratio pecuniae debitae, propterea quod pecuniam
qui retinet non dissolvit : qui reddidit non habet :
gratiam et qui rettulit, habet et qui habet dissolvit.
24 X. Quapropter memoriam vestri beneficii colam
benevolentia sempiterna, non solum, dum anima
spirabo mea, sed etiam cum me vita defecerit,
monumenta vestri in me beneficii permanebunt. In

---

[1] contineri *Pet.* : teneri *MSS.*
[2] c. a. l. *Pet.*

---

[a] See *Pro Plancio*, Chap. XXVIII. *n.*

reason that there is less labour involved in rising superior to the wicked than in attaining to the same level with the good ; and furthermore, one is not so strictly bound in duty to requite disservice as to recompense service. Animosity can be assuaged by personal appeal, or it can be renounced in consideration of public crises or the common welfare ; hindrances to the exaction of revenge may bid us stifle it, or it may be abated by lapse of years ; but duty forbids that any entreaty should induce us to ignore our benefactors, nor can any circumstances compel us to postpone our gratitude to political exigencies ; to allege impediments is no palliation of neglect, nor must the recollection of benefits be made contingent upon times or opportunities. Lastly, the man who is backward to pursue vengeance does but exercise his manifest right to act at his own discretion ; but reluctance to repay services so distinguished as those which you have conferred upon me is visited with condign censure, entailing, as it does, the reproach, not only of ingratitude, in itself a serious charge, but also that of impiety. Moreover, the rendering of a moral obligation stands on an altogether different footing from the payment of a debt in money.[a] He who keeps his money does not discharge his debt, he who pays his debt loses his money ; but he who repays a favour keeps it, and he who keeps it repays it by the very act of keeping.

24   X. This being so, I will cherish the recollection of your kindness by a goodwill that shall be eternal ; and the record of that kindness shall endure not merely for so long as I breathe the breath of life, but even when life shall have failed me. And in the

referenda autem gratia hoc vobis repromitto semperque praestabo, mihi neque in consiliis de re publica capiendis diligentiam neque in periculis a re publica propulsandis animum neque in sententia simpliciter ferenda fidem neque in hominum voluntatibus pro re publica laedendis libertatem nec in perferendo labore industriam nec in vestris commodis augendis grati
25 animi benevolentiam defuturam. Atque haec cura, Quirites, erit infixa animo meo sempiterna, ut cum vobis, qui apud me deorum immortalium vim et numen tenetis, tum posteris vestris cunctisque gentibus dignissimus ea civitate videar, quae suam dignitatem non posse se tenere, nisi me recuperasset, cunctis suffragiis iudicavit.

repayment of your favours I promise for my part, and shall ever be found true to my promise, that in the pursuit of my public policy I shall not be found lacking in earnestness, nor in courage in the protection of the state from the perils that threaten it, nor in loyalty in the honest expression of my convictions, nor in freedom in the frustration, for the public good, of private designs, nor in energy in the endurance of toil, nor in grateful goodwill in endeavouring to increase your general happiness. This ideal, fellow-citizens, shall be indelibly imprinted upon my heart, that I may be judged, not only by you, who are endowed in my thoughts with the power and sanctity of the immortal gods, but also by your descendants and by all nations, as fully worthy of a place in that community which expressed by its vote the unanimous conviction that, had it not won me back to itself, it could not possibly have retained its own proud position.

DE DOMO SUA AD PONTIFICES ORATIO

It will be advisable for the reader to have a summary to guide him through this diffuse and disordered speech. The following is a rough outline of the argument:—

§§ 1–32. C. replies to the attacks of Clodius in reference to the appointment of Pompey to the control of the food-supply.

§§ 32–42. "No citizen can be deprived of civic rights without due legal procedure. Clodius' tribunate is invalid, his adoption having been illegally carried out."

§§ 43–71. "Clodius' law decreeing C.'s banishment was unconstitutional and ridiculously phrased, and his allegation against C.'s 'senatus consultum' false."

1   I. Cum multa divinitus, pontifices, a maioribus nostris inventa atque instituta sunt, tum nihil praeclarius quam quod eosdem et religionibus deorum immortalium et summae rei publicae praeesse voluerunt, ut amplissimi et clarissimi cives rem publicam bene gerendo religiones, religiones ¹ sapienter interpretando rem publicam conservarent. Quod si ullo tempore magna causa in sacerdotum

----

¹ religiones *Pet.* : religionibus *MSS.*

ᵃ This seems to suggest that membership of the Pontifical College was confined to senators, but all the information we possess goes to prove the contrary ; see *De har. resp.* Chap. VII.; *Ad Att.* iv. 2.

THE SPEECH CONCERNING HIS HOUSE DELIVERED BEFORE THE COLLEGE OF PONTIFFS

[57]

1　I. GENTLEMEN OF THE PONTIFICAL COLLEGE : Among the many divinely-inspired expedients of government established by our ancestors, there is none more striking than that whereby they expressed their intention that the worship of the gods and the vital interests of the state should be entrusted to the direction of the same individuals,[a] to the end that citizens of the highest distinction and the brightest fame might achieve the welfare of religion by a wise administration of the state, and of the state by a sage interpretation of religion. And if, on any occasion in the past, a case of high importance has been submitted to the discretion and arbitrament

133

populi Romani iudicio ac potestate versata est, haec
profecto tanta est, ut omnis rei publicae dignitas,
omnium civium salus, vita, libertas, arae, foci, di
penates, bona, fortunae, domicilia vestrae sapientiae,
fidei, potestati commissa creditaque esse videantur.

2 Vobis hodierno die constituendum est utrum posthac
amentes ac perditos magistratus improborum ac
sceleratorum civium praesidio nudare an etiam
deorum immortalium religione armare malitis. Nam
si illa labes ac flamma rei publicae suum illum
pestiferum et funestum tribunatum, quem aequitate
humana tueri non potest, divina religione defenderit,
aliae caerimoniae nobis erunt, alii antistites deorum
immortalium, alii interpretes religionum requirendi :
sin autem vestra auctoritate sapientiaque, pontifices,
ea, quae furore improborum in re publica ab aliis
oppressa, ab aliis deserta, ab aliis prodita gesta sunt,
rescinduntur, erit causa cur consilium maiorum in
amplissimis viris ad sacerdotia deligendis iure ac
3 merito laudare possimus. Sed, quoniam ille demens,
si ea, quae per hos dies ego in senatu de re publica
sensi, vituperasset, aliquem se aditum ad aures
vestras esse habiturum putavit, omittam ordinem
dicendi meum ; respondebo hominis furiosi non

134

of the priests of the Roman people, surely the importance of the case now before you justifies the belief that to the wisdom and impartiality of your decision the whole prestige of the state, the well-being of all her citizens, their lives, their liberty, their altars, their hearths, their household gods, their property, their fortunes, and their dwellings, 2 are unreservedly entrusted. You on this day are called upon to decide whether from this time forward you desire that mad and unprincipled magistrates should be stripped of the protection afforded them by wicked and dastardly citizens, or actually armed with the awful sanction of the immortal gods. For if that plague-spot and devouring flame of the republic should succeed in defending by means of divine religion his iniquitous and ruinous tribunate, which he can defend on no ground of human justice, then we shall have to look around for a new ritual, new mediators between ourselves and the power of heaven, and new interpreters of the divine will. But if, on the other hand, your authority and wisdom is applied to the cancelling of what the madness of villains has achieved, now in the crushing of constitutional government, now in its desertion, and now in its betrayal, then we shall have good reason to give well-deserved approbation to the prudence of our ancestors in electing to the priestly offices the men 3 of highest distinction. But since that madman has thought that by pouring abuse upon all political courses recently advocated by me in the senate he could win some access to your ears, I shall depart in my speech from a natural arrangement ; and shall reply, I will not say to the speech of my

orationi, qua ille uti non potest, sed convitio, cuius exercitationem cum intolerabili petulantia tum etiam diuturna impunitate munivit.

II. Ac primum illud a te homine vaesano ac furioso requiro, quae te tanta poena tuorum scelerum flagitiorumque vexet, ut hos tales viros, qui non solum consiliis suis, sed etiam specie ipsa dignitatem rei publicae sustinent, quod ego in sententia dicenda salutem civium cum honore Cn. Pompeii coniunxerim, mihi esse iratos et aliter de summa religione hoc tempore sensuros ac me absente senserint arbitrere. 4 — Fuisti, inquit, tum apud pontifices superior, sed iam, quoniam te ad populum contulisti, sis inferior necesse est. — Itane vero ? quod in imperita multitudine est vitiosissimum, varietas et inconstantia et crebra tamquam tempestatum sic sententiarum commutatio, hoc tu ad hos transferas, quos ab inconstantia gravitas, a libidinosa sententia certum et definitum ius religionum, vetustas exemplorum, auctoritas litterarum monumentorumque deterret ? —Tune es ille, inquit, quo senatus carere non potuit, quem boni luxerunt, quem res publica desideravit ? quo restituto senatus auctoritatem restitutam puta-

---

infuriated opponent, for a speech is beyond his
capacity, but to his scurrility, his practice in which
has been reinforced not only by an intolerable
impudence, but also by a long-continued impunity.

II. And first I ask you, Clodius, infatuate lunatic
that you are, what Nemesis of your crimes and
enormities is it which is so powerfully deluding you
to believe that upright men such as these, who bear
up the state not merely by their wise deliberations,
but by the very impressiveness of their external
majesty, are incensed with me, because in a statement of my opinion I identified the welfare of the
state with the bestowal of honour upon Gnaeus
Pompeius, and that they are likely to hold at this
time views on essential matters of religion different
4 from those which they held in my absence ? " At
that time," he says, " you held a commanding
position in the eyes of the pontiffs ; but now that
you have passed to the popular side,[a] you must be
held to have degraded yourself." Is it indeed so ?
Would you wrest from their proper dwelling those
qualities which are the besetting sins of the ignorant
mob, fickleness, I mean, and inconstancy, and a
mind mutable as the weather, and would you attach
them to men whose high seriousness bids them
shrink from inconstancy, and who are deterred from
capricious changes of view by the strict and precise
ordinances of religion, by the precept of history, and
by the study of approved literary record ? " Are
you the man," so my opponent addresses me, " in-
dispensable to the senate, mourned by patriots,
yearned for by the republic, whose restoration we
thought would mean the restoration of senatorial
authority, and yet whose first act on your return

bamus, quam primum adveniens prodidisti ?—Nondum de mea sententia dico : impudentiae primum
respondebo tuae.

5   III. Hunc igitur, funesta reī publicae pestis, hunc
tu civem ferro et armis et exercitus terrore et
consulum scelere et audacissimorum hominum minis,
servorum dilectu, obsessione templorum, occupatione
fori, oppressione curiae, domo et patria, ne cum
improbis boni ferro dimicarent, cedere coëgisti, quem
a senatu, quem a bonis omnibus, quem a cuncta
Italia desideratum, arcessitum, revocatum conservandae rei publicae causa confiteris ? — At enim in
senatum venire in Capitolium turbulento illo die
6 non debuisti. — Ego vero neque veni et domo me
tenui, quam diu turbulentum tempus fuit, cum
servos tuos a te iam pridem ad bonorum caedem
paratos cum illa tua consceleratorum ac perditorum
manu armatos in Capitolium tecum venisse constabat:
quod cum mihi nuntiaretur, scito me domi mansisse
et tibi et gladiatoribus tuis instaurandae caedis potestatem non fecisse. Postea quam mihi nuntiatum
est, populum Romanum in Capitolium propter metum
atque inopiam rei frumentariae convenisse, ministros
autem scelerum tuorum perterritos, partim amissis
gladiis, partim ereptis diffugisse, veni non solum sine
ullis copiis ac manu, verum etiam cum paucis amicis.

ᵃ Piso and Gabinius.
ᵇ i.e. the day of the "food riots" which gave rise to
C.'s proposal mentioned in note on Chap. II. above.

was to betray it?" I defer the treatment of my own expressed opinion until I have replied to your impudent assertions.

5   III. Was this then, O fatal scourge of the state, was this the citizen whose retirement from his home and his country, to prevent an armed conflict between patriots and traitors, you endeavoured to procure by the power of the sword, by the menace of an army, by the guilt of the consuls,[a] by the threats of desperadoes, by a levy of slaves, by a blockade of the temples, by a seizure of the forum, and by the stifling of the senate, and yet whom you yourself avow to have been longed for, summoned, and recalled for the preservation of the state by the senate, by all men of sound views, and by an united Italy? "But," you object, "you did wrong in coming to the senate assembled on the Capitol on

6   that day of riot."[b] No, I reply, so far was I from attending the senate, that I shut myself up at home while the period of turbulence lasted, when it was a matter of general knowledge that the slaves, whom you had for a long time past equipped for the murder of patriots, had come armed with you to the Capitol, in company with your infamous crew of rascals and fellow-criminals. I do not mind telling you that on receipt of this news I remained at home instead of giving you and your gladiators a chance of reopening the slaughter. But when I was informed that the Roman people had been induced by their fears and by the scarcity of provisions to gather on the Capitol, while your instruments in crime had either lost their swords or been robbed of them, and had scattered in a panic, I came, with no forces and no armed retinue, but with

7 An ego, cum P. Lentulus consul, optime de me ac
de re publica meritus, cum Q. Metellus, qui, cum
meus inimicus esset, frater tuus, et dissensioni nostrae
et precibus tuis salutem ac dignitatem meam
praetulisset, me arcesserent in senatum, quum tanta
multitudo civium tam recenti officio suo me ad
referendam gratiam nominatim vocarent, non
venirem, cum praesertim te iam illinc cum tua
fugitivorum manu discessisse constaret ? Hic tu me
etiam custodem defensoremque Capitolii templorum-
que omnium hostem Capitolinum appellare ausus
es, quod cum in Capitolio senatum duo consules
haberent, eo venirem ? Utrum est tempus aliquod
quo in senatum venisse turpe sit ? an ea res erat
illa, de qua agebatur, ut rem ipsam repudiare
8 et eos, qui agebant, condemnare deberem ? IV.
Primum dico senatoris esse boni semper in senatum
venire, nec cum his sentio, qui statuunt minus bonis
temporibus in senatum ipsum non venire, non
intelligentes hanc suam nimiam perseverantiam
vehementer iis, quorum animum offendere voluerint,
gratam et iucundam fuisse. At enim non nulli
propter timorem, quod se in senatu tuto non esse
arbitrabantur, discesserunt. Non reprehendo, nec
quaero fueritne aliquid pertimescendum : puto suo
140

a mere handful of friends. Would you have me refuse to come, when I was being summoned to the senate by the consul Publius Lentulus, who had done signal service to myself and to the state, and by Quintus Metellus, who, though he was my opponent and your cousin, had postponed our differences and your prayers to the claims of my safety and dignity, and when so vast a throng of citizens were calling upon me by name to express my gratitude for the favour they had but recently conferred upon me, and when, above all, it was ascertained that you had taken yourself off with your band of renegades? Have you the effrontery to apply in this place the term " enemy of the Capitol " to me, who was the guardian and defender of the Capitol and all the temples, because I came to the Capitol when two consuls were holding a meeting of the senate there? Are there certain conjunctures when it is a misdemeanour to attend the senate, or did the nature of the matter under debate make it incumbent upon me to repudiate the matter and censure the debaters? IV. I assert, in the first place, that it is always the duty of a conscientious senator to attend the senate, nor do I hold with those who elect not to attend the senate in person when times are adverse, failing to realize that by their ill-considered obstinacy they do but play into the hands of those whose purpose they desire to baulk. But, it may be urged, members have often held aloof from attendance through apprehension, and a feeling that their presence in the senate was not compatible with safety. I pass no censure upon such, nor do I inquire into the reality of their fears. I hold that no man can dictate to

quemque arbitratu timere oportere. Cur ego non timuerim quaeris ? quia te illinc abisse constabat. Cur, cum viri boni non nulli putarint tuto se in senatu esse non posse, ego non idem senserim ? Cur, cum ego me sensissem tuto omnino in civitate esse non posse, illi remanserunt ? An aliis licet et recte licet in meo metu sibi nihil timere : mihi uni necesse erit et meam et aliorum vicem pertimescere ?

9 An quia non condemnavi sententia mea duo consules, sum reprehendendus ? Eos igitur ego potissimum damnare debui, quorum lege perfectum est, ne ego indemnatus atque optime de re publica meritus damnatorum poenam sustinerem ? Quorum etiam delicta propter eorum egregiam in me conservando voluntatem non modo me, sed omnes bonos ferre oporteret, eorum optimum consilium ego potissimum, per eos in meam pristinam dignitatem restitutus, meo consilio repudiarem ? At quam sententiam dixi ? Primum eam, quam populi sermo in animis nostris iam ante defixerat : deinde eam, quae erat superioribus diebus agitata in senatu : denique eam, quam senatus frequens tum, cum

---

^a P. Lentulus and Q. Metellus Nepos.

another when he shall or shall not feel fear. Do
you ask the reason for my own fearlessness? It
was because it was known that you had left the
scene. There were several good citizens who held
that they could not safely appear in the senate;
why then could I not hold the same view? Why
did they remain, when I personally had made up
my mind that continued existence as a citizen was
absolutely unsafe for me? Are others permitted,
and rightly permitted, to find no cause for personal
apprehension in what brings fear to me, and am I
alone to be compelled to fear vicariously for others
as well as individually for myself?

9   Again, if in the statement of my opinion I included
no condemnation of the two consuls,[a] am I for that
reason deserving of censure? Was it for me to
select as objects of my strictures those statesmen
whose measure had saved me, unsentenced as I
was, and a benefactor of the state, from undergoing
a penalty that attaches only to condemned criminals?
The marvellous zeal they displayed for my preservation made it incumbent not only upon me but
upon all patriots to bear with their shortcomings,
and was I of all men, who owed to them my restoration to my old proud position, to lend the weight
of my counsel to the repudiation of their salutary
policy? But what was the opinion which I *did* express? It was, in the first place, the opinion which
popular discussion had for long past embedded in
our minds; in the second place, it was the opinion
which had been weighed in the senate during the
previous days; and, in the third place, it was the
opinion which a full meeting of the senate had
adopted at the time when it expressed itself in

mihi est adsensus, secutus est : ut neque adlata sit
a me res inopinata ac recens, nec, si quod in sententia
vitium est, maius sit eius, qui dixerit, quam omnium,
10 qui probarint.—At enim liberum senatus iudicium
propter metum non fuit.—Si timuisse eos facis, qui
discesserunt, concede non timuisse eos, qui remanserunt : sin autem sine iis, qui tum afuerunt, nihil
decerni libere potuit, quum omnes adessent, coeptum
est referri de inducendo senatus consulto : ab
universo senatu reclamatum est. V. Sed quaero in
ipsa sententia, quoniam princeps ego sum eius atque
auctor, quid reprehendatur. Utrum causa novi
consilii capiendi non fuit, an meae partes in ea
causa non praecipuae fuerunt, an alio potius confu-
giendum fuit ? Quae vis, quae causa maior quam
fames esse potuit, quam seditio, quam consilia tua
tuorumque, qui facultate oblata ad imperitorum
animos incitandos renovaturum te tua illa funesta
11 latrocinia ob annonae causam putavisti ? Frumentum
provinciae frumentariae partim non habebant, partim
in alias terras, credo propter avaritiam [1] venditorum,
miserant, partim, quo gratius esset tum, cum in

---

[1] avaritiam *Pet. foll. Graevius* : varietatem *MSS.*

---

[a] These words are not in the original, but are inserted to
make the connexion clear.

agreement with me. Consequently, the matter which I introduced was neither unforeseen nor novel, and if the pronouncement was at fault, it is the fault rather of him who gave it expression than of all those who gave it their approbation. It may be objected that the freedom of the senate's judgement was hampered by intimidation ; but if you represent that those who had retired from the scene of action were actuated by fear, at least grant that fear had no influence with those who stood their ground. But if no freedom of vote was possible without those who were at the time absent, I would point out that the motion for the introduction of a formal resolution was only made when all were present ; and it was the whole senate that obstinately demanded it. V. But since I am its originator and author, what ground of censure, I ask, can be found in the actual pronouncement ? Was the occasion not such as to justify our embarking upon a new policy ? Was my rôle upon that occasion not that of a prot-agonist ? Or ought we to have looked rather to another quarter for safety ? What more justifying occasion could there have been than a famine, than faction, than the projects of you and your adherents, who thought that now that an opportunity was offered to you of inflaming the minds of the ignorant mob, you might make the price of grain a pretext for renewing the robbery which spelt ruin for them ?

11 The reason for the famine was [a] partly that the corn-growing provinces had no corn ; partly that it had been exported to other countries, the demands of the dealers being, as we are asked to believe, extortionate ; partly that it was being kept stored in custody, in order that its alleviating effect in the

ipsa **fame** subvenissent, custodiis **suis** clausum
continebant, ut sub novum mitterent. Res erat non
in opinione dubia, sed in praesenti atque ante
oculos proposito periculo, neque id coniectura pros-
piciebamus, **sed iam** experti videbamus. Nam cum
ingravesceret annona, ut iam plane inopia ac fames,
non caritas timeretur, concursus est ad templum
Concordiae factus, senatum illuc vocante Metello
consule. Qui si verus fuit, ex dolore hominum et
fame, certe consules causam suscipere, certe senatus
aliquid consilii capere potuit : sin causa fuit annona, seditionis quidem instimulator et concitator tu
fuisti, nonne id agendum nobis omnibus fuit, ut
12 materiem subtraheremus furori tuo ? Quid ? si
utrumque fuit, ut et fames stimularet homines et
tu in hoc ulcere[1] tamquam inguen exsisteres, nonne
fuit eo maior adhibenda medicina quae et illud
nativum et hoc inlatum[2] malum sanare posset ?
Erat igitur et praesens caritas et futura fames : non
est satis : facta lapidatio est. Si ex dolore plebei,
nullo incitante, magnum malum : si P. Clodii
impulsu, usitatum hominis facinerosi scelus : si
utrumque, ut et res esset ea, quae sua sponte
multitudinis animos incitaret, et parati atque **armati**

---

[1] ulcere *most mss.* : viscere *B.*
[2] inlatum *Pet.* : delictum *mss.*

actual throes of famine might be more gratifying ; it was to be produced as an unlooked-for surprise. The situation did not repose on vague rumour, but on a very present and palpable danger ; it existed, not in conjectural prophecy, but within our own actual range of vision and experience. When prices were rising so steadily, that we began to fear not mere dearness but actual destitution and famine, the mob flocked to the temple of Concord, whither the consul Metellus was summoning the senate. If this was a genuine result of resentment at the famine, at least the consuls could have taken the matter up, at least the senate could have initiated some measures. But if it was occasioned by the price of corn, and if it was you who were the goad and the instigator of agitation, was it not right that we should all make it our object to remove from you all that might act as fuel to your recklessness ? If, again, both of these combined were the cause, and if, when men were already goaded by the pangs of hunger, you were found to make the ulcer swell, did not this call for a yet more drastic remedy, calculated to heal the innate as well as the adventitious disease ? This, then, was the situation,— high prices in the present and the prospect of famine in the immediate future ; then, as though these were not sufficient evil, stone-throwing began. If this was a mere spontaneous expression of popular indignation, it would be bad enough ; if it was instigated by Publius Clodius, it would be no greater crime than what experience has led us to expect from a mischievous character ; but if both influences were present, if the occasion was such as naturally to stir the animosity of the mob, and if at the same

seditionis duces, videturne ipsa res publica et consulis auxilium implorasse et senatus fidem ? Atqui
utrumque fuisse perspicuum est : difficultatem
annonae summamque inopiam rei frumentariae, ut
homines non iam diuturnam caritatem, sed ut famem
plane timerent, nemo negat : hanc istum otii et
pacis hostem causam adrepturum fuisse ad incendia,
caedem, rapinas nolo, pontifices, suspicemini, nisi
13 videritis. Qui sunt homines a Q. Metello fratre tuo
consule in senatu palam nominati, a quibus ille se
lapidibus appetitum, etiam percussum esse dixit ?
L. Sergium et M. Lollium nominavit. Quis est iste
Lollius ? qui sine ferro ne nunc quidem tecum est :
qui te tribuno plebis, nihil de me dicam, sed qui
Cn. Pompeium interficiendum depoposcit. Quis est
Sergius ? armiger Catilinae, stipator tui corporis,
signifer seditionis, concitator tabernariorum, damna-
tus iniuriarum, percussor, lapidator, fori depopulator,
obsessor curiae. His atque eius modi ducibus cum
tu in annonae caritate in consules, in senatum, in
bona fortunasque locupletium per causam inopum
atque imperitorum repentinos impetus comparares,
cum tibi salus esse in otio nulla posset, cum
desperatis ducibus decuriatos ac descriptos haberes

time ring-leaders of sedition were waiting armed for their opportunity, do you not think that the very voice of the state implored the aid of the consul and the protection of the senate ? As a matter of fact, it is obvious that both causes were responsible : the oppressive prices of grain and the great scarcity of provisions, which made men apprehensive not merely now of a long period of dearness, but of absolute famine, are denied by none ; and that this was the pretext for pursuing his incendiarism, murder, and rapine which that enemy of peace and tranquillity was ready to grasp at, I would not have you, gentlemen, even suspect, unless you shall see it with your eyes. Who are the men whom the consul Quintus Metellus, your cousin, publicly named in the senate as having stoned, and even stabbed him ? Lucius Sergius and Marcus Lollius. Who is this Lollius ? He is a man who, not even now as he sits among you, is without his weapon, and who, when you were tribune of the plebs (I waive my own position), demanded the surrender of Gnaeus Pompeius for execution. Who is Sergius ? The squire of Catiline, the bodyguard of yourself, the standard-bearer of civil strife, the rallying-point of the shopkeepers ; he is a convicted law-breaker, an assassin, a stoner, a pillager of the forum, a blockader of the senate-house. Seeing that it was with these men and such as these as your lieutenants that, at a time of high prices, you were plotting a sudden onset upon the consuls, the senate, and the property and fortunes of the rich, alleging as a pretext the cause of the destitute and the ignorant, seeing that tranquillity offered you no loophole of safety, and seeing that you, with your desperate subordinates,

exercitus perditorum, nonne providendum senatui fuit ne in hanc tantam materiem seditionis ista funesta fax adhaeresceret ?

14 VI. Fuit igitur causa capiendi novi consilii. Videte nunc fuerintne partes meae praecipuae. Quem tum Sergius ille tuus, quem Lollius, quem ceterae pestes in lapidatione illa nominabant ? quem annonam praestare oportere dicebant ? nonne me ? Quid operarum illa concursatio nocturna ? non a te ipso instituta me frumentum flagitabat ? Quasi vero ego aut rei frumentariae praefuissem aut compressum aliquod frumentum tenerem aut in isto genere omnino quidquam aut curatione aut potestate valuissem. Sed homo ad caedem imminens meum nomen operis ediderat, imperitis iniecerat. Cum de mea dignitate in templo Iovis optimi maximi senatus frequentissimus, uno isto dissentiente, decrevisset, subito illo ipso die carissimam annonam 15 nec opinata vilitas consecuta est. Erant qui deos immortales—id quod ego sentio—numine suo reditum meum dicerent comprobasse. Non nulli autem illam rem ad illam rationem coniecturamque revocabant, qui, quod in meo reditu spes otii et concordiae sita videbatur, in discessu autem cotidianus seditionis timor, iam paene belli depulso

had at your back armies of rascals whom you had already told off to their several functions, was it not the duty of the senate to take measures to prevent your laying the torch of ruin to all that fuel that stood ready to burst into the flames of civil strife?

VI. The occasion, then, was such as to justify a new policy : consider now whether mine was not the rôle almost of a protagonist. In connexion with the incident of the stone-throwing, whose name was mentioned by your minion Sergius, or by Lollius, or by those other scourges? Who did they say should make himself responsible for the price of grain? Was it not myself? Again, was it not from me that your nocturnal troupe of partisans (personally coached by yourself) demanded corn? As if I, forsooth, had been placed in charge of supplies, or had made a corner in wheat, or had any authority at all in that direction by any powers either of control or of jurisdiction. And yet, with his whole mind bent on slaughter, he had proclaimed my name to his partisans, and openly hinted it to the ignorant mob. When a crowded senate, with his voice alone opposing, had passed in the temple of Jupiter Best and Greatest a decree for the restoration of my position, suddenly upon that very day the extreme dearness of corn gave way to an unexpected cheapness Some asserted (and I agree with them) that the immortal gods had given a clear intimation of their approval of my restoration, while there were many who applied to the result an inferential train of reasoning as follows : since, they argued, all hope of peace and tranquillity lay in my return, whereas my departure had meant a daily apprehension of turmoil, it was the almost total vanishing of the

metu commutatam annonam esse dicebant : quae
quia rursus in meo reditu facta erat durior, a me,
cuius adventu fore vilitatem boni viri dictitabant,
annona flagitabatur. VII. Ego denique non solum
ab operis tuis impulsu tuo nominabar, sed etiam
depulsis ac dissipatis tuis copiis a populo Romano
universo, qui tum in Capitolium convenerat, cum
illo die minus valerem, in senatum nominatim
16 vocabar. Veni exspectatus : multis iam sententiis
dictis rogatus sum sententiam : dixi rei publicae
saluberrimam, mihi necessariam. Petebatur a me
frumenti copia, annonae vilitas : possem aliquid in
ea re necne ratio non habebatur : flagitabar bonorum
expostulatione : improborum convitia sustinere non
poteram. Delegavi amico locupletiori, non quo illi
ita de me merito onus illud imponerem—succubuissem
enim potius ipse,—sed quia videbam id, quod omnes,
quod nos de Cn. Pompeio polliceremur, id illum fide,
consilio, virtute, auctoritate, felicitate denique sua
17 facillime perfecturum. Itaque sive hunc di immortales fructum mei reditus populo Romano tribuunt,
ut, quem ad modum discessu meo frugum inopia,
fames, vastitas, caedes, incendia, rapinae, scelerum

fear of war which was responsible for the change in prices; and since on my return they had again become more oppressive, it was to me, whose arrival loyal citizens had constantly asserted would produce cheapness, that they appealed to influence them. VII. The upshot of the matter is, that it was not merely your partisans who, acting on your suggestion, named me, but, after the defeat and scattering of your forces, it was the whole Roman people, who had gathered to the Capitol, who, since on that day I was in poor health, expressly demanded my 6 presence in the senate. My arrival was eagerly anticipated; and after several speeches had been made I was called upon to speak. The policy which I proposed was one that was highly salutary to the state and most necessary for myself. I was asked to procure plentiful supplies of corn, and a decrease in its price; but whether I had any powers in the matter or not was never taken into account. I was besieged by the urgent complaints of patriots; but it was the sarcasms of the disloyal that I found hard to bear. I entrusted the settlement of the demand to a friend who was wealthier than myself, not from a desire to shelve the responsibility upon one who had deserved so well of me,—rather would I have sunk beneath the burden myself,—but because I saw that Gnaeus Pompeius, by his loyalty, wisdom, courage, influence, and, last but not least, by his proverbial felicity, would realize with the greatest ease the hopes which we and all had reposed in him. 17 So, whether it be a happy result of my return bestowed by the immortal gods upon the Roman people, that even as at my retirement scarcity of provisions, famine, devastation, slaughter, conflagrations,

impunitas, fuga, formido, discordia fuisset, sic reditu
ubertas agrorum, frugum copia, spes otii, tranquillitas
animorum, iudicia, leges, concordia populi, senatus
auctoritas mecum simul reducta videantur, sive
egomet aliquid adventu meo, consilio, auctoritate,
diligentia pro tanto beneficio populi Romani praestare
debui, praesto, promitto, spondeo : nihil dico amplius,
hoc, quod satis est huic tempori, dico, rem publicam
annonae nomine in id discrimen quo vocabatur non
esse venturam.

18   VIII. Num igitur in hoc officio, quod fuit praecipue
meum, sententia mea reprehenditur ? Rem maximam fuisse et summi periculi non solum a fame, sed
etiam a caede, incendiis, vastitate nemo negat, cum
ad causam caritatis accederet iste speculator communium miseriarum, qui semper in rei publicae malis
sceleris sui faces inflammaret. Negat oportuisse
quidquam uni extra ordinem decerni. Non iam tibi
sic respondebo, ut ceteris : Cn. Pompeio plurima,
periculosissima, maxima, mari terraque bella extra
ordinem sunt commissa : quarum rerum si quem
poeniteat, eum victoriae populi Romani necesse est
19 poenitere. Non ita tecum ago. Cum his haec a me

ᵃ The commissions were : (1) against the pirates, by *lex
Gabinia*, 67 ; and (2) against Mithridates, by *lex Manilia*, 66.

robberies, impunity for criminals, exile, terror, and faction were rife, so on my return fertility, plenty, hope of tranquillity, security of mind, justice, constitutional government, popular concord, and senatorial authority seemed to be reinstalled with me ; or whether I personally on my arrival was in duty bound to devote all my ingenuity, influence, and energy to securing some requital for the Roman people for all their kindness ; whichever be the case, I do now guarantee, promise, and vow—I make no larger assertion, I assert only what is enough for the present time—that, so far as concerns the price of grain, the state will never arrive at that crisis to which it appeared to be tending.

18 VIII. Is it then in respect of this service, for which I was primarily responsible, that fault is found with that declaration of my policy ? That the task was one of supreme importance and of supreme peril, not only by reason of the actual famine, but also by reason of the workers of murder, arson, and spoliation, is denied by none, since to the factors that produced the high prices was added that keen observer of the universal distress, who never failed to kindle the torches of his wickedness at the miseries of the state. He denies the propriety of decreeing any extraordinary function to an individual. I will not answer this plea of yours as I would if any other were the pleader ; I will not point out that the extraordinary commissions on land and sea which have been entrusted to Gnaeus Pompeius surpass all others in number, in hazardousness, and in importance, and that if anyone regrets these commissions[a] he regrets the success of the Roman people. 19 I do not use this argument with you, though it is

155

haberi oratio potest, qui ita disputant, se, si qua res ad
unum deferenda sit, ad Cn. Pompeium delaturos
potissimum, sed se extra ordinem nihil cuiquam dare :
cum Pompeio datum sit, id se pro dignitate hominis
ornare et tueri solere.   Horum ego sententiam ne
laudem, impedior Cn. Pompeii triumphis, quibus ille,
cum esset extra ordinem ad patriam defendendam
vocatus, auxit nomen populi Romani imperiumque
honestavit : constantiam probo, qua mihi quoque
utendum fuit, quo ille auctore extra ordinem bellum
20 cum Mithridate Tigraneque gessit. Sed cum illis
possum tamen aliquid disputare : tua vero quae
tanta impudentia est, ut audeas dicere extra ordinem
dari nihil cuiquam oportere ? Qui cum lege nefaria
Ptolemaeum, regem Cypri, fratrem regis Alexandrini,
eodem iure regnantem, causa incognita publicasses
populumque Romanum scelere obligasses, cum in
eius regnum, bona, fortunas patrocinium huius imperii
immisisses, cuius cum patre, avo, maioribus societas
nobis et amicitia fuisset, huius pecuniae deportandae
et, si ius suum defenderet, bello gerendo M. Catonem

---

a Cyprus had been bequeathed to Rome under the will of
Ptolemy Auletes, king of Egypt, but had never been formally
annexed, and had until fifty-eight been ruled by the brother
of Ptolemy.   A. Clodius was prompted both by avarice (for
the island was wealthy) and by a desire to remove a
troublesome opponent, to send Cato to reduce it.   The king
committed suicide on Cato's arrival, and his property was
confiscated.

b Committed suicide after Utica, 46 ; for twenty years
an uncompromising opponent of monarchical tendencies.

a line that I can well adopt in my speech to gentlemen here who oppose the bestowal of extraordinary commissions upon any one, though they allow that if any special position must be conferred upon an individual, Gnaeus Pompeius is the man upon whom above all they would confer it, and state that it is a principle of action with them, since the commission has been given to Pompeius, to lend it a dignity and a support which are demanded by the merits of its holder. The opinions of these men I am prevented from approving owing to the triumphs of Gnaeus Pompeius, by which that great man, summoned by an extraordinary mandate to the defence of his country, added lustre to the name and honour to the empire of the Roman people ; though I do approve their consistency, a consistency of which I too have been called upon to avail myself, and which enabled our great general to carry out the extraordinary command which was given to him in the war against 20 Mithridates and Tigranes. With these I have at all events some common ground whereon to dispute ; but what impudence can rival yours when you dare to assert that no extraordinary powers should be given to anyone ? You, by an iniquitous law, holding no inquiry, and involving the Roman people in your criminal act, outlawed Ptolemy, the king of Cyprus,[a] who was brother to the king of Alexandria, and who held his kingdom upon a title equally good ; you inflicted the patronage of this empire upon the realm, the property, and the fortunes of one with whose father, grandfather, and ancestors we had been on terms of alliance and friendship; and after all this, you gave to Marcus Cato[b] supervision of the removal of his money, and the management of the war against

157

21 praefecisti. Dices: Quem virum? Sanctissimum,
prudentissimum, fortissimum, amicissimum rei publicae, virtute, consilio, ratione vitae mirabili ad laudem
et prope singulari! Sed quid ad te, qui negas esse
verum quemquam ulli rei publicae extra ordinem
praefici? IX. Atque in hoc solum inconstantiam
redarguo tuam; quem tu in ea re[1] non pro illius
dignitate produceres, sed pro tuo scelere subduceres,
quem tuis Sergiis, Lolliis, Titiis ceterisque caedis et
incendiorum ducibus obieceras, quem carnificem
civium, quem indemnatorum necis principem, quem
crudelitatis auctorem fuisse dixeras,—ad hunc honorem et imperium extra ordinem nominatim rogatione
tua detulisti; et tanta fuisti intemperantia, ut illius
22 tui sceleris rationem occultare non posses. Litteras
in contione recitasti, quas tibi a C. Caesare missas
diceres: CAESAR PULCRO, cum etiam es argumen-
tatus amoris esse hoc signum, quod cognominibus
tantum uteretur neque ascriberet PRO CONSULE aut
TRIBUNO PLEBIS: deinde gratulari tibi, quod M. Catonem a tribunatu tuo removisses et quod ei dicendi
in posterum de extraordinariis potestatibus liberta-

---

[1] in ea re *Pet.*: in eo MSS.

[a] *i.e.* in having conferred an extraordinary command upon
Cato, while professing disapproval of such commands on
principle.

158

21 him, should he defend his rights. " Ah ! " you will say, " but what a magnificent man ! The soul of uprightness, of sagacity, of fortitude, and of patriotism, whose virtues, principles, and whole philosophy of life give him a surpassing and almost unique title to fame ! " I grant it, but where is the relevancy of all this, since you assert, as you do, that it is wrong for any extraordinary public command to be given to any one ? IX. But in this act it is only your inconsistency [a] of which I disapprove ; by express nomination you, in your proposal, conferred an extraordinary distinction and command upon him whom you desired, not by so doing to promote to the position which his merits deserved, but to put out of the way, in order to give you a free hand for your misdeeds, him whom you had exposed to the attacks of your partisans of the type of Sergius, Lollius, and Titius, and your other princes of fire and slaughter, him who, as you asserted, had been an executioner of citizens, an instigator to the death of men against whom no verdict had been passed, and a supporter of cruelty. And so devoid of self-control were you, that you were unable to conceal your 22 criminal methods. At a mass meeting you recited a letter which you said had been sent to you by Caesar. The letter opened " my dear Pulcher," and you even adduced as a proof of his affection the fact that he employed your surname only, without the addition of " pro-consul " or " tribune of the plebs." There followed, so you pretend, congratulations on your having disencumbered your tribunate of Marcus Cato, and on having deprived him for the future of all opportunity of speaking his mind on the subject of extraordinary commands. Either

tem ademisses : quas aut numquam tibi ille litteras
misit aut, si misit, in contione recitari noluit : at,
sive ille misit sive tu finxisti, certe consilium tuum
de Catonis honore illarum litterarum recitatione
23 patefactum est. Sed omitto Catonem, cuius eximia
virtus, dignitas et in eo negotio, quod gessit, fides et
continentia tegere videretur improbitatem et legis
et actionis tuae : quid ? homini post homines natos
turpissimo, sceleratissimo, contaminatissimo quis illam
opimam fertilemque Syriam, quis bellum cum paca-
tissimis gentibus, quis pecuniam ad emendos agros
constitutam, ereptam ex sui[1] Caesaris rebus actis,
quis imperium infinitum dedit ? Cui quidem cum
Ciliciam dedisses, mutasti pactionem et Ciliciam ad
praetorem item extra ordinem transtulisti : Gabinio
pretio amplificato Syriam nominatim dedisti. Quid ?
homini taeterrimo, crudelissimo, fallacissimo, omnium
scelerum libidinumque maculis notatissimo, L. Pisoni,
nonne nominatim populos liberos, multis senatus
consultis, etiam recenti lege generi ipsius liberatos,
vinctos et constrictos tradidisti ? Nonne, cum ab
eo merces tui beneficii pretiumque provinciae meo
sanguine tibi esset persolutum, tamen aerarium cum
24 eo partitus es ? Itane vero ? tu provincias con-

[1] ex sui *Niebuhr* : vi MSS.

Caesar never sent you this letter, or, if he did send
it, he did not wish it to be recited at a mass meeting.
But whether he sent it or whether it is a mere fiction
of your own, the fact remains that your recitation
of it was a revelation of your motive in so distin-
23 guishing Cato.   But I will deal no further with Cato ;
for his splendid qualities, his great merits, and the
loyalty and self-control with which he executed his
commission, seemed to cast into the shade the un-
scrupulousness of your measure and of your policy.
But what follows ?   Who ever committed the rich
and fertile province of Syria, the administration of
a war with peaceable tribes, the funds which he
stole, though they had been set apart for the purchase of holdings in accordance with the measures
of his friend Caesar, and an unlimited command, to
the man who was of all men ever born the most vile,
the most wicked, the most polluted ?   It was to
such an one that you first assigned Cilicia ; then
you altered your bargain, and transferred Cilicia,
again by an extraordinary bestowal, upon a praetor ;
while to Gabinius you gave, at an enhanced price,
Syria by express nomination.   Again, did you not
expressly surrender free peoples bound hand and
foot, though they had been given their liberty by
many decrees of the senate and also by a recent
measure of his own son-in-law,[a] to Lucius Piso, the
most savage, cruel, and hypocritical of men, who
was deeply branded with the stains of all manner of
wickedness and lust ?   And though he had already
paid you full wage for services rendered and the
full price for the province in my blood, did you not,
in spite of this, share with him the contents of the
24 public chest ?   Can this indeed be true ?   Was the

sulares, quas C. Gracchus, qui unus maxime popularis
fuit, non modo non abstulit a senatu, sed etiam, ut
necesse esset quotannis constitui per senatus decreta,
lege sanxit, eas lege Sempronia per senatum decretas
rescidisti, extra ordinem, sine sorte, nominatim
dedisti, non consulibus, sed rei publicae pestibus :
nos, quod nominatim rei maximae, paene iam de-
speratae, summum virum, saepe ad extrema rei
publicae discrimina delectum, praefecimus, a te
reprehendemur ?

X. Quid tandem ? si, quae tum in illis rei publicae
tenebris caecisque nubibus et procellis, cum senatum a gubernaculis deiecisses, populum e navi ex-
turbasses, ipse archipirata cum grege praedonum
impurissimo plenissimis velis navigares : si, quae tum
promulgasti, constituisti, promisisti, vendidisti, perferre potuisses, ecqui locus orbi terrarum vacuus
extraordinariis fascibus atque imperio Clodiano
fuisset ?

25   Sed excitatus aliquando Cn. Pompeii,—dicam ipso
audiente, quod sensi et sentio, quoquo animo me
auditurus est,—excitatus, inquam, aliquando Cn.
Pompeii nimium diu reconditus et penitus abstrusus
animi dolor subvenit subito rei publicae civitatemque

assignment of the consular provinces, which Gaius
Gracchus, the unique example of an extreme democrat, not only did not take away from the senate,
but even enacted by legislation were year by year
to be assigned through the senate, annulled by you
after it had been decreed by the senate in accordance with the Sempronian law; and were those
provinces given by express nomination, extra-
ordinarily and without the lot, not to consuls, but to
public pests? And are we to be censured by you
for having nominated to the control of a vital matter
of state policy, which seemed insoluble, a great man
who had repeatedly in the past been chosen to cope
with the gravest crises of the state?

X. And what is the upshot of it all? Had you
been able, amid all the gloom and blinding clouds
and storms that then enveloped the state, when you
had hurled the senate from the helm, sent the
democracy by the board, and yourself, like a pirate
chief, with your abominable crew of robbers, sailed
forth with every stitch of canvas filled,—had you
been able then to carry out your proposals, deter-
minations, promises, and bargainings, what spot on
the round world would have been untroubled by
the symbols of extraordinary power and by the
plenipotentiaries of Clodius?

25 But the resentment of Gnaeus Pompeius,—and,
though it is in his hearing, I shall speak frankly what
I have felt and what I still feel, whatever may be
the sentiments with which he listens to me,—the
resentment of Gnaeus Pompeius, I say, which had
lain too long dormant in the deep recesses of his
mind, was roused at length, and came suddenly to
the aid of the republic, and bade her, cowed, en-

fractam malis, imminutam[1] ac debilitatam, abiectam
metu, ad aliquam spem libertatis et pristinae dignitatis erexit. Hic vir extra ordinem rei frumentariae
praeficiendus non fuit ? Scilicet tu helluoni spur-
catissimo, praegustatori libidinum tuarum, homini
egentissimo et facinorosissimo, Sex. Clodio, socio tui
sanguinis, qui sua lingua etiam sororem tuam a te
abalienavit, omne frumentum privatum et publicum,
omnes provincias frumentarias, omnes mancipes,
omnes horreorum claves lege tua tradidisti. Qua ex
lege primum caritas nata est, deinde inopia. Im-
pendebat fames, incendia, caedes, direptio : immine-
26 bat tuus furor omnium fortunis et bonis. Queritur
etiam importuna pestis, ex ore impurissimo Sex.
Clodii rem frumentariam esse ereptam summisque in
periculis eius viri auxilium implorasse rem publicam,
a quo saepe se et servatam et amplificatam esse
meminisset. Extra ordinem ferri nihil placet Clodio.
Quid ? de me quod tulisse te dicis, patricida, fratri-
cida, sororicida, nonne extra ordinem tulisti ? An de
peste civis, quem ad modum omnes iam di atque
homines iudicarunt, conservatoris rei publicae, quem
ad modum autem tute ipse confiteris, non modo
indemnati, sed ne accusati quidem, licuit tibi ferre

---

[1] imminutam *F. W. Schmidt* : mutatam MSS.

---

[a] Cic.'s first act on his return was to support a proposal
giving Pompey the organization of corn supplies for five
years.

[b] For the gratuitous distribution of corn to the poor.
Clodius was thus the prime source of what was later the
most demoralizing element in the life of the Imperial city.

[c] This may mean no more than "kinsman," but it is
a strange phrase.

[d] Rhetorical exaggeration.

feebled, and cringing though she was, to entertain
some hope of regaining her freedom and her ancient
pride. Was it wrong to give an extraordinary supervision over the corn-supply to this great man ?[a]
You, forsooth, passed a law[b] by which you made over
all supplies both public and private, all the corn-
supplying provinces, all the contractors, and all the
keys of the granaries to Sextus Clodius, a man deep
in destitution and crime, a foul glutton who sampled
your debaucheries for you, who shared your blood,[c]
and who by his tongue had estranged even your
sister from you,—a law whose first-fruits were high
prices, and whose aftermath was famine. Hunger,
incendiarism, murder, and pillaging hung over us ;
your reckless policy was a menace to the fortunes
and property of all. And the unconscionable
scoundrel actually grumbles that the administration
of supplies has been snatched from the filthy maw of
Sextus Clodius, and that in her gravest peril the
republic has implored the aid of a man who, she
remembers, has often preserved and glorified her.
Clodius is opposed to the passing of any extraordinary measure. What ! you slayer of father,
brother, and sister ![d] Was not the measure which
you say you passed concerning myself an extraordinary measure ? Had you any right to pass, I
will not say a law, but an iniquitous piece of party
legislation, to work the downfall of a citizen who
had recently by the unanimous verdict of gods and
men been declared the saviour of the state, and who,
as you yourself admit, so far from having been
condemned, had not even been arraigned, amid the

non legem, sed nefarium privilegium, lugente senatu, maerentibus bonis omnibus, totius Italiae precibus repudiatis, oppressa captaque re publica : mihi, populo Romano implorante, senatu poscente, temporibus rei publicae flagitantibus, non licuit de salute

27 populi Romani sententiam dicere ? Qua quidem in sententia si Cn. Pompeii dignitas aucta est, coniuncta cum utilitate communi, certe laudandus essem, si eius dignitati suffragatus viderer, qui meae saluti opem et auxilium tulisset. XI. Desinant, desinant homines iisdem machinis sperare me restitutum posse labefactari, quibus antea stantem perculerunt. Quod enim par amicitiae consularis fuit umquam in hac civitate coniunctius quam fuimus inter nos ego et Cn. Pompeius ? quis apud populum Romanum de illius dignitate illustrius, quis in senatu saepius dixit ? qui tantus fuit labor, quae simultas, quae contentio quam ego non pro illius dignitate susceperim ? qui ab illo in me honos, quae praedicatio de mea laude, quae remuneratio benevolentiae praetermissa est ?

28 Hanc nostram coniunctionem, hanc conspirationem in re publica bene gerenda, hanc iucundissimam vitae atque officiorum omnium societatem certi homines fictis sermonibus et falsis criminibus diremerunt, cum iidem illum, ut me metueret, me caveret,

mourning of the senate and the grief of all true
patriots, while the prayers of all Italy were dis-
dained, and while the republic lay crushed and
paralysed ? And had I no right, on the supplication
of the Roman people, the demand of the senate,
and the urgent appeal of the crisis through which
the state was passing, to declare my policy for the
salvation of the Roman people ? And if in this
declaration I enhanced the dignity of Gnaeus
Pompeius conjointly with the public weal, I should
surely deserve approbation, if it were seen that the
man to whose greatness I gave my vote was one
who had furthered and promoted my own welfare.
XI. Let my enemies once and for all resign the hope
that now after my restoration I can be undermined
by the same engines which they used to shatter
me when as yet I was unassailed. For what bond
between any friends of consular rank was ever closer
in this state than that which bound Gnaeus Pompeius
and myself one to the other ? Who has ever dwelt
upon his merits in more laudatory terms before the
Roman people, or more frequently before the senate ?
What toil, what **rivalry,** what controversy has ever
been so formidable that I have shrunk from facing
it, when his prestige was at stake ? And, on his
side, what opportunity of conferring distinction upon
myself, of advertising my glory, or of repaying my
kindly feelings towards him, has he ever omitted ?
There are men whom I could name who, by baseless
insinuations and false charges, have undermined our
close sympathy, our union for the wise administration of the state, and our delightful partnership in
all the round of life's duties. At one minute they
would warn him to be apprehensive and guarded

monerent, iidem apud me mihi illum uni esse inimicis-
simum dicerent, ut neque ego ab illo quae mihi
petenda essent satis audaciter petere possem neque
ille tot suspicionibus certorum hominum et scelere
exulceratus quae meum tempus postularet satis
29 prolixe mihi polliceretur. Data merces est erroris
mei magna, pontifices, ut me non solum pigeat
stultitiae meae, sed etiam pudeat : qui, cum me
non repentinum aliquod tempus meum, sed veteres
multo ante suscepti et provisi labores cum viro
fortissimo et clarissimo coniunxissent, sim passus a
tali amicitia distrahi neque intellexerim quibus aut ut
apertis inimicis obsisterem aut ut insidiosis amicis non
crederem. Proinde desinant aliquando me iisdem
inflare verbis : Quid sibi iste vult ? nescit quantum
auctoritate valeat, quas res gesserit, qua dignitate sit
30 restitutus ! Cur ornat eum, a quo desertus est ? Ego
vero neque me tum desertum puto, sed paene deditum : nec quae sint in illa rei publicae flamma gesta
contra me neque quo modo neque per quos pate-
faciundum mihi esse arbitror. Si utile rei publicae fuit
haurire me unum pro omnibus illam indignissimam
168

against me ; at another they would say in my hearing that his bitter enmity was directed solely against myself ; and the result was that I, for my part, was unable to claim from him with sufficient confidence what I was entitled to claim, while he, with his views jaundiced by a host of suspicions wickedly suggested by certain individuals, was backward in entering into such unreserved engagements with me as my situation required. I have paid a bitter penalty for my delusion, gentlemen ; my folly has brought me not sorrow alone, but shame, for although my connexion with that gallant and distinguished man was occasioned, not by any unforeseen conjuncture in my affairs, but by activities which I had undertaken and premeditated long before, I yet allowed myself to be severed from that noble friendship, nor did I realize whom I was resisting, in the belief that they were declared enemies, or whom I was refusing to trust, in the belief that their friendship was an ambuscade. Accordingly, let them finally resign their efforts to play upon my pride with their old phrases : " What is our friend's notion ? Does he fail to recognize the extent of his influence, the greatness of his achievements, the splendour which has attended his restoration ? Why does he contribute to the fame of one who has left him in the lurch ? " But I do not consider that I was then left in the lurch, though I do consider that I was all but betrayed ; nor do I think that I am called upon to disclose the nature, methods, and agents of the measures taken to thwart me during that public conflagration. If it was expedient for the state that I, and I alone, should drain on behalf of all the cup of humiliation and ruin, then it is also

calamitatem, etiam hoc utile est, quorum id scelere
conflatum sit me occultare et tacere.   Illud vero est
hominis ingrati tacere, itaque libentissime praedicabo,
Cn. Pompeium studio et auctoritate, atque[1] unum
quemque vestrum, opibus, contentione, precibus,
periculis denique praecipue pro salute mea laborasse.
XII. Hic tuis, P. Lentule, cum tu nihil aliud dies et
noctes nisi de salute mea cogitares, consiliis omnibus
interfuit : hic tibi gravissimus auctor ad instituendam,
fidelissimus socius ad comparandam, fortissimus
adiutor ad rem perficiendam fuit : hic municipia
coloniasque adiit : hic Italiae totius auxilium cupien-
tis imploravit : hic in senatu princeps sententiae fuit,
idemque cum sententiam[2] dixisset, tum etiam pro
31 salute mea populum Romanum obsecravit.   Qua re
istam orationem, qua es usus, omittas licet : post illam
sententiam, quam dixeram de annona, pontificum
animos esse mutatos : proinde quasi isti aut de Cn.
Pompeio aliter atque ego existimo sentiant aut quid
mihi pro exspectatione populi Romani, pro Cn.
Pompeii meritis erga me, pro ratione mei temporis
faciendum fuerit ignorent aut etiam, si cuius forte
pontificis animum, quod certo scio aliter esse, mea

---

[1] atque *I read for* aeque *of MSS.* :   aeque atque *Klotz.*
[2] sententiam *supplied by A. C. Clark.*

---

[a] C. is addressing Clodius ; see Chap. II.

expedient that I should cover with the veil of silence
the identity of those by whose treachery that cup
was mixed. But there is one fact which it would be
ingratitude to conceal, and consequently I shall most
joyfully avow that Gnaeus Pompeius by his zeal and
influence, and each individual of you by his resources,
his assiduity, his prayers, and last and chiefest by
the risks that he faced, laboured to procure my
restoration. XII. Night and day, Publius Lentulus,
your every thought was for my safety, yet you
formed no plan to which he did not contribute something ; his was the fortifying influence that enabled
you to initiate, his the unfailing sympathy that
enabled you to execute, his the stalwart support
that enabled you to effect your purposes. He it
was that made overtures to municipalities and
colonies ; he it was who implored the aid of united
Italy, which pined for me ; he was the prime mover
of the project in the senate, and he too it was who,
at the close of his speech on the motion, added an
appeal to the Roman people for my restoration. In
view of this, we will allow you [a] to drop the argument
you employed, when you urged that after I had pro-
pounded my corn policy the Pontifical College had
altered their attitude ; as though, indeed, their
sentiments regarding Gnaeus Pompeius were different from mine, or as though they did not know
what it was necessary for me to do, so as to act up
to the anticipations of the Roman people, the obligations which Gnaeus Pompeius had conferred upon
me, or the requirements of my situation ; or, again,
as if any member of the College whose susceptibilities were offended by my opinions (and I am
convinced that none were so offended) would be

sententia offendit, alio modo sit constituturus aut de
religione pontifex aut de re publica civis, quam eum
aut caerimoniarum ius aut civitatis salus coëgerit.

32   Intelligo, pontifices, me plura extra causam dixisse
quam aut opinio tulerit aut voluntas mea, sed quum
me purgatum vobis esse cuperem, tum etiam vestra
in me attente audiendo benignitas provexit orationem
meam.   Sed hoc compensabo brevitate eius orationis,
quae pertinet ad ipsam causam cognitionemque
vestram : quae cum sit in ius religionis et in ius rei
publicae distributa, religionis partem, quae multo est
verbosior, praetermittam, de iure rei publicae dicam.

33 Quid est enim aut tam adrogans quam de religione,
de rebus divinis, caerimoniis, sacris pontificum collegium docere conari aut tam stultum quam, si quis
quid in vestris libris invenerit, id narrare vobis aut
tam curiosum quam ea scire velle, de quibus maiores
nostri vos solos et consuli et scire voluerunt ?   XIII.
Nego potuisse iure publico, legibus iis, quibus haec
civitas utitur, quemquam civem ulla eius modi calamitate adfici sine iudicio : hoc iuris in hac civitate
etiam tum, cum reges essent, dico fuisse : hoc nobis
esse a maioribus traditum : hoc esse denique pro-

likely for that reason to arrive at a different decision, as pontiff upon religion, and as citizen upon politics, from that which was forced upon him by the laws of ritual and the welfare of the community.

2 I realize, gentlemen, that I have dwelt upon matters extraneous to the point at issue at greater length than the general feeling, or indeed my own inclination, would approve ; but I desired to be absolved of blame in your eyes, and, at the same time, the attentive hearing you have been good enough to lend me has induced me to extend the scope of my speech. I will, however, make amends for this by the brevity I shall observe in my treatment of the matter which is actually submitted to you for inquiry ; and since this is divided between a religious issue and a political issue, I shall pass over the section dealing with religion, which is much more diffuse than the other, and deal with the political issue.

3 For what act could be so presumptuous as to endeavour to instruct the Pontifical College in religion, in our relation to the divine powers, in ritual, or in sacrifice ; or so foolish, as to recount to you discoveries that have been made in your own books ; or so officious, as to wish to know matters whereon our ancestors desired that you should be the sole referees and the sole experts ? XIII. I assert that it was impossible, according to public equity and the constitution enjoyed by the state, for any citizen, without a trial, to have such disaster inflicted upon him as that in question ; that this right existed in this state even in the days of the kings, that it has been bequeathed to us by our ancestors, and is, finally, the peculiar mark of a free community,— the right, I mean, in accordance with which it is

prium liberae civitatis, ut nihil de capite civis aut de bonis sine iudicio senatus aut populi aut eorum, qui de quaque re constituti iudices sint, detrahi possit. 34 Videsne me non radicitus evellere omnes actiones tuas neque illud agere, quod apertum est, te omnino nihil gessisse iure, non fuisse tribunum plebis, hodie esse patricium ? Dico apud pontifices : augures adsunt : versor in medio iure publico.

Quod est, pontifices, ius adoptionis ? nempe ut is adoptet, qui neque procreare iam liberos possit et, cum potuerit, sit expertus. Quae deinde causa cuique sit adoptionis, quae ratio generum ac dignitatis, quae sacrorum quaeri a pontificum collegio solet. Quid est horum in ista adoptione quaesitum ? Adoptat annos viginti natus, etiam minor senatorem. Liberorumne causa ? At procreare potest. Habet uxorem, suscipiet ex ea liberos. Exheredabit igitur pater filium. Quid ? sacra Clodiae gentis cur intereunt quod in te est ? quae omnis notio pontificum, 35 cum adoptarere, esse debuit. Nisi forte ex te ita quaesitum est num perturbare rem publicam sedi-

---

a Or, possibly, " there are augurs present " ; for we do not know whether the augurs, as a body, attended the meetings of the pontiffs.

b The Romans attached great importance to the maintenance of the *sacra gentilicia*, as symbolizing the continuity of the family, and the departure from, or admission into, the family circle of any person was held to constitute a danger to their sanctity.

unlawful for any abatement of civic privilege or private property to be made without a verdict of senate, of people, or of the courts constituted to deal with each type of offence. Do you observe that I am not trying to annul all your proceedings root and branch? that I am not, in face of obvious realities, trying to prove that you have never once acted in accordance with right, or that you never were tribune of the plebs, or that you are to-day a patrician? It is the Pontifical College that I am addressing, and the augurs are present [a]; the very atmosphere which I breathe is one of public equity.

What, gentlemen, is the law relating to adoption? Clearly that the adoption of children should be permissible to those who are no longer capable of begetting children, and who, when they were in their prime, put their capacity for parenthood to the test. What pleas, then, what considerations of family, of credit, or of religion justify an adoption in any individual case,—this is the question commonly asked by the Pontifical College. Which of these was looked for in your case? A man twenty years of age or even less adopts a senator. Is it because he desires a child? But he is in a position to beget one. He has a wife; he will still rear children by her; and the father, by the act of adoption, will disinherit his son. Again, why should the religious traditions of the Clodii be extinguished, so far as you can extinguish them? [b] On this inquiry the whole attention of the pontiffs should have been centred when you were adopted, unless, indeed, the information they looked for from you was whether you wished to throw the state into the turmoil of civil strife, and whether your reason

tionibus velles et ob eam causam adoptari, non ut
eius filius esses, sed ut tribunus plebis fieres et
funditus everteres civitatem ? Respondisti, credo,
te ita velle. Pontificibus bona causa visa est :
approbaverunt. Non aetas eius, qui adoptabat, est
quaesita, ut in Cn. Aufidio, M. Pupio : quorum uterque nostra memoria, summa senectute, alter Oresten,
alter Pisonem adoptavit : quas adoptiones, sicut alias
innumerabiles, hereditates nominis, pecuniae, sacrorum secutae sunt. Tu neque Fonteius es, qui esse
debebas, neque patris heres, neque amissis sacris
paternis in haec adoptiva venisti. Ita perturbatis
sacris, contaminatis gentibus et quam deseruisti et
quam polluisti, iure Quiritium legitimo tutelarum et
hereditatium relicto, factus es eius filius contra fas,
36 cuius per aetatem pater esse potuisti. XIV. Dico
apud pontifices : nego istam adoptionem pontificio
iure esse factam : primum, quod eae vestrae sint
aetates, ut is, qui te adoptavit, vel filii tibi loco per
aetatem esse potuerit vel eo, quo fuit : deinde quod
causa quaeri solet adoptandi, ut et is adoptet, qui,

---

[a] A patrician could become *trib. plebis* only by being
adopted into a plebeian family.

[b] C. hints at immoral relations.

for being adopted was not that you might become the son of your adopter, but that, by becoming tribune of the plebs,[a] you might turn the state upside down. No doubt you replied that such was your desire. The Pontifical College thought your reason a just one, and gave their sanction. The age of the adopting party was never inquired into, as it was in the case of Gnaeus Aufidius and Marcus Pupius, who, as I recollect, in extreme old age, respectively adopted Orestes and Piso, and these adoptions, as in countless other cases, were followed by the adopted party inheriting the name, the wealth, and the family rites of his adopter. You are not a Fonteius, as you should be by rights, nor have you become the heir of your father by adoption, nor have you entered upon the rites of the family into which you have been adopted, to take the place of the paternal rites you have resigned. So, with the subversion of sacred rites, the pollution of families, of that which you have left as well as of that which you have contaminated, and with the scouting of the legally prescribed terms of wardship and inheritance among our citizens, you have set nature at defiance, and have become the son of a man whose father you might have been, on the score of your relative ages. **XIV.** Speaking as I do in the presence of the Pontifical College, I assert that your adoption did not take place in accordance with pontifical rules : firstly, because your relative ages are such that your adopter might, in respect of this, have stood to you in the relation of a son, or in the relation in which he actually did stand to you[b] ; and secondly, because the reason why a sufficient cause for the adoption is customarily required is that the

quod natura iam adsequi non potest, legitimo **et**
pontificio iure quaerat, et ita adoptet, ut ne quid aut
de dignitate generum aut de sacrorum religione
minuatur : illud in primis, ne qua calumnia, ne qua
fraus, ne quis dolus adhibeatur : ut haec simulata
adoptio filii quam maxime veritatem illam suscipien-
37 dorum liberorum imitata esse videatur. Quae maior
calumnia est quam venire imberbum adolescentulum,
bene valentem ac maritum : dicere se filium senatorem populi Romani sibi velle adoptare : id autem
scire et videre omnes, non ut ille filius instituatur, sed
ut e patriciis exeat et tribunus plebis fieri possit,
idcirco adoptari ? neque id obscure : nam adoptatum
emancipari statim, ne sit eius filius, qui adoptarit :
cur ergo adoptabat ? Probate genus adoptionis :
iam omnium sacra interierint, quorum custodes vos
esse debetis, iam patricius nemo relinquetur. Cur
enim quisquam vellet tribunum plebis se fieri non
licere, angustiorem sibi esse petitionem consulatus,
in sacerdotium cum possit venire, quia patricio non
sit is locus, non venire ? Ut cuique aliquid acciderit,

---

[a] By the Licinian Rogations (367 B.C.) one consul must
be a plebeian.
[b] *i.e.* those open to plebeians only.

adopter may be one who seeks to gain by the statutory and pontifical laws what he can no longer gain in the course of nature, and that the method of adoption may be such that neither the dignity of the families nor the sanctity of religion suffers any detraction ; but the chief reason is, to preclude the employment of chicanery, fraud, or subterfuge, and to enable this artificial expedient of adoption to reproduce as nearly as possible the responsibilities of actual parenthood. What more striking example of evasion than that a beardless stripling, married and in excellent health, should come before you and say that he wishes to adopt as his son a senator of the Roman people, and that all should be perfectly aware of and awake to the fact that the motive of the adoption was not that the adopted party might become the son of the adopter, but that he might leave the patrician body and so be in a position to become tribune of the plebs ? And he took no trouble to conceal his motive ; for no sooner had he been adopted than he was emancipated, that he might not continue to be the son of his adopter. What, then, was the adopter's motive ? Do but once sanction this form of adoption, and you will find in a very short while that all family religion, for the protection of which you are responsible, will die out, and not a patrician will be left. For why should a man acquiesce in his ineligibility to election as tribune of the plebs, in limited chances of successful candidature for the consulship,[a] and in his inability, owing to the fact that such a position is not open to a patrician, to be appointed to a priesthood,[b] when he has a possibility of removing that inability ? Similar adoptions will take place in future whenever circum-

qua re commodius sit esse plebeium, simili ratione
38 adoptabitur. Ita populus Romanus brevi tempore
neque regem sacrorum neque flamines nec Salios
habebit nec ex parte dimidia reliquos sacerdotes
neque auctores centuriatorum et curiatorum comitiorum auspiciaque populi Romani, si magistratus
patricii creati non sint, intereant necesse est, cum
interrex nullus sit, quod et ipsum patricium esse et a
patriciis prodi necesse est. Dixi apud pontifices
istam adoptionem nullo decreto huius collegii pro-
batam, contra omne pontificium ius factam pro
nihilo esse habendam : qua sublata intelligis totum
tribunatum tuum concidisse.

39   XV. Venio ad augures, quorum ego libros, si qui
sunt reconditi, non scrutor : non sum in exquirendo
iure augurum curiosus : haec, quae una cum populo
didici, quae saepe in contionibus responsa sunt, novi.
Negant fas esse agi cum populo, cum de caelo servatum sit. Quo die de te lex curiata lata esse dicatur,
audes negare de caelo esse servatum ? Adest
praesens vir singulari virtute, constantia, gravitate
praeditus, M. Bibulus : hunc consulem illo ipso die
contendo servasse de caelo.—Infirmas igitur tu acta

---

a See *De har. resp.* Chap. VII. *n.*
b Special priests of special deities.
c The ancient college of priests of Mars.
d Not true to the Roman constitution of Cic.'s day ; he
is appealing to an earlier usage in order to show Clodius'
proceedings in a more unfavourable light.
e Patrician nominated to hold consular elections, when
a consul had died or resigned.
f Consul with Caesar 59.

stances render it more advantageous to a man to be a plebeian; and the result will be that in a short time the Roman people will have no King of Rites,[a] no Flamens,[b] no Salii,[c] and it will lose half its remaining priests, and will be without any authoritative conveners for the Centuriate and Curiate assemblies[d]; while, if patrician magistrates are not elected, the auspices of the Roman people will inevitably vanish, for there will be no Interrex,[e] inasmuch as that officer is bound to be a patrician and to be appointed by patricians. I have stated in the presence of the pontiffs that your adoption was sanctioned by no decree of this College, was entered upon in defiance of all pontifical regulations, and must be held to be null and void; and you must realize that, your adoption invalidated, your whole tribunate falls to the ground.

XV. I proceed now to the augurs, into whose books, such of them at least as are secret, I forbear to pry. I am not curious to inquire into augural regulations. There are some, however, of which I share the knowledge with the populace, which have often been revealed, in answer to inquiry, in mass meetings, and with these I am familiar. These assert that proceedings in assembly are sacrilegious when observation of the heavens is in progress. Have you the audacity to deny that such observation was in progress on the day when, as is asserted, the law dealing with your case was passed in the Curiate assembly? We have with us to-day Marcus Bibulus,[f] a gentleman of exceptional uprightness, firmness of will, and seriousness of purpose; he, as consul, had, I affirm, on that very day undertaken observation of the heavens. "Do you then," asks Clodius, "invalidate

181

C. Caesaris, viri fortissimi ?—Minime. Neque enim
mea iam quidquam interest exceptis iis telis, quae ex
40 illius actionibus in meum corpus immissa sunt. Sed
haec de auspiciis, quae ego nunc perbreviter attingo,
acta sunt a te. Tu tuo praecipitante iam et debilitato
tribunatu auspiciorum patronus subito exstitisti : tu
M. Bibulum in contionem, tu augures produxisti : a
te interrogati augures responderunt, cum de caelo
servatum sit, cum populo agi non posse : tibi M.
Bibulus quaerenti se de caelo servasse respondit,
idemque in contione dixit, ab Appio tuo fratre
productus, te omnino, quod contra auspicia adoptatus
esses, tribunum non fuisse. Tua denique omnis actio
posterioribus mensibus fuit : omnia, quae C. Caesar
egisset, quod contra auspicia essent acta, per senatum
rescindi oportere : quod si fieret, dicebas te tuis
umeris me custodem urbis in urbem relaturum.
Videte hominis amentiam . . . [1] per suum tribunatum
41 Caesaris actis illigatus teneretur. Si et sacrorum
iure pontifices et auspiciorum religione augures totum
evertunt tribunatum tuum, quid quaeris amplius ? an
etiam apertius aliquod ius populi atque legum ?

XVI. Hora fortasse sexta diei questus sum in
iudicio, cum C. Antonium, collegam meum, defen-

---

[1] *A gap in the* MSS. *here*: quasi non ipse *supplied by Halm.*

[a] There is evidently a gap in the MSS. in this sentence,
but the connexion seems clear ; it was lunacy in C. to
rescind Caesar's acts when one of those acts was his own
election as tribune.

the gallant Caesar's proceedings?" By no means; for none of them any longer affect my interests, with the exception of those measures of his which were aimed with hostile intent against my own person. But it was you who treated the auspices, which I do but lightly touch upon, in this way. It was you who, in your already tottering and emasculated tribunate, suddenly stood forth as the protector of the auspices; you who brought Marcus Bibulus and the augurs before the mass meeting; it was in reply to your inquiries that the augurs answered that proceedings in assembly are sacrilegious when observation of the heavens is in progress; it was your question that Marcus Bibulus met by an assertion that he had observed the heavens, and also stated at a mass meeting, before which he was brought by your brother Appius, that you were not a tribune at all, inasmuch as you had been adopted in defiance of the auspices. You, finally, were responsible for all the agitation of the ensuing months in favour of the repeal by the senate of the whole of Gaius Caesar's proceedings, on the ground that they had been carried out in defiance of the same auspices; and you said that, in the event of their repeal, you would bring me back to the city shoulder-high as the city's preserver. What lunacy in the fellow! Why, his own tribunate held him fettered to Caesar's measures![a] If the pontiffs use the law of ritual, and the augurs the sanctity of the auspices, wherewith to overthrow your entire tribunate, for what more do you look? Is there anything in public equity or statutory law which is more self-evident?

XVI. It was perhaps at the sixth hour of the day that, in a trial where I was defending my colleague

derem, quaedam de re publica, quae mihi visa sunt
ad illius miseri causam pertinere. Haec homines
improbi ad quosdam viros fortes longe aliter atque a
me dicta erant detulerunt. Hora nona illo ipso die
tu es adoptatus. Si, quod in ceteris legibus trinum
nundinum esse oportet, id in adoptione satis est
trium esse horarum, nihil reprehendo : sin eadem
observanda sunt, iudicavit senatus M. Drusi legibus,
quae contra legem Caeciliam et Didiam latae essent,
12 populum non teneri. Iam intelligis omni genere
iuris, quod in sacris, quod in auspiciis, quod in legibus
sit, te tribunum plebis non fuisse. At ego hoc totum
non sine causa relinquo. Video enim quosdam clarissimos viros, principes civitatis, aliquot locis iudicasse
te cum plebe iure agere potuisse : qui etiam de me
ipso, cum tua rogatione funere elatam rem publicam
esse dicerent, tamen id funus, etsi miserum atque
acerbum fuisset, iure indictum esse dicebant. Quod
de me civi ita de re publica merito tulisses,
funus te indixisse rei publicae : quod salvis auspiciis
tulisses, iure egisse dicebant. Qua re licebit, ut
opinor, nobis eas actiones non infirmare, quibus

---

a Consul with Cic. 63; defended by Cic. on a charge
of extortion 59.

b Probably Caesar is meant here, and in § 42 below,
" quosdam clarissimos viros."

c By *lex Caecilia et Didia* 98, which enacted that a
measure must be published (*promulgari*) three *nundinae*,
before the voting-day. The same period applied to
adoptions.

Gaius Antonius,[a] I complained of certain political abuses, which I thought affected my unhappy client's case. These complaints were reported by scoundrels to certain worthy gentlemen [b] in terms very far removed from those which I had used. At the ninth hour on that same day your adoption took place. If an interval of three hours is sufficient, in the case of an adoption, to correspond to the three weeks that must elapse in all other legislation,[c] then I make no word of protest. But if that interval is of universal compulsion, I would point out that the senate pronounced that the laws of Marcus Drusus were not binding upon the people, because they were passed in defiance of the laws of Caecilius and Didius. Perhaps by this time you realize that by every description of law, the laws of ritual, of the auspices, and of the constitution, you were never tribune of the plebs. But I waive all this, not without good reason. For I note that certain very eminent men, leading spirits in the state, have on several occasions pronounced that you would have been within your rights in bringing the matter before an assembly of the people ; and these also have asserted, with reference to myself, that though the introduction of your measure marked the obsequies of the dead republic, yet nevertheless that death was legally inflicted, painful and distressing though it was. In that the measure you had passed was directed against a citizen and a benefactor of the state, you had, in their opinion, signed the state's death-warrant ; but in that it was passed without violence to the auspices, you had not transgressed the law. So I think that we may be permitted to allow the validity of those enactments on which your tribunate is based, and

illi actionibus constitutum tuum tribunatum comprobaverunt.

43 Fueris sane tribunus plebis tam iure legeque quam fuit hic ipse P. Servilius, vir omnibus rebus clarissimus atque amplissimus : quo iure, quo more, quo exemplo legem nominatim de capite civis indemnati tulisti ? XVII. Vetant leges sacratae, vetant xii tabulae leges privatis hominibus irrogari : id est enim privilegium. Nemo umquam tulit : nihil est crudelius, nihil perniciosius, nihil quod minus haec civitas ferre possit. Proscriptionis miserrimum nomen illud et omnis acerbitas Sullani temporis quid habet quod maxime sit insigne ad memoriam crudelitatis ? Opinor, poenam in cives Romanos nominatim sine iudicio **44** constitutam. Hanc vos igitur, pontifices, iudicio atque auctoritate vestra tribuno plebis potestatem dabitis, ut proscribere possit quos velit ? quaero enim quid sit aliud nisi proscribere : VELITIS IUBEATIS UT M. TULLIUS IN CIVITATE NE SIT BONAQUE EIUS UT MEA SINT. Ita enim re, etsi aliis verbis tulit. Hoc plebei scitum est ? haec lex ? haec rogatio est ? hoc vos pati potestis ? hoc ferre civitas, ut singuli cives singulis versiculis e civitate tollantur ? Equidem

---

^a The earliest code of Roman law (450).

^b Our language possessing no word for *privilegium*, I venture to use the derivative, of which the Oxford Dictionary quotes a 16th century example in this sense : " 1548 Elyot Dict. *Privilegium*, ' a lawe concernying priuate persons, also a priuate or speciall lawe, a priuilege.' "

which have won for it the sanction of such good judges.

But let us freely grant that your tribunate was as securely grounded upon equity and law as was that of Publius Servilius himself, who is present, a man of universal distinction and honour. Still, on what equitable principle, what tradition, or what precedent, did you base the express measure you passed concerning the civil status of an uncondemned citizen? XVII. Those laws the violation of which involves a curse, as well as the Twelve Tables,[a] forbid the passing of measures which assail private individuals; for such a measure is a "privilege."[b] No one has ever passed such measures; for no act could be more cruel, more mischievous, more abhorrent to the sense of our community. What is the most notable title possessed by the unhappy word proscription, and by all the anguish which accompanied the régime of Sulla, to be perpetuated in the annals of savagery? Surely the fact that, without a trial, penalties were enacted against expressly named Roman citizens. Will you then, gentlemen, by the official pronouncement of your verdict in open court, grant to a tribune of the plebs the power of proscribing whom he wishes? For what else, I ask, if not proscription, do these words involve: "That it may please you, and that you may command, that Marcus Tullius be no more a citizen, and that his goods be mine"? For this was the effect, if not the actual phrase, of his enactment. Is this a resolution of the people, this a law, this a bill? Can you endure, can the state tolerate this, that the mere stroke of a pen should suffice to erase the name of a citizen from the roll? For myself, I

187

iam perfunctus sum : nullam vim, nullum impetum
metuo : explevi animos invidorum : placavi odia improborum : saturavi etiam perfidiam et scelus prodi-
torum : denique de mea causa, quae videbatur
perditis civibus ad invidiam esse proposita, iam omnes
urbes, omnes ordines, omnes di atque homines iudi-
45 caverunt. Vobismet ipsis, pontifices, et vestris liberis
ceterisque civibus pro vestra auctoritate et sapientia
consulere debetis. Nam cum tam moderata iudicia
populi sint a maioribus constituta, primum ut ne
poena capitis cum pecunia coniungatur, deinde ne
improdicta die quis accusetur, ut ter ante magistratus accuset intermissa die quam multam irroget
aut iudicet, quarta sit accusatio trinum nundinum
prodicta die, quo die iudicium sit futurum, tum multa
etiam ad placandum atque ad misericordiam reis
concessa sunt ; deinde exorabilis populus, facilis
suffragatio pro salute, denique etiam si qua res illum
diem aut auspiciis aut excusatione sustulit, tota causa
iudiciumque sublatum est : haec cum ita sint in re,
ubi crimen est, ubi accusator, ubi testes, quid
indignius quam qui neque adesse sit iussus neque
citatus neque accusatus, de eius capite, liberis,
188

have already played out my part; I fear no more violence, no more assaults; I have glutted the intent of envy; I have appeased the hatred of the malevolent; I have gorged to repletion the treachery and wickedness of traitors; and, lastly, my cause, which profligate citizens thought was set as a mark for their rancour to shoot at, has now had verdict pronounced upon it by all cities, all classes, and all 45 gods and men. It is for you, gentlemen, to take such measures for yourselves, your children, and your fellow-citizens, as shall be in keeping with your dignity and your wisdom. For on the one hand, the popular courts established by our ancestors are carefully regulated, first to prevent personal penalties being inflicted conjointly with financial penalties, secondly to prevent the accusation of anyone without notice being given, but demanding that the magistrate shall lay his accusation thrice, with an interval of a day between each accusation, before he inflicts a fine or gives his verdict, while the fourth accusation shall convey an intimation that the trial will take place three days from the day on which it is laid; and, on the other hand, defendants are conceded many opportunities of procuring sympathy and arousing favour; the populace is always susceptible of entreaty, and it is easy to make interest with a view to acquittal; and finally, if the day named is cancelled by reason of unfavourable auspices or on any other pretext, the whole process and the trial itself are also cancelled. Seeing that these regulations apply in a case where there is a formal charge, an accuser, and witnesses, what can be more outrageous than that hirelings assassins, ne'er-do-wells, and scoundrels should give a vote upon the civil status, the children, and the whole

fortunis omnibus conductos et sicarios et egentes et
perditos suffragium ferre et eam legem putari ?
46 XVIII. Ac, si hoc de me potuit, quem honos, quem
dignitas, quem causa, quem res publica tuebatur,
cuius denique pecunia non expetebatur, cui nihil
oberat praeter conversionem status et inclinationem
communium temporum, quid tandem futurum est iis,
quorum vita remota ab honore populari et ab hac
illustri gratia est, pecuniae autem tantae sunt, ut eas
nimium multi, egentes, sumptuosi, nobiles con-
47 cupiscant ? Date hanc tribuno plebis licentiam et
intuemini paullisper animis iuventutem et eos
maxime, qui imminere iam cupiditate videntur in
tribuniciam potestatem : collegia, medius fidius, tribunorum plebis tota reperientur hoc iure firmato,
quae coëant de hominum locupletissimorum bonis,
praeda praesertim populari et spe largitionis oblata.

At quid tulit legum scriptor peritus et callidus ?
VELITIS IUBEATIS UT M. TULLIO AQUA ET IGNI INTER-
DICATUR ? Crudele, nefarium, ne in sceleratissimo
quidem civi sine iudicio ferendum. Non tulit UT
INTERDICATUR. Quid ergo ? UT INTERDICTUM SIT. O
caenum, o portentum, o scelus ! hanc tibi legem

---

[a] The argument of this paragraph rests upon a frivolous
cavil against Clodius' use of the perfect instead of the present
tense.

[b] Sextus ; see *De har. resp.* Chap. VI.

fortunes of one who has not been ordered to come up for trial nor arraigned nor accused, and that 46 this vote should be held to be a law ? XVIII. And if so great were his powers against me, though I was protected by official position, a great reputation, a good cause, and considerations of public weal, whose property, lastly, was not coveted, and whose sole embarrassment was the perturbed conditions and general downward tendency of the times, what is likely to be the fate of those who have passed lives secluded from the honours that the people can bestow and from a dazzling popularity, but whose wealth is considerable enough to be lusted after by too many 47 of our spendthrift and penniless nobility ? Once grant this licence to a tribune of the plebs, and if you will but take a mental survey of our rising generation, and especially of those whose evil ambitions lead them even now to cast greedy eyes upon the tribunician power, I do most solemnly warn you that whole boards of plebeian tribunes will appear, ready to conspire with such men for the property of wealthy persons, especially when their hoped-for booty is destined for the mob and there is a prospect of a general bounty.

But what did the expert and astute formulator of laws enact ?[a] " That it may please you, that you may command, that Marcus Tullius be interdicted from fire and water ? " A cruel, a shocking measure this, and one not to be tolerated, be the citizen who is its victim never so far gone in crime ! But the actual phrase was not " that he be interdicted." How then did it run ? " That an interdict *have* been passed upon him." O abominable and monstrous wickedness ! Behold ! Clodius[b] has formulated a

Clodius scripsit, spurciorem lingua sua, ut interdictum
sit, cui non sit interdictum ? Sexte noster, bona
venia, quoniam iam dialecticus es et haec quoque
liguris, quod factum non est, ut sit factum, ferri ad
populum aut verbis ullis sanciri aut suffragiis con-
48 firmari potest ? Hoc tu scriptore, hoc consiliario, hoc
ministro omnium non bipedum solum, sed etiam
quadrupedum impurissimo rem publicam perdidisti :
neque tu eras tam excors tamque demens, ut nescires
Clodium esse qui contra leges faceret, alios qui leges
scribere solerent, sed neque eorum neque ceterorum,
in quibus esset aliquid modestiae, cuiusquam tibi
potestas fuit : neque tu legum scriptoribus iisdem
potuisti uti quibus ceteri neque operum architectis,
neque pontificem adhibere quem velles, postremo ne
in praedae quidem societate mancipem aut praedem
extra tuorum gladiatorum numerum aut denique
suffragii latorem in ista tua proscriptione quemquam
nisi furem ac sicarium reperire potuisti.

49   XIX. Itaque cum tu florens ac potens per medium
forum scortum populare volitares, amici illi tui, te
uno amico tecti et beati, qui se populo commiserant,
ita repellebantur, ut etiam Palatinam tuam perderent.

---

law for you in phrase more vile than his own vile tongue, for he enacts that an interdict *have* been passed upon one upon whom an interdict has not been passed! I ask your kind pardon, my good Sextus, since you have lately turned logician, and are smacking your lips over your performances in this direction as well as in others, but is it possible to propose to the assembly, or to ratify in any form of words, or to corroborate by vote, an enactment enjoining the existence of a state of affairs which does not exist? This was the man, fouler than all two-footed or even all four-footed creatures, whom you employed as secretary, expert adviser, and right-hand man, for the destruction of the republic; and yet you were not so senseless and so infatuated as not to know that it was Clodius' part to act in defiance of the laws, and the business of others to formulate them. But you had no power of command over any of these, or indeed over any others, who had any vestige of self-respect; you were unable to employ either as legal secretaries or as architects *a* those whom others were accustomed so to employ; you could not consult the pontiff whom you desired; and, finally, even in the distribution of your booty you could find no agent, and no sponsor, outside the muster of your gladiators, and none save a thief and an assassin to put your proscriptive measure to the vote.

48

49 XIX. So when, in the heyday of your affluence and power, you were flitting, a public prostitute, through the midst of the forum, your fine friends, who owed solely to their friendship with you their safety and their wealth, were so disgusted that they even lost the votes of your Palatine tribe;

Qui in iudicium venerant, sive accusatores erant sive rei, te deprecante damnabantur. Denique etiam ille novicius Ligus, venalis ascriptor et subscriptor tuus, cum M. Papirii sui fratris esset testamento et iudicio improbatus, mortem eius se velle persequi dixit: nomen Sex. Propertii detulit. Accusare alienae dominationis scelerisque socius propter 50 calumniae metum non est ausus. De hac igitur lege dicimus, quasi[1] iure rogata videatur: cuius quam quisque partem tetigit, digito, voce, praeda, suffragio, quocumque venit, repudiatus convictusque discessit.

Quid, si iis verbis scripta est ista proscriptio, ut se ipsa dissolvat? est enim, QUOD M. TULLIUS FALSUM SENATUS CONSULTUM RETTULERIT. Si igitur rettulit falsum senatus consultum, tum est rogatio: si non rettulit, nulla est. Satisne tibi videtur a senatu iudicatum me non modo non ementitum esse auctoritatem eius ordinis, sed etiam unum post urbem conditam diligentissime senatui paruisse? Quot modis doceo legem istam, quam vocas, non esse legem? Quid, si etiam pluribus de rebus una sortitione[2] tulisti, tamenne arbitraris, id, quod M. Drusus in legibus suis plerisque, nobilissimus ille vir, M. Scauro

---

[1] quasi *Madvig*: quae *MSS.*
[2] *So Halm*: sortitu retulisti *MSS.*

---

[a] I reproduce literally this illogical expression.
[b] Presumably the decree dealing with the Catilinarian conspirators.
[c] The *lex Caecilia et Didia* (see Chap. XVI.) forbade the inclusion of separate measures in a single bill.

while those who were engaged in lawsuits, whether as accusers or accused, suffered an adverse verdict if you interceded on their behalf. And finally, your neophyte Ligur, whose signature and subservience were at your disposal for a consideration, disappointed in the will of his brother, Marcus Papirius, and unsuccessful in his litigation, expressed a desire to avenge his brother's death. He laid a charge against Sextus Propertius ; but, fellow-victim as he was of the unscrupulous ascendancy of another, he did not dare to pursue his action, as he feared to be arraigned for bad faith. We have been speaking of this law on the assumption that its proposal was in order, and yet whoever touched it even remotely with the tip of a finger, with a single word, a single penny of perquisite,[a] or a single vote, whatever point of it he approached, retired from the encounter discomfited and baffled.

But what if your proscription was made in such terms that it destroys itself? It runs, " inasmuch as Marcus Tullius has adduced a spurious decree of the senate."[b] Well, if he did adduce a spurious decree, then your bill stands ; if not, it is nullified. Do you think that the senate has not stated with sufficient clearness that so far from having falsified the authority of that order, I was actually the one man who obeyed the senate with a scrupulousness unknown since the city's foundation ? By how many methods can I demonstrate that the measure of yours which you call a law was none at all ? Furthermore, even though you did pass a measure dealing with several matters by a single casting of lots,[c] do you in spite of this think that you, a man stained with every form of crime and debauchery, could win, with such

et L. Crasso consiliariis non obtinuerit, id te posse,
hominem omnium facinorum et stuprorum, Decumis
51 et Clodiis auctoribus obtinere ? Tulisti de me, ne
reciperer, non ut exirem : quem tu ipse non poteras
dicere non licere esse Romae. XX. Quid enim
diceres ? Damnatum ? Certe non. Expulsum ?
Qui licuit ? Sed tamen ne id quidem est scriptum,
ut exirem : poena est, qui receperit : quam omnes
neglexerunt : eiectio nusquam est. Verum sit.
Quid ? operum publicorum exactio : quid ? nominis
inscriptio tibi num aliud videtur esse ac meorum bonorum direptio ? praeterquam quod ne id quidem per
legem Liciniam, ut ipse tibi curationem ferres, facere
potuisti ? Quid ? hoc ipsum, quod nunc apud pontifices agis, te meam domum consecrasse, te monumentum fecisse in meis aedibus, te signum dedicasse
eaque te ex una rogatiuncula fecisse, unum et idem
videtur esse atque id, quod de me ipso nominatim
52 tulisti ? Tam hercule est unum, quam quod idem tu
lege una tulisti, ut Cyprius rex, cuius maiores huic
populo socii atque amici semper fuerunt, cum bonis

---

[a] Clodius was probably appointed to superintend the
construction of the building to be erected on the site of
Cic.'s house.
[b] By which the proposer of a law instituting any office
was debarred from holding that office.

men as Decumus and Clodius to back you, what the exemplary Marcus Drusus failed in many of his enactments to win, even with the expert advice of Marcus Scaurus and Lucius Crassus ? In your measure you forbade that anyone should give me shelter, not that I should leave the city ; for not even you could assert that I had no right to be at Rome. XX. For what could you say ? That I had been condemned ? Assuredly not that. Banished, then ? How could that have been permissible ? But the law did not even contain a clause ordering me to leave ; penalties are enacted against all who harboured me, and these penalties were universally set at naught ; there is no mention anywhere of my being turned out. But, granting that you are right in this, what of your supervision of public constructions ?[a] What of your posting of your name ? Do you think that these amount to anything short of the plundering of my property ? This is quite apart from the fact that even your appointing yourself to an administrative office was prohibited by the law of Licinius.[b] Again, to come to the actual plea you are now offering to the pontiffs, that you have consecrated my house, that you have erected a monument in my private apartment, and dedicated a statue, and that you have done all this on the strength of one puny bill,—do you think that this plea is inseparable from and identical with your measure dealing expressly with myself ? Yes, they were as inseparable, no doubt, as were the measures which, on another occasion, you embodied in the same law, enacting that the king of Cyprus, whose ancestors were always friends and allies of this people, should be disposed of, with all his property, by the

197

omnibus sub praeconem subiiceretur et exsules Byzantium reducerentur.—Eidem, inquit, utraque de re
negotium dedi.—Quid ? si eidem negotium dedisset,
ut in Asia cistophorum flagitaret, inde iret in His-
paniam, cum Romam decessisset, consulatum ei
petere liceret, cum factus esset, provinciam Syriam
obtineret, quoniam de uno homine scriberet, una res
53 esset ? Quod si iam populus Romanus de ista re
consultus esset et non omnia per servos latronesque
gessisses, nonne fieri poterat ut populo de Cyprio rege
placeret, de exsulibus Byzantiis displiceret ? Quae
est, quaeso, alia vis, quae sententia Caeciliae legis et
Didiae nisi haec, ne populo necesse sit in coniunctis
rebus compluribus aut id, quod nolit, accipere, aut id,
quod velit, repudiare ?

Quid ? si per vim tulisti, tamenne lex est ? aut
quidquam iure gestum videri potest, quod per vim
gestum esse constet ? An, si in ipsa latione tua,
capta iam urbe, lapides iacti, si manus collata non est,
idcirco tu ad illam labem atque eluviem civitatis sine
54 summa vi pervenire potuisti ? XXI. Cum in tribunali Aurelio conscribebas palam non modo liberos,
sed etiam servos, ex omnibus vicis concitatos, vim

---

[a] Coins of Pergamum, of a sacred Ark with figures.

[b] "As if the affairs of Cyprus and Ptolemy were not a
sufficient employment, he (Clodius) ordered him (Cato) to
restore the Byzantine exiles." (Plut. *Cato Minor*, 34.)

[c] C. means: "Though only stones were thrown and there
was no hand-to-hand fighting, can you argue that you
attained your end without violence?"

[d] See *Ad Quir.*, Chap. V. *n.*

auctioneer, and that the exiles should be restored to Byzantium. "But," he objects, "I entrusted the execution of the measures to the same person." But supposing he had entrusted to one individual the duties, first of dunning for silver Ark-bearers[a] in Asia, then of going to Spain, had then allowed him to stand for the consulship after his departure for Rome, and, after his election, had given him the province of Syria; would all these be a single matter, just because the law in which they were embodied had reference to a single person? If the Roman people had been consulted upon the subject at the time, instead of everything being done through the medium of slaves and robbers, is it not conceivable that, while accepting the measure dealing with the king of Cyprus, the people might have rejected that which dealt with the Byzantine exiles?[b] What other force or significance, pray, has the law of Caecilius and Didius but this, that the people may not be called upon, by voting on several matters in gross, either to accept what it dislikes, or refuse what it wants?

Furthermore, if you employed force to carry your measure, is it, in spite of this, a law? Do you think that the result of any operation which might has effected can be thought to be founded upon right? Or if at the actual voting, when the city was in your hands, there was throwing of stones, but no actual fighting, could you on that account have brought about the ruin and destruction of the state, without a resort to extreme violence?[c] XXI. Presumably you were not preparing violence when at the tribunal of Aurelius[d] you were openly enrolling not only free men but even slaves, whom

tum videlicet non parabas ? Cum edictis tuis taber-
nas claudi iubebas, non vim imperitae multitudinis,
sed hominum honestorum modestiam prudentiamque
quaerebas ? Cum arma in aedem Castoris compor-
tabas, nihil aliud nisi uti ne quid per vim agi
posset machinabare ? Cum vero gradus Castoris con-
vellisti ac removisti, tum, ut modeste tibi agere
liceret, homines audaces ab eius templi aditu atque
ascensu reppulisti ? Cum eos, qui in conventu
virorum bonorum verba de salute mea fecerant,
adesse iussisti eorumque advocationem manibus,
ferro, lapidibus discussisti, tum profecto ostendisti
55 vim tibi maxime displicere. Verum haec furiosa vis
vaesani tribuni plebis facile superari frangique potuit
virorum bonorum vel virtute vel multitudine. Quid ?
cum Gabinio Syria dabatur, Macedonia Pisoni,
utrique infinitum imperium, ingens pecunia, ut tibi
omnia permitterent, te adiuvarent, tibi manum,
copias, tibi suos spectatos [1] centuriones, tibi pecuniam,
tibi familias compararent, te suis sceleratis contionibus sublevarent, senatus auctoritatem irriderent,
equitibus Romanis mortem proscriptionemque mini-
tarentur, me terrerent minis, mihi caedem et dimica-
tionem denuntiarent, meam domum refertam viris
bonis per amicos suos complerent proscriptionis metu,
me frequentia nudarent virorum bonorum, me prae-

[1] spectatos *Pet.* : speratos ***most*** *MSS.*

you had summoned from every quarter in the city ; when you issued proclamations ordering that the shops should be closed, you were not calling upon the ignorant mob to have recourse to force, but to honest gentlemen to show restraint and prudence. When you were storing weapons at the temple of Castor, you were merely contriving means to prevent violent proceedings ; when you tore up and carted away the steps of that temple, you did but debar presumptuous characters from access and ascent thereto, so that you might have freedom for your own law-abiding proceedings ; by ordering those who, at a gathering of patriots, had passed resolutions in favour of my restitution, to present themselves, and by scattering their adherents by blows, weapons, and stones, you no doubt displayed your strong dislike of violence. But surely all this reckless violence of one insane tribune of the plebs could easily have been overpowered and broken by the bravery or superior numbers of honest men. I suppose that when Syria was being given to Gabinius and Macedonia to Piso, in both cases with unlimited authority and vast sums of money, that they might give you perfect freedom of action, might further your schemes, might provide you with retainers, troops, their own centurions of tried loyalty, money, and whole households of slaves, that by their shameless harangues they might relieve you of your embarrassments, mock at the authority of the senate, menace Roman knights with death and outlawry, terrify me with threats, call down murder and strife upon my head, use their friends to fill my house, thronged, as it was, by patriotic citizens, with the fear of proscription, denude me of my troops of high-minded fol-

sidio spoliarent senatus, pro me non modo pugnare
amplissimum ordinem, sed etiam plorare et supplicare mutata veste prohiberent, ne tum quidem vis
56 erat ? XXII. Quid igitur ego cessi aut qui timor
fuit ? non dicam, in me : fac me timidum esse natura:
quid illa tot virorum fortissimorum milia ? quid nostri
equites Romani ? quid senatus ? quid denique omnes
boni ? Si nulla erat vis, cur me flentes potius
prosecuti sunt, quam aut increpantes retinuerunt
aut irati reliquerunt ? An hoc timebam, si mecum
ageretur more institutoque maiorum, ut possem prae-
57 sens sustinere ? Utrum si dies dicta esset, iudicium
mihi fuit pertimescendum an sine iudicio privilegium ?
Iudicium in causa tam turpi ? Scilicet homo, qui
causam, si iam esset ignota, dicendo non possem
explicare. An quia causam probare non poteram,
cuius tanta bonitas est, ut ea ipsa non modo se, sed
etiam me absentem per se probarit ? An senatus, an
ordines omnes, an ii, qui cuncta ex Italia ad me revo-
candum convolaverunt, segniores me praesente ad
me retinendum et conservandum fuissent in ea causa,
quam ipse iam parricida talem dicat fuisse, ut me ab
omnibus ad meam pristinam dignitatem exspectatum

---

a Nothing can be made of the text as it stands, but the
sense is tolerably clear.

lowers, despoil me of the protection of the senate, and forbid that august order not merely to fight on my behalf, but even to change their garments as a symbol of grief and supplication,—I suppose not even this constituted violence ? XXII. And I,—what position did I relinquish ? What timidity was found,—I will not say in me ; let us grant that I am naturally timorous,—but what of those many thousands of gallant gentlemen, what of our Roman knights ? What of the senate ? What of the whole body of patriots ? If no violence had been employed, why was it that they escorted me forth with tears instead of barring my way with execrations or deserting me in anger ? Or had I misgivings of my ability to withstand the danger face to face, if proceedings were taken against me in the traditional and established method ? Which had I the better reason to fear ? A trial, supposing that a charge were laid against me ? Or, instead of a trial, a law touching myself alone ? A trial, indeed ? No doubt my case was so bad, and my powers so mean, that I could not have made a clear statement of circumstances the details of which were at the time not generally known.[a] Was it because I could not have made a good case for myself, when, as a matter of fact, my case was so good that its own unsupported merits were enough to justify, not only itself, but even me, though I was absent ? If I had remained, would the senate, or all the orders of the state, or all those who rallied from the whole of Italy to procure my recall, have worked less fervently to retain and preserve me in a cause so popular that, as even this enemy of his country querulously admits, the whole world was summoning me with ardent expectation

58 atque revocatum queratur? An vero in iudicio periculi nihil fuit: privilegium pertimui ne, mihi praesenti si multa irrogaretur, nemo intercederet? Tam inops autem ego eram ab amicis aut tam nuda res publica a magistratibus? Quid? si vocatae tribus essent, proscriptionem non dicam in me, ita de sua salute merito, sed omnino in ullo civi comprobavissent? An, si ego praesens fuissem, veteres illae copiae coniuratorum tuique perditi milites atque egentes et nova manus sceleratissimorum consulum corpori meo pepercissent? qui cum eorum omnium crudelitati scelerique cessissem, ne absens quidem luctu meo mentes eorum satiare potui.

59 XXIII. Quid enim vos uxor mea misera violarat, quam vexavistis, raptavistis, omni crudelitate lacerastis? Quid mea filia, cuius fletus adsiduus sordesque lugubres vobis erant iucundae, ceterorum omnium mentes oculosque flectebant? Quid parvus filius, quem, quam diu afui, nemo nisi lacrimantem confectumque vidit, quid fecerat, quod eum totiens per insidias interficere voluistis? Quid frater meus? qui cum aliquanto post meum discessum ex provincia venisset neque sibi vivendum nisi me restituto putaret, cum eius maeror, squalor incredibilis et

204

58 to resume my former proud position? Or, on the other hand, while I had no danger to apprehend from a trial, did I dread legislation against my person, for fear lest no veto might be interposed if it should be proposed to inflict a fine upon me, being at the time present? But was I so destitute of aid from friends, or was the republic so devoid of magistrates? Or supposing that the tribes had been summoned to vote, would they have sanctioned proscription against any citizen whatsoever, far less against me, to whom they were so deeply obliged for their preservation? Or, if I had been present, would your troop of veteran conspirators, your needy and desperate soldiery, and your retinue of recruits furnished by those abandoned consuls, have kept their hands from my person, seeing that, though I had retired before the wicked brutality of all of them, even when I was far away I could not glut their souls by any grief of mine?

59 XXIII. For what harm had you suffered at the hands of my unhappy wife, whom you had harassed, plundered, and tortured by every artifice of brutality? Or from my daughter, whose ceaseless tears and sorrowful weeds filled you with joy, though there was not an eye or heart in all the world else that could view them unmoved? Or from my little son, who, as long as I was absent from him, was never seen save weeping and prostrated? What had he done, that you should have desired so often to lay plots against his life? What had you suffered from my brother? Some time after my retirement he had come from his province, counting life not worth living except on the terms of my restoration; his desolation, that baffled all belief and beggared all

205

inauditus, omnibus mortalibus miserabilis videbatur,
60 quotiens est ex vestro ferro ac manibus elapsus ? Sed
quid ego vestram crudelitatem expromo, quam in
ipsum me ac meos adhibuistis : qui parietibus, qui
tectis, qui columnis ac postibus meis hostificum quoddam et nefarium, omni imbutum odio bellum intu-
listis ? Non enim te arbitror, cum post meum discessum omnium locupletium fortunas, omnium provinciarum fructus, tetrarcharum ac regum bona spe
atque avaritia devorasses, argenti et supellectilis
meae cupiditate esse caecatum : non existimo Cam-
panum illum consulem cum saltatore collega, cum
alteri totam Achaiam, Thessaliam, Boeotiam, Graeciam, Macedoniam omnemque barbariam, bona
civium Romanorum condonasses, alteri Syriam, Baby-
lonem, Persas, integerrimas pacatissimasque gentes,
ad diripiendum tradidisses, illos tam cupidos liminum
61 meorum et columnarum et valvarum fuisse. Neque
porro illa manus copiaeque Catilinae caementis ac
testis tectorum meorum se famem suam expleturas
putaverunt : sed ut hostium urbes nec omnium
hostium, verum eorum, quibuscum acerbum bellum
internicivumque suscepimus, non praeda adducti, sed
odio solemus exscindere, quod, in quos propter eorum
crudelitatem inflammatae mentes nostrae fuerunt,
cum horum etiam tectis et sedibus residere aliquod
bellum semper videtur : . . .
62 XXIV. Nihil erat latum de me : non adesse eram
iussus, non citatus afueram : eram etiam tuo iudicio

---

a Piso ; see *In senatu*, Chap. VII. n.
b The completion of the comparison is missing in the
MSS.

experience, was an object of pity to every mortal soul ; but how often did he escape by an hair's 0 breadth from your swords and your clutches ! But why disclose the savagery you displayed towards me and my dear ones, when you have waged a bitter and sacrilegious war, instinct with the extremity of hatred, against my very walls, roofs, pillars, and door-posts ? For I refuse to believe that, after my retirement, when you had devoured with greedy anticipation the fortunes of all the wealthy, the produce of all the provinces, and the possessions of tetrarchs and kings, you were blinded by a lust for my plate and my furniture ; I cannot think that that Campanian *a* consul and his dancer colleague, to the former of whom you had consigned all Achaea, Thessaly, Boeotia, Greece, Macedonia, all Barbary, and the property of Roman citizens, and to the latter's plundering hands Syria, Babylon, and Persia, peoples utterly loyal and entirely peaceable,— I cannot think that they were so covetous of my 1 portals, my columns, and my doors. Why, the troops and retainers of Catiline never thought that they could sate their hunger upon the masonry and tiles of my dwelling ; but as in the case of the cities of our foes, and not all our foes, but those against whom we have started bitter and internecine war-fare, it is our practice to raze them to the ground, with the end not of booty but of revenge, because we hold that some sediment of war lingers even in the buildings and abodes of those whose savagery has inflamed our minds against them, so also . . . *b*

62 XXIV. No measure had been passed bearing on myself ; I had not been called upon to appear ; I had not failed to answer any summons. Even in

civis incolumis, cum domus in Palatio, villa in Tusculano, altera ad alterum consulem, transferebatur :
scilicet eos consules vocabant [1] : columnae mar-
moreae ex aedibus meis inspectante populo Romano
ad socrum consulis portabantur : in fundum autem
vicini consulis non instrumentum aut ornamenta
villae, sed etiam arbores transferebantur, cum ipsa
villa non praedae cupiditate—quid enim erat praedae ?—sed odio et crudelitate funditus everteretur.
Domus ardebat in Palatio non fortuito, sed oblato
incendio : consules epulabantur et in coniuratorum
gratulatione versabantur, cum alter se Catilinae
delicias, alter Cethegi consobrinum fuisse diceret.
33 Hanc ego vim, pontifices, hoc scelus, hunc furorem
meo corpore opposito ab omnium bonorum cervicibus
depuli omnemque impetum discordiarum, omnem diu
collectam vim improborum, quae inveterata com-
presso odio atque tacito iam erumpebat nancta tam
audaces duces, excepi meo corpore. In me uno
consulares faces, iactae manibus tribuniciis, in me
omnia, quae ego quondam rettuderam, coniurationis
nefaria tela adhaeserunt. Quod si, ut multis fortissimis viris placuit, vi et armis contra vim decertare
voluissem, aut vicissem cum magna internicione
improborum, sed tamen civium, aut interfectis bonis

---

[1] sc. eos cos. voc. *Pet.*: senatus consules vocabant *P* :
senatus consulta volabant *G*.

your judgement I was a citizen untainted, when my house on the Palatine and my country mansion at Tusculum were being made over one to each of the two consuls (the nominal consuls, that is to say), when the marble columns were being taken down from my apartments and handed over to the consul's mother-in-law, while to the consul's estate adjoining were transferred not merely the furniture or ornaments of the mansion, but even the very trees, while the mansion itself was razed to the foundations as a sacrifice not to the greed of booty—for what did it amount to as booty?—but to merciless hatred. My house on the Palatine was ablaze, by no mere accident, but by deliberate arson; the consuls were feasting and enjoying the congratulations of their fellow-conspirators, one of them asserting that he had been Catiline's minion, and the other that he 63 was cousin to Cethegus. This was the savagery, gentlemen, this the criminality, this the recklessness, which I warded from the heads of all patriots by the shield of my body; I in my person met the full onset of civil strife, all the pent-up lawlessness of traitors, which for long had smouldered with a secret rankling hate, and which, now that it had found leaders so shameless, was bursting from its concealment. Against me alone by the hands of the tribunes were hurled the brands of the consuls; in me were fixed all the impious shafts of conspiracy which I had once blunted. If I had done as many gallant gentlemen urged, and had chosen to meet violence in the field, either I should have proved victorious at the cost of a tremendous carnage of men who, though traitors, were yet citizens, or all patriots would have been exterminated (and they could have prayed for

209

omnibus, quod illis optatissimum erat, una cum re
64 publica concidissem. Videbam vivo senatu populoque Romano celerem mihi summa cum dignitate
reditum, nec intellegebam fieri diutius posse, ut mihi
non liceret esse in ea re publica, quam ipse servassem.
Quod si non liceret, audieram et legeram clarissimos
nostrae civitatis viros se in medios hostes ad per-
spicuam mortem pro salute exercitus iniecisse : ego
pro salute universae rei publicae dubitarem hoc
meliore condicione esse quam Decii, quod illi ne
auditores quidem suae gloriae, ego etiam spectator
meae laudis esse potuissem ?

XXV. Itaque infractus furor tuus inanes faciebat
impetus. Omnem enim vim omnium sceleratorum
acerbitas mei casus exceperat. Non erat in tam
immani iniuria tantisque ruinis novae crudelitati
65 locus. Cato fuerat proximus. Quid ageres ? non
erat ut qui modus odiis[1] fuerat, idem esset iniuriae ?
Quid posses ? extrudere ad Cypriam pecuniam ?
praeda perierit : alia non deerit : hinc modo aman-
dandus est.[2] Sic M. Cato invisus quasi per beneficium Cyprum relegatur. Eiiciuntur duo, quos videre
improbi non poterant, alter per honorem turpissimum,

---

[1] odiis *A. C. Clark* : amoribus *Pet.* : moribus MSS.
[2] *So Pet. foll. Müller ; the text of the* MSS. *here is hopeless.*

---

[c] At the battles of Veseris (340) and Sentinum (295).
[b] C. here turns to Clodius.
[c] Cato.

no better fate), and I, and the republic with me,
4 should have been laid low. I saw, while the senate
and the Roman people yet lived, the prospect of a
speedy and honourable return; and I thought it inconceivable that it would any longer be illegal for
me to exist in the republic which I myself had saved.
But if it were still to be illegal, I had heard and
had read how distinguished compatriots of ours had
dashed into the thick of the foe upon indubitable
death in order to save the army; and was I, when
the safety of the whole state was to be won, to
shrink from playing this part under better conditions
than the Decii[a] enjoyed, inasmuch as while they
could not even hear of the fame they had won, I
might have been in a position to be even the spectator
of my own renown?

XXV. It was the check, then, that I gave to your[b]
mad career which rendered all your attacks fruitless; for my bitter calamities had stemmed the full
shock of all the forces of wickedness; and in so
shocking an outrage, so dire a fall, there was no
5 room for any new phase of brutality. Cato had been
my closest adherent. What line of conduct were
you to pursue? It was not to be thought of that
you should affront all those against whom you felt
animosity. What then could you do? Get him out
of the way by sending him to collect money from
Cyprus? But your booty would be as good as lost
to you. Well, you will be at no loss to find more;
but he must at all costs be removed from the scene.
So the hated Marcus Cato is banished to Cyprus
under show of having a favour bestowed upon him.
There were two, of whom traitors could not endure
the sight, and these were driven forth, one[c] by the

66 alter per honestissimam calamitatem. Atque ut sciatis non hominibus istum, sed virtutibus hostem semper fuisse, me expulso, Catone amandato, in eum ipsum se convertit, quo auctore, quo adiutore in contionibus ea, quae gerebat, omnia, quaeque gesserat, se et fecisse et facere dicebat : Cn. Pompeium, quem omnium iudicio longe principem esse civitatis videbat, diutius furori suo veniam daturum non arbitrabatur. Qui ex eius custodia per insidias regis amici filium, hostem, captivum, surripuisset, et ea iniuria virum fortissimum lacessisset, speravit iisdem se copiis cum illo posse confligere, quibuscum ego noluissem bonorum periculo dimicare, et primo quidem adiutoribus consulibus, postea fregit foedus Gabinius, Piso tamen

67 in fide mansit. Quas iste tum caedes, quas lapidationes, quas fugas fecerit, quam facile ferro cotidianisque insidiis, cum iam a firmissimo robore copiarum suarum relictus esset, Cn. Pompeium foro curiaque privarit domique continuerit vidistis. Ex quo iudicare potestis quanta vis illa fuerit oriens et congre-

a Himself.
b C. again addresses the Pontifices.   *c* Pompey.
d The son of Tigranes, brought to Rome by Pompey ; see Plut. *Pompey*, xlviii.

conferring of a distinction which was a deep insult, the other[a] by the infliction upon him of a disaster 66 which was to his eternal credit. And that you[b] may realize that it is not persons but high qualities that inspire his consistent hatred, I would remind you that, as soon as I had been expelled and Cato removed, he turned round upon the very man[c] whose agency and assistance in mass meetings had enabled him, as he himself admitted, to carry out all his projects in the past, and still continued to enable him ; on the other hand, he did not think it likely that Gnaeus Pompeius, whom every one judged, as he saw, to be far the most powerful man in the state, would long continue to condone his reckless proceedings. Clodius by a plot had seduced from his tutelage an enemy captive, the son of a friendly king,[d] and by this outrage had challenged that gallant gentleman ; and then he deemed that he could sustain a conflict with him by means of the same forces which I had refused to use in a struggle that would have involved peril to patriots. At the outset, indeed, he was backed by the consuls ; but later Gabinius broke his engagement, though Piso 67 remained loyal to him. You have seen the carnage, the stone-throwing, and the banishments for which he was responsible ; you know how easily, even after he had been deserted by the leading stalwarts among his followers, he forbade Gnaeus Pompeius access to the forum and the senate-house by his arms and his daily ambushes, and penned him in his own house ; and upon this knowledge you are able to base an estimate of the formidable nature of his assaults when they were united and in the ascendant, seeing that even when they

gata, cum haec Cn. Pompeium terruerit iam dis-
tracta et exstincta.

68   XXVI. Haec vidit in sententia dicenda Kalendis
Ianuariis vir prudentissimus et cum rei publicae,
cum mihi, tum etiam veritati amicissimus, L. Cotta,
qui legem de meo reditu ferendam non censuit : qui
me consuluisse rei publicae, cessisse tempestati, ami-
ciorem vobis ceterisque civibus quam mihi exstitisse,
vi, armis, dissensione hominum ad caedem instituta
novoque dominatu pulsum esse dixit : nihil de meo
capite potuisse ferri, nihil esse iure scriptum aut
posse valere, omnia contra leges moremque maiorum,
temere, turbulente, per vim, per furorem esse gesta.
Quod si illa lex esset, nec referre ad senatum consulibus nec sententiam dicere sibi licere : quorum
utrumque quum fieret, non oportere ut de me lex
ferretur decerni, ne illa, quae nulla esset, esse
lex iudicaretur. Sententia verior, gravior, melior,
utilior rei publicae nulla esse potuit.   Hominis enim
scelere et furore notato similis a re publica labes in
69 posterum demovebatur.   Neque hoc Cn. Pompeius,
qui ornatissimam de me sententiam dixit, vosque,

ᵃ Consul 65 B.C., censor 63 B.C. ; see Chap. XXXVII.

were disunited and crushed Pompeius was terrified by them.

XXVI. It was because he was cognisant of this, as he stated in the speech which he delivered on the Kalends of January, that Lucius Cotta,[a] a man of supreme tact and a devoted friend of the state, of myself, and of the truth, disapproved of legislation which should bring about my return. He asserted that I had studied the welfare of the republic, had yielded to the storm, had proved a better friend to you and to the community at large than to myself, and that my banishment had been brought about by armed violence, and by a reign of strife and massacre that had been purposely stimulated. It was impossible, he asserted, to pass a measure concerning my civil status ; not a line had been legally formulated so as to possess validity ; the whole process had been against the constitution and against precedent, ill-considered, seditious, over-bearing, infatuated. He pointed out that if Clodius' measure were a law, it would be illegal for the consuls to bring the question before the senate or for him to express an opinion upon it; and seeing that both of these were being done, a resolution that a law should be introduced dealing with my case would be ill-advised, since the measure which was null and void might be pronounced to be a legal enactment. No policy could have been more just, more dignified, more wise, or more beneficial to the republic. A brand was set on the man's unbridled wickedness, and all possibility of a repetition of the mischief was removed from the state for evermore. That the law was not valid, but was rather a piece of inflammatory opportunism, an interdict of wickedness spoken by the lips of frenzy,

pontifices, qui me vestris sententiis auctoritatibusque
defendistis, non vidistis, legem illam esse nullam
atque esse potius flammam temporis, interdictum
sceleris, vocem furoris, sed prospexistis, ne quae
popularis in nos aliquando invidia redundaret, si sine
populi iudicio restituti videremur. Eodemque consilio M. Bibuli, fortissimi viri, senatus sententiam
secutus est, ut vos de mea domo statueretis, non quo
dubitaret quin ab isto nihil legibus, nihil religionibus,
nihil iure esset actum, sed ne quis oreretur aliquando
in tanta ubertate improborum qui in meis aedibus
aliquam religionem residere diceret. Nam legem
quidem istam nullam esse, quotienscumque de me
senatus sententiam dixit, totiens iudicavit, quoniam
quidem scripto illo istius sententiam dicere vetabatur.
70 Atque hanc rem par illud simile, Piso et Gabinius,
vidit : homines legum iudiciorumque metuentes,
quum frequentissimus senatus eos ut de me referrent cotidie flagitaret, non se rem improbare dicebant,
sed lege istius impediri. Erat hoc verum. Nam
impediebantur, verum ea lege, quam idem iste de
Macedonia Syriaque tulerat. XXVII. Hanc tu, P.
Lentule, neque privatus neque consul legem esse
umquam putasti. Nam tribunis plebis referentibus

was not lost upon Gnaeus Pompeius, who stated his views in terms highly complimentary to myself, nor upon you, gentlemen, who defended me by your expressed opinions and your moral influence; but you took precautions against any future outburst of popular resentment against me, if at any time it should be considered that my restoration had not been sanctioned by the popular will. It was with the same idea that the senate adopted the motion of the gallant Marcus Bibulus that you should pronounce upon the question of my house, not that it had any doubt that Clodius' proceedings had been utterly unconstitutional, sacrilegious, and disorderly, but because in times that were so prolific of traitors they wished to prevent anyone from standing forth one day and saying that some vestige of sanctity still hovered about my house. For the senate never pronounced any opinion in my case without at the same time adjudging that Clodius' law was null and void, since by the terms of his law they were forbidden to pronounce an opinion. This fact did not escape the notice of that well-matched pair, Piso and Gabinius; being scrupulous observers of laws and decisions, they declared, when daily urged by a full senate to propose a measure dealing with me, that, though the proposal had their approval, they were prevented by Clodius' law from supporting it. That was true; they were prevented, but it was by the law which this same Clodius had carried dealing with Macedonia and Syria. XXVII. But the former law you, Publius Lentulus, judged never to be a law at all, either when you were consul or when you were a private citizen. For as consul-elect you repeatedly spoke on motions

sententiam de me designatus consul saepe dixisti:
ex Kalendis Ianuariis, quoad perfecta res est, de me
rettulisti, legem promulgasti, tulisti: quorum tibi,
si esset illa lex, nihil liceret. At etiam Q. Metellus,
collega tuus, clarissimus vir, quam legem esse homines alienissimi a P. Clodio iudicarent, Piso et
Gabinius, eam nullam esse frater P. Clodii, quum de
71 me ad senatum tecum una rettulit, iudicavit. Sed
vero isti, qui Clodii leges timuerunt, quem ad modum
ceteras observarunt? Senatus quidem, cuius est
gravissimum iudicium de iure legum, quotienscumque
de me consultus est, totiens eam nullam esse iudicavit.
Quod idem tu, Lentule, vidisti in ea lege, quam de me
tulisti. Nam non est ita latum, ut mihi Romam venire
liceret, sed UT VENIREM. Non enim voluisti id, quod
licebat, ferre ut liceret, sed me ita esse in re publica,
magis ut arcessitus imperio populi Romani viderer
quam ad administrandam civitatem restitutus.

72   Hunc tu etiam, portentosa pestis, exsulem appellare ausus es, cum tantis sceleribus esses et flagitiis
notatus, ut omnem locum quo adisses exsilii similli-
mum redderes? Quid est enim exsul? Ipsum per
se nomen calamitatis, non turpitudinis. Quando

concerning me proposed by the tribunes of the plebs; from the Kalends of January until your aim had been successfully achieved, you introduced, promulgated, and carried motions dealing with me; none of which could you legally have done, were Clodius' enactment valid. Furthermore, the measure which was pronounced to be valid by Piso and Gabinius, who had no connexion at all with Publius Clodius, was pronounced to be null and void by your colleague, the distinguished Quintus Metellus, Publius Clodius' cousin, when in conjunction with you he brought a motion in my case before the senate. But what respect for laws in general was displayed by those who were so meticulous in dealing with the laws of Clodius? The senate, indeed, whose decision on a question of legal validity outweighs every other, was never consulted in my case without pronouncing against the validity of Clodius' law, a fact which you too, Lentulus, must have observed in the deliberation upon the law dealing with me which you introduced. For your law enacted not that I should be permitted to come to Rome, but that I should come; for you did not wish to enact that it should be lawful for me to do that which was already lawful, but that my position in the state should suggest that I had been ordered back by the Roman people rather than restored to active political life.

And was it such a man as I am, O baneful prodigy that you are, whom you dared to describe as an exile, branded as you were with crimes and enormities so heinous that you made every spot you approached like a place of banishment? For what is an exile? In itself the name implies misfortune, not disgrace.

igitur est turpe ? re vera, quum est poena peccati :
opinione autem hominum etiam, si est poena damnati.
Utrum igitur peccato meo nomen subeo an re iudicata ? Peccato ? Iam neque tu id dicere audes,
quem isti satellites tui felicem Catilinam nominant,
neque quisquam eorum, qui solebant. Non modo
iam nemo est tam imperitus qui ea, quae gessi in
consulatu, peccata esse dicat, sed nemo est tam
inimicus patriae qui non meis consiliis patriam con-
73 servatam esse fateatur. XXVIII. Quod enim est in
terris commune tantum tantulumve consilium quod
non de meis rebus gestis ea, quae mihi essent opta-
tissima et pulcherrima, iudicarit ? Summum est
populi Romani populorumque et gentium omnium ac
regum consilium senatus : decrevit ut omnes, qui
rem publicam salvam esse vellent, ad me unum
defendendum venirent, ostenditque nec stare potuisse rem publicam, si ego non fuissem, nec futuram
74 esse ullam, si non redissem. Proximus est huic
dignitati ordo equester : omnes omnium publicorum
societates de meo consulatu ac de meis rebus gestis
amplissima atque ornatissima decreta fecerunt.
Scribae, qui nobiscum in rationibus monumentisque
publicis versantur, non obscurum de meis in rem
publicam beneficiis suum iudicium decretumque esse

When, then, does it convey disgrace ? It conveys an actual disgrace when it comes as a retribution for misdoing, and a disgrace in the eyes of society as well when it is the punishment that follows upon an adverse verdict. Is it then as a result of my misdoing that I incur the name, or by the issue of an action at law ? Misdoing of mine ? To-day neither will you, whom your minions dub " Catiline in Luck," dare to use this word, nor will any of those who used it in the past. Not merely is there no one so ill-instructed as to apply the word " misdoing " to the achievements of my consulship, but there is no one so ill-disposed to his country as to refuse to admit that it was by my counsels that that country was 73 preserved. XXVIII. For what public deliberative body is there, important or unimportant, in the whole world, whose verdict upon my achievements has not been such as to meet my highest desires and my proudest ambitions ? The supreme deliberative body of the Roman people, and indeed of all peoples, nations, and kings, is the senate ; and the senate decreed that all who had the safety of the republic at heart should rally to my sole defence, and intimated that the state could not have survived had I not existed, and would be annihilated should I 74 not be restored. Immediately below this exalted body is the equestrian order ; and all the companies for the collection of all the public revenues which this order contained passed resolutions concerning my consulship and my achievements which were most laudatory and enthusiastic. The secretaries, who assist us in the charge of public accounts and records, endeavoured to express in unmistakable terms their judgement and conclusion upon my ser-

voluerunt.   Nullum est in hac urbe collegium, nulli
pagani aut montani, quoniam plebei quoque urbanae
maiores nostri conventicula et quasi concilia quaedam
esse voluerunt, qui non amplissime non modo de
75 salute mea, sed etiam de dignitate decreverint.   Nam
quid ego illa divina atque immortalia municipiorum
et coloniarum et totius Italiae decreta commemorem,
quibus tamquam gradibus mihi videor in caelum
ascendisse, non solum in patriam revertisse ?   Ille
vero dies qui fuit, cum te, P. Lentule, legem de me
ferente populus Romanus ipse vidit sensitque quantus
et quanta dignitate essem [1] ?   Constat enim nullis
umquam comitiis campum Martium tanta celebritate,
tanto splendore omnis generis hominum, aetatum,
ordinum floruisse.   Omitto civitatium, nationum,
provinciarum, regum, orbis denique terrarum de meis
in omnes mortales meritis unum iudicium unumque
consensum : adventus meus atque introitus in urbem
qui fuit ? utrum me patria sic accepit, ut lucem
salutemque redditam sibi ac restitutam accipere
debuit, an ut crudelem tyrannum, quod vos, Catilinae
76 gregales, de me dicere solebatis ?   Itaque ille unus
dies, quo die me populus Romanus a porta in Capitolium atque inde domum sua celebritate laetitiaque
comitatum honestavit, tantae mihi iucunditati fuit,
ut tua mihi conscelerata illa vis non modo non

[1] esset *Pet.*

---

a Manutius says that by these are meant the inhabitants
of the villages in the Ager Romanus, who were reckoned
among the city tribes.

b This may mean the dwellers on the hills (in Rome) ;
but these were mostly inhabited by the rich.

c Or, reading *esset*, " its own."

vices to the state. There is no guild in this city, no community, whether of the villages *a* or the highlands *b* (for it was the will of our ancestors that the city proletariate too should have its committees and councils of a kind), which did not register most complimentary decrees dealing not only with my restora-
75 tion but also with my merits. Why should I enlarge upon the heaven-inspired and never-to-be-forgotten decrees of the municipalities and colonies, and indeed of the whole of Italy,—a ladder, for so I account them, whereby not merely did I return to my country, but climbed to heaven? But what a day was that, Publius Lentulus, when the Roman people itself saw you proposing a measure dealing with me, and when it realized my *c* greatness and my *c* eminent merits? For it is generally recognized that at no previous meeting of the assembly had the Field of Mars ever shone with so brilliant a concourse of all ranks, all ages, and all orders of men. I forbear to mention the unanimity of judgement and opinion with regard to my services displayed by communities, tribes, provinces, kings, and, in a word, by all the world, and pass to my arrival at and entry into the city. What was its character? Did my country welcome me as she was bound to welcome the light of her salvation returned and restored to her ; or did she welcome me as a cruel tyrant, to use the term applied to me by you cronies of
76 Catiline? Why, that day, and that alone, whereon the Roman people graced my return by their thronging and enraptured escort from the gate to the Capitol and thence to my house, was a source of such deep gratification to me, that it may well seem that instead of quelling your lawless depravity

propulsanda, sed etiam excitanda[1] fuisse videatur.
Qua re illa calamitas, si ita est appellanda, exussit hoc
genus totum maledicti, ne quisquam iam audeat
reprehendere consulatum meum tot, tantis, tam
ornatis iudiciis, testimoniis, auctoritatibus compro-
batum. XXIX. Quod si in isto tuo maledicto probrum non modo mihi nullum obiectas, sed etiam
laudem illustras meam, quid te aut fieri aut fingi
dementius potest ? Uno enim maledicto bis a me
patriam servatam esse concedis : semel, cum id feci,
quod omnes non negent immortalitati, si fieri potest.
mandandum, tu supplicio puniendum putasti : iterum,
cum tuum multorumque praeter te inflammatum
in bonos omnes impetum meo corpore excepi, ne
eam civitatem, quam servassem inermis, armatus in
discrimen adducerem.

77 Esto : non fuit in me poena ulla peccati : at fuit
iudicii. Cuius ? quis me umquam ulla lege interro-
gavit ? quis postulavit ? quis diem dixit ? Potest
igitur damnati poenam sustinere indemnatus ? est
hoc tribunicium ? est populare ? quamquam ubi tu
te popularem, nisi cum pro populo fecisti, potes
dicere ? Sed cum hoc iuris a maioribus proditum
sit, ut nemo civis Romanus aut libertatem aut civita-

---

[1] excitanda *Halm* : emendanda, emenda *MSS.*

---

[a] An ironical reference to the participation of Clodius,
disguised as a woman, in the rites of Bona Dea (for whom
see Dict. Class. Ant.).

1 ought to have encouraged it. Thus my misfortune, if misfortune it must be called, has silenced all slander of this kind, so that no one any more is so hardy as to cast aspersions on my consulship, sealed as it is with the approval of so many authoritative and distinguished judgements, testimonies, and official pronouncements. XXIX. But if in all your campaign of scurrility not merely do you fail to fasten any reproach upon me, but even shed lustre upon my fame, what thing more senseless than you are can exist or be conceived? For in a single abusive utterance you twice admit that it was I who saved my country: first, when I had performed a deed which all admit deserved a place on the deathless record of history, if it may so be, whereas you expressed an opinion that it should be visited with death; and secondly, when I met with my own body the infuriated onset against law-abiding citizens of you and many beside you, that I might not, by having resort to arms, endanger a state which unarmed I had preserved.

77 So far so good; it was for no misdoing that I suffered retribution. Then perhaps it was the result of an action at law. But of what action? Who has ever brought me to book under any law? Who has applied for a writ against me or named a day for trial? But can a man uncondemned undergo a penalty which is the sequel only of a condemnation? Is such a thing compatible with the tribunate or with democracy? And yet what act of yours can you point to as democratic, save your performance of sacrifice on the people's behalf?[a] But inasmuch as it is a right which we have received by the tradition of our ancestors that no Roman citizen should

tem possit amittere, nisi ipse auctor factus sit : quod
tu ipse potuisti in tua causa discere—credo enim,
quamquam in illa adoptatione legitime factum est
nihil, tamen te esse interrogatum, AUCTORNE ESSES, UT
IN TE P. FONTEIUS VITAE NECISQUE POTESTATEM HABERET,
UT IN FILIO,—quaero, si aut negasses aut tacuisses, si
tamen id xxx curiae iussissent, num id iussum esset
ratum ?   Certe non.   Quid ita ? quia ius a maioribus
nostris, qui non ficte et fallaciter populares, sed vere
et sapienter fuerunt, ita comparatum est, ut civis
Romanus libertatem nemo posset invitus amittere.
78 Quin etiam, si decemviri sacramentum in libertatem
iniustum iudicassent, tamen quotienscumque vellet
quis, hoc in genere solo rem iudicatam referri posse
voluerunt : civitatem vero nemo umquam ullo populi
iussu amittet invitus.   XXX. Qui cives Romani in
colonias Latinas proficiscebantur, fieri non poterant
Latini, nisi erant auctores facti nomenque dederant :
qui erant rerum capitalium condemnati, non prius
hanc civitatem amittebant, quam erant in eam recepti,
quo vertendi, hoc est mutandi, soli causa venerant.
Id autem ut esset faciundum, non ademptione civitatis, sed tecti et aquae et ignis interdictione facie-
79 bant.   Populus Romanus L. Sulla dictatore ferente

---

^a The *Comitia Curiata*, by whom adoptions must be sanc-
tioned.
^b *Sc. Stlitibus Iudicandis*, a standing board of plebeian
lawyers, which dealt with cases involving citizenship.
^c This chapter is difficult to follow, but seems to pursue
the point that neither Cicero nor any other Roman could lose
liberty or citizenship save by his own act.

be able to lose his freedom or his citizenship save by a deliberate act on his part, a fact that you might have been enabled to learn in your own case (for I suppose, even though your adoption was utterly illegal at every point, you were nevertheless asked whether it was with your full consent that Publius Fonteius received powers of life and death over you as over a son),—inasmuch as this is so, supposing that you had returned the answer " no " or given no answer at all to that question, would the decree have been ratified all the same if the thirty parishes *a* had voted for it ? Most assuredly it would not. Why so ? Because our ancestors, who were democratic not from pose or hypocrisy, but genuinely and wisely, ordained it as a right that no Roman citizen should be able to lose his freedom against his will.

78 Moreover their intent was that, even if the Commission of Ten *b* had given an unjust decision affecting the liberty of anyone, a man might still, in this kind of case alone, bring up again for decision, as often as he wished, a case on which a verdict had already been given ; but no one by any decree of the people will ever lose his liberty against his will. XXX. Those again who, being Roman citizens,*c* migrated to Latin colonies, could not become Latins unless they deliberately chose to do so, and sent in their names for enrolment. Those who had been condemned on capital charges did not lose citizenship of this state until they had been accepted as citizens of the state whither they had gone in order to " turn," that is to say change, their soil. And that this might be practicable, they had resort not to deprivation of citizenship, but to interdiction from hospitality, water,

79 and fire. On a motion made by the dictator Lucius

comitiis centuriatis municipiis civitatem ademit:
ademit eisdem agros : de agris ratum est : fuit enim
populi potestas : de civitate ne tam diu quidem valuit,
quam diu illa Sullani temporis arma valuerunt. An
vero Volaterranis, cum etiam tum essent in armis,
L. Sulla victor, re publica recuperata, comitiis centuriatis, civitatem eripere non potuit, hodieque
Volaterrani non modo cives, sed etiam optimi cives
fruuntur nobiscum simul hac civitate : consulari
homini P. Clodius, eversa re publica, civitatem adi-
mere potuit concilio advocato, conductis operis non
solum egentium, sed etiam servorum, Fidulio principe,
80 qui se illo die confirmat Romae non fuisse ?   Quod si
non fuit, quid te audacius, qui eius nomen [1] incideris ?
quid desperatius, qui ne ementiendo quidem potueris
auctorem adumbrare meliorem ? Sin autem is
primus scivit, quod facile potuit, qui propter inopiam
tecti in foro pernoctasset, cur non iuret se Gadibus
fuisse, cum tu te fuisse Interamnae probaveris ? Hoc
tu igitur homo popularis iure munitam civitatem
et libertatem nostram putas esse oportere, ut, si,

---

[1] *After* nomen *Müller inserts* in aes.

[a] The name of the first voter in the *tribus praerogativa*
(see *Dict. sub verb.*) was engraved at the top of the bronze
tablet on which a law was inscribed.

[b] Mod. Cadiz, always used to signify remoteness ; cp.
Hor. *Od.* ii. 6. 1.

[c] E. of Latium, mod. Terni.

Sulla before the assembly of the Centuries the Roman
people deprived certain municipalities of the citizenship, depriving them at the same time of territories.
The deprivation of territory was ratified, for that
came within the scope of the popular jurisdiction ;
but the deprivation of citizenship remained valid for
not even as long as Sulla's armed régime was in
power.   Lucius Sulla, after his triumphant restoration of the republic, was unable through the assembly
of the Centuries to wrest their citizenship from the
people of Volaterrae, though they were at the time
under arms, so that to-day that people are not
merely citizens, but are on the first footing of citizenship, and are in equal enjoyment of the franchise
with ourselves ; and was Publius Clodius able, after
subverting the republic, to rob of his citizenship a
man of consular rank, by the mere summoning of a
meeting, and the hiring of gangs, not merely of
ne'er-do-wells but even of slaves, with Fidulius as
their ring-leader, who states that on that day he
was not at Rome ? But if he was not at Rome,
what greater audacity than yours to have had his
name engraved [a] ? What more desperate plight than
to have been unable even by lying to draft a more
reputable promoter of your measure ? But if he
was the first to give his vote, as indeed is easily
conceivable, seeing that, being without a roof to
cover him, he had spent the night in the forum,
why should he not swear that he was at Gades,[b]
when you on one occasion endeavoured to prove
that you were at Interamna [c] ? And is this the right
which you, pillar of our democracy, think should be
the bulwark of our citizenship and our freedom, the
right of each one of us to lose our franchise, if, when

229

tribuno plebis rogante VELITIS IUBEATISNE, Fidulii
centum se velle et iubere dixerint, possit unus quisque
nostrum amittere civitatem ? Tum igitur maiores
nostri populares non fuerunt, qui de civitate et
libertate ea.iura sanxerunt, quae nec vis temporum
nec potentia magistratuum nec res iam iudicata nec
denique universi populi Romani potestas, quae ceteris
81 in rebus est maxima, labefactare possit. At tu etiam,
ereptor civitatis, legem de iniuriis publicis tulisti
Anagnino nescio cui Menullae pergratam, qui tibi ob
eam legem statuam in meis aedibus posuit, ut locus
ipse in tanta tua iniuria legem et inscriptionem
statuae refelleret : quae res municipibus Anagninis
ornatissimis multo maiori dolori fuit quam quae idem
ille gladiator scelera Anagniae fecerat. XXXI. Quid ?
si ne scriptum quidem umquam est in ista ipsa rogatione, quam se Fidulius negat scivisse, tu autem, ut
acta tui praeclari tribunatus hominis dignitate co-
82 honestes, auctoritatem amplecteris :—sed tamen, si
nihil de me tulisti quo minus essem non modo in
civium numero, sed etiam in eo loco, in quo me
honores populi Romani collocarunt, tamenne eum tua
voce violabis, quem post nefarium scelus consulum
superiorum tot vides iudiciis senatus, populi Romani,
totius Italiae honestatum ? quem ne tunc quidem,

---

a In Latium, mod. Anagni ; nothing is known of the affair
alluded to.   *b* *i.e.* Piso and Gabinius.

the tribune of the plebs asks, "Is it your will and command?" a hundred men of Fidulius' stamp say that it is their will and command? If this is so, then there was no true democratic spirit in our ancestors, who laid down laws of franchise and freedom with the intent that neither phases of lawlessness, nor ascendancy of magistrates, nor verdicts recorded, nor even the authority of the whole Roman people, paramount in all else, should avail to undermine them. Yet even you, the spoiler of men's civic rights, carried a measure for the redressing of public wrongs to the particular gratification of some fellow or other of Anagnia^a named Menulla, who in gratitude for this measure set up a statue to you in my house, so that the very place which you had so deeply wronged was a standing refutation of your law and the inscription below the statue ; and this act was a far deeper mortification to the people of Anagnia than were the crimes which that gladiator had wrought at Anagnia. XXXI. But supposing that that actual bill of yours, of which Fidulius disclaims all knowledge, though you, in order to dignify the proceedings of your egregious tribunate by the support of an influential individual, lay claim to him as prime mover, has no such clause in it,—supposing that, in spite of your claim, you carried no motion to oust me, not merely from my place as a citizen, but from the position in which I have been placed by the distinctions which the Roman people have conferred upon me,—will you nevertheless sully by your utterances one whom you see to have been honoured, after the profane wickedness of past consuls,^b by so many pronouncements of the senate, the Roman people, and the whole of Italy, and to whom

cum aberam, negare poteras esse tua lege senatorem ? Ubi enim tuleras, ut mihi aqua et igni interdiceretur ? quod C. Gracchus de P. Popilio, Saturninus
de Metello tulit, homines seditiosissimi de optimis ac
fortissimis civibus, non ut esset interdictum, quod ferri
non poterat, tulerunt, sed ut interdiceretur. Ubi
cavisti ne meo me loco censor in senatum legeret ?
quod de omnibus, etiam quibus damnatis interdictum
83 est, scriptum est in legibus. Quaere hoc ex Clodio,
scriptore legum tuarum : iube adesse : latitat
omnino, sed si requiri iusseris, invenient hominem
apud sororem tuam occultantem se capite demisso.
Sed si patrem tuum, civem me dius fidius egregium
dissimilemque vestri, nemo umquam sanus exsulem
appellavit, qui, cum de eo tribunus plebis promul-
gasset, adesse propter iniquitatem illius Cinnani
temporis noluit eique imperium est abrogatum—si in
illo poena legitima turpitudinem non habuit propter
vim temporum, in me, cui dies dicta numquam est,
qui reus non fui, qui numquam sum a tribuno plebis
citatus, damnati poena esse potuit, ea praesertim,
quae ne in ipsa quidem rogatione praescripta est ?

^a See *Ad Quirites*, Chap. III. n.
^b See *Pro Plancio*, Chap. XXVIII. n.
^c Sextus.   ^d 86–84.

not even in my absence could you deny the title of
senator under the terms of your law ? For on what
occasion had you carried a motion that I should be
debarred from fire and water ? This was a motion
that Gaius Gracchus carried against Publius Popilius,[a]
and Saturninus against Metellus,[b] turbulent individuals, that is to say, against upright and gallant
citizens ; but their measures were not that an
interdict should *have* been passed, which would have
been an impossible measure, but that it should be
passed. Where was your clause to forbid the censor
from choosing me to fill the place in the senate which
I myself had vacated ? Clauses affecting this are
included in all measures of outlawry, even when
that penalty follows upon the adverse finding of a
court. Inquire of Clodius,[c] who draws up your laws
for you ; bid him appear. He is skulking away out
of sight ; but do but order search to be made for
him, and the fellow will be discovered secreting himself shamefacedly at your sister's house. But if no
one in his senses ever applied the name of exile to
your father, who was a splendid citizen, indeed, and
utterly unlike you and your brother, and who, when
the tribune of the plebs promulgated a measure
dealing with him, refused to answer the charge
owing to the lawlessness that prevailed in those
days when Cinna ruled,[d] and was deprived of his
command,—if in his case a legally-inflicted penalty
carried with it no stigma, because it was enacted in
turbulent times, could there have been any penalty
after conviction, above all one not enacted even in
the actual bill, in my case, who had never been cited
to appear on a fixed day, who was never defendant
in a suit, and never summoned to appear by a

84 XXXII. Ac vide quid intersit inter illum iniquissi-
mum patris tui casum et hanc fortunam condicionem-
que nostram.   Patrem tuum, civem optimum, clarissimi viri filium, qui si viveret, qua severitate fuit, tu
profecto non viveres, L. Philippus censor avunculum
suum praeteriit in recitando senatu.   Nihil enim
poterat dicere quare rata non essent, quae erant acta
in ea re publica, in qua se illis ipsis temporibus
censorem esse voluisset : me L. Cotta, homo censorius, in senatu iuratus dixit se, si censor tum esset,
cum ego aberam, meo loco senatorem recitaturum
85 fuisse.   Quis in meum locum iudicem subdidit ? quis
meorum amicorum testamentum discessu meo fecit
qui mihi non idem tribuerit, quod si adessem ? quis
me non modo civis, sed socius recipere contra tuam
legem et iuvare dubitavit ?   Denique universus
senatus multo ante quam est lata lex de me, gratias
agendas censuit civitatibus iis, quae M. Tullium :
tantumme ? immo etiam, civem optime de re
publica meritum, recepissent.   Et tu unus pestifer
civis eum restitutum negas esse civem, quem eiectum
234

tribune of the plebs ?   XXXII. And pray note the
contrast between the scandalous injustice of your
father's fate and the circumstances of my own career.
That excellent citizen, your father, who was himself
the son of a renowned gentleman,—if he, with his
austere character, were alive to-day, *you* would certainly not be alive,—was passed over in the reading
of the list of senators by the censor Lucius Philippus,
who was his own nephew.   For he could allege no
reason why ratification should be withheld from enactments which had been passed at a crisis in public
affairs when, though the times were what they were,
he had wished to be censor himself ; whereas in
my case, Lucius Cotta, an ex-censor, declared under
oath in the senate that if he had been censor
during the period of my absence, he would have duly
read my name among those of the other senators.
5 Who substituted another name on the list of jurymen
for my own ?   Who was there among my friends who
made his will at the time of my retirement, and did
not make exactly the same bequest to me as he
would have done if I had still been on the scene ?
What citizen was there, nay, what member of an
allied community, who hesitated to give me shelter
and assistance in defiance of your law ?   Last of all,
the whole senate, long before the passing of any
measure dealing with me, resolved that a vote of
thanks be accorded to those states which had given
shelter to Marcus Tullius,—was that all ?   By no
means—" a citizen who," so the resolution proceeded,
" has deserved highly of the republic."   And is
yours, pestilential citizen that you are, the sole voice
to deny citizenship after his restoration to a man
who, even when an outcast, was ever accounted by

universus senatus non modo civem, sed etiam egre-
86 gium civem semper putavit ? At vero, ut annales
populi Romani et monumenta vetustatis loquuntur,
Kaeso ille Quinctius et M. Furius Camillus et C.
Servilius Ahala, cum essent optime de re publica
meriti, tamen populi incitati vim iracundiamque
subierunt, damnatique comitiis centuriatis cum in
exsilium profugissent, rursus ab eodem populo placato
sunt in suam pristinam dignitatem restituti. Quod
si his damnatis non modo non imminuit calamitas
clarissimi nominis gloriam, sed etiam honestavit—
nam etsi optabilius est cursum vitae conficere sine
dolore et sine iniuria, tamen ad immortalitatem
gloriae plus adfert desideratum esse a suis civibus
quam omnino numquam esse violatum,—mihi sine
ullo iudicio populi profecto, cum amplissimis omnium
iudiciis restituto maledicti locum aut criminis obtine-
87 bit ? Fortis et constans in optima ratione civis P.
Popilius semper fuit : tamen eius in omni vita nihil
est iam ad laudem illustrius quam calamitas ipsa.
Quis enim iam meminisset eum bene de re publica
meritum, nisi et ab improbis expulsus esset et per
bonos restitutus ? Q. Metelli praeclarum imperium
in re militari fuit, egregia censura, omnis vita
plena gravitatis : tamen huius viri laudem ad sempiternam memoriam temporis calamitas propagavit.

---

[a] Son of Cincinnatus, Livy iii. 2.
[b] Livy v. 32.   [c] Livy iv. 14.

the whole senate as not merely a citizen, but even a citizen of distinction? And yet, as the records of the Roman people and their ancient annals tell us, Kaeso Quinctius[a] and Marcus Furius Camillus[b] and Gaius Servilius Ahala,[c] though they had deserved highly of the republic, bowed before the animosity and violence of a populace that had been roused against them; condemned by the assembly of the Centuries, they fled into exile, but once again the same populace, with its wrath appeased, recalled them to their previous dignity. But if the fall of these men, condemned though they were, so far from impairing the glory of their famous names, even gave them added lustre,—for though we should rather pray to finish life's course free from sorrow and injustice, it is still a greater title to an immortality of renown that one's absence should be felt by one's fellow-citizens than that one should have been altogether immune from outrage,—shall I, who went forth at the bidding of no people's verdict, but amid the enthusiastic opinions of all, find that my restoration is to be occupied as a vantage-ground for malicious and accusatory tongues? In pursuing his lofty policy Publius Popilius showed himself invariably courageous and steadfast; but nothing in all his career so illumines his merits as his actual downfall. For who at this time would remember the services he conferred upon the state, had he not been banished by traitors and restored by the efforts of patriots? As a military commander Quintus Metellus was brilliant, as a censor he was exemplary, earnestness was the note of his whole career; yet what has perpetuated this hero's renown to eternal recollection has been his fall.

XXXIII. Quod si illis, qui expulsi sunt inique, sed
tamen legibus, reducti inimicis interfectis, rogationibus tribunicis, non auctoritate senatus, non comitiis centuriatis, non decretis Italiae, non desiderio
civitatis, iniuria inimicorum probro non fuit : in me,
qui profectus sum integer, afui simul cum re publica,
redii cum maxima dignitate te vivo, fratre tuo altero
consule reducente, altero praetore patiente, tuum
88 scelus meum probrum putas esse oportere ? Ac si
me populus Romanus incitatus iracundia aut invidia e
civitate eiecisset idemque postea mea in rem publicam beneficia recordatus se collegisset, temeritatem
atque iniuriam suam restitutione mea reprehendisset,
tamen profecto nemo tam esset amens qui mihi tale
populi iudicium non dignitati potius quam dedecori
putaret esse oportere. Nunc vero cum me in
iudicium populi nemo omnium vocarit, condemnari
non potuerim, qui accusatus non sim, denique ne
pulsus quidem ita sim, ut, si contenderem, superare
non possem, contraque a populo Romano semper sim
defensus, amplificatus, ornatus, quid est qua re quis-
89 quam mihi se ipsa populari ratione anteponat ? An

XXXIII. These great men were banished unjustly,
though not illegally; their return was permitted by
the death of their opponents, and was enacted by
bills of the tribunes, not by senatorial authority, nor
by the assembly of the centuries, nor the decrees of
Italy, nor the yearning of their compatriots; and if
the wrongs done them by their enemies were no
slur upon them, do you think that I, who went forth
unstained, taking the republic with me, and who
returned at the height of my prestige, while you yet
lived, with one of your cousins, a consul, supporting
my restoration, and your brother, a praetor, acqui-
escing in it, can justly find in your crime my own
disgrace? Had the Roman people been wrought
upon by anger or jealousy to eject me from the
state, and had they been later brought to a better
frame of mind by a recollection of my benefits to the
republic, so as by my recall to pass censure upon
their own ill-considered injustice, even so I am quite
sure that no one would be so stupid as not to consider that such expression of the popular will should
redound rather to the enhancement of my reputation
than to my discredit. But since, as things are, there
is not a man on earth who has summoned me to
submit myself to a verdict of the people and since,
not having been accused, it has been impossible for
me to be condemned, and since, lastly, the conditions
even of my banishment have not been such that I
could not have won the day if I had contended the
matter, but on the contrary I have always been
championed, exalted, and distinguished by the Roman
people, what grounds can anyone have for claiming
precedence for himself over me in the popular
estimation? Or do you count that body to be the

tu populum Romanum esse putas illum, qui constat
ex iis, qui mercede conducuntur ? qui impelluntur ut
vim adferant magistratibus, ut obsideant senatum :
optent cotidie caedem, incendia, rapinas ? Quem tu
tamen populum nisi tabernis clausis frequentare non
poteras, cui populo duces Lentidios, Lollios, Plagu-
leios, Sergios praefeceras. O speciem dignitatemque
populi Romani quam reges, quam nationes exterae,
quam gentes ultimae pertimescant, multitudinem
hominum ex servis, ex conductis, ex facinerosis, ex
90 egentibus congregatam ! Illa fuit pulcritudo populi
Romani, illa forma, quam in campo vidisti tum, cum
etiam tibi contra senatus totiusque Italiae auctoritatem et studium dicendi potestas fuit. Ille populus
est dominus regum, victor atque imperator omnium
gentium, quem illo clarissimo die, scelerate, vidisti
tum, cum omnes principes civitatis, omnes ordinum
atque aetatum omnium suffragium se non de civis,
sed de civitatis salute ferre censebant : cum denique
homines in campum non tabernis, sed municipiis
91 clausis venerunt. XXXIV. Hoc ego populo, si tum
consules aut fuissent in re publica aut omnino non
fuissent, nullo labore tuo praecipiti furori atque impio
sceleri restitissem. Sed publicam causam contra vim
armatam sine populi praesidio suscipere nolui : non
quo mihi P. Scipionis, fortissimi viri, vis in Ti.
Graccho [1] privati hominis displiceret, sed Scipionis

---

[1] *So Müller* : vis intima *most* MSS.

---

[a] Who led the attack on Tib. Gracchus 133.

Roman people, which is formed of those who are hired for pay, who are goaded on to employ violence against the magistrates, to blockade the senate, and to fix their daily hopes upon slaughter, fire, and robbery? But even such a body as this you were unable to assemble without closing the shops, and had appointed as ring-leaders over it men of the stamp of Lentidius, Lollius, Plaguleius, and Sergius. To think that the pride and majesty of the Roman people, dreaded by kings, foreign tribes, and nations at the end of the earth, should be represented by a mob of men mustered from slaves, hirelings, criminals, and desperadoes! This was the Roman people whose beauty and brilliance met your gaze in the Campus on that day when even you found licence to speak against the authority and the ideals of the senate and of an united Italy! This the people, master of kings, victor and ruler over all nations, which you, villain, surveyed on that proud day when all the leading men of the state, and all people of all ranks and ages of life, gave a vote which they held to be a vote upon the welfare not of a citizen but of the civic body; when, in a word, not the shops alone, but whole country towns were closed, that the world might gather at the Campus. XXXIV. This is the people who, had there been any consuls at that time in the state, or even had there been no consuls at all, would have enabled me without effort to withstand your headstrong frenzy and profane wickedness. But without a bodyguard of the people I was reluctant to undertake the people's cause against armed lawlessness; not that I disapproved of the extreme of lawlessness employed in the case of Tiberius Gracchus by the gallant Publius Scipio,[a] when he acted in a private

factum statim P. Mucius consul, qui in gerenda re
putabatur fuisse segnior, gesta multis senatus consultis non modo defendit, sed etiam ornavit : mihi
aut te interfecto cum consulibus aut te vivo et tecum
92 et cum illis armis decertandum fuit. Erant eo tempore multa etiam alia metuenda. Ad servos, medius
fidius, res publica venisset : tantum homines impios
ex vetere illa coniuratione inustum nefariis mentibus
bonorum odium tenebat.

Hic tu me etiam gloriari vetas : negas esse ferenda
quae soleam de me praedicare, et homo facetus
inducis etiam sermonem urbanum ac venustum, me
dicere solere esse me Iovem, eumdemque dictitare
Minervam esse sororem meam. Non tam insolens
sum, quod Iovem esse me dico, quam ineruditus, quod
Minervam sororem Iovis esse existimo. Sed tamen
ego mihi sororem virginem ascisco : tu sororem tuam
virginem esse non sisti. Sed vide ne tu te soleas
Iovem dicere, quod tu iure eamdem sororem et
93 uxorem appellare possis. XXXV. Et quoniam hoc
reprehendis, quod solere me dicas de me ipso gloriosius praedicare, quis umquam audivit, cum ego de

---

ᵃ *i.e.* of Catiline.

ᵇ To whom C. had a special devotion. " Taking a statue
of Minerva, which he had long kept in his house . . ., [he]
carried it to the Capitol, and dedicated it there with this
inscription, 'To Minerva, the Protectress of Rome.'"
Plutarch, *Cicero* (trans. Langhorne).

capacity; on that occasion Publius Mucius the consul, who was considered to have been somewhat lacking in energy when the deed was in contemplation, when it had been accomplished immediately defended Scipio's action by several decrees in the senate, and even complimented him upon it; but in my case I had the prospect of an armed struggle with the consuls had you been slain, or, had you survived, with you and them combined. At that time there were many other dangers as well to be apprehended. Upon slaves, in all solemnity I say it, would have fallen the government of the state, so bitter was the hatred against men of sound views which possessed unscrupulous persons, and which had been seared into their abominable minds as a result of that now long-past conspiracy.[a]

In this connexion you go so far as to bid me cease from boasting; you declare that the assertions I am in the habit of making concerning myself are intolerable, and, with a pretty turn of wit, you come forward with an elegant and humorous jest to the effect that I am accustomed to call myself Jupiter, and also to assert that Minerva[b] is my sister. My insolence in calling myself Jupiter is not so great as my ignorance in thinking that Minerva is Jupiter's sister. But I at least do claim virginity for my sister; you have not permitted your sister to be a virgin. But I would warn you against the practice of applying the name of Jupiter to yourself, since in your case, as in his, you may use the term of sister and that of wife with regard to the same lady.

XXXV. And since you blame me for being too boastful in sounding my own praises, who, I would ask you, has ever heard me speak of myself, save

me nisi coactus ac necessario dicerem? Nam si,
cum mihi furta, largitiones, libidines obiiciuntur,
ego respondere soleo meis consiliis, periculis, laboribus
patriam esse servatam, non tam sum existimandus
de gestis rebus gloriari quam de obiectis confiteri.
Sed si mihi ante haec durissima rei publicae tempora
nihil umquam aliud obiectum est, nisi crudelitas mea
unius temporis, quum a patria perniciem depuli,
quid? me huic maledicto utrum non respondere an
94 demisse respondere decuit? Ego vero etiam rei
publicae semper interesse putavi me illius pulcher-
rimi facti, quod ex auctoritate senatus consensu bonorum omnium pro salute patriae gessissem, splendorem
verbis dignitatemque retinere, praesertim cum mihi
uni in hac re publica, audiente populo Romano, opera
mea hanc urbem et hanc rem publicam esse salvam
iurato dicere fas fuisset. Exstinctum est iam illud
maledictum crudelitatis, quod me non ut crudelem
tyrannum, sed ut mitissimum parentem, omnium
civium studiis desideratum, repetitum, arcessitum
95 vident. Aliud exortum est. Obiicitur mihi meus
ille discessus: cui ego crimini respondere sine mea
maxima laude non possum. Quid enim, pontifices,
debeo dicere? Peccati me conscientia profugisse?
Ad id, quod mihi crimini dabatur, non modo peccatum
244

under the constraint of an inevitable necessity? For if, when crimes of theft, corruption, and passion are imputed to me, I am in the habit of replying that it was by my forethought, at my risk, and through my exertions that my country was saved, it must be considered that I am not so much boasting of my own exploits, as stating facts in answer to charges. But if, until the recent hard crisis through which the state has passed, no crime has been imputed to me save one isolated act of cruelty, when I warded destruction from our country, which, I ask, was the more dignified course? —to make no reply at all to these aspersions, or to make answer to them with a bowed head? But I have always thought it to be in the interest of the state that I should maintain by every word of mine the splendour and magnificence of the noble deed I had achieved for my country's well-being by the union of patriots and through the support of the senate, especially in view of the fact that I was the only citizen to whom it was permitted to say on oath, in the hearing of the Roman people, that it was through my efforts that this city and this republic still stood. The malignant imputations of cruelty have by now been hushed, because it is seen that I have been yearned for, demanded, and appealed to by the ardent longing of all citizens, not as a cruel tyrant, but as a tender parent. But a new imputation has arisen in its place. My retirement is cast in my teeth; and to this charge I cannot reply without highly exalting my own merits. For what, gentlemen, must I say? That consciousness of misdoing urged me into exile? But the charge that was laid at my door, so far from being a misdoing, was the

245

non erat, sed erat res post natos homines pulcherrima.
Iudicium populi pertimuisse ?   At id nec propositum
ullum fuit et, si fuisset, duplicata gloria discessissem.
Bonorum mihi praesidium defuisse ?   Falsum est.
Me mortem timuisse ?   Turpe est.   XXXVI. Dicendum igitur est id, quod non dicerem nisi coactus—
nihil enim umquam de me dixi sublatius asciscendae
laudis causa potius quam criminis depellendi,—dico
96 igitur et quam possum maxima voce dico : Cum
omnium perditorum et coniuratorum incitata vis,
duce tribuno plebis, consulibus auctoribus, adflicto
senatu, perterritis equitibus Romanis, suspensa ac
sollicita tota civitate, non tam in me impetum faceret,
quam per me in omnes bonos, me vidisse, si vicissem,
tenues rei publicae reliquias, si victus essem, nullas
futuras.   Quod cum iudicassem, deflevi coniugis
miserae discidium, liberorum carissimorum solitudinem, fratris absentis amantissimi atque optimi casum,
subitas fundatissimae familiae ruinas, sed his omnibus
rebus vitam anteposui meorum civium remque publicam concidere unius discessu quam omnium interitu
occidere malui.   Speravi, id quod accidit, me iacentem

grandest deed in the history of the human race. That I dreaded prosecution before the people ? But such a prosecution was never even contemplated, and had it taken place I should have emerged from it with my reputation doubly enhanced. Shall I then say that the patriotic party failed in my protection ? It would be false. XXXVI. Or that I feared death ? That would be cowardly. I must say, then, what I would not say save under compulsion,—for any self-congratulatory remarks I have ever uttered have been made rather to repel insinuations than to claim credit for myself,—I say, then, and with all the emphasis I can use, that when, under the leadership of a tribune of the plebs and with the support of the consuls, with the senate humiliated, the Roman knighthood cowed, and the whole community agitated and distraught, the carefully stimulated lawlessness of desperadoes and conspirators was launching an assault not so much upon myself as upon all good patriots through me, I saw that, should I prove victorious, some frail vestiges of a republic would yet remain, but, should I be defeated, it would become utterly extinct. Having come to this conclusion, I was heart-broken at the prospect of separation from my unhappy wife, of the destitution of my beloved children, of the blow that would fall upon my excellent and affectionate brother who was far away, and of the unforeseen wreck of a family whose sense of security had been so complete ; but all these possibilities came second in my thoughts to the lives of my fellow-citizens, and I thought it better that the state should falter through the retirement of one, than that it should fall through the destruction of all. I hoped, and my hopes have been realized,

247

posse vivis viris fortibus excitari : si una cum bonis
interissem, nullo modo posse rem publicam [1] recreari.
97 Accepi, pontifices, magnum atque incredibilem
dolorem : non nego, neque istam mihi ascisco
sapientiam, quam non nulli in me requirebant, qui
me animo nimis fracto esse atque adflicto loque-
bantur. An ego poteram, cum a tot rerum tanta
varietate divellerer, quas idcirco praetereo, quod ne
nunc quidem sine fletu commemorare possum, in-
fitiari me esse hominem et communem naturae sen-
sum repudiare ? Tum vero neque illud meum factum
laudabile nec beneficium ullum a me in rem publicam
profectum dicerem, si quidem ea rei publicae causa
reliquissem, quibus aequo animo carerem, eamque
animi duritiam, sicut corporis, quod cum uritur, non
sentit, stuporem potius quam virtutem putarem.
98 XXXVII. Suscipere tantos animi dolores atque ea,
quae capta urbe accidunt victis, stante urbe, unum
perpeti et iam se videre distrahi a complexu suorum,
disturbari tecta, diripi fortunas, patriae denique
causa patriam ipsam amittere, spoliari populi Romani
beneficiis amplissimis, praecipitari ex altissimo dignitatis gradu, videre praetextos inimicos, nondum
morte complorata, arbitria petentes funeris : haec
omnia subire conservandorum civium causa atque id,[2]
cum dolenter adsis non tam sapiens quam ii, qui

---

[1] rem publicam *suppl. by Nägelsbach.*
[2] id *Pet.* : ita MSS.

that if brave men yet survived, my humiliation might be retrieved ; but if I should perish, and the patriotic party with me, I saw no prospect of a resurrection for the republic. Bitter beyond all belief, gentlemen, was the anguish that I felt. I do not gainsay this, nor do I arrogate to myself that philosophic spirit, the absence of which was a disappointment to many who said that I betrayed an excessive discomfiture and prostration of mind. But, torn as I was by so many conflicting reflexions, which I pass over because even at this time I cannot dwell upon them without tears, could I have disowned my humanity, and repudiated those natural sentiments which are common to us all ? In that case, I could not now describe my action as praiseworthy or say that I was the source of any benefit to the republic, if I had but abandoned, for the republic's sake, what I felt no pang at losing; I should hold that such mental apathy, like the physical apathy which does not feel the sting of fire, was brute insensibility rather than bravery. XXXVII. To undergo such deep grief of heart, and to endure in loneliness all the suffering of the conquered inhabitants of a captured city that survives her capture, to see one's self torn from the clasp of one's kin, dwelling shattered, property plundered, and, bitterest of all, country forfeited for country's sake ; to be deprived of the proudest bestowals of the Roman people, to be sent hurtling down from the pinnacle of majesty, to see foes in the garb of office demanding the funeral dues even before the lamentations for death have arisen ; to endure to be a broken-hearted eyewitness of all this, in order to save the lives of compatriots, facing it not with the philosophy of those to

nihil curant, sed tam amans tuorum ac tui quam communis humanitas postulat, ea laus praeclara atque divina est. Nam qui ea, quae numquam cara ac iucunda duxit, animo aequo rei publicae causa deserit, nullam benevolentiam insignem in rem publicam declarat : qui autem ea relinquit rei publicae causa, a quibus cum summo dolore divellitur, ei cara patria 99 est, cuius salutem caritati anteponit suorum. Qua re disrumpatur licet ista furia atque pestis,[1] audiat haec ex me, quoniam lacessivit : bis servavi rem publicam,[2] qui consul togatus armatos vicerim, privatus consulibus armatis cesserim. Utriusque temporis fructum tuli maximum : superioris, quod ex senatus auctoritate et senatum et omnes bonos meae salutis causa mutata veste vidi, posterioris, quod et senatus et populus Romanus et omnes mortales et privatim et publice iudicarunt sine meo reditu rem publicam salvam esse non posse.

100 Sed hic meus reditus, pontifices, vestro iudicio continetur. Nam si vos me in meis aedibus collocatis, id quod in omni mea causa semper studiis, consiliis, auctoritatibus sententiisque fecistis, video me plane ac sentio restitutum : sin mea domus non modo mihi non redditur, sed etiam monumentum praebet inimico doloris mei, sceleris sui, publicae

---

[1] pestis *suppl. by Pet.*
[2] rem publicam *suppl. by Kayser.*

whom nothing matters, but with the deep love for
your dear ones and yourself which is imperative to
our universal humanity ;—this, indeed, is a glory
transcending, nay, divine. For he who for the sake
of the common weal abandons with indifference that
which he has never held dear or delightful gives
proof of no exceptional unselfishness in the state's
interests ; but the man who, for the common weal,
relinquishes that, the severance from which racks
his heart with bitter grief, he is the true lover of
his country, whose well-being he places before the
demands of private affection. So, even though that
plague and tormentor be mortified even to bursting,
he shall hear this from me, since he has challenged me
to it,—twice have I saved the state : first, when as
consul in the garb of peace I overcame armed forces,
and next, when as a private citizen I gave ground
before armed consuls. From both occasions I have
reaped a rich harvest : from the former, in that I
saw both the senate and all good patriots with official
garb discarded, by senatorial order, for my preservation ; from the latter, in that the senate, the Roman
people, and the whole human race testified by official
and unofficial pronouncements that, unless I should
be restored, the republic could not be saved.

But the reality of this restoration depends, gentlemen, upon your verdict. For if you reinstall me in
my house, an end to which throughout all my case
your inclinations, counsels, influence, and resolutions
have always tended, then I fully realize that my
restitution will be absolute. But if my house, so far
from being restored to me, even serves my enemy
as a memorial of my humiliation, of his own wickedness, and of the public disaster, who will look upon

calamitatis, quis erit qui hunc reditum potius quam poenam sempiternam putet ? In conspectu prope totius urbis domus est mea, pontifices : in qua si manet illud non monumentum urbis, sed sepulcrum, inimico nomine inscriptum, demigrandum mihi potius aliquo est quam habitandum in ea urbe, in qua tropaea et de me et de re publica videam constituta.

1 XXXVIII. An ego tantam aut animi duritiam habere aut oculorum impudentiam possim, ut cuius urbis servatorem me esse senatus omnium adsensu totiens iudicarit, in ea possim intueri domum meam eversam non ab inimico meo, sed ab hoste communi et ab eodem exstructam et positam in oculis civitatis, ne umquam conquiescere possit fletus bonorum ? Sp. Maelii regnum appetentis domus est complanata, et, quia illud aequum accidisse populus Romanus Maelio iudicavit, nomine ipso Aequimaelii iustitia poenae comprobata est : Sp. Cassii domus ob eamdem causam eversa atque in eo est loco aedis posita Telluris. In Vacci pratis domus fuit M. Vacci, quae publicata est et eversa, ut illius facinus memoria et nomine loci notaretur. M. Manlius cum ab ascensu Capitolii Gallorum impetum reppulisset, non fuit contentus beneficii sui gloria : regnum appetisse est iudicatus : ergo eius domum eversam duobus lucis convestitam

---

ᵃ At a time of famine (440) bought corn from Etruria, and distributed it among the poor. Accused of aiming at the kingship, and slain by Servilius Ahala (Livy iv. 13, 15).

ᵇ A purely fanciful etymology.

ᶜ Proposed a law (486) giving plebeians the right to occupy public lands. Put to death on the same charge as Sp. Maelius (Livy ii. 41).

ᵈ A native of Fundi in Latium, who had a house in Rome. In 330 roused his fellow-citizens to war against Rome, and being taken prisoner was put to death (Livy viii. 19).

ᵉ Livy vi. 20.

this as a restoration, and not rather an unending
punishment ? My house, gentlemen, stands full in
view of well-nigh the whole city ; and if it abides
in the city, not as the city's monument, but as her
sepulchre, inscribed with an enemy's name, then I
must migrate elsewhere rather than dwell in a city
where I witness the erection of trophies over myself
and over the republic. XXXVIII. Or could my
heart be so dulled to all feeling, or my eyes so lost
to all sense of shame, as to endure to gaze upon my
house overturned in the very city whose saviour I
was so often pronounced to be by the senate, in
agreement with the whole community,—overturned
by no private enemy of mine, but by a public foe,
who had also raised another edifice upon its site in
full view of all citizens, that so the tears of all true
patriots might know no respite ? Spurius Maelius [a]
aimed at the tyranny, and his house was levelled
with the ground ; and since the Roman people pronounced that Maelius' penalty was on a level with
his offence, the justice of the punishment was acknowledged by the very name " Level of Maelius," [b]
which was applied to the site. For the same reason
Spurius Cassius' [c] house was razed, and a temple
erected to Earth upon the spot. On Vaccus' [d] Meads
stood the house of Marcus Vaccus, which was confiscated and razed, so that the very name of the place
emblazoned the ignominy of his name to all posterity.
Marcus Manlius,[e] after having repelled the assault
of the Gauls upon the approach to the Capitol, was
not content with the fame of the service he had
rendered ; he was judged to have aimed at the
tyranny, and therefore his house was razed, and
the site planted with two copses, as you see it to

videtis. Quam igitur maiores nostri sceleratis ac
nefariis civibus maximam poenam constitui posse
arbitrati sunt, eamdem ego subibo ac sustinebo, ut
apud posteros nostros non exstinctor coniurationis et
102 sceleris, sed auctor et dux fuisse videar ?   Hanc vero,
pontifices, labem turpitudinis et inconstantiae poterit
populi Romani dignitas sustinere vivo senatu, vobis
principibus publici consilii, ut domus M. Tullii
Ciceronis cum domo M. Fulvii Flacci ad memoriam
poenae publice constitutae coniuncta esse videatur ?
M. Flaccus, quia cum C. Graccho contra salutem rei
publicae fecerat, ex senatus sententia est interfectus :
eius domus eversa et publicata est : in qua porticum
post aliquanto Q. Catulus de manubiis Cimbricis fecit.
Ista autem fax ac furia patriae, cum urbem Pisone
et Gabinio ducibus cepisset, occupasset, teneret, uno
eodemque tempore et clarissimi viri mortui monumenta delebat et meam domum cum Flacci domo
coniungebat, ut, qua poena senatus adfecerat ever-
sorem civitatis, eadem iste oppresso senatu adficeret
eum, quem patres conscripti custodem patriae iu-
103 dicassent.   XXXIX. Hanc vero in Palatio atque in
pulcherrimo urbis loco porticum esse patiemini,

---

* M. Fulvius Flaccus, consul 125, tribune 122, slain with
C. Gracchus 121.

this day. And shall I encounter and endure the selfsame penalty which our ancestors considered to be the severest that could be enacted against criminal and sacrilegious citizens, with the result that in the eyes of our future generations I shall be thought to have been not the queller of conspiracy and crime, but its promoter and chief agent? Will the prestige of the Roman people, while the senate yet lives, and while you direct its public counsels, be able to survive the stain of ignominy and inconsistency that will attach to it, when it becomes known that the house of Marcus Tullius Cicero was associated with that of Fulvius Flaccus *a* in suffering a fate which perpetuated the memory of a publicly enacted penalty? Marcus Flaccus was put to death by a resolution of the senate because in conjunction with Gaius Gracchus he had acted counter to the welfare of the state; his house was razed and the site confiscated; and shortly afterwards Quintus Catulus erected a portico there from the spoils taken from the Cimbri. And when that flaming fury of his country had, under the direction of Piso and Gabinius, captured and seized the city, which he held in his grip, at one and the same time he erased the memorial of a distinguished hero who was dead, and united my house in the same fate with that of Flaccus; with the result that, having crushed the senate, he visited one whom the conscript fathers had pronounced to be the guardian of his country with the self-same punishment that the senate had inflicted upon the subverter of the community. XXXIX. And will you brook that this portico should stand on the Palatine, yes, in the city's fairest spot, to be an ineradicable memorial

255

furoris tribunicii, sceleris consularis, crudelitatis
coniuratorum, calamitatis rei publicae, doloris mei
defixum indicium ad memoriam omnium gentium
sempiternam ? quam porticum pro amore, quem
habetis in rem publicam et semper habuistis, non
modo sententiis, sed, si opus esset, manibus vestris
disturbare cuperetis : nisi quem forte illius castissimi
sacerdotis superstitiosa dedicatio deterret.

104   O rem, quam homines soluti ridere non desinant,
tristiores autem sine maximo dolore audire non
possint ! Publiusne Clodius, qui ex pontificis maximi domo religionem eripuit, is in meam intulit ?
Huncine vos, qui estis antistites caerimoniarum et
sacrorum, auctorem habetis et magistrum publicae
religionis ? O di immortales !—vos enim haec audire
cupio,—P. Clodius vestra sacra curat ? vestrum
numen horret ? res omnes humanas religione vestra
contineri putat ? Hic non illudit auctoritati horum
omnium, qui adsunt, summorum virorum ? non vestra,
pontifices, gravitate abutitur ? Ex isto ore religionis
verbum excidere aut elabi potest ? quam tu eodem
ore accusando senatum, quod severe de religione
105 decerneret, impurissime taeterrimeque violasti. XL.
Aspicite, pontifices, hominem religiosum et, si vobis
videtur, quod est bonorum pontificum, monete eum
modum quemdam esse religionis : nimium esse super-

to all future generations of all races of a tribune's
recklessness, a consul's wickedness, the barbarity of
conspirators, the ruin of the republic, and of my own
grief?—a portico which, out of the affection you
bear, and have ever borne, to the state, you would
yearn to shatter, not alone by your votes, but, if
need were, with your very hands, were it not that
some perchance find misgivings roused within them
because of the superstitious dedication of this most
spotless of priests.

104   What a situation, calculated to arouse the un-
quenchable laughter of the frivolous, but which the
serious cannot hear of without the deepest mortification! Has Publius Clodius, who robbed the house
of the supreme pontiff of its sanctity, conferred
sanctity upon mine? Is this the man whom you,
who are the overseers of ritual and sacrifice, have
as the guide and director of the state religion?
Ye immortal gods (for I desire that what I say
should reach your ears), is it indeed Publius Clodius
who makes your sacrifices his care, who quakes before
your power, and who thinks that all human affairs
are swayed by the observance paid to you? Surely
the fellow does but mock at the authority of all the
great men here present; surely he does but do outrage, gentlemen, to your august presence. What
word of religion can fall or slip inadvertently from his
lips, those same lips wherewith he has so abominably
and outrageously polluted religion, in that he
accused the senate of being too austere in its decrees
105 upon religion? XL. Look, gentlemen, upon this
model of religious scrupulosity, and if you think it
advisable, act as good priests should, and admonish
him that there are limits to scrupulosity; that it is

stitiosum non oportere.   Quid tibi necesse fuit anili
superstitione, homo fanatice, sacrificium, quod alienae
domi fieret, invisere ?   quae autem te tanta mentis
imbecillitas tenuit, ut non putares deos satis posse
placari, nisi etiam muliebribus religionibus te im-
plicuisses ?   quem umquam audisti maiorum tuorum,
qui et sacra privata coluerunt et publicis sacerdotiis
praefuerunt, cum sacrificium Bonae deae fieret,
interfuisse ?   Neminem, ne illum quidem, qui caecus
est factus.   Ex quo intelligitur multa in vita falso
homines opinari : cum ille, qui nihil viderat sciens
quod nefas esset, lumina amisit, istius, qui non solum
aspectu, sed etiam incesto flagitio et stupro caerimonias polluit, poena omnis oculorum ad caecitatem
mentis est conversa.   Hoc auctore tam casto, tam
religioso, tam sancto, tam pio potestis, pontifices, non
commoveri, cum suis dicat se manibus domum civis
optimi evertisse et eam iisdem manibus consecrasse ?

106   Quae tua fuit consecratio ?   Tuleram, inquit, ut
mihi liceret.   Quid ? non exceperas, ut, si quid ius
non esset rogari, ne esset rogatum ?   Ius igitur
statuetis esse unius cuiusque vestrum sedes, aras,

---

[a] Appius Claudius Caecus (censor 312) who became blind
in old age.

not right to be too superstitious. Where was the
necessity, fanatic that you are, of being so haggishly
superstitious as to attend a sacrifice that was
taking place at another man's house? What was
the stupendous insanity that led you to think that
the gods could not be satisfactorily appeased unless
you too should mix yourself up in women's celebra-
tions? Your ancestors were assiduous in their
performance of private rites and their surveillance
of state priesthoods, but of whom of them have you
heard that he intruded at the celebration of the
sacrifice to the Benign Goddess? Of no one, not
even of him who was stricken blind.[a] This enables
us to realize how wrong are many popular theories
about life. The man who had never knowingly
looked upon sin was deprived of his eyesight; while
this fellow, who violated the sacred rites not only
by looking upon them, but by monstrous lewdness
and debauchery, finds that retribution for the sin
of his bodily eye takes wholly the shape of blindness
of the understanding. Dealing as you are with an
agent so highly moral, so scrupulous, so upright, and
so conscientious, can your hearts, gentlemen, fail to
be stirred when you hear him say that with his own
hands he has overthrown the house of an exemplary
citizen, and that with his own hands he has consecrated it?

6   And what a consecration was that? "But," he
objects, "I had carried a motion giving me legal
powers." What! Had you failed to insert the saving
clause that if anything illegal was proposed, it should
be held that it had not been proposed? Will you
then, gentlemen, decide that it is legal that the dwellings, altars, hearths, and household gods of each one

focos, deos penates subiectos esse libidini tribuniciae ?
in quem quisque per homines concitatos irruerit,
quem impetu perculerit, huius domum non solum
adfligere, quod est praesentis insaniae quasi tempe-
statis repentinae, sed etiam in posterum tempus
107 sempiterna religione obligare ? XLI. Equidem sic
accepi, pontifices, in religionibus suscipiendis caput
esse interpretari quae voluntas deorum immortalium
esse videatur : nec est ulla erga deos pietas nisi sit
honesta de numine eorum ac mente opinio, ut expeti
nihil ab iis quod sit iniustum atque inhonestum arbitrere. Hominem invenire ista labes tum, cum omnia
tenebat, neminem potuit cui meas aedes addiceret,
cui traderet, cui donaret : ipse cum loci illius,
cum aedium cupiditate flagraret ob eamque causam
unam funesta illa rogatione sua vir bonus domi-
num se in meis bonis esse voluisset, tamen illo ipso in
furore suo non est ausus meam domum, cuius cupiditate inflammatus erat, possidere : deos immortales
existimatis, cuius labore et consilio sua ipsi templa
tenuerunt, in eius domum adflictam et eversam per
hominis sceleratissimi nefarium latrocinium immi-
108 grare voluisse ?   Civis est nemo tanto in populo extra
contaminatam illam et cruentam P. Clodii manum,

of you should be placed at the tender mercies of a tribune's caprice, and that it is right to inflict upon the house of one who has been assaulted through deliberately incited agents, and stricken down by violence, not mere destruction, which might argue the momentary madness aroused by a sudden tempest, but the entail, immutable through all future time, of an irredeemable sanctity?

XLI. I, gentlemen, have always understood that in the contraction of religious obligations the main task is to interpret what is the apparent will of the immortal gods; and a right fulfilment of duty to the gods is impossible without a disinterested conviction as to their designs and purposes, combined with a belief that they grant no petitions which are unjust or unseemly. Even when he held everything in the hollow of his hand, that plague-spot could find no human soul who would accept proprietorship, trusteeship, or even the gift of my house. Fired as he was by lust for the site and for the house, and having for this reason alone conceived the desire of using that fatal bill of his to install himself as owner in my property, the worthy gentleman, in spite of all, in the midst of his reckless career, had not the courage to enter upon possession of my house, which had kindled his covetousness; and think you that the immortal gods desired to bestow their presence upon the house, stricken and shattered as it was by the sacrilegious piracy of an abandoned scoundrel, belonging to one by whose energy and wisdom they still possessed their own temples? In all this vast people, save only for the polluted and ensanguined crew of Publius Clodius, no citizen was found to lay a finger upon

qui rem ullam de meis bonis attigerit, qui non pro
suis opibus in illa tempestate me defenderit. At qui
aliqua se contagione praedae, societatis, emptionis
contaminaverunt, nullius neque privati neque publici
iudicii poenam effugere potuerunt. Ex his igitur
bonis, ex quibus nemo rem ullam attigit qui non
omnium iudicio sceleratissimus haberetur, di immortales domum meam concupiverunt? Ista tua
pulcra Libertas deos penates et familiares meos lares
expulit, ut se ipsa tamquam in captivis sedibus
109 collocaret? Quid est sanctius, quid omni religione
munitius quam domus unius cuiusque civium? Hic
arae sunt, hic foci, hic di penates, hic sacra, religiones,
caerimoniae continentur : hoc perfugium est ita
sanctum omnibus, ut inde abripi neminem fas sit.
XLII. Quo magis est istius furor ab auribus vestris
repellendus, qui quae maiores nostri religionibus tuta
nobis et sancta esse voluerunt, ea iste non solum
contra religionem labefactavit, sed etiam ipsius religionis nomine evertit.

110 At quae dea est? Bonam esse oportet, quoniam
quidem est abs te dedicata. Libertas, inquit, est.
Eam tu igitur domi meae collocasti, quam ex urbe
tota sustulisti? Tu cum collegas tuos, summa
potestate praeditos, negares liberos esse, cum in
templum Castoris aditus esset apertus nemini, cum

any particle of my property, or who did not defend me at that crisis, as his means allowed. But of all those who defiled themselves by touching booty, partnership, or sale, none has been able to escape the penalty either of a public or of a private trial. No one, I say, laid a finger upon any particle of my property who was not pronounced by the universal verdict to be an utter villain, and is it to be thought that out of this property the immortal gods had set their hearts upon my house? Did your darling Liberty drive out my household gods and the spirits of my family, that she might establish herself in what was virtually a captive's dwelling? What is more sacred, what more inviolably hedged about by every kind of sanctity, than the home of every individual citizen? Within its circle are his altars, his hearths, his household gods, his religion, his observances, his ritual; it is a sanctuary so holy in the eyes of all, that it were sacrilege to tear an owner therefrom. XLII. All the more, then, should we remove out of your hearing the madness of this reprobate, who has not merely undermined, in defiance of religion, that which our ancestors desired religion should guard and sanctify to our use, but has actually employed the plea of religion under which to overturn it.

But who is your goddess? A " Benign Goddess " she must needs be, since it was you who enshrined her. " Liberty," replies Clodius. What! Have you installed at my house her whom you have ousted from the whole city? You denied freedom of action to your colleagues who were entrusted with supreme authority; you allowed none to have free access to the temple of Castor; you ordered, in the hearing of

hunc clarissimum virum, summo genere natum,
summis populi beneficiis usum, pontificem et consularem et singulari bonitate et modestia praeditum,
quem satis mirari quibus oculis aspicere audeas non
queo, audiente populo Romano a pedisequis con-
culcari iuberes, cum indemnatum me exturbares
privilegiis tyrannicis irrogatis, cum principem orbis
terrae virum inclusum domi contineres, cum forum
armatis catervis perditorum hominum possideres,
Libertatis simulacrum in ea domo collocabas, quae
domus erat ipsa indicium crudelissimi tui dominatus
111 et miserrimae populi Romani servitutis ? Eumne
potissimum Libertas domo sua debuit pellere, qui
nisi fuisset, in servorum potestatem civitas tota
venisset ? XLIII. At unde est inventa ista Libertas ? quaesivi enim diligenter. Tanagraea quaedam
meretrix fuisse dicitur. Eius non longe a Tanagra
simulacrum e marmore in sepulcro positum fuit. Hoc
quidam homo nobilis, non alienus ab hoc religioso
Libertatis sacerdote, ad ornatum aedilitatis suae
deportavit. Etenim cogitarat omnes superiores
muneris splendore superare. Itaque omnia signa,
tabulas, ornamentorum quod superfuit in fanis et
communibus locis, tota e Graecia atque insulis omnibus honoris populi Romani causa sane frugaliter
112 domum suam deportavit. Is postea quam intellexit
posse se interversa aedilitate a L. Pisone consule

---

[a] It is uncertain to whom this refers.
[b] Pompey.
[c] Appius Clodius, brother of Publius.

264

the Roman people, this distinguished gentleman,[a] of the highest birth, on whom the people had bestowed its loftiest honours, a pontiff and an ex-consul, a man of singular kindliness and irreproachability, whose gaze I cannot sufficiently wonder how you can have the face to meet, to be trampled upon by your lackeys; you hustled me forth uncondemned by means of arbitrary measures directed expressly against myself; you kept the first gentleman in the world[b] penned up in his house; you occupied the forum with armed troops of desperate men; and were you the man to set up an image of Liberty in a house which was itself a standing indictment of your brutal despotism and the piteous degradation of the Roman people? Was it for Liberty to drive from his house him of all men whose existence was the only thing that prevented the state from falling utterly under the power of slaves? XLIII. But where did you find your Liberty? After making careful inquiry, I learn that rumour has it that she was a certain courtesan of Tanagra, a marble statue of whom stood upon a tomb not far from that city. A certain nobleman,[c] not unconnected with our punctilious priest of Liberty, had carried this statue off to adorn the entertainment he intended to give as aedile; for indeed he had made up his mind to surpass all his predecessors in the magnificence of his exhibition. So, with true economy, and for the greater glory of the Roman people, he carried off to his house all the statues, pictures, and ornaments that still remained in shrines and public buildings throughout the whole of Greece and the islands. Realizing, however, that, if he renounced the aedileship, there was a chance of his being

265

praetorem renuntiari, si modo eadem prima littera competitorem habuisset aliquem, aedilitatem duobus in locis, partim in arca, partim in hortis suis, collocavit : signum de busto meretricis ablatum isti dedit, quod esset signum magis istorum quam publicae libertatis. Hanc deam quisquam violare audeat, imaginem meretricis, ornamentum sepulcri, a fure sublatam, a sacrilego collocatam ? haec me domo mea pellet ? haec ultrix adflictae civitatis, rei publicae spoliis ornabitur ? haec erit in eo monumento, quod positum est, ut esset indicium oppressi senatus ad

113 memoriam sempiternam turpitudinis ? O Q. Catule, —patremne appellem ante an filium ? Recentior enim memoria filii est et cum meis rebus gestis coniunctior,—tantumne te fefellit, cum mihi summa et cotioie maiora praemia in re publica fore putabas ? negabas fas esse duo consules esse in hac civitate inimicos rei publicae. Sunt inventi qui senatum tribuno furenti constrictum traderent, qui pro me patres conscriptos deprecari et populo supplices esse edictis atque imperio vetarent, quibus inspectantibus domus mea disturbaretur, diriperetur, qui denique ambustas fortunarum mearum reliquias suas domos

114 comportari iuberent. Venio nunc ad patrem. Tu,

---

[a] Making it easier to tamper with the voting-tablets, whereon the names of candidates were written in abbreviated form.

[b] Consul with Marius 102, and co-operator with him in the conquest of the Cimbri and Teutones. From the spoils of this campaign he built on the Capitol a portico, which Clodius had destroyed. See Chap. XLIV.

[c] Consul 78 ; leader of the senatorial party.

returned praetor by Lucius Piso the consul, if only
it might turn out that there was a rival candidate
with the same initial letter as himself,[a] he invested
the funds set aside for his aedileship partly by
storing them in his coffers, and partly by spending them on his park ; he took the statue of
the courtesan from its pedestal and presented it to
Clodius, that it might symbolize the "liberty" of
Clodius and his like rather than that of the state.
Would anyone dare to desecrate this goddess, a
courtesan's likeness, which had decked a tomb, been
removed by a thief, and set up by a sacrilegious
hand ? Shall it be such an one as she who drives
me from my house ? Shall she, the avengeress of a
stricken state, be adorned with the spoils of the
republic ? Shall she find a place in a memorial raised
to be a witness to the eternal disgrace of the senate's
degradation ? O Quintus Catulus ! [b]—shall I address
the father first, or his son [c] ? I will address the son,
for his memory is more recent, and he was more
closely connected with my own achievements,—were
you so wide of the mark, in thinking that I should
win great and daily greater rewards in my public life ?
You said that it was a shocking thing that there
should be two consuls in this state who were foes
to the republic ; but there were not lacking those
who were ready to hand over the senate bound to
a reckless tribune, to issue peremptory manifestoes
forbidding the conscript fathers to intercede on
my behalf by appeals to the people, who looked on
calmly while my house was shattered and plundered,
and who, finally, ordered that the charred wreckage
of my property should be transferred to their own
houses. I pass now to the father. You, Quintus

Q. Catule, M. Fulvii domum, cum is fratris tui socer
fuisset, monumentum tuarum manubiarum esse
voluisti, ut eius, qui perniciosa rei publicae consilia
cepisset, omnis memoria funditus ex oculis hominum
ac mentibus tolleretur. Hoc si quis tibi aedificanti
illam porticum diceret, fore tempus, cum is tribunus
plebis, qui auctoritatem senatus, iudicium bonorum
omnium neglexisset, tuum monumentum consulibus
non modo inspectantibus, verum adiuvantibus distur-
baret, everteret, idque cum eius civis, qui rem publicam ex senatus auctoritate consul defendisset, domo
coniungeret, nonne responderes id nisi eversa civitate
accidere non posse ?

115   XLIV. At videte hominis intolerabilem audaciam
cum proiecta quadam et effrenata cupiditate. Monumentum iste umquam aut religionem ullam excogi-
tavit ? Habitare laxe et magnifice voluit duasque et
magnas et nobiles domos coniungere. Eodem puncto
temporis, quo meus discessus isti causam caedis
eripuit, a Q. Seio contendit ut sibi domum venderet :
cum ille id negaret, primo se luminibus eius esse
obstructurum minabatur. Adfirmabat Postumus se
vivo illam domum istius numquam futuram. Acutus
adolescens ex ipsius sermone intellexit quid fieri
oporteret : hominem veneno apertissime sustulit :

Catulus, since Marcus Fulvius had been your brother's father-in-law, chose his house to be the shrine of your spoils, with the intent that the memory of anyone who should adopt a policy ruinous to the republic should be utterly erased from the vision and the minds of men. Had anyone told you, as you were building that portico, that a time would come when your monument would be demolished and overthrown by a tribune of the plebs who had ignored the majesty of the senate and the opinions of all good citizens, and that the consuls would not merely look on at, but even assist in, the work, and that the house of a citizen who, as consul, had defended the republic with the senate's support would be associated with yours in this fate, would you not have answered that that result would be impossible, unless the whole fabric of our society were at the same time overthrown ?

XLIV. But observe how the man's intolerable effrontery is joined to a spirit of over-reaching and unbridled covetousness. Did *he* ever dream of memorials or of any kind of sanctity ? *His* ideal was to live in an unhampered sumptuousness, and to unite two great and noble mansions.[a] At the very moment when my retirement had robbed him of a pretext for murdering me, he pressed Quintus Seius to sell him his house ; when Seius refused to do so, he first threatened that he would obstruct his lights ; but Postumus [b] still swore that his house would never belong to Clodius while he himself was yet alive. The owner's words gave our astute young friend a suggestion as to what course he must pursue ; he barefacedly poisoned Seius, and put him out of the way ; and then, when all other bidders were

emit domum licitatoribus defatigatis prope dimidio
116 carius quam aestimabatur. Quorsum igitur haec
oratio pertinet ? Domus illa mea prope tota vacua
est : vix pars aedium mearum decima ad Catuli
porticum accessit. Causa fuit ambulatio et monumentum et ista Tanagraea oppressa libertate Libertas. In Palatio, pulcherrimo prospectu, porticum
cum conclavibus pavimentatam trecentum pedum
concupierat, amplissimum peristylum, cetera eius
modi, facile ut omnium domos et laxitate et dignitate
superaret. Et homo religiosus cum aedes meas idem
emeret et venderet, tamen illis tantis tenebris non
est ausus suum nomen emptioni illi ascribere. Posuit
Scatonem illum, hominem sua virtute egentem, ut
is, qui in Marsis, ubi natus est, tectum, quo imbris
vitandi causa succederet, iam nullum haberet, aedes
in Palatio nobilissimas emisse se diceret. Inferiorem
aedium partem adsignavit non suae genti Fonteiae,
sed Clodiae, quam reliquit : quem in numerum ex
multis Clodiis nemo nomen dedit nisi aut egestate
aut scelere perditus. XLV. Hanc vos, pontifices,
tam variam, tam novam in omni genere voluntatem,
impudentiam, audaciam, cupiditatem comprobabitis ?

wearied out, bought the house at a price half as high again as its true value. Well, how does this incident bear upon the point at issue? Nearly the whole site of my house is still unconsecrated; for scarce a tenth part of the building has been added to Catulus' portico. The reason was that Clodius wished to extend his own promenade, and raise his own shrine with the lady of Tanagra doing duty for Liberty—liberty, incidentally, having been crushed. He had set his heart upon building upon the Palatine a paved portico three hundred feet long with apartments opening from it and commanding a magnificent view, possessing a spacious colonnade and other such accessories, with the intent to surpass all other men's houses in roominess and imposing appearance. And though our scrupulous friend was at once the purchaser and the seller of my house, yet he did not dare, in the deep gloom that reigned, to attach his own name to the purchase. He put forward the notorious Scato, whose virtues, no doubt, had brought him into destitution, with the result that a man who, in his birthplace among the Marsi, had no longer a roof to retire to that he might shelter from the rain, now alleged that he had bought the noblest house upon the Palatine. The more low-lying part of the house he made over, not to his own family of Fonteius, but to that of Clodius, which he had relinquished; but of the many who bore the name of Clodius none applied for a place on the list of assignees who was not over his ears in poverty or crime. XLV. And will you, gentlemen, set the seal of your sanction upon intentions, impudence, effrontery, and covetousness, so shifting and so unparalleled in any walk of life?

117 Pontifex, inquit, adfuit. Non te pudet, cum apud
pontifices res agatur, pontificem dicere et non collegium pontificum adfuisse, praesertim cum tribunus
plebis vel denuntiare potueris vel etiam cogere ?
Esto : collegium non adhibuisti. Quid ? de collegio
quis tandem adfuit ? Opus erat[1] enim auctoritate,
quae est in his omnibus, sed tamen auget et aetas et
honos dignitatem : opus erat etiam scientia, quam si
omnes consecuti sunt, tamen certe peritiores vetustas
118 facit. Quis ergo adfuit ? Frater, inquit, uxoris
meae. Si auctoritatem quaerimus, etsi id est aetatis,
ut nondum consecutus sit, tamen quanta est in adolescente auctoritas, ea propter tantam coniunctionem
adfinitatis minor est putanda. Sin autem scientia est
quaesita, quis erat minus peritus quam is, qui paucis
illis diebus in collegium venerat ? qui etiam tibi erat
magis obstrictus beneficio recenti, cum se fratrem
uxoris tuae fratri tuo germano antelatum videbat ;
etsi in eo providisti ne frater te accusare possit.
Hanc tu igitur dedicationem appellas, ad quam non
collegium, non honoribus populi Romani ornatum
pontificem, non denique adolescentem quemquam

[1] opus erat *corr. by Markland for* posuerat *of* MSS.

---

[a] We know nothing of this alleged power of the tribunes.
[b] L. Pinarius Natta.

7 " But," interposes Clodius, " a pontiff was present."
Seeing that it is before the pontiffs that the case
is being tried, are you not ashamed to say that a
pontiff, and not the College of Pontiffs, was present,
especially as your powers as tribune allowed you to
order, and even to compel,[a] their presence ? Very
well, you did not call in the College. And of the
College, who, pray, was present ? You needed such
moral support as can be found in all these gentlemen,
though at the same time individual dignity is enhanced by age and distinction ; you needed, too,
knowledge, and though this has been attained by
all, it is nevertheless undoubted that length of years
8 lends added skill. Who, then, was present ? " My
wife's brother,"[b] he replies. If it is moral weight for
which we are looking, he is not yet of an age to have
gained this ; still, however considerable be the moral
weight which that young man possesses, the close
connexion with Clodius which his marriage involves
must lead us to disparage that weight in our minds.
But if knowledge is the object of our search, who
was possessed of less technical qualifications than
one who had only entered the College during the
few previous days ? Moreover, he was yet more
closely bound to you by recent kindness, since he
saw that he, your wife's brother, had been preferred
to your own brother by blood ; though with regard
to this you have taken all precautions that your
brother may have no power to accuse you. Do
you, then, apply the name of dedication to a ceremony to which you were unable to invite either the
College of Pontiffs, or any single pontiff who had had
distinctions of the Roman people conferred upon
him, or even any young man who possessed any

scientem,[1] cum haberes in collegio familiarissimos,
adhibere potuisti ? Adfuit is, si modo adfuit, quem tu
119 impulisti, soror rogavit, mater coëgit. Videte igitur,
pontifices, quid statuatis in mea causa de omnium
fortunis, verbone pontificis putetis, si is postem
tenuerit et aliquid dixerit, domum unius cuiusque
consecrari posse, an istae dedicationes et templorum
et delubrorum religiones ad honorem deorum immortalium sine ulla civium calamitate a maioribus
nostris constitutae sint ? Est inventus tribunus
plebis qui consularibus copiis instructus omni impetu
furoris in eum civem irruerit, quem perculsum ipsa
120 res publica suis manibus extolleret. XLVI. Quid ?
si qui similis istius—neque enim iam deerunt qui imi-
tari velint—aliquem mei dissimilem, cui res publica
non tantum debeat, per vim adflixerit, domum eius
per pontificem dedicaverit, id vos ista auctoritate
constituetis ratum esse oportere ? Dicitis : Quem
reperiet pontificem ? Quid ? pontifex et tribunus
plebis idem esse non potest ? M. Drusus, ille clarissimus vir, tribunus plebis, pontifex fuit : ergo si is Q.
Caepionis, inimici sui, postem aedium tenuisset et
pauca verba fecisset, aedes Caepionis essent dedi-

---

[1] scientem *suppl. by Lambinus.*

knowledge, though the College contained many who were your intimate friends? And his presence, if he was present at all, was due to your insistence, your sister's prayers, your mother's compulsion. Bethink you, then, gentlemen, how you decide in my case upon the well-being of all; will you conclude that the mere word of a pontiff, who has but laid his hand upon the door-post and pronounced a formula, avails to consecrate the house of any individual, or have your dedications, and the sanctity of your temples and your shrines, been designed by our ancestors for the honour of the immortal gods, without entailing any detriment to our citizens? There has been found a tribune of the plebs, who, with the forces of the consuls marshalled in his support, launched the full fury of his madness upon a citizen whom the republic, with her own hands, upraised from his prostration. XLVI. Well then, tell me this. Suppose a man like Clodius— and indeed there will in future be no lack of would-be imitators of him—has brutally assailed one who bears no resemblance to myself, in that he has laid the state under no such heavy debt, and has employed a pontiff to dedicate his house, will you decide with the full weight of your authority that such proceedings must be ratified? You object, gentlemen, by asking, "What pontiff will such a man find?" I reply by asking, "Is it not possible for the same man to be at once pontiff and tribune of the plebs?" The renowned Marcus Drusus, when tribune of the plebs, was also pontiff. If he, therefore, had laid his hands upon the door-post of the house of Quintus Caepio, his enemy, and had spoken a brief formula, would Caepio's house have been duly

275

121 catae ? Nihil loquor de pontificio iure, nihil de ipsius verbis dedicationis, nihil de religione, caerimoniis : non dissimulo me nescire ea, quae, etiam si scirem, dissimularem, ne aliis molestus, vobis etiam curiosus viderer : etsi effluunt multa ex vestra disciplina, quae etiam ad nostras aures saepe permanant. Postem teneri in dedicatione oportere videor audisse templi : ibi enim postis est, ubi templi aditus et valvae. Ambulationis postes nemo umquam tenuit in dedicando : simulacrum autem aut aram si dedicasti, sine religione loco moveri potest. Sed iam hoc dicere tibi non licebit, quoniam pontificem postem tenuisse dixisti.

122 Quamquam quid ego de dedicatione loquor ? aut quid de vestro iure et religione contra quam proposueram disputo ? XLVII. Ego vero, si omnia solemnibus verbis, veteribus et traditis [1] institutis acta esse dicerem, tamen me rei publicae iure defenderem. An, cum tu eius civis discessu, cuius unius opera senatus atque omnes boni civitatem esse incolumem totiens iudicassent, oppressam taeterrimo latrocinio cum duobus sceleratissimis consulibus rem

[1] traditis *Madvig* : praeditis MSS.

dedicated ? I say nothing about the prerogatives of pontiffs, or the forms of the actual ceremony of dedication, or of sanctity, and all the ritual attached to it ; I will not attempt to hide my ignorance of all this ; indeed, even were I not ignorant, I should conceal my knowledge, lest I should seem to others pedantic, and to you even interfering ; though it is true that there are many details of your lore that often leak out, and even penetrate to our ears. I think I have heard it said that in the dedication of a temple the hand should be laid upon the door-post ; for the door-post is at the place of access to the temple by the folding doors. But no one has ever, in process of dedication, laid a hand upon the door-post of a promenade ; and if you have dedicated any statue or altar that it may contain, it can be removed from its position without sacrilege. But you, Clodius, cannot assert as much in the present case, for you have told us that a pontiff *did* lay his hand upon the door-post.

And yet why do I speak of the ceremony of dedication, or enter upon a controversy regarding your rights and the sanctity which I have set myself to refute ? XLVII. For my own part, even were I to confess that everything had been duly performed by the prescribed formula and the ancient and traditional observances, I should nevertheless defend myself by appealing to the rights of the republic. Otherwise, could the resurgent republic have power to survive your proceedings, in having, after the retirement of a citizen by whose unaided efforts the senate and all loyal men had declared that the state had been protected from harm, crushed and overpowered the commonwealth by your abominable

publicam teneres, domum eius, qui patriam a se
servatam perire suo nomine noluisset, per pontificem
aliquem dedicasses, posset recreata res publica sus-
123 tinere ?   Date huic religioni aditum, pontifices : iam
nullum fortunis communibus exitum reperietis.   An
si postem tenuerit pontifex et verba ad religionem
deorum immortalium composita ad perniciem civium
transtulerit, valebit in iniuria nomen sanctissimum
religionis : si tribunus plebis verbis non minus priscis
et aeque solemnibus bona cuiuspiam consecrarit, non
valebit ?   Atqui C. Atinius patrum memoria bona
Q. Metelli, qui eum ex senatu censor eiecerat, avi tui,
Q. Metelle, et tui, P. Servili, et proavi tui, P. Scipio,
consecravit, foculo posito in Rostris adhibitoque
tibicine.   Quid tum ? num ille furor tribuni plebis
ductus ex non nullis perveterum temporum exemplis
fraudi Metello fuit, summo illi et clarissimo viro ?
124 Certe non fuit.   Vidimus hoc idem Cn. Lentulo
censori tribunum plebis facere.   Num qua igitur is
bona Lentuli religione obligavit ?   Sed quid ego
ceteros ?   Tu, tu, inquam, capite velato, contione
advocata, foculo posito, bona tui Gabinii, cui regna

---

[a] C. A. Labeo, *trib. plebis* 133.
[b] *Sc.* Macedonicus.

depredations in common with the two reprobate consuls, and in having employed some pontiff to dedicate the house of one who had refused to allow the country which he had preserved to perish on his account ? Do but throw open the door to this kind of consecration, gentlemen, and you will never find an issue from our universal plight. Shall the sacred name of religion lend authority to an outrage if a pontiff has laid his hand upon a door-post, and misapplied to the undoing of citizens a form of words designed for the worship of the immortal gods ; and shall that name fail to lend its authority if a tribune of the plebs has used a formula no less time-honoured and of equal solemnity to devote to the gods the property of any one ? And yet our fathers could remember how Gaius Atinius,[a] with brazier duly placed upon the rostra and with flute-player in attendance, so devoted the property of Quintus Metellus,[b] who, in his capacity of censor, had ejected him from the senate,—your grandfather, Quintus Metellus, and yours, Publius Servilius, and your great-grandfather, Publius Scipio. And what was the result ? Were these mad proceedings, inspired by several examples afforded by our earliest history, detrimental to that great and renowned gentleman Metellus ? Assuredly not. We have seen the censor Gnaeus Lentulus treated in the same manner by a tribune of the plebs ; and was that tribune able by so doing to put any religious embarrassment upon the property of Lentulus ? But why mention other instances ? It was you—you, I say—who, with muffled head, in the presence of the meeting you had summoned, with the brazier in position, consecrated the property of your friend Gabinius, to whom you had

omnia Syrorum, Arabum Persarumque donaras, con-
secrasti. Quod si tum nihil est actum, quid in meis
bonis agi potuit ? Sin est ratum, cur ille gurges,
helluatus tecum simul rei publicae sanguine, ad
caelum tamen exstruit villam in Tusculano visceribus
aerarii : mihi meas ruinas, quarum ego similem totam
urbem esse passus non sum, aspicere non licuit ?

125 XLVIII. Omitto Gabinium : quid ? exemplo tuo
bona tua nonne L. Ninnius, vir fortissimus atque optimus, consecravit ? quod si, quia ad te pertinet, ratum
esse negas oportere, ea iura constituisti in praeclaro
tribunatu tuo, quibus in te conversis recusares, alios
everteres : sin ista consecratio legitima est, quid est
quod profanum in tuis bonis esse possit ? An consecratio nullum habet ius, dedicatio est religiosa ?
Quid ergo illa tua tum obtestatio tibicinis ? quid
foculus ? quid preces ? quid verba[1] prisca voluerunt ?
ementiri, fallere, abuti deorum immortalium numine
ad hominum timorem voluisti ? Nam si est illud
ratum, mitto Gabinium : tua domus certe et quidquid
habes aliud, Cereri est consecratum. Sin ille tibi
ludus fuit, quid te impurius, qui religiones omnes

---

[1] verba *suppl. by Halm.*

---

[a] See *In senatu*, Chap. II.

made a present of all the realms of Syria, Arabia, and Persia. If none of your actions was valid in that case, what validity could there have been in your actions with regard to *my* property? And if your actions in his case still hold good, why is it that, in spite of all, that prodigal, having glutted his appetite along with you upon the blood of the republic, rears a villa in Tusculum up to the skies out of the bowels of the treasury, while I, who refused to allow the entire city to share a like fate, have not been permitted even to look upon the ruins of mine? XLVIII. I leave Gabinius and pass to another question. Did not Lucius Ninnius,[a] the bravest and best of men, take his cue from you when he consecrated your property? If you assert that his proceedings, so nearly affecting you as they do, should be held to be ineffective, you created in your memorable tribunate a precedent, to which you take exception when it is applied against you, but which you apply against others to their undoing. If your consecration possesses legal validity, what of your own property can be held to be unconsecrated? Or are we to consider that, while a consecration has no binding force, a dedication is inviolably sacred? What then was the efficacy of your employment of a flute-player as witness on that occasion, of your brazier, your prayers, and your time-honoured formula? Why did you desire to lie, to deceive, and to misapply the majesty of the immortal gods to the intimidation of men? If that act holds good,—I waive your proceedings against Gabinius,—there can be no doubt that your house and anything else that you possess has been devoted to Ceres; but if it was a mere farce, what can be more loathsome than your

126 pollueris **aut** ementiundo aut stuprando ?—Iam fateor, inquit, me in Gabinio nefarium fuisse.—Quippe vides poenam illam a te in alium institutam in te ipsum esse conversam. Sed homo omnium scelerum flagitiorumque documentum, quod in Gabinio fateris, cuius impudicitiam pueritiae, libidines adolescentiae, dedecus et egestatem reliquae vitae, latrocinium consulatus vidimus, cui ne ista quidem **ipsa** calamitas iniuria potuit accidere, id in me infirmas, et gravius esse dicis, quod uno adolescente quam quod contione tota teste fecisti ?

127 Dedicatio magnam, inquit, habet religionem. XLIX. Nonne vobis Numa Pompilius videtur loqui ? Discite orationem, pontifices, et vos flamines : etiam tu, rex, disce a gentili tuo : quamquam ille gentem istam reliquit, sed tamen disce ab homine religionibus dedito ius totum omnium religionum. Quid ? in dedicatione nonne et quis dedicet et quid et quo modo quaeritur ? An tu haec ita confundis et perturbas, ut quicumque velit, quod velit, quo modo velit possit dedicare ? Quis eras tu, qui dedicabas ? quo iure ? qua lege ? quo exemplo ? qua potestate ? ubi te isti rei populus Romanus praefecerat ? Video enim esse

---

* L. Claudius ; see *De har. resp.* Chap. VI. **n.**

defilement of all sanctities either by falsehood or by immorality? "I am ready to confess now," he says, "that in the case of Gabinius I acted impiously." Yes, for you realize that the penalty you enacted against another has recoiled upon your own head. But, embodiment in human form, as you are, of all crime and enormity, do you claim validity in my case for an act to which you disallow it in the case of Gabinius, whose immoral boyhood, whose licentious youth, whose ignominy and destitution in subsequent life, and whose rapacity as consul we have witnessed, and who would suffer no more than his deserts even were your own disaster to fall upon him; and do you assign greater weight to an act which you performed in the presence of a single youth than to that which was performed in the presence of a whole meeting?

"A dedication," he asserts, " has a grave binding force." XLIX. The pronouncement of a veritable Numa Pompilius, is it not? Lay his words to heart, gentlemen of the Pontifical College, and you too, Flamens; and do you also, King of Rites,[a] learn of this scion of your family (he has relinquished your family, but still learn of him)—learn of this devotee of religious observances all religion's every law. But, I ask you, do we not inquire with regard to a ceremony of dedication who is the dedicator, and what and how he dedicates? Or would you so far subvert and confound these principles as to assert that agent, object, and form of dedication are all alike matters of choice? Who were you, the dedicator? Where was your title, your legal authority, your precedent, your jurisdiction? On what occasion had the Roman people given you superintendence of this business? For I note that there is an ancient law enacted by

legem veterem tribuniciam quae vetet iniussu plebis
aedes, terram, aram consecrari : neque tum hoc ille
Q. Papirius, qui hanc legem rogavit, sensit neque
suspicatus est, fore periculum ne domicilia aut
possessiones indemnatorum civium consecrarentur.
Neque enim id fieri fas erat neque quisquam fecerat
neque erat causa cur prohibendo non tam deterrere
128 videretur quam admonere.   Sed quia consecrabantur
aedes, non privatorum domicilia, sed quae sacrae
nominantur, consecrabantur agri, non ita ut nostra
praedia, si qui vellet, sed ut imperator agros de
hostibus captos consecraret, statuebantur arae quae
religionem adferrent ipsi ei loco, qua essent conse-
cratae, haec, nisi plebs iussisset, fieri vetuit.   Quae
si tu interpretaris de nostris aedibus atque agris
scripta esse, non repugno, sed quaero quae lex lata
sit, ut tu aedes meas consecrares, ubi tibi haec
potestas data sit, quo iure feceris.   Neque ego nunc
de religione, sed de bonis omnium nostrum, nec
de pontificio, sed de iure publico disputo.   L. Lex
Papiria vetat aedes iniussu plebis consecrari.   Sit
sane hoc de nostris aedibus ac non de publicis templis.
Unum ostende verbum consecrationis in ipsa tua lege,

---

a Nothing is known of this law.
b The point of this argument is very obscure.

284

a tribune to forbid the consecration without popular mandate of any building, land, or altar ; and at that time Quintus Papirius, who proposed this law,[a] never dreamed or suspected that a situation would arise involving danger of consecration to the dwellings or properties of uncondemned citizens. As a matter of fact, such a situation was inconceivable ; no one had ever done such a thing ; and he had no reason to include a prohibition which would seem to be not so much a deterrent as a suggestion. But since the buildings which it was customary to consecrate were not private dwellings, but those to which the name sacred is applied, and since the consecration of land, which the law envisaged, was not the consecration of our estates by anyone who wished, but that performed by a general upon lands conquered from an enemy, and since the altars commonly set up were such as lent a sanctity to the place wherein they had been consecrated, Papirius forbade such consecrations, unless the people had first given a mandate for them.[b] If you interpret the terms of the law to refer to our houses and lands, I do not join issue with you ; I merely ask what legislation permitted you to consecrate my house, whence you derived the necessary authority, and on what ground of right you acted. And I am not now dealing with religion, but with the property of us all ; not with the rights of the pontiffs, but with the rights of the people. L. The law of Papirius forbids the consecration of a building without a mandate from the people. Let it by all means be conceded that this refers to our private houses and not to the public temples. Still, show us one single reference to consecration in your actual law, if law it can be called,

285

si illa lex est ac non vox sceleris et crudelitatis tuae.
129 Quod si tibi tum in illo rei publicae naufragio omnia
in mentem venire potuissent aut si tuus scriptor in illo
incendio civitatis non syngraphas cum Byzantiis
exsulibus et cum legatis Brogitari faceret, sed vacuo
animo tibi ista non scita, sed portenta conscriberet,
esses omnia si minus re, at verbis legitimis consecutus.
Sed uno tempore cautiones fiebant pecuniarum,
foedera feriebantur provinciarum, regum appella-
tiones venales erant, servorum omnium vicatim cele-
brabatur tota urbe descriptio, inimici in gratiam re-
conciliabantur, imperia scribebantur nova iuventuti,
Q. Seio venenum misero parabatur, de Cn. Pompeio,
propugnatore et custode imperii, interficiendo consilia inibantur, senatus ne quid esset, ut lugerent
semper boni, ut capta res publica consulum prodi-
tione, vi tribunicia teneretur. Haec cum tot tantaque agerentur, non mirum est, praesertim in furore
animi et caecitate, multa illum et te fefellisse.
130 At videte quanta sit vis huius Papiriae legis in re
tali, non qualem tu adfers, sceleris plenam et furoris.
Q. Marcius censor signum Concordiae fecerat idque
in publico collocarat. Hoc signum C. Cassius censor

---

a See *De har. resp.* Chap. XIII. *n.*
b 164.

and not rather an expression of your wickedness and cruelty. But if at that time of shipwreck for the state you could have recollected everything, or if your secretary, when society was ablaze, had not been drawing up notes of hand with Byzantine exiles and the emissaries of Brogitarus,[a] but had been compiling for you your decrees, or more truly monstrosities, with mind undistracted, you might then have met every requirement, if not actually, at least with the proper legal terms. But, all at the same time, securities for money were being taken, engagements for provinces were being compounded, royal titles were being offered for sale, a busy telling-off of all the slaves to their beats in the several quarters of the whole city was in progress, opponents were being reconciled to you, new commands were being apportioned to your stalwarts, the poison was being prepared for poor Quintus Seius, schemes were being set on foot for the murder of Gnaeus Pompeius, the bulwark and protector of the empire, for the annihilation of the senate, the perpetual mortification of loyal men, the capture of the republic through the treachery of the consuls, and its enslavement to tribunician lawlessness. In the midst of so many absorbing interests, especially in view of the blind recklessness of your mood, it is not surprising that there was much that both he and you overlooked.

But mark how forcible a cogency is possessed in such a matter as this by the law of Papirius, a cogency not inspired, as is that which you assert, by a mood of passionate wickedness. Quintus Marcius[b] the censor had had a statue of Concord made, and had set it up publicly. This statue was transferred to

287

cum in curiam transtulisset, collegium vestrum consuluit num quid esse causae videretur quin id signum curiamque Concordiae dedicaret. LI. Quaeso, pontifices, et hominem cum homine et tempus cum tempore et rem cum re comparate. Ille erat summa modestia et gravitate censor: hic tribunus plebis scelere et audacia singulari. Tempus illud erat tranquillum et in libertate populi et gubernatione positum senatus: tuum porro tempus libertate populi Romani oppressa, senatus auctoritate deleta. Res illa plena iustitiae, sapientiae, dignitatis. Censor enim, penes quem maiores nostri, id quod tu sustulisti, iudicium senatus de dignitate esse voluerunt, Concordiae signum

131 volebat in curia curiamque ei deae dedicare. Praeclara voluntas atque omni laude digna. Praescribere enim se arbitrabatur, ut sine studiis dissensionis sententiae dicerentur, si sedem ipsam ac templum publici consilii religione Concordiae devinxisset. Tu cum ferro, cum metu, cum edictis, cum privilegiis, cum praesentibus copiis perditorum, absentis exercitus terrore et minis, consulum societate et nefario foedere servitute oppressam civitatem teneres, Libertatis signum posuisti magis ad ludibrium impudentiae quam ad simulationem religionis.

---

the senate-house by his successor Gaius Cassius,[a] who consulted your College as to whether they thought that there was any reason to prevent his dedicating both statue and senate-house to Concord. LI. Compare, I beg of you, gentlemen, character with character, period with period, and circumstances with circumstances. Cassius was a censor of the highest morality and dignity ; Clodius is a tribune of the plebs, unparalleled in criminal effrontery. In the former case the times were peaceful, established upon popular liberty and senatorial direction ; your days, on the other hand, Clodius, were marked by the crushing of the liberty of the Roman people and the extinction of the senate's authority. His act breathed a spirit of justice, sagacity, and high-mindedness ; he was a censor, holding an office which (though you have abolished all this) our ancestors desired should have control over senators and their rank; and he wished to dedicate a statue of Concord in the senate-house, and to dedicate the senate-house itself to this goddess. His wish was a lofty one, and worthy of all praise ; for he thought that in imposing the sanctity of Concord upon the very home and shrine of public deliberations, he was inculcating the lesson that declarations of policy should be untainted by the controversies of partisanship. You, on the other hand, though by the sword, by threats, by manifestos, by party legislation, by attending troops of ruffians, by the menace and terror of an absent army, and by the conspiracy and impious compact of the consuls, you held the state in the grip of a humiliating despotism, you set up a statue of Liberty, by way not so much of making a hypocritical pretence of religion, as of laughing in your sleeve at your own

Ille in curia quae poterat sine cuiusquam incommodo dedicari : tu in civis optime de re publica meriti cruore ac paene ossibus simulacrum non libertatis publicae, sed licentiae collocasti. Atque ille tamen 132 ad collegium rettulit : tu ad quem rettulisti ? Si quid deliberares, si quid tibi aut piandum aut instituendum fuisset religione domestica, tamen instituto ceterorum vetere ad pontificem detulisses : novum delubrum cum in urbis clarissimo loco nefando quodam atque inaudito instituto inchoares, referendum ad sacerdotes publicos non putasti ? At si collegium pontificum adhibendum non videbatur, nemone horum tibi idoneus visus est, qui aetate, honore, auctoritate antecellunt, ut cum eo de dedicatione communicares ? Quorum quidem tu non contempsisti, sed pertimuisti dignitatem LII. An tu auderes quaerere ex P. Servilio aut ex M. Lucullo, quorum ego consilio atque auctoritate rem publicam consul ex vestris manibus ac faucibus eripui, quibusnam verbis aut quo ritu, primum hoc dico, civis domum consecrares, deinde civis eius, cui princeps senatus, tum autem ordines omnes, deinde Italia tota, post cunctae gentes testimonium huius urbis atque

lack of compunction. Cassius placed his statue in
the senate-house, the dedication of which involved
embarrassment to none; you set up a likeness,
not of a people's liberty, but of its licence, in the
blood, nay, well-nigh in the very bones of a citizen
who had done signal service to the republic. Yet
he submitted his dedication to the sacred College;
132 and to whom did you submit yours? If, in the
sphere of your family worship, you had cherished
any project, or had been called upon to make any
expiation or innovation, you would still have adhered
to the immemorial practice of the rest of the world,
and have laid the question before a pontiff; and did
you think that there was no need for any reference
to the priests of the state, when by an impious and
unheard-of process you were inaugurating a new
shrine upon the most renowned spot in the city?
At least, if you did not think it necessary to call in
the College of Pontiffs, did you consider that there was
no individual of their number, pre-eminent as they
are in age, distinction, and dignity, to whom you
might appropriately impart your project of dedication? But it was not contempt, but rather fear
of their lofty qualities, that deterred you. LII. Or
would you have the face to inquire of Publius
Servilius or of Marcus Lucullus, on whose advice
and authority I, as consul, snatched the republic
out of your clutches and your very jaws, by what
form of words or ceremony—I mention this only
at the outset—you could consecrate the house of a
citizen, and furthermore of a citizen to whom the
leader of the senate, after him all the orders in
the state, after them the whole of Italy, and next
all the races of the earth, had given testimony that
291

133 imperii conservati dedissent? Quid diceres, o
nefanda et perniciosa labes civitatis? Ades, ades,
Luculle, Servili, dum dedico domum Ciceronis, ut
mihi praeeatis postemque teneatis. Es tu quidem
cum audacia tum impudentia singulari, sed tibi
tamen oculi, vultus, verba cecidissent, quum te viri,
qui sua dignitate personam populi Romani atque
auctoritatem imperii sustinerent, verbis gravissimis
proterruissent neque sibi fas esse dixissent, furori
interesse tuo atque in patriae parricidio exsultare.

134 Quae cum videres, tum te ad tuum adfinem non
delectum a te, sed relictum a ceteris contulisti.
Quem ego tamen credo, si est ortus ab illis, quos
memoriae proditum est ab ipso Hercule, perfuncto
iam laboribus, sacra didicisse, in viri fortis aerumnis
non ita crudelem fuisse, ut in viventis etiam et
spirantis capite bustum suis manibus imponeret : qui
aut nihil dixit nec fecit omnino poenamque hanc
maternae temeritatis tulit, ut mutam in delicto
personam nomenque praeberet, aut, si dixit aliquid
verbis haesitantibus postemque tremebunda manu
tetigit, certe nihil rite, nihil caste, nihil more institutoque perfecit. Viderat ille Murenam, vitricum

---

[a] For descent of the Pinarii from H. see Livy i. 7.

[b] By asserting the "dedication" of C.'s house he makes
it (though the phrase is startling) C.'s "tomb." *Caput*
is used in a double sense = (1) "head," literally, (2) "status
as a citizen," metaphorically.

[c] I cannot discover to what C. alludes.

it was he who preserved this city and this empire?
What would you say, O abominable and mischievous
plague-spot of the state? " You are here, Lucullus,
and you, Servilius, are here, to dictate the responses
to me, and to lay your hands upon the door-
post, while I dedicate the house of Cicero!" Your
effrontery and shamelessness are no doubt without
any parallel, but even your gaze, countenance, and
utterance would have faltered, cowed as you would
have been by the solemn pronouncements of the
men who by their dignity upheld the character of
the Roman people and the majesty of their empire,
and who would have declared it to be impious to
participate in your folly, and to gloat over the
treacherous overthrow of their country. Realizing
this, you forthwith betook yourself to your kinsman
by marriage, not that you had fixed your choice
upon him, but because all the world beside had
deserted him. Yet I cannot believe that he, if he
really be descended from those who, as legend
relates, were instructed in sacred rites by Hercules [a]
after he had performed his labours, was so hard-
hearted towards a brave man in his hour of distress
as to entomb [b] with his own hands the head of a
living and breathing man. No, but either he said
and did nothing whatsoever, and suffered retribution
for his mother's indiscretion [c] by playing a dumb
part and merely lending his name to the crime that
was being committed, or, supposing that he did
stammer out a few broken words, and did lay a
quaking hand upon the door-post, we may be quite
sure that nothing was done properly or correctly
or according to the prescribed tradition. He had
seen how Murena, his stepfather, when consul-

suum, consulem designatum, ad me consulem cum
Allobrogibus communis exitii indicia adferre : audierat ex illo se a me bis salutem accepisse, separatim
135 semel, iterum cum universis. Qua re quis est qui
existimare possit huic novo pontifici, primam hanc
post sacerdotium initum religionem instituenti vocemque mittenti, non et linguam obmutuisse et manum
obtorpuisse et mentem debilitatam metu concidisse,
praesertim cum ex collegio tanto non regem, non
flaminem, non pontificem videret fierique particeps
invitus alieni sceleris cogeretur et gravissimas poenas
adfinitatis impurissimae sustineret ?

136 LIII. Sed ut revertar ad ius publicum dedicandi,
quod ipsi pontifices semper non solum ad suas caerimonias, sed etiam ad populi iussa accommodaverunt,
habetis in commentariis vestris, C. Cassium censorem de signo Concordiae dedicando ad pontificum
collegium rettulisse eique M. Aemilium pontificem
maximum pro collegio respondisse, nisi eum populus
Romanus nominatim praefecisset atque eius iussu
faceret, non videri eam posse recte dedicari. Quid ?
cum Licinia, virgo Vestalis, summo loco nata,

elect, in company with the Allobrogians, laid before me in my consulship information with regard to the threatened overthrow of society; from his lips he had heard how I had twice been responsible for the preservation of his life, first when a separate danger menaced him personally, and again when he was involved with the whole community. Who is there, then, who can bring himself to think that this novice in the pontificate, presiding at the first religious ceremony and uttering the first religious formula since his induction to the priesthood, did not find his tongue grow dumb, his hand become palsied, and his mind unnerved and faltering for terror, especially when he looked upon none of his numerous colleagues, no King of Rites, no flamen, no pontiff, and when he was reluctantly constrained to become a party to another's guilt, and endured a grievous penalty for the sin of his abandoned kinswoman?

LIII. But let me return to the official rules that govern dedicatory ceremonies, rules which the pontiffs themselves have invariably adapted not merely to their own ritual, but also to the decrees of the people. You will find in your records that the censor Gaius Cassius submitted to the Pontifical College his project for the dedication of a statue to Concord, and that the reply made to him by the supreme pontiff, Marcus Aemilius, on behalf of the College was, that they did not think that the dedication could be correctly carried out, unless the Roman people should give him express authority in the matter, so that it should be at their mandate that he acted. Again, when Licinia, a Vestal Virgin of noble birth, distinguished by the most sacred of

sanctissimo sacerdotio praedita, T. Flaminino Q.
Metello consulibus aram et aediculam et pulvinar
sub Saxo dedicasset, nonne eam rem ex auctoritate
senatus ad hoc collegium Sex. Iulius praetor rettulit ?
cum P. Scaevola, pontifex maximus, pro collegio
respondit, QUOD IN LOCO PUBLICO LICINIA, CAII FILIA,
INIUSSU POPULI DEDICASSET, SACRUM NON VIDERIER.
Quam quidem rem quanta tractaverit severitate
quantaque diligentia senatus ex ipso senatus consulto facile cognoscetis. SENATUS CONSULTUM.

137 Videtisne praetori urbano negotium datum, ut
curaret ne id sacrum esset, et ut, si quae essent
incisae aut inscriptae litterae, tollerentur ? O
tempora ! o mores ! Tum censorem, hominem sanctissimum, simulacrum Concordiae dedicare pontifices in
templo inaugurato prohibuerunt, post autem senatus
in loco augusto consecratam iam aram tollendam ex
auctoritate pontificum censuit neque ullum est passus
ex ea dedicatione litterarum exstare monumentum :
tu, procella patriae, turbo ac tempestas pacis atque
otii, quod in naufragio rei publicae, tenebris offusis,
demerso populo Romano, everso atque eiecto senatu,

---

^a A rock on the slope of the Aventine, where there was
a temple of Bona Dea ; see Ovid, *Fasti*, v. 148.
^b 123.
^c *Sc.* Balearicus.

priestly offices, dedicated an altar, an oratory, and
a sacred couch under the Rock *a* in the consulship *b*
of Titus Flaminius and Quintus Metellus,*c* did not
Sextus Julius the praetor, on the senate's authority,
refer the question to the decision of this College?
On that occasion Publius Scaevola, the supreme
pontiff, answered on behalf of the College that
"that which Licinia, daughter of Gaius, had dedicated in a public place was not deemed by them to
be sacred." You will have no difficulty in realizing,
by an examination of the senate's actual decree,
how sternly and how punctiliously they dealt with
the affair. (*The Decree of the Senate is read.*)

You observe, do you not, that herein the city
praetor has the function assigned to him of seeing
that no sanctity attached to what had been dedicated,
and that any letters that had been engraved or
inscribed thereon should be erased. The times are
indeed changed, and moral standards with them!
Then a censor, a pattern of uprightness, was forbidden by the pontiffs to dedicate in a consecrated
temple an image of Concord, and on a later occasion
the senate, prompted by the authority of the
pontiffs, determined that an altar which had already
been consecrated at a revered spot must be removed,
and did not permit a single letter upon what had
been dedicated to stand as a witness. You, on the
other hand, the storm upon which your country is
tossed, the raging whirlwind that robs us of peace
and repose, did you dream that, at a time when the
state was suffering shipwreck, when a cloud of gloom
was shed about us, when the Roman people were
sunk beneath the waves, and when the senate was
overthrown and cast overboard, your acts of pull-

dirueris, aedificaris, religione omni violata, religionis
tamen nomine contaminaris, in eius civis aedibus, qui
urbem suis laboribus ac periculis conservasset, monumentum deletae rei publicae collocaris † ad equitum
notam, ad dolorem bonorum † omnium sublato Q.
Catuli nomine incideris, id sperasti rem publicam
diutius quam, quoad mecum simul expulsa careret
his moenibus, esse laturam ?

138 Ac si, pontifices, neque is, cui licuit, neque id, quod
fas fuit, dedicavit, quid me attinet iam illud tertium,
quod proposueram, docere, non iis institutis ac verbis, quibus caerimoniae postulant, dedicasse ? LIV.
Dixi a principio nihil me de scientia vestra, nihil de
sacris, nihil de abscondito iure pontificum dicturum.
Quae sunt adhuc a me de iure dedicandi disputata,
non sunt quaesita ex occulto aliquo genere litterarum,
sed sumpta de medio, ex rebus palam per magistratus
actis ad collegiumque delatis, ex senatus consulto,
ex lege. Illa interiora iam vestra sunt, quid dici,
139 quid praeiri, quid tangi, quid teneri ius fuerit. Quae
si omnia e Ti. Coruncanii scientia, qui peritissimus
pontifex fuisse dicitur, acta esse constarent aut si M.
Horatius ille Pulvillus, qui, cum eum multi propter

ᵃ Nothing can be made of the text here ; I give the
general sense.
   ᵇ The first plebeian to be Pontifex Maximus, about 254.
   ᶜ See Livy ii. 8. In the first year of the republic he was
in the act of dedicating the Capitol (' postem iam tenenti '),
when his enemies announced to him the death of his son.
" He was only so far distracted by the intelligence, as to
order that the body should be buried."

ing down and building up, of polluting all religion, and yet defiling your deeds by the name of religion, of planting a monument of the extinction of the republic in the dwelling of him who by his labours had preserved the city at the risk of his life, and of removing the name of Quintus Catulus, and inscribing in its place a stigma that spells the grief of loyal men,[a]—did you dream that the republic would tolerate such acts longer than while it remained banished with me and expelled from these walls?

But if, gentlemen, the agent of the dedication was unauthorized, and its object an improper object, what need for me to demonstrate the third point which I had in view, namely, that the dedication was not performed in accordance with those usages and formulas which are demanded by ritual? LIV. I said at the outset that I should base no assertion upon my own knowledge, upon religious observance, or upon the secret regulations of the pontiffs. The arguments dealing with the rules of dedication which I have hitherto adduced have been culled from no esoteric treatise; they are drawn from a common stock, from open proceedings of magistrates in which they have deferred to the College, from senatorial decrees, and from the statutes. As to the questions that remain, the correct words to be uttered, responses to be dictated, and objects to be touched or held, these are your own intimate concern. Were it beyond all doubt that all these details had been carefully observed in accordance with the knowledge of Tiberius Coruncanius,[b] who is said to have been the most expert of pontiffs; or if the famous Horatius Pulvillus,[c] who, though many men were moved by jealousy

invidiam fictis religionibus impedirent, restitit et constantissima mente Capitolium dedicavit, huius modi alicui dedicationi praefuisset, tamen in scelere religio non valeret, ne valeat id, quod imperitus adolescens, novus sacerdos, sororis precibus, matris minis adductus, ignarus, invitus, sine collegis, sine libris, sine auctore, sine fictore, furtim, mente ac lingua titubante fecisse dicatur, praesertim cum iste impurus atque impius hostis omnium religionum, qui contra fas et inter viros saepe mulier et inter mulieres vir fuisset, ageret illam rem ita raptim et turbulente, uti neque mens neque vox neque lingua
140 consisteret. LV. Delatum tum est ad vos, pontifices, et post omnium sermone celebratum, quem ad modum iste praeposteris verbis, ominibus obscaenis, idemtidem se ipse revocans, dubitans, timens, haesitans omnia aliter ac vos in monumentis habetis et pronuntiarit et fecerit. Quod quidem minime mirum est, in tanto scelere tantaque dementia ne audaciae quidem locum ad timorem comprimendum fuisse. Etenim si nemo umquam praedo tam barbarus atque immanis fuit qui cum fana spoliasset, deinde aram aliquam in littore deserto somniis stimulatus aut religione aliqua consecraret, non horreret animo, cum divinum numen scelere violatum placare pre-

---

[a] Lit. "moulder"; "so called," says Varro, "because they moulded the cakes" (fictores dicti a fingendis libis).

to interfere with his actions on false pleas of religious hindrances, still stood his ground and with unfaltering resolution dedicated the Capitol, had presided over a dedication like that of Clodius, even so there could be no valid sanctity conferred where the circumstances were criminal; allow not, then, validity to the alleged proceedings of an ignorant youth, a novice in the priesthood, who was influenced by a sister's prayers and a mother's threats, who acted without knowledge, without consent, without colleagues, without books, with none to support you, none to bake the cakes of sacrifice,[a] but surreptitiously, and with mind and tongue that wavered; more especially, seeing that that polluted and unnatural foe of all things holy, who had shocked propriety by often behaving as a woman among men and as a man among women, was managing the business with such feverish and disorderly haste, that he too worked with faltering purpose and stammering tongue. LV. Information was carried to you, gentlemen, and later it became a subject of universal comment, how Clodius, with a distorted formula, and amid inauspicious omens, constantly correcting himself, with a fearful and faltering hesitation, pronounced phrases and performed rites entirely different from those contained in your treatises of ritual. And indeed it is little to be wondered at that, in wickedness so outrageous and so infatuated, not effrontery itself should have had scope to quell his terrors. For truly if no robber, who, after desecrating temples, had later been prompted by dreams or scruples to consecrate some altar upon a desolate shore, was ever so barbarous and so inhuman as not to shudder in spirit, when compelled to appease by his prayers

cibus cogeretur, qua tandem istum perturbatione
mentis omnium templorum atque tectorum totiusque
urbis praedonem fuisse censetis, cum pro detesta-
tione tot scelerum unam aram nefarie consecraret ?

141 Non potuit ullo modo—quamquam et insolentia
dominatus extulerat animos et erat incredibili
armatus audacia—non in agendo ruere ac saepe
peccare, praesertim illo pontifice et magistro qui
cogeretur docere ante quam ipse didicisset. Magna
vis est quum in deorum immortalium numine tum
vero in ipsa re publica. Di immortales suorum templorum custodem ac praesidem sceleratissime pulsum
quum viderent, ex suis templis in eius aedes immi-
grare nolebant. Itaque istius vaecordissimi mentem
cura metuque terrebant. Res vero publica quamquam erat exterminata mecum, tamen obversabatur
ante oculos exstinctoris sui et ab istius inflammato
atque indomito furore iam tum se meque repetebat.
Qua re quid est mirum, si iste metu exagitatus,[1]
furore instinctus, scelere praeceps, neque institutas
caerimonias persequi neque verbum ullum sollemne
potuit effari ?

142 LVI. Quae cum ita sint, pontifices, revocate iam
animos vestros ab hac subtili nostra disputatione ad
universam rem publicam, quam antea cum viris fortibus multis, in hac vero causa solis vestris cervicibus
sustinetis. Vobis universi senatus perpetua auctori-

<hr>

[1] metu exagitatus *Pet.* : metus MSS.

the godhead whom his crime had assailed, how great, think you, must have been the disquiet of mind suffered by that robber of all temples, houses, and indeed of the whole city, when, to avert the consequences of so many misdeeds, he consecrated a single altar,—and consecrated that sacrilegiously? For all that the pride of his new-won mastery had puffed up his soul, for all that he stood sheathed in incredible hardihood, yet in performance he could not but make many slips and blunders, especially as the pontiff who directed him was constrained to dictate a ritual which as yet he himself had not learned. Great is the power that resides in the dispensation of the immortal gods, yes, and in the republic itself. The immortal gods, when they saw the guardian and champion of their temples outrageously expelled, refused to remove themselves from those temples into his house. They therefore wrought upon his insensate mind with panic and apprehension. As for the republic, though it had shared my banishment, its phantom yet loomed before the eyes of its suppressor, and was even then demanding me (yes! and itself) back from his fiery and irrepressible fury. What wonder, then, that with fear hounding him, with infatuation inspiring him, and with crime hurrying him upon his ruin, he was unable to carry out the prescribed ritual, or to pronounce a single word of the accustomed formula?

LVI. Since this is so, gentlemen, divert your minds at last from the minutiae of my argument to a broad survey of that republic, the responsibilities of which many gallant heroes have in the past helped you to bear, but which at the present juncture you have supported solely upon your own backs. It is to you

tas, cui vosmet ipsi praestantissime semper in mea
causa praefuistis, vobis Italiae magnificentissimus ille
motus municipiorumque concursus, vobis campus
centuriarumque una vox omnium, quarum vos principes atque auctores fuistis, vobis omnes societates,
omnes ordines, omnes, qui aut re aut spe denique
sunt bona, omne suum erga meam dignitatem
studium et iudicium non modo commissum, verum
143 etiam commendatum esse arbitrabuntur. Denique
ipsi di immortales, qui hanc urbem atque hoc imperium tuentur, ut esset omnibus gentibus posterita-
tique perspicuum divino me numine esse rei publicae redditum, idcirco mihi videntur fructum reditus
et gratulationis meae ad suorum sacerdotum potestatem iudiciumque revocasse. Hic est enim reditus,
pontifices, haec restitutio in domo, in sedibus, in aris,
in focis, in dis penatibus recuperandis. Quorum si
iste suis sceleratissimis manibus tecta sedesque convellit, ducibusque consulibus tamquam urbe capta
hanc unam domum quasi acerrimi propugnatoris sibi
delendam putavit, tamen illi di penates ac familiares
mei per vos in meam domum mecum erunt restituti.
144 LVII. Quocirca te, Capitoline, quem propter beneficia populus Romanus Optimum, propter vim Maxi-

that the perpetual authority of the senate, to which you yourselves have always throughout my case given a magnificent lead, it is to you that the magnanimous demonstrations of Italy and the united support of the corporate towns, it is to you that the Campus and the unopposed voice of all the Centuries, who have had you for their mentors and directors, it is to you that all associations, all classes, in a word, all whose welfare has been realized or is in prospect of realization, think that all their good wishes and favourable opinions towards my merits have been, not committed merely, but commended. Finally, the immortal gods themselves, who watch over this city and this empire, seem to have submitted to the jurisdiction and discretion of their priests the full harvestage of my restoration and the acclamations that accompanied it, solely in order that it might be manifest to all nations and to all future generations that my restitution to the republic was due to divine providence. Herein, gentlemen, consists a true return and a true restoration,—to possess once more house, home, altars, hearths, and household gods ; and though with impious hands he has torn down the roofs and resting-places of those gods, and though, as if this were a city he had captured under the consuls' leadership, he has thought it his duty to single out for destruction the house of its most ardent champion, nevertheless the gods of my household and my family will find that by your aid they are once again restored with me to my home.

LVII. Wherefore I beseech and supplicate thee, God of the Capitol, to whom the Roman people has given the name of Best by reason of the blessings thou hast vouchsafed, and of Greatest by reason of

mum nominavit, teque, Iuno Regina, et te, custos
urbis, Minerva, quae semper adiutrix consiliorum
meorum, testis laborum exstitisti, precor atque quaeso, vosque, qui maxime me repetistis atque revo-
castis, quorum de sedibus haec mihi est proposita
contentio, patrii penates familiaresque, qui huic urbi
et rei publicae praesidetis, vos obtestor, quorum ego a
templis atque delubris pestiferam illam et nefariam
flammam depuli, teque, Vesta mater, cuius castissi-
mas sacerdotes ab hominum amentium furore et
scelere defendi, cuiusque ignem illum sempiternum
non sum passus aut sanguine civium restingui aut
145 cum totius urbis incendio commisceri : ut, si in illo
paene fato rei publicae obieci meum caput pro vestris
caerimoniis atque templis perditissimorum civium
furori atque ferro et si iterum, cum ex mea contentione interitus bonorum omnium quaereretur, vos
sum testatus, vobis me ac meos commendavi, meque
atque meum caput ea condicione devovi, ut, si et eo
ipso tempore et ante in consulatu meo commodis
meis omnibus, emolumentis, praemiis praetermissis,
cura, cogitatione, vigiliis omnibus nihil nisi de salute
meorum civium laborassem, tum mihi re publica
aliquando restituta liceret frui : sin autem mea consilia patriae non profuissent, ut perpetuum dolorem
avulsus a meis sustinerem, hanc ego devotionem
capitis mei, cum ero in meas sedes restitutus, tum
146 denique convictam esse et commissam putabo. Nam

ᵃ C. appeals to Jupiter, Juno, and Minerva as the special
deities of the Capitol.   The two last had "side-chapels" in
the temple of Jupiter Optimus Maximus.
306

thy might, and thee, Queen Juno, and thee, guardian of our city, Minerva,[a] who hast ever shown thyself the helper of my designs and the witness of my devotion ; and ye too, who above all sought for and demanded my return, for the recovery of whose abode I have set myself this present encounter, ye ancestral gods of the household and the family, who preside over this city and this republic, I conjure ye, from whose temples and shrines I warded those pestilential and impious flames ; and thee, Vesta our Mother, whose chaste priestesses I have protected from the madness, frenzy, and wickedness of men, and whose undying fire I have not suffered to be quenched in the blood of citizens, nor to be commingled with the whole city's conflagration ; that if, when the state so nearly met her doom, I offered my own head to the reckless weapons of the ungodly on behalf of your rites and temples, and if later, when, by reason of my opposition, the destruction of all true patriots was aimed at, I called ye to witness, commended to ye myself and mine, and vowed to ye my life and myself, engaging that if, both at that very time and before in my consulship, I had forgone all my privileges, profits, and rewards, and toiled with all my pains, thoughts, and vigilance, for no other end than the welfare of my fellow-citizens, I might then one day be permitted to look with joy upon the republic restored ; but that if my measures availed nothing for my country's good, I might be torn from my dear ones, and be bowed beneath an unending sorrow ; then this dedication of my life I shall not consider to have been indubitably accepted until the day whereon I find myself restored to my dwelling.   For as it is, gentlemen, I am deprived not

nunc quidem, pontifices, non solum domo, de qua cognostis, sed tota urbe careo, in quam videor esse restitutus. Urbis enim celeberrimae et maximae partes adversum illud non monumentum, sed vulnus patriae contuentur. Quem cum mihi conspectum morte magis vitandum fugiendumque esse videatis, nolite, quaeso, eum, cuius reditu restitutam rem publicam fore putastis, non solum dignitatis ornamentis, sed etiam urbis patriae usu velle esse privatum. LVIII. Non me bonorum direptio, non tectorum excisio, non depopulatio praediorum, non praeda consulum ex meis fortunis crudelissime capta permovet: caduca semper et mobilia haec esse duxi, non virtutis atque ingenii, sed fortunae et temporum munera: quorum ego non tam facultatem umquam et copiam expetendam putavi, quam et in utendo rationem et in carendo patientiam. Etenim ad nostrum usum prope modum iam est definita moderatio rei familiaris: liberis autem nostris satis amplum patrimonium paterni nominis ac nostrae memoriae relinquemus: domo per scelus erepta, per latrocinium occupata, per religionis vim sceleratius etiam aedificata quam eversa, carere sine maxima ignominia rei

alone of my house, which is the subject of your inquiry, but of the whole city, to which, on a superficial view, I have been restored. For the chiefest and most frequented districts of the city are confronted by the vision of what I will not describe as a memorial, but rather as a scar upon our country. And since you realize, as you must, that I must needs shun and avoid the sight of this more than death, forbear, I beg of you, to decree that he, whose restoration you hoped would mean the restoration of the republic, should be deprived not only of the external trappings of dignity, but even of the enjoyment of living in the city which is his home.   LVIII. It is not the plundering of my property nor the demolition of my house nor the ravaging of my estates nor the booty that the consuls have so pitilessly taken from my fortunes that greatly moves me ; these I have always accounted transient and fleeting, the bestowal not of virtue and genius but of chance and circumstance ; and it is not so much opportunities for acquiring and amassing these that I have thought desirable, but rather philosophy in their enjoyment and steadfastness in their loss.   For truly our power to dispose of our private goods extends as a rule for no longer than our power to enjoy them ; and the inheritance we shall leave to our children will be bounteous enough, if it consists but of their ancestral name and their father's memory ; but the house which has been wrested from me by crime, seized by brigandage, and built over by lawlessness masquerading as religion, even more wickedly than it was overthrown, cannot be lost to me without the infliction of the direst disgrace upon the state, and the deepest grief and ignominy

147 publicae, meo dedecore ac dolore non possum. Quapropter, si dis immortalibus, si senatui, si populo Romano, si cunctae Italiae, si provinciis, si exteris nationibus, si vobismet ipsis, qui in mea salute principem semper locum auctoritatemque tenuistis, gratum et iucundum meum reditum intelligitis esse, quaeso obtestorque vos, pontifices, ut me, quem auctoritate, studio, sententiis restituistis, nunc, quoniam senatus ita vult, manibus quoque vestris in sedibus meis collocetis.

upon myself. If, therefore, you conceive that my restoration is a source of pleasure and gratification to the immortal gods, to the senate, to the Roman people, to all Italy, to the provinces, to foreign nations, and to your own selves, who have always been first and most influential in working for my welfare, I beg and conjure you, gentlemen, as I have been restored by your influence, enthusiasm, and suffrages, so now also, since it is the will of the senate, let it be your hands that install me in my own home.

ORATIO
DE HARUSPICUM RESPONSIS [1]

Introductory Note.—Early in 56 a strange noise was reported to have been heard in the Ager Latiniensis, a district near Rome. The Senate referred the matter to the Soothsayers, who pronounced that expiation must be offered to the gods for (*a*) neglect and impiety in the conduct of public games, (*b*) profanation of hallowed sites, (*c*) assassination of ambassadors, (*d*) violation of oaths, (*e*) neglect and impiety in the conduct of an ancient sacrifice.

In the interval between this and the speech *De domo sua* the Senate had decided against Clodius' alleged consecration of the site of C.'s house, and had restored it to its former owner, and Clodius, who was aedile for the year, affirmed that it was to this site that the Soothsayers referred.

In this speech C. gives the following explanations of the offences to be expiated: (*a*) the games alluded to were the Megalesia, on which occasion Clodius had packed the theatre with his gangs of slaves, though only freemen should

1 I. Hesterno die, patres conscripti, quum me et vestra dignitas et frequentia equitum Romanorum praesentium, quibus senatus dabatur, magno opere commosset, putavi mihi reprimendam esse P. Clodii impudicam impudentiam, quum is publicanorum causam stultissimis interrogationibus impediret, P. Tullioni Syro navaret operam atque ei se, cui totus

<hr>

[1] *Asconius gives* responso.

a At a debate in the Senate, of which we know nothing save what we are told here.

312

THE SPEECH CONCERNING
THE RESPONSE OF THE SOOTHSAYERS

[DELIVERED BEFORE THE SENATE, 56]

have been admitted, (b) the site alluded to was not his house, but that of Seius, of which Clodius was in possession after having murdered its owner, the house having contained a shrine and altars, (c) the ambassadors alluded to were Theodosius and Plator, the former of whom had been killed by Clodius, and the latter by Piso, his associate, (d) the perjury alluded to was that of the jury which had acquitted Clodius when he was manifestly guilty of sacrilege, and (e) the sacrifice alluded to was that of the Bona Dea, which Clodius had polluted.

A modern authority (Heitland, *Roman Republic*, vol. iii. p. 187 n.) says of the speech, " That Cicero's speech *De haruspicum responso* is the edited copy of that actually delivered, I do not venture to affirm. But I find it very difficult to attribute it to a forger. It does not stand on a high level, I freely admit."

I. CONSCRIPT FATHERS : Yesterday,[a] under the influence of the profound emotions inspired in me by your lofty demeanour and by the concourse of Roman knights, to whom you had vouchsafed an audience, I considered it to be my duty to repress the shameless impudence displayed by Publius Clodius in endeavouring to obstruct the business dealing with the collectors of revenue by his fatuous questions, in espousing the cause of Publius Tullio the Syrian, and in displaying his wares, before your

313

venierat, etiam vobis inspectantibus venditaret.
Itaque hominem furentem exsultantemque continui,
simul ac periculum iudicii intendi : duobus inceptis
verbis omnem impetum gladiatoris ferociamque com-
2 pressi.   Ac tamen ignarus ille qui consules essent, ex-
sanguis atque aestuans, se ex curia repente proripuit
cum quibusdam fractis iam atque inanibus minis et
cum illius Pisoniani temporis Gabinianique terrori-
bus.   Quem quum egredientem insequi coepissem,
cepi equidem fructum maximum et ex consurrectione
omnium vestrum et ex comitatu publicanorum.   Sed
vaecors repente sine suo vultu, sine colore, sine voce
constitit : deinde respexit et simul atque Cn. Lentulum consulem aspexit, concidit in curiae paene
limine, recordatione, credo, Gabinii sui desiderioque
Pisonis.   Cuius ego de effrenato et praecipiti furore
quid dicam ? an [1] potest gravioribus a me verbis
vulnerari quam est statim in facto ipso a gravissimo
viro, P. Servilio, confectus ac trucidatus ?   Cuius si
iam vim et gravitatem illam singularem ac paene
divinam adsequi possem, tamen non dubito quin ea
tela, quae coniecerit inimicus, quam ea, quae collega
patris emisit, leviora atque hebetiora esse videantur.
3   II. Sed tamen mei facti rationem exponere illis
volo, qui hesterno die dolore me elatum et iracundia

[1] an *Pet.*

---

a P. Servilius Isauricus, consul with Ap. Clodius Pulcher
79.

very eyes, to this man, to whom he had sold himself body and soul. In pursuit of this end, I menaced him with the threat of action at law, and so checked forthwith his extravagant exultation; indeed, two words had not escaped me before I had silenced his contumacious outburst. But he was not altogether silenced; for, totally regardless of the character of our consuls, he suddenly flung himself pale and fuming from the senate-house, crying empty threats that broke into stuttering upon his lips, and imprecating upon us the terrors of the régime of Piso and Gabinius. Making as though to follow him as he departed, I was deeply gratified by your rising to a man from your seats, while the collectors prepared to accompany me. But on a sudden, dumfounded, pale, and speechless, with the scowl dying from his brow, he halted; then he cast a backward glance, and as his gaze fell upon the consul Gnaeus Lentulus, he fell to the ground almost on the threshold of the senate-house, overcome, no doubt, by the recollection of his beloved Gabinius and by yearning for his lost Piso. How can I describe his unbridled and headstrong infatuation? Can any expressions I have at my command wound him more trenchantly than those whereby, at the actual time, Publius Servilius, that exemplary gentleman, summarily demolished and made an end of him? But even were I able to match his unrivalled and wellnigh superhuman energy and seriousness, I have no doubt that the missiles directed against Clodius by an enemy would seem blunter and less weighty than those discharged by his father's colleague.[a]

3 II. I wish, however, to demonstrate the propriety of my conduct for the benefit of those who considered

longius prope progressum arbitrabantur quam sapientis hominis cogitata ratio postulasset. Nihil feci iratus, nihil impotenti animo, nihil non diu consideratum ac multo ante meditatum. Ego enim me, patres conscripti, inimicum semper esse professus sum duobus, qui me, qui rem publicam cum defendere deberent, servare possent, cumque ad consulare officium ipsis insignibus illius imperii ad meam salutem non solum auctoritate, sed etiam precibus vestris vocarentur, primo reliquerunt, deinde prodiderunt, postremo oppugnarunt praemiisque nefariae pactionis funditus una cum re publica oppressum exstinctumque voluerunt, quique suo ductu et imperio cruento illo atque funesto supplicia neque a sociorum moenibus prohibere neque hostium urbibus inferre potuerunt: excisionem, inflammationem, eversionem, depopulationem, vastitatem etiam sua cum praeda meis omnibus tectis atque agris intu-

4 lerunt. Cum his furiis et facibus, cum his, inquam, exitiosis prodigiis ac paene huius imperii pestibus bellum mihi inexpiabile dico esse susceptum, neque id tamen ipsum tantum quantum meus ac meorum, sed tantum quantum vester atque omnium bonorum dolor postulavit. III. In Clodium vero non est hodie meum maius odium quam illo die fuit, cum illum

that under the stress of resentment and indignation I went yesterday to perhaps greater lengths than those to which a wise man by his reasoned principles might have been called upon to go. Nothing that I did was done in anger or upon uncontrolled impulse ; there was nothing that I had not long pondered and rehearsed some considerable time before. For I, conscript fathers, have always avowed my hostility to two men, who, though it was in their duty to defend, and in their power to preserve the republic and myself, and though they were summoned to the responsibilities of the consulship by the very external emblems of that lofty position, and to the cause of my protection not only by your authority but by your prayers, first deserted their trust, then betrayed, and finally assailed it, and designed to use the profits of their traitorous trafficking to effect my utter humiliation and annihilation along with that of the state ; and who, to their own profit, visited upon all my houses and estates those inflictions, in the shape of destruction, fire, demolition, harrying and rapine, which they were unable, by their leadership and their blood-stained and fatal tenure of power, to ward from the walls of our allies, or launch 4 against the cities of our foemen. With these furies and fire-brands, yes, with these pernicious portents who brought all but pestilence upon this empire, I do admit that I have entered upon implacable warfare : a war, albeit, which is itself not bitter enough to satisfy my resentment and that of those belonging to me, though it satisfies your own and that of all sound patriots.

III. But for Clodius my hatred is no greater to-day than it was on that day when I discovered that he

ambustum religiosissimis ignibus cognovi muliebri
ornatu ex incesto stupro atque ex domo pontificis
maximi emissum. Tum, inquam, tum vidi ac multo
ante prospexi quanta tempestas excitaretur, quanta
impenderet procella rei publicae. Videbam illud
scelus tam importunum, audaciam tam immanem
adolescentis furentis, nobilis, vulnerati non posse
arceri otii finibus : erupturum illud malum aliquando,
5 si impunitum fuisset, ad perniciem civitatis. Non
multum mihi sane post ad odium accessit. Nihil enim
contra me fecit odio mei, sed odio severitatis, odio
dignitatis, odio rei publicae. Non me magis violavit
quam senatum, quam equites Romanos, quam omnes
bonos, quam Italiam cunctam : non denique in me
sceleratior fuit quam in ipsos deos immortales :
etenim illos eo scelere violavit, quo nemo antea : in
me fuit eodem animo, quo etiam eius familiaris
Catilina, si vicisset, fuisset. Itaque eum numquam
a me esse accusandum putavi, non plus quam stipitem
illum, qui quorum hominum esset nesciremus, nisi se
Ligurem ipse esse diceret. Quid enim hunc per-
sequar, pecudem ac beluam, pabulo inimicorum meorum et glande corruptum ? qui si sensit quo se scelere

---

[a] Clodius' violation of the rites of Bona Dea, to which
reference is made in this speech *passim*.
[b] Aelius Ligur, who opposed the motion for Cic.'s return ;
also means 'Ligurian,' the Ligurians being proverbial for
deceit.

had burnt his fingers in the fires of awful rites, and
had been dismissed in his woman's garb from the
house of the supreme Pontiff which he had made the
scene of vile adultery.ᵃ It was then, then I say,
that I marked and anticipated long before its arrival
the fierce hurricane that was being roused, the
furious tempest that was brewing to imperil the
state. I saw that criminality so savage and
effrontery so monstrous, displayed by a maddened
and exasperated young nobleman, could not be kept
within the limits of a peaceful existence ; but that
one day, if it were allowed to go unchecked, the
plague would break forth, fraught with ruin to the
5 community. True, indeed, that as regards myself
there was · little addition afterwards to his hate ; he
did nothing through hatred of me, but through
hatred of austerity, of dignity, of the republic ;
it was not me he attacked, so much as the senate,
the Roman knights, the general body of patriots,
and the whole of Italy ; in fact the crimes he committed against me were no more shocking than
those which he committed against the immortal
gods. Them indeed he assailed with an impiety
hitherto unknown ; but his animosity against me
was no greater than that which would have actuated
his friend Catiline, had he triumphed. Consequently
I never thought myself called upon to accuse him,
any more than to accuse that blockhead whom we
should be at a loss how to classify, were it not that
he characterized himself for us by his name of
Ligur.ᵇ For what need that I should vent my spleen
upon such brute cattle as Clodius, who had browsed
to his own bane upon the fodder and acorns of my
enemies ? If he has realized the nature of the sin

devinxerit, non dubito quin sit miserrimus : sin autem id non videt, periculum est ne se stuporis excusatione defendat. Accedit etiam, quod exspectatione omnium fortissimo et clarissimo viro, T. Annio, devota et constituta ista hostia esse videtur : cui me praeripere desponsam iam et destinatam laudem, cum ipse eius opera et dignitatem et salutem recuperarim, valde est iniquum. IV. Etenim, ut P. ille Scipio natus mihi videtur ad interitum exitiumque Karthaginis, qui illam a multis imperatoribus obsessam, oppugnatam, labefactam, paene captam aliquando, quasi fatali adventu solus evertit, sic T. Annius ad illam pestem comprimendam, exstinguendam, funditus delendam natus esse videtur et quasi divino munere donatus rei publicae. Solus ille cognovit quem ad modum armatum civem, qui lapidibus, qui ferro alios fugaret, alios domi contineret, qui urbem totam, qui curiam, qui forum, qui templa omnia caede incendiisque terreret, non modo vinci, verum etiam vinciri oporteret. Huic ego et tali et ita de me ac de patria merito viro numquam mea voluntate praeripiam eum praesertim reum, cuius ille inimicitias non solum suscepit propter salutem meam, verum etiam appetivit. Sed si etiam nunc illaqueatus iam omnium legum periculis, irretitus odio bonorum omnium, exspectatione supplicii iam non diuturna implicatus, feretur tamen haesitans

^a Milo ; see *In senatu*, Chap. VIII. n.
^b Clodius was killed by Milo three years after the date of this speech. This passage may be read as a prophecy of this, but it more probably refers to a prosecution of Clodius by Milo.

that has enthralled him, I cannot doubt that he is
the most wretched of men ; but if he is blind to this,
he may attempt to defend himself by pleading
6 congenital dulness of wit. There is this too : the
universal anticipation seems to have marked him
down and allotted him as a victim to Titus Annius,[a]
that bravest and most renowned of men ; and it
would be most improper, in view of the fact that it is
to his efforts that I myself owe the recovery of my
position and my security, for me to filch from him
a glory which is already his by promise and destiny.
IV. For indeed, even as the great Publius Scipio
appears to me to have been destined from birth to
work the doom and destruction of Carthage, which
he alone, after many generals had besieged, attacked,
shaken, and all but captured it, overthrew by what
seemed a direct mission of fate, so Titus Annius
seems to have 'been designed from birth and
presented to the state as a heaven-sent gift, for the
purpose of foiling, abolishing, and utterly extirpating
that pestilence. He alone knows the proper method
of not merely defeating but also of fettering an armed
citizen, who intimidated some by stones or steel, who
penned others in their houses, and who terrified with
fire and slaughter the whole city, the senate-house,
7 and all the temples. Never of my own free will shall I
deprive so noble a gentleman, whose services to the
state and to myself are so eminent, of the man he
accuses, above all when he is one whose enmity
he not merely braved, but even coveted, in the cause
of my restoration.[b] But if even now, hampered
though he be by manifold legal liabilities, enmeshed
in the hatred of all loyal men, racked by the anticipation of a retribution that cannot now be long deferred,

et in me impetum impeditus facere conabitur, re-
sistam et aut concedente aut etiam adiuvante Milone
eius conatum refutabo, velut hesterno die, cum mihi
stanti tacens minaretur, voce tantum attigi legum
initium et iudicii : consedit ille : conticui. Diem
dixisset, ut iecerat[1] : fecissem ut ei statim tertius a
praetore dies diceretur. Atque hoc sic moderetur et
cogitet, si contentus sit iis sceleribus, quae commisit,
esse se iam consecratum Miloni : si quod in me telum
intenderit, statim me esse adrepturum arma iudiciorum atque legum.

8   Atque paullo ante, patres conscripti, contionem
habuit, quae est ad me tota delata : cuius contionis
primum universum argumentum sententiamque au-
dite. Cum riseritis impudentiam hominis, tum a me
de tota contione audietis. V. De religionibus sacris
et caerimoniis est contionatus, patres conscripti,
Clodius : P. inquam Clodius sacra et religiones
negligi, violari, pollui questus est. Non mirum, si
hoc vobis ridiculum videtur. Etiam sua contio risit
hominem, quo modo ipse gloriari solet, ducentis
confixum senati consultis, quae sunt omnia contra

---

[1] iecerat *Ernesti* : fecerat MSS.

---

a " The shortest term of notice allowed by the law "
(Long).

he shall still, though with many misgivings, be yet
borne onward, and if, in spite of all his embarrassments, he shall yet try to assail me, I will stand my
ground, and with Milo's permission, perhaps even
with his assistance, I shall baffle his endeavours,
even as yesterday, when he hurled unspoken threats
at me as I stood speaking, I cowed him by my first
syllables of reference to the law and legal proceedings. He sat down; I spoke no further word.
Had he given me notice of prosecution, as he had
threatened that he would, I would have contrived
to make the praetor summon him on the spot for the
third day from that.[a] So let him be guided by the
reflection, if he is content with the crimes he has
already committed, that he has already been marked
down for Milo ; and that, if he launches any missile
against me, I shall at once have resort to the weapon
of law and legal proceedings.

8   Now a short while ago, conscript fathers, he held
a mass meeting, the proceedings of which were
fully reported to me. Let me first give you an
account of the topics discussed and the resolutions
passed ; then, when you have laughed at the
fellow's effrontery, I will proceed to give you a
detailed narrative of the meeting. V. Religious
observances and rites, conscript fathers, were the
matters which Clodius, if you please, laid before his
mass meeting ; yes, Publius Clodius complained of
the neglect, the violation, the desecration, of rites
and sanctities ! It is not surprising that to you
this should seem a fit subject for laughter ; why,
his own meeting laughed at the thought that a
fellow who, as he himself often brags, was paralysed
by a hundred decrees of the senate, all of them

illum pro religionibus facta, hominemque eum, qui
pulvinaribus Bonae deae stuprum intulerit, eaque
sacra, quae viri oculis ne imprudentis quidem aspici
fas est, non solum aspectu virili, sed flagitio stupro-
que violarit, in contione de religionibus neglectis
9 conqueri. Itaque nunc proxima contio eius ex-
spectatur de pudicitia. Quid enim interest utrum ab
altaribus religiosissimis fugatus de sacris et religionibus conqueratur an ex sororum cubiculo egressus
pudorem pudicitiamque defendat ? Responsum haruspicum hoc recens de fremitu in contione recitavit,
in quo cum aliis multis scriptum etiam illud est, id
quod audistis, LOCA SACRA ET RELIGIOSA PROFANA
HABERI. In ea causa esse dixit domum meam, a
religiosissimo sacerdote, P. Clodio, consecratam.
10 Gaudeo mihi de toto hoc ostento, quod haud scio an
gravissimum multis his annis huic ordini nuntiatum
sit, datam non modo iustam, sed etiam necessariam
causam esse dicendi. Reperietis enim ex hoc toto
prodigio atque responso nos de istius scelere ac furore
ac de impendentibus periculis maximis prope iam
11 voce Iovis optimi maximi praemoneri. Sed primum
expiabo religionem aedium mearum, si id facere vere
324

pronounced against him for sacrilege, who had made the sacred banquet of the Good Goddess the scene of his adultery, and who had polluted rites, which it is a crime for a man's eyes to gaze upon even inadvertently, not only by his male presence, but by shocking licentiousness, should protest at a mass meeting against a want of regard for religion. So now we look forward with keen anticipation to his next meeting on the subject of chastity. Chased from altars of the deepest sanctity, he raises his voice in protest on behalf of rites and sanctities; and surely it would be an act only in keeping with such conduct that he should come forth from his sister's chamber to champion honour and chastity. He read to the meeting that response recently delivered by the soothsayers with regard to the strange noise that was heard, wherein the statement you yourselves have heard was comprised with many others, to the effect that " sacred and hallowed sites were being turned to secular purposes." In the course of his argument he asserted that my house had been consecrated by that most scrupulous of priests, Publius Clodius. I am glad to have been given an opportunity, which is not only appropriate but quite irresistible, of speaking on the general theme of this prodigy, which I am inclined to believe is the most solemn that has been announced to this order for many years past; for you will find that this prodigy and the response occasioned thereby are nothing but a warning to us, uttered almost by the voice of Jupiter Best and Greatest, concerning Clodius' mad wickedness and the terrible dangers that threaten us. But first I will extricate my house from its alleged sanctity, if I can do so truly,

ac sine cuiusquam dubitatione potero : sin scrupulus tenuissimus residere alicui videbitur, non modo patienti, sed etiam libenti animo portentis deorum immortalium religionique parebo.

VI. Sed quae tandem est in hac urbe tanta domus ab ista suspicione religionis tam vacua atque pura ? Quamquam vestrae domus, patres conscripti, ceterorumque civium multo maxima ex parte sunt liberae religione, tamen una mea domus iudiciis omnibus liberata in hac urbe sola est. Te enim appello, Lentule, et te, Philippe : ex hoc haruspicum responso decrevit senatus, ut de locis sacris religiosis ad hunc ordinem referretis. Potestisne referre de mea domo ? quae, ut dixi, sola in hac urbe omni religione, omnibus iudiciis liberata est : quam primum inimicus ipse in illa tempestate ac nocte rei publicae, quum cetera scelera stilo illo impuro, Sex. Clodii ore tincto, conscripsisset, ne una quidem attigit littera religionis : deinde eamdem domum populus Romanus, cuius est summa potestas omnium rerum, comitiis centuriatis omnium aetatum ordinumque suffragiis eodem iure
12 esse iussit, quo fuisset. Postea vos, patres conscripti, non quo dubia res esset, sed ut huic furiae, si diutius in

---

ᵃ See *De domo sua*, Chap. XVIII.

and so as to leave no shadow of doubt in anyone; but if any should feel at the end that he still has the most minute misgiving, I shall not merely be content, but I shall even be delighted, to comply with the portents of the immortal gods and the obligations which they impose.

VI. But, I would ask you, what house is there in all this great city which is so utterly void and free of this suspicion of sanctity as is my own? It is true that your houses, conscript fathers, and those of the general body of citizens are, in the vast majority of cases, free from sanctity, but mine is the only house in this city which has been absolved therefrom by every variety of judicial decision. I appeal to you, Lentulus, and to you, Philippus. As a result of this response of the soothsayers the senate decreed that a vote of this body should be taken on the subject of hallowed and consecrated sites. But can you possibly take a vote upon my house, which, as I have already said, is the only one in this city which has been absolved from all sanctity by every variety of judicial decision? In the first place my enemy himself, in that dark and stormy night of the state, never wrote a single letter attaching sanctity to that house, though with that pen that he dipped in the vile effrontery of Sextus Clodius[a] he had exhausted the whole catalogue of crimes; in the second place, the Roman people, whose authority is universal and paramount, decreed by the votes of all ages and orders given in the Assembly of the Centuries that the legal standing of this house should remain as it had always been; and finally you, conscript fathers, decreed that the question of the sanctity of my house should be

hac urbe, quam delere cuperet, maneret, vox interdiceretur, decrevistis, ut de mearum aedium religione
ad pontificum collegium referretur. Quae tanta
religio est, qua non in nostris dubitationibus atque in
maximis superstitionibus unius P. Servilii aut M.
Luculli responso ac verbo liberemur ? De sacris
publicis, de ludis maximis, de deorum penatium
Vestaeque matris caerimoniis, de illo ipso sacrificio,
quod fit pro salute populi Romani, quod post Romam
conditam huius unius casti tutoris religionum scelere
violatum est, quod tres pontifices statuissent, id
semper populo Romano, semper senatui, semper ipsis
dis immortalibus satis sanctum, satis augustum, satis
religiosum esse visum est. At vero meam domum P.
Lentulus consul et pontifex, P. Servilius, M. Lucullus,
Q. Metellus, M'. Glabrio, M. Messalla, L. Lentulus
flamen Martialis, P. Galba, Q. Metellus Scipio, C.
Fannius, M. Lepidus, L. Claudius rex sacrorum, M.
Scaurus, M. Crassus, C. Curio, Sex. Caesar flamen
Quirinalis, Q. Cornelius, P. Albinovanus, Q. Terentius, pontifices minores, causa cognita, duobus locis
dicta, maxima frequentia amplissimorum ac sapien-
tissimorum civium astante, omni religione una mente
13 omnes liberaverunt. VII. Nego umquam post sacra
constituta, quorum eadem est antiquitas, quae ipsius
urbis, ulla de re, ne de capite quidem virginum Vesta-

ᵃ To Bona Dea.
ᵇ A religious official who inherited the sacred functions of
the king.
ᶜ The Sabine god of war, whose worship was especially
connected with the Quirinal.

referred to the Pontifical College, not that there was any doubt about the matter, but in order that an interdict might be put upon this fury's utterance, should he remain any longer in this city which he was bent upon destroying. What sanctity can be so potent, that amid all our doubts and gravest scruples the plain pronouncement of Publius Servilius alone or of Marcus Lucullus cannot absolve us therefrom? In all matters of public rites, of the great games, of the ceremonies of the household gods and of Vesta the Mother, and even of that sacrifice *a* which is offered up for the welfare of the Roman people, a sacrifice which since Rome was founded has never been violated save by the wickedness of this spotless protector of sanctities, the decision of three Pontifices has always been considered by the Roman people, by the senate, and by the immortal gods themselves, to be sufficiently sacred, venerable, and binding. But my house has been unanimously absolved from all sanctity by Publius Lentulus, consul and pontiff, by Publius Servilius, Marcus Lucullus, Quintus Metellus, Manius Glabrio, Marcus Messalla, Lucius Lentulus the flamen of Mars, Publius Galba, Quintus Metellus Scipio, Gaius Fannius, Marcus Lepidus, Lucius Claudius the King of Rites,*b* Marcus Scaurus, Marcus Crassus, Gaius Curio, Sextus Caesar flamen of Quirinus,*c* Quintus Cornelius, Publius Albinovanus, Quintus Terentius, sub-pontiffs, after two separate hearings of the case, in the presence of a vast throng of wise and influential citizens. VII. I assert that never, since religion, which is coeval with the city itself, was established, has so numerous a meeting of the College pronounced upon any matter, no, not

lium, tam frequens collegium iudicasse : quamquam
ad facinoris disquisitionem interest adesse quam
plurimos : ita est enim interpretatio illa pontificum,
ut eidem potestatem habeant iudicum : religionis
explanatio vel ab uno pontifice perito recte fieri
potest, quod idem in iudicio capitis durum atque iniquum est : tamen sic reperietis frequentiores pontifices de mea domo quam umquam de caerimoniis
virginum iudicasse. Postero die frequentissimus
senatus, te consule designato, Lentule, sententiae
principe, P. Lentulo et Q. Metello consulibus referentibus statuit, cum omnes pontifices, qui erant
huius ordinis, adessent, cumque alii, qui honoribus
populi Romani antecedebant, multa de collegii iudicio
verba fecissent omnesque iidem scribendo adessent,
domum meam iudicio pontificum religione liberatam
14 videri.   De hoc igitur loco sacro potissimum videntur
haruspices dicere, qui locus solus ex privatis locis
omnibus hoc praecipue iuris habet, ut ab ipsis, qui
sacris praesunt, sacer non esse iudicatus sit ?   Verum
referte : quod ex senatus consulto facere debetis.
Aut vobis cognitio dabitur, qui primi de hac domo
sententiam dixistis et eam religione omni liberastis,

even upon the lives of Vestal Virgins. It is, no doubt, important for the proper investigation of a crime that the inquiry should be attended by as many persons as possible ; for pontifical pronouncements are of such a nature that the powers of their College are as great as those of our juries. But while the interpretation of a point in religion can be validly given by a single expert pontiff, the application of this principle to a capital trial would involve harshness and injustice. You will thus find, however, that the meetings of the Pontifical College that gave judgement upon my house were more numerously attended than any of those that dealt with the ritual of the Vestals. On the following day a crowded senate decreed upon your suggestion, Lentulus, who were consul-elect, and upon the motion of the consuls Publius Lentulus and Quintus Metellus, all the pontiffs who were members of this order being present, and after others, who held high offices of the Roman people, had discussed the judgement of the College at some length, that the pontifical pronouncement had absolved my house from sanctity ; and the formulated decree was subscribed 14 to by all those I have mentioned. And is it to be concluded that the soothsayers alluded to this consecrated site rather than to any other, though it alone of all private sites possesses the peculiar privilege of having been declared, by the overseers of consecration themselves, free from consecration ? Give upon this matter the true vote which is demanded of you by that decree of the senate. Either the inquiry will rest with you, who were the first to pronounce an opinion concerning this house, and who declared it to be totally absolved of sanctity ;

aut senatus ipse iudicabit, qui uno illo solo antistite
sacrorum dissentiente frequentissimus antea iudicavit, aut, id quod certe fiet, ad pontifices reiicietur,
quorum auctoritati, fidei, prudentiae maiores nostri
sacra religionesque et privatas et publicas commenda-
runt. Quid ergo ii possunt aliud iudicare ac iudi-
caverunt ? Multae sunt domus in hac urbe, patres
conscripti, atque haud scio an paene cunctae iure
optimo, sed tamen iure privato, iure hereditario, iure
auctoritatis, iure mancipi, iure nexi : nego esse ullam
domum aliam aeque privato iure atque optima lege,
publico vero omni praecipuo et humano et divino iure
15 munitam : quae primum aedificatur ex auctoritate
senatus, pecunia publica, deinde contra vim nefariam
huius gladiatoris tot senati consultis munita atque
saepta est. VIII. Primum negotium iisdem magistratibus est datum anno superiore, ut curarent ut sine
vi aedificare mihi liceret, quibus in maximis periculis
universa res publica commendari solet : deinde cum
ille saxis et ignibus et ferro vastitatem meis sedibus
intulisset, decrevit senatus eos, qui id fecissent, lege
de vi, quae est in eos, qui universam rem publicam
oppugnassent, teneri. Vobis vero referentibus, o
post hominum memoriam fortissimi atque optimi
consules, decrevit idem senatus frequentissimus, qui

---

^a *i.e.* by assignment to a creditor on the part of an
insolvent debtor.
^b The consuls.

or the decision will belong to the senate, which has already given its decision in full house, with but one dissentient voice—that of yonder hierophant ; or, which is bound in any case to occur, the question will be referred to the pontiffs, to whose authority, loyalty, and wisdom our ancestors entrusted all matters of religion and of private and public observance. And what verdict can they give other than that which they have already given ? There are many houses in this city, conscript fathers, nearly all of them, I imagine, held upon incontrovertible legal title, but held upon private title, hereditary title, title of possession, of purchase, or of distraint.[a] But I deny that there is any other house which is protected at once by an incontestable private title, and also by every important public title either of divine or of human origin, seeing that it, in the first place, is erected at the public expense by authority of the senate, and seeing that, secondly, it has been fortified and barricaded by senatorial decrees to withstand the lawless assaults of this gladiator. VIII. Last year, in the first place, the duty of securing freedom for me to build without molestation was assigned to the same magistrates[b] to whom the well-being of the whole community is usually entrusted in supreme crises ; and, in the second place, in view of the fact that Clodius had attempted to devastate my dwelling with stones, fire, and the sword, the senate decreed that the guilty persons should be amenable to the law of assault, which is enacted against those who have assailed the republic at large. Yes, it was upon your motion, O bravest and best of all consuls in human memory, that the senate again in full con-

meam domum violasset, contra rem publicam esse
16 facturum. Nego ullo de opere publico, de monumento, de templo tot senatus exstare consulta quot
de mea domo, quam senatus unam post hanc urbem
constitutam ex aerario aedificandam, a pontificibus
liberandam, a magistratibus defendendam, a iudicibus puniendam putarit. P. Valerio pro maximis in
rem publicam beneficiis data domus est in Velia publice, at mihi in Palatio restituta : illi locus, at mihi
etiam parietes atque tectum : illi quam ipse privato
iure tueretur, mihi quam publice magistratus omnes
defenderent. Quae quidem ego si aut per me aut ab
aliis haberem, non praedicarem apud vos, ne nimis
gloriari viderer : sed cum sint mihi data a vobis,
cum ea attemptentur eius lingua, cuius antea manu
eversa vos mihi et liberis meis manibus vestris reddidistis, non ego de meis, sed de vestris factis loquor,
nec vereor ne haec mea vestrorum beneficiorum praedicatio non grata potius quam adrogans videatur.
.7 Quamquam, si me tantis laboribus pro communi salute
perfunctum efferret aliquando ad gloriam in refutan-
dis maledictis hominum improborum animi quidam
dolor, quis non ignosceret ? Vidi enim hesterno die
quemdam murmurantem : quem aiebant negare ferri

---

^a Consul in the first year of the republic 509.

course decreed that whosoever should lay violent hands upon my house should be guilty of an act 16 against the state. I assert that there is no public work, no monument, and no temple concerning which so many senatorial decrees have been registered as my house, the only house since the foundation of the city which the senate has thought fit should be erected from the public treasury, absolved by the pontiffs, protected by the magistrates, and avenged by the juries. In recognition of his signal services to the republic Publius Valerius [a] was presented by the state with a house upon the Velian hill, but my house upon the Palatine was restored by the state ; he was furnished with a site, but I was furnished with walls and roof as well ; he was given a house to defend by his own efforts and upon his own private title, mine was to be defended as a matter of public interest by all the magistrates. Had I to thank myself for this, or had I received it from any other source, I should not thus proclaim it to you, lest I should seem over-boastful ; but as it is, since it is to you that I owe this gift, and since his tongue is now assailing what his hand before overthrew, though it has since been restored by your hands to me and to my children, it is not of my own deeds but of yours that I am speaking, and I have no fear lest my present eulogy of your kindness should seem prompted rather by self-satisfaction than by 17 gratitude. And yet if, after having faced such bitter toils for the welfare of the community, a sense of resentment, as I refuted the slanders of the unscrupulous, should lead me so far to forget myself as to boast, who would not pardon me ? Yesterday I marked one that muttered beneath his breath ;

me posse, quia cum ab hoc eodem impurissimo
parricida rogarer cuius essem civitatis, respondi me,
probantibus et vobis et equitibus Romanis, eius esse,
quae carere me non potuisset. Ille, ut opinor,
ingemuit. Quid igitur responderem ? quaero ex eo
ipso, qui ferre me non potest. Me civem esse Romanum ? Litterate respondissem. An tacuissem.
Desertum negotium. Potest quisquam vir in rebus
magnis cum invidia versatus satis graviter in inimici
contumeliis sine sua laude respondere ? At ipse non
modo respondet quidquid potest, cum est lacessitus,
sed etiam gaudet se ab amicis quid respondeat
admoneri.

18 IX. Sed quoniam mea causa expedita est, videamus
nunc quid haruspices dicant. Ego enim fateor me et
magnitudine ostenti et gravitate responsi et una
atque constanti haruspicum voce vehementer esse
commotum : neque is sum, qui, si cui forte videor plus
quam ceteri, qui aeque atque ego sunt occupati,
versari in studio litterarum, his delecter aut utar
omnino litteris, quae nostros animos deterrent atque
avocant a religione. Ego vero primum habeo auctores ac magistros religionum colendarum maiores

and I was told that he murmured that I was intolerable, because, when this same loathsome traitor asked me to what state I belonged, I answered, amid the plaudits of yourselves and of the Roman knights, "To a state which could not exist without me." My reply drew a groan from the man, I believe. And what other reply could I have given? I put the question to that very man who finds me intolerable. Should I have replied that I was a citizen of Rome? I should have answered to the letter of his question. Ought I to have remained speechless? It would have signified surrender. Is there any man, whose weighty activities have gained him enemies, who can reply with adequate impressiveness to the insults of an opponent without glorifying himself? But Clodius himself, when challenged, not only makes any reply that occurs to him, but is only too relieved that he has friends ready to prompt him how to answer.

18 IX. But since the question affecting myself has been satisfactorily disposed of, let us now consider what the soothsayers say. For I must admit that I have been deeply impressed both by the awe-inspiring nature of the prodigy and the solemnity of its interpretation, and the firm and unwavering utterances of the soothsayers; and indeed, though I may perhaps appear to some to be a greater student of literature than others whose lives are as full of distractions as my own, my natural bent does not lead me to find any pleasure in, or indeed any use whatsoever for, such literature as tends to discourage and withdraw our minds from religion. In the first place, speaking for myself, I look for authority and guidance in religious observance to our ancestors, whose

nostros : quorum mihi tanta fuisse sapientia videtur,
ut satis superque prudentes sint, qui illorum pruden-
tiam, non dicam adsequi, sed quanta fuerit perspicere
possint : qui statas sollemnesque caerimonias ponti-
ficatu, rerum bene gerundarum auctoritates augurio,
fatorum veteres praedictiones Apollinis vatum libris,
portentorum explanationes Etruscorum disciplina
contineri putaverunt : quae quidem tanta est, ut
nostra memoria primum Italici belli funesta illa principia, post Sullani Cinnanique temporis extremum
paene discrimen, tum hanc recentem urbis inflam-
mandae delendique imperii coniurationem non
19 obscure nobis paullo ante praedixerint. Deinde, si
quid habui otii, etiam cognovi, multa homines doctos
sapientesque et dixisse et scripta de deorum immortalium numine reliquisse : quae quamquam divinitus
perscripta video, tamen eius modi sunt, ut ea maiores
nostri docuisse illos, non ab illis didicisse videantur.
Etenim quis est tam vaecors qui aut cum suspexit in
caelum, deos esse non sentiat et ea, quae tanta
mente fiunt, ut vix quisquam arte ulla ordinem rerum
ac necessitudinem persequi possit, casu fieri putet,
aut cum deos esse intellexerit, non intelligat eorum

---

[a] As there was no early philosophic writing in Latin, this
must refer to the Greek philosophers. If it does so refer,
the statement here made becomes startling !

wisdom seems to me to have been so unquestionable that those who are able, I will not say to reach the level of, but only to have gained an insight into, their sagacity, themselves possess sagacity which is sufficient, and more than sufficient. In their view, all prescribed and liturgical ceremonies depended upon the Pontificate, and all regulations determining auspicious action upon augury ; they thought that the ancient prophecies of the oracle of Apollo were comprised in the books of the seers, and all interpretations of prodigies in the lore of the Etruscans ; and indeed the efficacy of this last is shown by the fact that even in our memory unmistakable predictions were given shortly before each event, first of the calamitous outbreak of the Italian war, later of the perilous days of Sulla and Cinna that so nearly proved fatal, and more recently still, of the conspiracy to burn and destroy the city. In the second place, such leisure as I have had has enabled me to learn that wise and inspired men have uttered numerous maxims and left behind them numerous writings dealing with the deity of the immortal gods ; and though I realize that these works are inspired of heaven, still their nature is such that our ancestors seem to have taught the writers rather than learned from them.[a] And, indeed, who is so witless that, when he gazes up into heaven, he fails to see that gods exist, and imagines that chance is responsible for the creations of an intelligence so transcendent that scarce can the highest artistry do justice to the immutable dispositions of the universe ? Or who, once convinced that divinity does exist, can fail at the same time to be convinced that it is by its power that this great

numine hoc tantum imperium esse natum et auctum et retentum ? Quam volumus licet, patres conscripti, ipsi nos amemus, tamen nec numero Hispanos nec robore Gallos nec calliditate Poenos nec artibus Graecos nec denique hoc ipso huius gentis ac terrae domestico nativoque sensu Italos ipsos ac Latinos, sed pietate ac religione atque hac una sapientia, quod deorum numine omnia regi gubernarique perspeximus, omnes gentes nationesque superavimus.

20   X. Qua re ne plura de re minime loquar dubia, adhibete animos et mentes vestras, non solum aures, ad haruspicum vocem admovete : QUOD IN AGRO LATINIENSI AUDITUS EST STREPITUS CUM FREMITU. Mitto haruspices, mitto illam veterem ab ipsis dis immortalibus, ut hominum fama est, Etruriae traditam disciplinam : nos nonne haruspices esse possumus ? EXAUDITUS IN AGRO PROPINQUO ET SUBURBANO EST STREPITUS QUIDAM RECONDITUS ET HORRIBILIS FREMITUS ARMORUM. Quis est ex gigantibus illis, quos poëtae ferunt bellum dis immortalibus intulisse, tam impius qui hoc tam novo tantoque motu non magnum aliquid deos populo Romano praemonstrare et praecinere fateatur ? De ea re scriptum est : POSTILIONES [1] ESSE IOVI, SATURNO, NEPTUNO, TELLURI, DIS CAELESTI-

21   BUS. Audio quibus dis violatis expiatio debeatur, sed

----

[1] postiliones *Orelli's corr. for more familiar* postulationes *of* MSS.

----

[a] It is uncertain where these were ; Manutius says " in the suburbs." The adjective in this pecular form seems not to be found except in this speech.

empire has been created, extended, and sustained ? However good be our conceit of ourselves, conscript fathers, we have excelled neither Spain in population, nor Gaul in vigour, nor Carthage in versatility, nor Greece in art, nor indeed Italy and Latium itself in the innate sensibility characteristic of this land and its peoples ; but in piety, in devotion to religion, and in that special wisdom which consists in the recognition of the truth that the world is swayed and directed by divine disposal, we have excelled every race and every nation.

X. Wherefore, to speak at no further length upon a matter that admits of no doubt, give me your attention, and apply your minds, and not your ears alone, to this sentence in the pronouncement of the soothsayers : " Inasmuch as a rumbling and a noise have been heard in the Latin Lands.ᵃ " I will dispense with the soothsayers ; I will dispense with the lore which, as popular rumour has it, was committed to Etruria by the immortal gods ; for cannot we ourselves be our own soothsayers ? " In the immediate outskirts of the city there has been heard a subterranean rumbling and an awful noise as of arms." Who, even from among those giants who, as the poets tell us, waged war against the immortal gods, is so impious as not to confess that in this strange and dire upheaval the gods are prophesying and predicting some mighty destiny for the Roman people ? " Arrears of sacrifice are due to Jupiter, Saturn, Neptune, Earth, and to the gods of heaven " : that is how the pronouncement in connexion with this event runs. I am told here the names of the gods whose dishonour imposes upon us the duty of expiation, but I have yet to

hominum quae ob delicta quaero. LUDOS MINUS
DILIGENTER FACTOS POLLUTOSQUE. Quos ludos ? Te
appello, Lentule,—tui sacerdotii sunt tensae, curri-
cula, praecentio, ludi, libationes epulaeque ludorum,
—vosque, pontifices, ad quos epulones Iovis optimi
maximi, si quid est praetermissum aut commissum,
adferunt, quorum de sententia illa eadem renovata
atque instaurata celebrantur : qui sunt ludi minus
diligenter facti ? quando aut quo scelere polluti ?
Respondebis et pro te et pro collegis tuis, etiam pro
pontificum collegio, nihil cuiusquam aut negligentia
contemptum aut scelere esse pollutum : omnia
sollemnia ac iusta ludorum, omnibus rebus obser-
vatis, summa cum caerimonia esse servata.

22   XI. Quos igitur haruspices ludos minus diligenter
factos pollutosque esse dicunt ? eos, quorum ipsi di
immortales atque illa mater Idaea te, te, Cn. Lentule,
cuius abavi manibus esset accepta, spectatorem esse
voluit. Quod ni tu Megalesia illo die spectare
voluisses, haud scio an vivere nobis atque his de rebus
iam queri non liceret. Vis enim innumerabilis incitata ex omnibus vicis collecta servorum ab hoc aedile
religioso repente e fornicibus ostiisque omnibus in

ᵃ A deity worshipped in Phrygia as Cybele, identified
with Cretan Rhea ; her cult was introduced into Rome (204)
by P. Scipio Africanus. The Megalesia were held in her
honour (Apr. 4–9).
ᵇ Clodius.

learn in what human misdoings this dishonour consists.* " The games have been performed with laxity, and have been desecrated." What games ? I appeal to you, Lentulus, for to your sacred office belong the processional chariots and cars, the preliminary chant, the games, and the libations and banquets attached thereto, and to you, pontiffs, to whom all faults of ceremonial omission and commission are reported by the sacred stewards of Jupiter Best and Greatest, and upon whose judgement those ceremonies are recommenced and repeated. What are these games that have been performed with laxity, and when or by what crime have they been desecrated ? You will answer on behalf of yourselves and your colleagues, and indeed of the whole Pontifical College, that there has been no oversight due to anyone's neglect, no desecration due to anyone's crime ; all the prescriptions and regulations of the games have been observed with irreproachable scruple and punctilious ceremony.

XI. What games, then, are these which the soothsayers assert to have been performed with laxity and to have been desecrated ? They are the games of which the immortal gods themselves and the great Idaean Mother *a* willed that you, you, Gnaeus Lentulus, whose grandsire's grandsire with his own hands welcomed her, should be a spectator. For had you not on that day chosen to view the games of the Great Mother, it is my belief that we should not have been permitted to survive and raise our present protest. For innumerable bands of slaves that had been mustered by this scrupulous aedile *b* from every quarter of the city, and had been incited for the occasion, were suddenly let loose upon us

scaenam signo dato immissa irrupit. Tua tum, tua,
Cn. Lentule, eadem virtus fuit, quae in privato
quondam tuo proavo : te, nomen, imperium, vocem,
aspectum, impetum tuum stans senatus equitesque
Romani et omnes boni sequebantur, cum ille servorum eludentium multitudini senatum populumque
Romanum vinctum ipso consessu et constrictum
spectaculis atque impeditum turba et angustiis tradi-
23 disset. An si ludius constitit aut tibicen repente
conticuit aut puer ille patrimus et matrimus si tensam
non tenuit, si lorum omisit, aut si aedilis verbo aut
simpuvio aberravit, ludi sunt non rite facti, eaque
errata expiantur et mentes deorum immortalium
ludorum instauratione placantur : si ludi ab laetitia
ad metum traducti, si non intermissi, sed perempti
atque sublati sunt, si civitati universae scelere eius,
qui ludos ad luctum conferre voluit, exstiterunt dies
illi pro festis paene funesti, dubitabimus quos ille
24 fremitus nuntiet ludos esse pollutos ? Ac si volumus
ea, quae de quoque deo nobis tradita sunt, recordari,
hanc matrem magnam, cuius ludi violati, polluti,

---

[a] *i.e.* " flaws in matters of form invalidate the proceedings,
much more a general disturbance."

344

from every archway and entry, and at a given signal
burst on to the stage. Then it was that you, yes,
you, Lentulus, showed the same courage as your
great-grandfather showed of old in a private capacity ;
it was you, your name, your authority, your utterance, your majestic presence, and your resolute
vigour, in support of which the senate and the
knights of Rome and all true patriots rose to their
feet, when Clodius exposed that senate and that
Roman people to the mercies of a mob of jeering
slaves, imprisoned and rendered powerless as they
were in the tightly packed seats of the auditorium,
and hampered by the confusion of the narrow exits.
What ?   If the dancer has stood still, or if the flute-
player has suddenly become mute, if the boy whose
father and mother are alive has not kept to his
chariot or has let the rein slip, if the aedile made a
mistake in the formula or in the handling of the
sacred vessel, then the games have not been duly
performed, expiation is offered for the mistakes, and
the feelings of the immortal gods are appeased by
a recommencement of the games ; and when the
spirit of the games has been changed from joy to
terror, when they have been not merely interrupted,
but irreparably ruined, and when its dates, for the
whole state, have become, not festal, but fatal,
through the wickedness of one who wished to turn
merry-making to mourning, shall we have any doubt
what games are those which this noise declares to
have been desecrated ?[a]   Further, if we will only
call to mind the traditions we have received concerning our several deities, we shall surely remember
to have heard that this Great Mother, whose games
have been polluted, desecrated, and even made an

paene ad caedem et ad funus civitatis conversi sunt, hanc, inquam, accepimus agros et nemora cum quodam strepitu fremituque peragrare. XII. Haec igitur vobis, haec populo Romano et scelerum indicia ostendit et periculorum signa patefecit.

Nam quid ego de illis ludis loquar, quos in Palatio nostri maiores ante templum in ipso matris magnae conspectu Megalesibus fieri celebrarique voluerunt? qui sunt more institutisque maxime casti, sollemnes, religiosi, quibus ludis primum ante populi consessum senatui locum P. Africanus iterum consul ille maior dedit, ut eos ludos haec lues impura polluerit : quo si qui liber aut spectandi aut etiam religionis causa accesserat, manus adferebantur : quo matrona nulla adiit propter vim consessumque servorum : ita ludos eos, quorum religio tanta est, ut ex ultimis terris arcessita in hac urbe consederit : qui uni ludi ne verbo quidem appellantur Latino, ut vocabulo ipso et appetita religio externa et matris magnae nomine suscepta declaretur, hos ludos servi fecerunt, servi spectaverunt, tota denique hoc aedile servorum Megalesia 25 fuerunt. Pro di immortales ! qui magis nobiscum loqui possetis, si essetis versareminique nobiscum? ludos esse pollutos significastis ac plane dicitis. Quid

---

a *Illis* here is difficult. It suggests a mention of some games other than the Megalesia, and Livy says that it was in connexion with the Ludi Romani that P. Scipio made these arrangements (xxxiv. 54).

occasion of massacre and fatality to the community, yes, that even she walks abroad through our fields and woods to the accompaniment of strange murmurs and rumblings. XII. Surely, then, it is none other than she who has manifested these intimations of guilt and displayed these signals of danger to the Roman people.

For why enlarge upon those games,[a] which our ancestors decreed should be performed and celebrated on the Palatine before the temple and under the very eyes of the Great Mother upon the days known as Megalesia ; games which are by tradition and by usage pious, solemn, and venerable beyond all others ; games whereat the elder Publius Africanus, when consul for the second time, gave the first view to the senate before the people had assembled ; and all this, that these same games might be desecrated by this loathsome blight ? Yes! games where any freeman who came as spectator or even out of piety was mishandled, where no matron dared approach, for fear of violence from the throngs of slaves. So these games, the sanctity whereof is so deep that it has been summoned from distant lands and planted in this city, the only games which are not even called by a Latin name, that their very title might indicate the domestication of a foreign cult, adopted in honour of the Great Mother, these games, I say, were performed by slaves, viewed by slaves, and were indeed converted under Clodius'
25 aedileship into a Megalesia of slaves. Ye immortal gods ! how could ye speak with us more clearly, if ye were with us and moving in our midst ? Ye have signified and ye openly declare that the games have been desecrated. What greater example of pollution,

347

magis inquinatum, deformatum, perversum, contur-
batum dici potest quam omne servitium, permissu
magistratus liberatum, in alteram scaenam immissum,
alteri praepositum, ut alter consessus potestati servorum obiiceretur, alter servorum totus esset ? Si
examen apium ludis in scaenam caveamve venisset,
haruspices acciendos ex Etruria putaremus : videmus
universi repente examina tanta servorum immissa in
populum Romanum saeptum atque inclusum et non
commovemur ? Atque in apium fortasse examine
nos ex Etruscorum scriptis haruspices, ut a servitio
26 caveremus, monerent. Quod igitur ex aliquo dis-
iuncto diversoque monstro significatum caveremus, id
cum ipsum sibi monstrum est, et cum in eo ipso
periculum est, ex quo periculum portenditur, non
pertimescemus ? Istius modi Megalesia fecit pater
tuus ? istius modi patruus ? Is mihi etiam generis
sui mentionem facit, quum Athenionis aut Spartaci
exemplo ludos facere maluerit quam Gaii aut Appii
Claudiorum ? Illi cum ludos facerent, servos de
cavea exire iubebant : tu in alteram servos immisisti,
ex altera liberos eiecisti. Itaque qui antea voce
praeconis a liberis semovebantur, tuis ludis non voce,
sed manu liberos a se segregabant. XIII. Ne hoc
quidem tibi in mentem veniebat, Sibyllino sacerdoti,

---

[a] Athenio, leader of slave war in Sicily 104 : Spartacus,
leader of gladiatorial revolt in Campania 73.

dishonour, distortion, and confusion can be quoted, than that the whole of our slave population, liberated by permission of a magistrate, should have been let loose upon one stage and given control of another, with the result that the audience of one was exposed to the mercy of slaves, while that of the other was composed of slaves alone? Had a swarm of bees come upon the stage or into the auditorium at the games, we should think it necessary to summon soothsayers from Etruria; and do we feel no alarm when not a man of us but sees such numerous swarms of slaves launched suddenly upon the Roman people packed within the walls of a building? Indeed, were a swarm of bees actually in question, the soothsayers might perchance warn us, after reference to their Etrurian books, to beware of our slave population. Were this warning manifested to us by some alien and allegorical portent we should take precautions accordingly; and, when the portent is itself what it portends, and when an event is at once an augury of peril and a peril in itself, are we not terrified? Was it after this fashion that your father held the Megalesia, or your uncle? Does Clodius actually call my attention to his birth, though he has preferred, in his performance of the games, to model himself upon Athenio or Spartacus,[a] rather than upon a Gaius or an Appius of those whose name he bears? When *they* held the games, they bade slaves depart from the auditorium; *you* let slaves loose upon one auditorium, and ejected freemen from the other. Those who of old were separated from the free upon a herald's proclamation, at your games separated the free from themselves not by proclamation but by force. XIII. Did not even this ever occur to you, priest of

haec sacra maiores nostros ex vestris libris expetisse ?
si illi sunt vestri, quos tu impia mente conquiris,
violatis oculis legis, contaminatis manibus attrectas.
27 Hac igitur vate suadente quondam, defessa Italia
Punico bello atque ab Hannibale vexata, sacra ista
nostri maiores ascita ex Phrygia Romae collocarunt :
quae vir is accepit, qui est optimus populi Romani
iudicatus, P. Scipio, femina autem, quae matronarum
castissima putabatur, Q. Claudia : cuius priscam illam
severitatem mirifice tua soror existimatur imitata.
Nihil te igitur neque maiores tui coniuncti cum his religionibus neque sacerdotium ipsum, quo est haec tota
religio constituta, neque curulis aedilitas, quae
maxime hanc tueri religionem solet, permovit quo
minus castissimos ludos omni flagitio pollueres, dede-
28 core maculares, scelere obligares ? Sed quid ego id
admiror ? qui, accepta pecunia, Pessinuntem ipsum,
sedem domiciliumque matris deorum, vastaris et
Brogitaro Gallograeco, impuro homini ac nefario,
cuius legati te tribuno dividere in aede Castoris tuis
operis nummos solebant, totum illum locum fanumque
vendideris ? sacerdotem ab ipsis aris pulvinaribusque
detraxeris ? omnia illa, quae vetustas, quae Persae,

---

^a In Phrygia.
^b Son-in-law of Deiotarus, tetrarch of Galatia.

the Sibyl that you are, that it was from your books
that our ancestors derived this rite ?—if, indeed,
those books can be called yours, which you search with
impious purpose, peruse with jaundiced vision, and
27 handle with contaminated fingers.   And it was upon
the representations of this prophetess that once, when
Italy was worn out by the Carthaginian war and
harassed by Hannibal, our ancestors appropriated
these rites from Phrygia and established them
at Rome. They were welcomed by the man who
was judged to be the most exemplary among the
Roman people, Publius Scipio, and by the woman
who was held to be the chastest of the matrons,
Quinta Claudia, whose antique severity your sister
is considered to have reproduced to admiration.
And did not the association of your ancestors with
these rites, or the priestly office from which this cult
receives its exclusive authority, or the curule aedileship which has ever been its chief protection, prevail
upon you to forbear from desecrating by every
enormity, staining by every indignity, and stigmatiz-
ing by every crime, games of the most hallowed
28 sanctity ? But why should this excite my surprise,
when I remember that you were induced by a bribe
actually to devastate Pessinus,[a] the very seat and
dwelling-place of the Mother of the gods ; that to
Brogitarus [b] the Gallograecian, an impious and abandoned man, whose emissaries, when you were tribune,
used to distribute money to your gangs in · the
temple of Castor, you sold the whole region of
Pessinus with its shrine ; that you dragged its priest
from the very altars and sacred couches ; that you
overthrew everything that had at all times been held
in deep devotion by past generations, by Persians,

351

CICERO

quae Syri, quae reges omnes, qui Europam Asiamque
tenuerunt, semper summa religione coluerunt, per-
verteris ? quae denique nostri maiores tam sancta
duxerunt, ut cum refertam urbem atque Italiam
fanorum haberemus, tamen nostri imperatores maximis et periculosissimis bellis huic deae vota facerent
eaque in ipso Pessinunte ad illam ipsam principem
29 aram et in illo loco fanoque persolverent. Quod
cum Deiotarus religione sua castissime tueretur,
quem unum habemus in orbe terrarum fidelissimum
huic imperio atque amantissimum nostri nominis,
Brogitaro, ut ante dixi, addictum pecunia tradidisti.
Atque hunc tamen Deiotarum, saepe a senatu regali
nomine dignum existimatum, clarissimorum imperatorum testimoniis ornatum, tu etiam regem appellari
cum Brogitaro iubes. Sed alter est rex iudicio senatus per nos, pecunia Brogitarus per te appellatus :
. . .[1] alterum putabo regem, si habuerit unde tibi
solvat quod ei per syngrapham credidisti. Nam cum
multa regia sunt in Deiotaro tum illa maxime, quod
tibi nummum nullum dedit, quod eam partem legis
tuae, quae congruebat cum iudicio senatus ut ipse
rex esset, non repudiavit, quod Pessinuntem per
scelus a te violatum et sacerdote sacrisque spoliatum
recuperavit, ut in pristina religione servaret, quod
caerimonias ab omni vetustate acceptas a Brogitaro

[1] *Many edd. print a lacuna here.*

---

[a] The Latin can also bear the meaning " Brogitarus
has been dunned through you for a debt " : this double
meaning cannot be brought out in translation.

by Syrians, and by all kings who have ever held rule
in Europe and in Asia, and to which even our own
ancestors attributed such sanctity that, though we
had at our disposal the city and Italy, both rich in
sacred places, our generals made vows to this goddess
in their greatest and most perilous wars, vows which
they discharged in Pessinus itself, laying their offerings
before the principal altar of the shrine in that place.

29 And though this shrine was devotedly watched over
with characteristic piety by Deiotarus, whose unflinching loyalty to our empire and ardent attachment
to our authority has been absolutely peerless, you
adjudicated it and delivered it over to Brogitarus,
as I have already mentioned, for a money payment.
Moreover, though this Deiotarus has repeatedly been
adjudged by the senate to be worthy of the title of
king, and though he has been distinguished by the
recommendations of our most brilliant generals, you
actually order that he shall share that title with
Brogitarus. The former, however, owes his kingly
title, through us, to the senatorial pronouncement,
while Brogitarus owes his, through you, to the price
which he paid you.[a] . . . I shall believe the other
to be a king when he has found the means to pay
you what you advanced him under a note of hand.
Deiotarus has many kingly qualities, but in nothing
has he shown his character more than in his refusal
to give you a single penny ; in not repudiating that
clause in your law which agreed with the senate's
pronouncement in according him the name of king ;
in his recovery of Pessinus, which you had wickedly
desecrated and deprived of its priest and its rite,
that he might maintain it in its time-honoured cult ;
in his not permitting ceremonies which were the

pollui non sinit mavultque generum suum munere tuo
quam illud fanum antiquitate religionis carere. Sed
ut ad haec haruspicum responsa redeam, ex quibus
est primum de ludis, quis est qui id non totum in
istius ludos praedictum et responsum esse fateatur ?

30 Sequitur de locis sacris, religiosis. XIV. O impudentiam miram ! de mea domo dicere audes ?
Committe vel consulibus vel senatui vel collegio
pontificum tuam. Ac mea quidem his tribus omnibus
iudiciis, ut dixi antea, liberata est. At in iis aedibus,
quas tu, Q. Seio, equite Romano, viro optimo, per te
apertissime interfecto, tenes, sacellum dico fuisse et
aras. Tabulis hoc censoriis, memoria multorum

31 firmabo ac docebo. Agatur modo haec res, quod ex
eo senatus consulto, quod nuper est factum, referri ad
vos necesse est, habeo quae de locis religiosis velim
dicere. Cum de domo tua dixero, in qua tamen ita
est inaedificatum sacellum, ut alius fecerit, tibi tantum modo sit demoliendum, tum videbo num mihi necesse sit de aliis etiam aliquid dicere. Putant enim
ad me non nulli pertinere magmentarium [1] Telluris

---

[1] magm. *Mommsen for* dementarium *of most* MSS., *which
is a vox nihili.*

---

[a] See note p. 350.
[b] C. here addresses the Senate; in the next sentence
he turns again to Clodius. Long says here, "There is no
difficulty in translating the rest of the chapter, but it is
unintelligible." I fear I can do no more than endorse
Long's statement.

bequest of an unbroken past to be polluted by
Brogitarus; and in preferring that his son-in-law[a]
should lose your bounty rather than that this shrine
should lose its immemorial sanctity. But, to return
to these responses of the soothsayers, the first clause
of which deals with the games, who is there who
will not admit that it is the games administered
by Clodius to which the declaration and response
exclusively refer?

30 There follows the question of consecrated sites,
the violation of which is an offence against religion.
XIV. O miracle of shamelessness! Have you the
face to bring my house into the discussion? Rather
resign your own house, to the consuls, or to the senate,
or to the College of Pontiffs, as you please. Mine,
at all events, has been exonerated by pronouncements
of all these three, as I have already shown. But in
the house which you are enabled to occupy by your
bare-faced murder of that excellent gentleman and
Roman knight, Quintus Seius, stood, so I assert, a
shrine and altars. I will demonstrate this beyond
all doubt by reference to the registers of the censors
31 and the recollection of many persons. Do[b] but let
this question be discussed (and in accordance with
the decree of the senate which has been recently
passed the matter must inevitably come up before
you), and I am prepared to say somewhat concerning
inviolable sites. When I have finished speaking about
your house (I call it yours, but the shrine which it
holds is built into it in such a way that, while another
constructed it, all you can do is to demolish it), then
I shall see whether it is necessary for me to make
any further reference to other houses as well. Now
there are many who hold that I am responsible for

355

aperire. Nuper id patuisse dicunt et ego recordor. Nunc sanctissimam partem ac sedem maximae religionis privato dicunt vestibulo contineri. Multa me movent, quod aedes Telluris est curationis meae, quod is, qui illud magmentarium sustulit, meam domum iudicio pontificum liberatam secundum fratrem suum iudicatam esse dicebat : movet me etiam in hac caritate annonae, sterilitate agrorum, inopia frugum religio Telluris et eo magis, quod eodem ostento Telluri 32 postulio deberi dicitur. Vetera fortasse loquimur : quamquam hoc si minus civili iure perscriptum est, lege tamen naturae communi iure gentium sanctum est, ut nihil mortales a dis immortalibus usu capere possint. XV. Verum tamen antiqua negligimus : etiamne ea negligemus, quae fiunt cum maxime, quae videmus ? L. Pisonem quis nescit his temporibus ipsis maximum et sanctissimum Dianae sacellum in Caeliculo sustulisse ? Adsunt vicini eius loci : multi sunt etiam in hoc ordine, qui sacrificia gentilicia, illo ipso in sacello, stato loco, anniversaria factitarint. Et quaerimus di immortales quae loca desiderent,

---

ᵃ *Magmentarium*, a rare and archaic word connected with *mactus, mactare*.

ᵇ *i.e.* acquisition of ownership by long use or possession.

ᶜ Part of the Caelian Hill, sometimes called " Caelius Minor " (Mart. xii. 8).

356

the fact that the sanctuary [a] in the temple of Earth was exposed to public view. It is said that this exposure took place recently, and I myself recollect it. *Now* it is said that the most sacred part and the spot which is most hallowed is within the limits of a private vestibule. Many considerations weigh with me : first, the temple of Earth comes within the sphere of my administration ; next, the man who did destroy that sanctuary [a] was in the habit of asserting that my house, which had been exonerated by the pronouncement of the pontiffs, had been adjudged in his brother's favour. I am also influenced, in the present dearness of corn, failure of crops, and scarcity of provisions, by my devotion to the cult of Earth, the more so because we are told that this prodigy points to arrears of sacrifice being due to Earth. I may perhaps be speaking in an old-fashioned strain ; but though not a written law of the civil code, it is none the less a legal ordinance of nature and of the equity which is shared by all nations, that mortals can take by right of usufruct [b] nothing that belongs to the immortal gods. XV. But, neglecting antiquity as we do, shall we also neglect what takes place as never before, what goes on now before our eyes ? Surely there can be none of us who does not know that in these very days Lucius Piso has destroyed a magnificent and venerable shrine of Diana, situated on the lesser Caelian.[c] There are those here whose dwellings adjoin the site ; and moreover there are many members of this order who have performed the annual sacrifices of their clan in this very shrine, which was the place appointed for such. And do we ask what sites are those of which the immortal gods

quid significent, de quo loquantur ? A Sex. Serrano sanctissima sacella suffossa, inaedificata, oppressa, summa denique turpitudine foedata esse nescimus ?

33 Tu meam domum religiosam facere potuisti ? Qua mente ? quam amiseras. Qua manu ? qua disturbaras. Qua voce ? qua incendi iusseras. Qua lege ? quam ne in illa quidem impunitate tua scripseras. Quo pulvinari ? quod stupraras. Quo simulacro ? quod ereptum ex meretricis sepulcro in imperatoris monumento collocaras. Quid habet mea domus religiosi, nisi quod impuri et sacrilegi parietem tangit ? Itaque ne quis meorum imprudens introspicere tuam domum possit ac te sacra illa tua facientem videre, tollam altius tectum, non ut ego te despiciam, sed tu ne aspicias urbem eam, quam delere voluisti.

34 XVI. Sed iam haruspicum reliqua responsa videamus. ORATORES CONTRA IUS FASQUE INTERFECTOS. Quid est hoc ? de Alexandrinis esse video sermonem : quem ego non refuto. Sic enim sentio, ius legatorum, quum hominum praesidio munitum sit, tum etiam divino iure esse vallatum. Sed quaero ab illo,

---

a See *De domo sua*, Chap. XLIII.
b Assassinated through the intrigues of Ptolemy.

358

eel themselves deprived ? Do we ask what is the meaning or theme of their utterance ? Are we ignorant that Sextus Serranus has undermined, or walled up, or overthrown, or even defiled with the lowest infamy, shrines of the deepest sanctity ? Could *you*, Sir, attach inviolability to my house ? What reflection could you have acted upon, you, who had abandoned all reflection ? What agency of yours effected this, when you had been an agent but for its destruction ? Where was the voice that declared its sanctity, when yours had but given the word for its conflagration ? Or where the law that enacted it, when you had indited none such, even in the days of your impunity ? Where was the sacrificial couch ? You had employed it but for adultery. Where the image ? One that you had filched from a harlot's tomb and planted upon a great general's monument.[a] What other inviolability does my house possess, save that it adjoins the walls of an impure and sacrilegious man ? Wherefore, that none of my dear ones may be able inadvertently to look through the windows of your house, and see you performing those rites of yours, I will raise its stories higher, not that I may look down upon you, but that you may not gaze upon the city which you desired to destroy.

XVI. Let us now consider the remaining answers of the soothsayers. " Ambassadors have been slain contrary to law human and divine." What is the meaning of this ? I see that it is popularly referred to the Alexandrian legates[b] ; and I do not gainsay the opinion. For I hold that ambassadorial rights, fortified as they are by human protection, are also reinforced by divine ordinance. But I ask him who, when

359

qui omnes indices tribunus e carcere in forum effudit,
cuius arbitrio sicae nunc omnes atque omnia venena
tractantur, qui cum Hermarcho Chio syngraphas
fecit, ecquid sciat unum acerrimum adversarium Her-
marchi, Theodosium, legatum ad senatum a civitate
libera missum, sica percussum ? quod non minus
quam de Alexandrinis indignum dis immortalibus
35 esse visum certo scio. Nec confero nunc in te unum
omnia. Spes maior esset salutis, si praeter te nemo
esset impurus : plures sunt : hoc et tu tibi confidis
magis et nos prope iure diffidimus. Quis Platorem
ex Orestide, quae pars Macedoniae libera est,
hominem in illis locis clarum ac nobilem, legatum
Thessalonicam ad nostrum, ut se ipse appellavit,
imperatorem venisse nescit ? quem ille propter
pecuniam, quam ab eo extorquere non poterat, in
vincla coniecit et medicum intromisit suum qui
legato, socio, amico, libero foedissime et crudelissime venas incideret. Secures suas cruentari scelere
noluit : nomen quidem populi Romani tanto scelere
contaminavit, ut id nulla re possit nisi ipsius supplicio
expiari. Quales hunc carnifices putamus habere, qui
etiam medicis suis non ad salutem, sed ad necem
utatur ?

36 XVII. Sed recitemus quid sequatur. FIDEM IUS-
QUE IURANDUM NEGLECTUM. Hoc quid sit per se ipsum

---

^a We know nothing of these *legati* save what we are
told here.

^b Piso ; he " had certainly been saluted as Imperator
by his soldiers, but the senate had not recognized him as
such " (Klotz).

tribune, let loose a flood of informers from prison upon the forum, him at whose mandate alone the dagger and the poisoned draught go about their work, him who made out the notes of hand with Hermarchus the Chian, whether he has any knowledge of the fact that Theodosius,[a] the bitterest of all the enemies of Hermarchus, was stabbed with a dagger when acting as the ambassador of a free community to the senate. I am perfectly sure that this act was no less shameful in the eyes of the immortal gods than the murder of the Alexandrians. Not that I now impute all these crimes solely to you. We should have better assurance of well-being if none save you were tainted: but there are others; and this fact, which increases your confidence, makes us, almost justly, less confident. Is it not an acknowledged fact that one Plator,[a] a noble and a celebrity in his own land, came from Orestis, a free district of Macedonia, to Thessalonica upon a mission to our " general," [b] as he calls himself? Or that Clodius, failing to extort from him a sum of money, threw him into prison, and dispatched thither his physician that he might most abominably and brutally open the veins of an ambassador, who was our independent ally and friend? He would not stain his axes with the blood of outrage; but he defiled the name of the Roman people with outrage so foul, that there are no means of expiating it save by the condign punishment of the perpetrator. What manner of men are we to think are his executioners, when he employs even his physicians not to save life, but to take it?

XVII. But let us read on and see what follows. " Fealty and oath has been neglected." The meaning of this clause, if taken independently, I find

non facile interpretor, sed ex eo, quod sequitur, suspicor de tuorum iudicum manifesto periurio dici, quibus olim erepti essent nummi, nisi a senatu praesidium postulassent. Qua re autem de his dici suspicer haec causa est, quod sic statuo, et illud in hac civitate esse maxime illustre atque insigne periurium et te ipsum tamen in periurii crimen ab iis, quibuscum coniurasti, non vocari.

37 Et video in haruspicum responsum haec esse subiecta : SACRIFICIA VETUSTA OCCULTAQUE MINUS DILIGENTER FACTA POLLUTAQUE. Haruspices haec loquuntur an patrii penatesque di ? Multi enim sunt, credo, in quos huius maleficii suspitio cadat. Quis praeter hunc unum ? Obscure dicitur quae sacra polluta sint ? quid planius, quid religiosius, quid gravius dici potest ? VETUSTA OCCULTAQUE. Nego ulla verba Lentulum, gravem oratorem ac disertum, saepius, cum te accusaret, usurpasse quam haec, quae nunc ex Etruscis libris in te conversa atque interpretata dicuntur. Etenim quod sacrificium tam vetustum est quam hoc, quod a regibus aequale huius urbis accepimus ? Quod autem tam occultum quam id, quod non solum curiosos oculos excludit, sed etiam errantes ? quo non modo improbitas, sed ne impru-

---

a *i.e.* the jury who sat when Clodius was prosecuted for impiety in the Bona Dea affair.

b Showing, *i.e.*, that Clodius had bribed *and paid*. But *tamen* in the Latin adds to the obscurity.

difficulty in explaining, but the context leads me to suspect that the reference is to the perjury which is universally admitted to have been practised by jurymen of yours,[a] who once would have had their money wrested from them by force had they not appealed to the protection of the senate. And the reason for my suspicion that it is to this that the response refers is that this, as I hold, is the most glaring and outstanding instance of perjury of which this state has record, and that, in spite of this, no charge of perjury is laid against yourself by those with whom you conspired.[b]

7 I see that this further addition has been made to the response of the soothsayers : " Ancient and secret sacrifices have been performed with laxity, and have been desecrated." Is it the soothsayers who utter these words, or the gods of our ancestors and of our households ? For we are to believe that there are many on whom suspicion of this mis-demeanour may fall. But on whom could it fall save on Clodius alone ? Is it stated ambiguously what rites are those that have been desecrated ? What statement could be clearer, more peremptory, or more impressive ? " Ancient and secret." Why, when that grave and eloquent orator Lentulus accused you, there were no words of which he made more frequent use than these which are now quoted from the Etruscan books, and interpreted as pointing directly at you. And indeed what sacrifice is so ancient as that which we received from our kings, and which is coeval with our city ? Or what so secret as that which fences itself against the eyes not only of the inquisitive, but even of the idle, and to which access is debarred, not merely from wickedness, but

dentia quidem possit intrare ? quod quidem sacrificium nemo ante P. Clodium omni memoria violavit,
nemo umquam adiit, nemo neglexit, nemo vir aspicere non horruit : quod fit per virgines Vestales, fit
pro populo Romano, fit in ea domo, quae est in imperio, fit incredibili caerimonia, fit ei deae, cuius ne
nomen quidem viros scire fas est : quam iste idcirco
Bonam dicit, quod in tanto sibi scelere ignoverit.
XVIII. Non ignovit, mihi crede, non. Nisi forte tibi
esse ignotum putas, quod te iudices emiserunt ex-
cussum et exhaustum, suo iudicio absolutum, omnium
condemnatum, aut quod oculos, ut opinio illius re-
38 ligionis est, non perdidisti. Quis enim ante te sacra
illa vir sciens viderat, ut quisquam poenam quae
sequeretur id scelus scire posset ? an tibi luminis
obesset caecitas plus quam libidinis ? ne id quidem
sentis, coniventes illos oculos abavi tui magis optan-
dos fuisse quam hos flagrantes sororis ? Tibi vero,
si diligenter attendes, intelliges hominum poenas
deesse adhuc, non deorum. Homines te in re foe-
dissima defenderunt : homines turpissimum nocen-
tissimumque laudarunt : homines prope confitentem
iudicio liberaverunt : hominibus iniuria tui stupri
illata in ipsos dolori non fuit : homines tibi arma alii

ᵃ Cic. nicknamed Clodia by the Homeric epithet βοῶπις,
" ox-eyed " (Ad Att. ii. 9). See also note on Ap. Claudius
Caecus, De domo sua, Chap. XL.

even from inadvertency ? A sacrifice, too, which none in all history violated before Publius Clodius, none ever approached, none made light of ; a sacrifice from the sight of which no man but shrank with horror ; a sacrifice performed by Vestal Virgins on behalf of the Roman people, performed in the house of a magistrate and with the most exact ceremonial, in honour of a goddess whose very name men are not permitted to know, whom Clodius addresses as " Good " on the ground that she has forgiven his fearful wickedness. XVIII. No, believe me, she has not forgiven you ; unless, indeed, you imagine yourself forgiven because your judges, having shaken the last penny from your pockets, sent you forth acquitted by their verdict, though condemned by that of the world at large, or because you did not suffer loss of sight, which sacrilege against that rite is popularly held to involve. But what man before you had deliberately looked upon those rites, so that we might be informed as to what penalty was the natural consequence of such a crime ? Or could blinded sight be a sterner retribution upon you than your blind lust ? Is even this lost upon you, that your ancestor's sightless eyes were more desirable possessions than your sister's " wells of fire *a* " ? In your case, if you will mark my words closely, you will find that it is human, and not divine, retribution that has hitherto been lacking. It was by mortals that you were defended in this loathsome business, from mortals that your deep guilt and degradation drew praise, mortals who gave you a verdict of acquittal though you all but avowed your sin, mortals who expressed no resentment at the affront which your adultery had inflicted upon them, mortals who

365

in me, alii post in illum invictum civem dederunt:
hominum beneficia prorsus concedo tibi iam maiora
39 non esse quaerenda. A dis quidem immortalibus
quae potest homini maior esse poena furore atque
dementia ? nisi forte in tragoediis, quos vulnere ac
dolore corporis cruciari et consumi vides, graviores
deorum immortalium iras subire quam illos, qui
furentes inducuntur, putas. Non sunt illi eiulatus et
gemitus Philoctetae tam miseri, quamquam sunt
acerbi, quam illa exsultatio Athamantis et quam
senium matricidarum. Tu, cum furiales in contionibus voces mittis, cum domos civium evertis,
cum lapidibus optimos viros foro pellis, cum ar-
dentes faces in vicinorum tecta iactas, cum aedes
sacras inflammas, cum servos concitas, cum sacra
ludosque conturbas, cum uxorem sororemque non
discernis, cum quod ineas cubile non sentis, tum
baccharis, tum furis, tum das eas poenas, quae solae
sunt hominum sceleri a dis immortalibus constitutae.
Nam corporis quidem nostri infirmitas multos subit
casus per se : denique ipsum corpus tenuissima de
causa saepe conficitur : deorum tela in impiorum
mentibus figuntur. Qua re miserior es, cum in
omnem fraudem raperis oculis, quam si omnino oculos
non habueris.
40 XIX. Sed quoniam de iis omnibus, quae haruspices

a Pompey.
b A character in Greek tragedies now lost. He was
stricken with madness by Hera, and killed his son
Learchus.

put into your hands weapons to be used either against me, or, later, against our invincible fellow-citizen[a]; mortals, I grant you freely, have done you benefits that could not be exceeded. But what punishment could be visited upon a man by the immortal gods severer than madness and infatuation? Unless, indeed, you can think that those tragic heroes you see upon the stage, tortured and worn by the anguish of physical wounds, are meeting a direr visitation of divine anger than those who are represented to us raving. The shrieks and groans of Philoctetes, heart-rending though they be, do not speak such wretchedness as the exulting cries of Athamas[b] or the remorse of long-lived matricides. When you utter your frenzied phrases at mob-meetings, when you overturn the houses of citizens, when you drive honest men with stones from the forum, when you hurl blazing torches on your neighbours' roofs, when you set fire to sacred buildings, when you stir up slaves, when you throw sacrifices and games into turmoil, when you know no distinction between wife and sister, when you bethink you not what bed-chamber you enter, then, then it is that *you* rave in delirium, and undergo the only punishments determined by the immortal gods to requite the wickedness of men. The very frailty of our physical structure exposes it to many disasters; and, indeed, often the structure is even destroyed by the slightest of influences; but it is against the *minds* of the wicked that the darts of the gods are launched. Wherefore you are more wretched when your eyes only serve to hurry you into all manner of crime than if you had no eyes at all.

XIX. But since we have now said enough with

commissa esse dicunt, satis est dictum, videamus quid
iidem haruspices iam a dis immortalibus dicant
moneri. Monent : NE PER OPTIMATIUM DISCORDIAM
DISSENSIONEMQUE PATRIBUS PRINCIPIBUSQUE CAEDES
PERICULAQUE CREENTUR, AUXILIOQUE DIVINITUS DE-
FICIANTUR, †QUA RE AD UNUM IMPERIUM PROVINCIAE
REDEANT EXERCITUSQUE DEMINUTIOQUE ACCEDAT.† [1] Haruspicum verba sunt haec omnia : nihil addo de meo.
Quis igitur optimatium discordiam molitur ? Idem
iste, nec ulla vi ingenii aut consilii sui, sed quodam
errore nostro : quem quidem ille, quod obscurus non
erat, facile perspexit. Hoc enim etiam turpius ad-
flictatur res publica, quod ne ab eo quidem vexatur,
ut tamquam fortis in pugna vir acceptis a forti adversario vulneribus adversis honeste cadere videatur.
41 Ti. Gracchus convellit statum civitatis : qua gravitate vir ! qua eloquentia ! qua dignitate ! nihil ut a
patris avique Africani praestabili insignique virtute,
praeterquam quod a senatu desciverat, deflexisset.
Secutus est C. Gracchus : quo ingenio ! qua eloquentia ! quanta vi ! quanta gravitate dicendi ! ut
dolerent boni non illa tanta ornamenta ad meliorem
mentem voluntatemque esse conversa. Ipse Saturninus ita fuit effrenatus et paene demens, ut auctor

[1] qua re . . . accedat: *the MSS. are hopeless here ; we
should perhaps read with Lambinus* ad unius imperium res
redeat (*see Chap. XXV.*), *which I translate.*

---

[a] See critical note.
[b] Adherent of Marius ; *trib. plebis* 100.

368

regard to the misdoings alleged by the soothsayers to have been committed, let us see what is the warning which these soothsayers assert is given to us by the immortal gods. The warning is this: " Let not death and danger be wrought for the fathers and for statesmen by reason of the discord and division of the nobles, and let them not be bereft of divine power ; and let the state lapse not to the rule of one." [a] I have quoted the sentence of the soothsayers to the letter, inserting not a syllable of my own. Well, who is fomenting discord among the nobles ? Clodius again, and he is enabled to do this not by any powers of intellect or political skill, but by a spirit of delusion which is upon *us* ; he has been quick to recognize this spirit, and indeed its presence was palpable. For the very fact that not even Clodius assails the republic openly only makes her degradation the more humiliating ; were he to do so, she would at least seem to fall honourably, even as the brave warrior who, doing battle with a foeman no less brave, takes all his wounds in front. The stability of the community was shattered by Tiberius Gracchus, so distinguished by strength of character, by eloquence, and by reputation, that, save for his desertion of the senatorial cause, he had swerved not in the least degree from the eminent and remarkable qualities of his father and his grandfather Africanus. His policy was followed by Gaius Gracchus, whose genius, eloquence, vigour, and impressive utterances only inspired patriots with regret that such superb endowments were not applied to better purposes and ambitions. Saturninus [b] himself was so unrestrained, and almost unbalanced, that he wielded an extraordinary influence, and was a

esset egregius et ad animos imperitorum excitandos inflammandosque perfectus. Nam quid ego de Sulpicio loquar? cuius tanta in dicendo gravitas, tanta iucunditas, tanta brevitas fuit, ut posset vel ut prudentes errarent vel ut boni minus bene sentirent perficere dicendo. Cum his conflictari et pro salute patriae cotidie dimicare erat omnino illis, qui tum rem publicam gubernabant, molestum, sed habebat ea molestia quamdam tamen dignitatem.

42 XX. Hic vero, de quo ego ipse tam multa nunc dico, proh di immortales! quid est? quid valet? quid adfert, ut tanta civitas, si cadet, quod di omen obruant! a viro tamen confecta videatur? qui post patris mortem primam illam aetatulam suam ad scurrarum locupletium libidines detulit, quorum intemperantia expleta in domesticis est germanitatis stupris volutatus: deinde iam robustus provinciae se ac rei militari dedit atque ibi piratarum contumelias perpessus, etiam Cilicum libidines barbarorumque satiavit: post exercitu L. Luculli sollicitato per nefandum scelus fugit illim Romaeque recenti adventu suo cum propinquis suis decidit ne reos faceret, a Catilina pecuniam accepit ut turpissime praevaricaretur. Inde cum Murena se in Galliam contulit, in qua provincia mortuorum testamenta conscripsit, pupillos necavit, nefarias cum multis scelerum

[a] P. S. Rufus, *trib. plebis* 88, one of the most powerful orators of his day.

[b] When campaigning against Tigranes in Armenia 68.

consummate exciter and inflamer of the unschooled mind. What need to speak of Sulpicius,[a] whose oratorical style was marked by such weight, charm, and terseness, that his words could lead even the wise astray, and undermine the loyalty even of the loyal ? To grapple with such men as these, to join issue with them daily for our country's sake, was a task which the statesmen of the day found wholly burdensome ; and yet the very fact of its being burdensome lent it a certain dignity.

XX. But as for this fellow upon whom even I myself am now spending so many words, what is he, ye gods ! What power does he possess, what influence does he exert, in virtue of which this great state may be said, should it fall (which heaven forfend !), at least to have been overthrown by a Man ? After his father's death he surrendered the early years of his callow youth to the evil passions of wealthy debauchees, and when he had sated their incontinency he wallowed in domestic adultery in defiance of natural kinship. In due course, with the growth of physical vigour, he entered upon provincial duties and a military career, and incidentally endured the insults of pirates and glutted the lusts even of Cilicians and barbarians. Then, after having endeavoured, with abominable wickedness, to sap the loyalty of the army of Lucius Lucullus,[b] he fled thence and came to Rome, where, shortly after his arrival, he compounded with his kinsfolk, whom he had threatened with arraignment, and received a bribe from Catiline to join him in a nefarious collusion. He then proceeded with Murena to Gaul, and in this province he forged dead men's wills, murdered wards, and formed many criminal

371

pactiones societatesque conflavit : unde ut rediit,
quaestum illum maxime fecundum uberemque cam-
pestrem totum ad se ita redegit, ut homo popularis
fraudaret improbissime populum, idemque vir cle-
mens divisores omnium tribuum domi ipse suae
43 crudelissima morte mactaret. Exorta est illa rei
publicae, sacris, religionibus, auctoritati vestrae,
iudiciis publicis funesta quaestura : in qua idem iste
deos hominesque, pudorem, pudicitiam, senatus
auctoritatem, ius, fas, leges, iudicia violavit. Atque
hic ei gradus—o misera tempora stultasque nostras
discordias !—P. Clodio gradus ad rem publicam hic
primus fuit et aditus ad popularem iactationem atque
ascensus. Nam Ti. Graccho invidia Numantini
foederis, cui feriendo, quaestor C. Mancini consulis
cum esset, interfuerat, et in eo foedere improbando
senatus severitas dolori et timori fuit : eaque res
illum fortem et clarum virum a gravitate patrum
desciscere coëgit.   C. autem Gracchum mors frater-
na, pietas, dolor, magnitudo animi ad expetendas
domestici sanguinis poenas excitavit. Saturninum,
quod in annonae caritate quaestorem a sua frumen-
taria procuratione senatus amovit eique rei M.

---

a Persons employed by candidates to distribute bribes
at the elections.

372

compacts and associations. Returning from that province, he harvested into his own pockets all the rich and fruitful profits of the Campus ; yet we find this idol of the people unscrupulously defrauding the people, and this humane gentleman heartlessly butchering at his own house the distributors *a* of all the tribes. Then began that quaestorship, so fraught with disaster to the republic, to the ceremonies and observances of religion, to your authority, and to the public administration of justice ; during his tenure of this he scouted gods and men, honour, chastity, the senate's authority, equity, right, the constitution, and the courts. This position—O the misery of the times in which we live, and the folly of our discords ! —this position was the first step taken by Clodius in his political career, the first rung of the ladder of demagogic self-glorification. Tiberius Gracchus had been a party to the signing of the treaty at Numantia while acting as quaestor to the Consul Mancinus ; and the unpopularity he gained from this, together with the uncompromising attitude of the senate in withholding their assent from this treaty, inspired him with resentment and apprehension, a combination of circumstances which compelled that gallant and distinguished man to sever himself from the lofty policy of the fathers. Gaius Gracchus, on the other hand, was stirred by his brother's death, his natural affections, his grief, and his indomitable spirit, to wreak vengeance for the shedding of the blood of his house. Saturninus, as we know, became a democrat from indignation at the act of the senate, which, under the stress of a temporary dearness of corn, took from him, as quaestor, his administration of supplies, and trans-

Scaurum praefecit, scimus dolore factum esse popularem. Sulpicium ab optima causa profectum Gaio-
que Iulio consulatum contra leges petenti resisten-
tem longius quam voluit popularis aura provexit.

44 XXI. Fuit in his omnibus causa, etsi non iusta—nulla
enim potest cuiquam male de re publica merendi
iusta esse causa,—gravis tamen et cum aliquo animi
virilis dolore coniuncta. P. Clodius a crocota, a
mitra, a muliebribus soleis purpureisque fasceolis, a
strophio, a psalterio, a flagitio, a stupro est factus
repente popularis. Nisi eum mulieres exornatum
ita deprehendissent, nisi ex eo loco, quo eum adire
fas non fuerat, ancillarum beneficio emissus esset,
populari homine populus Romanus, res publica cive
tali careret. Hanc ob amentiam in discordiis nostris,
de quibus ipsis his prodigiis recentibus a dis immortalibus admonemur, adreptus est unus ex patriciis, cui
45 tribuno plebis fieri non liceret. Quod anno ante
frater Metellus et concors etiam tum senatus, senatus
principe Cn. Pompeio sententiam dicente excluserat
acerrimeque una voce ac mente restiterat, id post
discidium optimatium, de quo ipso nunc monemur,
ita perturbatum itaque permutatum est, ut, quod

---

^a G. J. Caesar Strabo stood for the consulship before he
had been praetor, 88 ; see note on Sulpicius, Chap. XIX.
above.

ferred it to Marcus Scaurus ; while Sulpicius, whose
resistance to the illegal candidature for the consulship
of Gaius Julius *a* had at the outset been fully justified,
was ultimately carried by the breeze of popular
support to greater lengths than he had purposed
4 to go.   XXI. The courses which all these adopted
were determined by reasons, not indeed such as to
justify those courses—for no reason can ever justify disservice to the state,—but at all events cogent reasons,
combined with sentiments of high-spirited resentment ; but Publius Clodius suddenly emerged from
his saffron robe, his frontlet, his womanish slippers
and purple hose, his breast-band, his psaltery, and
his monstrous debaucheries — a fully-fledged demagogue.   Had it been others than women who
had caught him in this finery, had not the good
offices of maid-servants permitted him to depart
from a place which it was impious for him to have
approached, the Roman people would now be without their demagogue, and the state without such a
model of civic virtue.   Thanks to the infatuation of
our present civil strife, which is the subject of the
warning recently given us by the immortal gods
through these very prodigies now in question, the
one man who had no business to become tribune of
the plebs has been snatched from the patrician body.
45 The strenuous, concerted, and unanimous opposition
and resistance which had been offered in the previous
year by his cousin Metellus and a senate which was
even then united, and which was supported by a
speech which Gnaeus Pompeius, leader of the
senate, delivered, was, after the split among the
nobles, which is what we are now warned against,
so utterly disintegrated and altered that what

frater consul ne fieret obstiterat, quod adfinis et
sodalis clarissimus vir, qui illum reum non laudarat,
excluserat, id is consul efficeret in discordiis principum, qui illi unus inimicissimus esse debuerat, et eo
fecisse auctore se diceret, cuius auctoritatis neminem
posset poenitere. Iniecta fax est foeda ac luctuosa
rei publicae : petita est auctoritas vestra, gravitas
amplissimorum ordinum, consensio bonorum omnium,
totus denique civitatis status. Haec enim certe
petebantur, cum in me cognitorem harum omnium
rerum illa flamma illorum temporum coniiciebatur.
Excepi et pro patria solus exarsi, sic tamen, ut vos
iisdem ignibus circumsaepti me primum ictum pro
46 vobis et fumantem videretis. XXII. Non sedaban-
tur discordiae, sed etiam crescebat in eos odium, a
quibus nos defendi putabamur. Ecce iisdem auctoribus, Pompeio principe, qui cupientem Italiam, flagi-
tantes vos, populum Romanum desiderantem non
auctoritate sua solum, sed etiam precibus ad meam
salutem excitavit, restituti sumus. Sit discordiarum
finis aliquando : a diuturnis dissensionibus conquies-
camus. Non sinit eadem ista labes : eas habet
contiones, ea miscet ac turbat, ut modo se his, modo

---

^a Pompey, whose son married a niece of Clodius, and who
had deprecated action against Clodius in the Bona Dea affair.
  ^b Caesar.
  ^c *i.e.* Caesar alleged that he was acting at Pompey's
instigation.　　　　^d Alluding to Catiline's conspiracy.

Clodius' cousin, when consul, had striven to prevent, and what his distinguished kinsman and comrade,[a] who had not approved that he should be put on his trial, had opposed, was during the feud between our leaders brought about by that consul[b] who might have been expected to be Clodius' worst foe, while he also said that the authority upon which he had acted was such that none could be dissatisfied with it.[c] A torch foul and fraught with sorrow was hurled at the state; it was aimed at your authority, at the dignity of the highest orders, the union of all patriots, in a word, at the whole fabric of our society. These at all events were the ultimate aim, when the incendiarism of the times vented their fury upon me, who was the detecter of all these.[d] I met the flame; I blazed alone for my country; but nevertheless those flames hedged you about on all sides, and I was but the first victim whom you saw smitten and smoking to save you. XXII. And so far from our discords being allayed, hatred even waxed strong against those by whom it was thought we were being championed. And now, behold, I have been restored, and my restoration has been due to the proposals of these same men, and to the lead given by Pompeius, who, when Italy longed for me, when you demanded me, and when the Roman people yearned for me, roused all of them, not only by his authority but even by his entreaties, to procure my deliverance. Now at length let there be an end to our discords; let us find repose from our protracted quarrels. But that same breeder of pestilence will not permit this; his mass meetings, his subversive and turbulent activities, are but the means whereby

377

vendat illis, nec tamen ita, ut se quisquam, si ab isto
laudatus sit, laudatiorem putet, sed ut eos, quos non
amant, ab eodem gaudeant vituperari. Atque ego
hunc non miror—quid enim faciat aliud ?—illos homines sapientissimos gravissimosque miror, primum,
quod quemquam clarum hominem atque optime
de re publica saepe meritum impurissimi voce hominis violari facile patiuntur, deinde si existimant
perditi hominis profligatique maledictis posse, id quod
minime conducit ipsis, cuiusquam gloriam dignitatemque violari, postremo quod non sentiunt id, quod
tamen mihi iam suspicari videntur, illius furentes ac
47 volaticos impetus in se ipsos posse converti. Atque
ex hac nimia non nullorum alienatione a quibusdam
haerent ea tela in re publica, quae quam diu haere-
bant in uno me, graviter equidem, sed aliquanto levius
ferebam. An iste nisi primo se dedisset iis, quorum
animos a vestra auctoritate seiunctos esse arbitrabatur, nisi eos in caelum suis laudibus praeclarus
auctor extolleret, nisi exercitum C. Caesaris—in quo
fallebat, sed eum nemo redarguebat, — nisi eum,
inquam, exercitum signis infestis in curiam se im-
missurum minitaretur, nisi se Cn. Pompeio adiutore,
M. Crasso auctore, quae faciebat facere clamaret,
nisi consules causam coniunxisse secum, in quo

he sells himself now to this party and now to that;
but with and through it all, no one counts praise
from Clodius any addition to his praise; they do
but rejoice to hear him vilify those whom they
dislike. And indeed it is not him I wonder at;
for how else could he act? I wonder rather at these
sage and serious persons: first, that they tolerate
that any man of renown who has often done high
service to the republic should be assailed by the
utterance of a vile scoundrel; secondly, that they
should think it possible that the slanders of an
abandoned profligate (and indeed it would be small
gain to themselves if it did so) should impair any
man's credit and reputation; and lastly, that they
do not realize (though I think they are beginning
to suspect it) that his irrational and desultory
attacks may recoil upon their own heads. And one
fruit of this unreasonable estrangement between
party and party is that those darts which, though
painful in all conscience, yet lost somewhat of their
sting when they were fixed in me alone, are now
fixed in the republic. Again, had not Clodius at
the outset surrendered himself to men whose
sympathies, as he thought, were alienated from your
authority; did he not, expert judge of character
that he is, exalt their praises to heaven; did
he not threaten that Gaius Caesar's army—herein
he tried to deceive us, but none refuted him—that
this army would be let loose by him upon the
senate-house prepared for hostile action; did he not
brag that his proceedings were abetted by Gnaeus
Pompeius and instigated by Marcus Crassus; did
he not assert (the only assertion he made which
was not a lie) that the consuls had made common

uno non mentiebatur, confirmaret, tam crudelis mei,
tam sceleratus rei publicae vexator esse potuisset?

48 XXIII. Idem postea quam respirare vos a metu
caedis, emergere auctoritatem vestram ex fluctibus
illis servitutis, reviviscere memoriam ac desiderium
mei vidit, vobis se coepit subito fallacissime venditare.
Tum leges Iulias contra auspicia latas et hic et in
contionibus dicere: in quibus legibus inerat curiata
illa lex, quae totum eius tribunatum continebat:
quam caecus amentia non videbat: producebat
fortissimum virum, M. Bibulum: quaerebat ex eo C.
Caesare leges ferente de caelo semperne servasset?
Semper se ille servasse dicebat. Augures interro-
gabat quae ita lata essent rectene lata essent? Illi
vitio lata esse dicebant. Ferebant in oculis hominem
quidam boni viri et de me optime meriti, sed illius, ut
ego arbitror, furoris ignari. Longius processit: in
ipsum Cn. Pompeium, auctorem, ut praedicare est
solitus, consiliorum suorum, invehi coepit: inibat

49 gratiam a non nullis. Tum vero elatus spe est,
posse se, quoniam togatum domestici belli exstincto-
rem nefario scelere foedasset, illum etiam, illum
externorum bellorum hostiumque victorem adfligere:
tum est illa in templo Castoris scelerata et paene

---

[a] Those enacted in Caesar's consulship 59.

[b] Consul with Caesar 59.

[c] We learn from *Pro Milone*, Chap. VII., that a slave of
Clodius had been arrested while carrying a dagger with
which to assassinate Pompey.

cause with him,—could he ever have harassed me so unmercifully, and the state so abominably? XXIII. Then again, when he saw that you were relieved of your apprehensions of massacre, that your authority was raising its head above the waves of servitude, and that yearning memories of me were stirring afresh in men's hearts, he suddenly began, like the arrant swindler that he is, to display his wares to you; then he asserted both in this house and at mass meetings that the Julian laws *a* had been carried in defiance of the auspices; among these was the law carried in the Assembly of the Curies which comprised all the acts of his tribunate, though he was so blinded by frenzy that he never remarked this. He brought forward that gallant gentleman Marcus Bibulus,*b* and asked him whether he had been assiduous in observing the sky, while Caesar was introducing his laws. Bibulus replied in the affirmative. He questioned the augurs as to whether legislation so carried had been validly carried; they replied that there was a flaw in the process. The fellow was looked upon with favour by certain men of sound views who had done me good service, but who, as I think, were blind to his recklessness. He went to yet further lengths; he began to attack Gnaeus Pompeius himself, the inspirer, as he was in the habit of proclaiming, of his policy; he began to ingratiate himself with not a few. Then indeed he was fired with a hope that, since by an impious crime he had humiliated the civilian queller of intestine war, he could assail *him* too, yes, him who had waged triumphant war against foreign foes; then that crime-stained dagger *c* that so nearly achieved the extinction of

deletrix huius imperii sica deprehensa : tum ille, cui
nulla hostium diutius urbs umquam fuit clausa, qui
omnes angustias, omnes altitudines moenium obiectas
semper vi ac virtute perfregit, obsessus est ipse domi,
meque non nulla imperitorum vituperatione timidi-
tatis meae consilio et facto suo liberavit. Nam si Cn.
Pompeio, viro uni omnium fortissimo, quicumque nati
sunt, miserum magis fuit quam turpe, quam diu ille
tribunus plebis fuit, lucem non aspicere, carere publico, minas eius perferre, cum in contionibus diceret
velle se in Carinis aedificare alteram porticum quaeque Palatio responderet, certe mihi exire domo mea
ad privatum dolorem fuit luctuosum, ad rationem rei
50 publicae gloriosum. XXIV. Videtis igitur hominem
per se ipsum iam pridem adflictum ac iacentem per-
niciosis optimatium discordiis excitari, cuius initia
furoris dissensionibus eorum, qui tum a vobis seiuncti
videbantur, sustentata sunt. Reliqua iam praecipi-
tantis tribunatus etiam post tribunatum obtrectatores eorum atque adversarii defenderunt, ne a re
publica rei publicae pestis removeretur restiterunt,
etiam ne causam diceret, etiam ne privatus esset.
Etiamne in sinu atque in deliciis quidam optimi viri

[a] A district between the Caelian and the Esquiline, now
S. Pietro in Vincoli. Pompey had a house there, and
Clodius threatened to treat this house as he had treated C.'s.
[b] Caesar, Pompey, and Crassus.
[c] Bibulus, Cato, and Domitius.

this empire was found upon him in the temple of
Castor; then that great man, against whom no
hostile city had barred her gates for long, he who
by his energy and valour had burst his way through
every breach, however narrow, and scaled every
wall, however high, was actually besieged in his own
house, and by the course he chose to pursue absolved
me from the reproach of cowardice which had been
fastened upon me by many who were unacquainted
with the facts. For if Gnaeus Pompeius, the bravest
of all men born, found it not so much ignominious
as miserable not to look upon the daylight, while
Clodius was tribune of the plebs, to resign his public
activities, and to endure Clodius' threats, when he
said in mass meetings that he intended to build a
second portico in the Carinae[a] to correspond with that
on the Palatine, then surely, though it was a grievous
personal blow for me to be banished from my home,
yet at the same time, inasmuch as it was a course that
accorded with the interest of the republic, it was
glorious. XXIV. So now you see the fellow roused
by the mischievous dissensions of the nobles from
the long prostration and impotence to which his
own conduct had brought him, though at the outset
the first essays of his madness were nourished upon
the differences of those[b] who at the time seemed
to be out of sympathy with you. The remaining
acts of his tribunate, when it had begun to rush head-
long upon ruin, were defended, even after he was
tribune no longer, by the belittlers and opponents[c]
of those whom I have just mentioned; they opposed
the removal from the state of the state's curse,
they opposed his arraignment, even his reduction
to private status. Is it possible that certain men,

viperam illam venenatam ac pestiferam habere potuerunt ? quo tandem decepti munere ? Volo, in-
quiunt, esse qui in contione detrahat de Pompeio.
Detrahat ille vituperando ? Velim sic hoc vir summus atque optime de mea salute meritus accipiat, ut
a me dicitur : dicam quidem certe quod sentio. Mihi,
me dius fidius, tum de illius amplissima dignitate
detrahere, cum eum maximis laudibus efferebat,
51 videbatur. Utrum tandem C. Marius splendidior,
cum eum C. Glaucia laudabat, an cum eumdem
iratus postea vituperabat ? an ille demens et iam
pridem ad poenam exitiumque praeceps, foedior aut
inquinatior in Cn. Pompeio accusando quam in universo senatu vituperando fuit ? quod quidem miror,
cum alterum gratum sit iratis, alterum esse tam
bonis civibus non acerbum. Sed ne id viros optimos
diutius delectet, legant hanc eius contionem, de qua
loquor : in qua Pompeium ornat an potius deformat ?
certe laudat et unum esse in hac civitate dignum
huius imperii gloria dicit et significat se illi esse amicissimum et reconciliationem esse gratiae factam.
52 Quod ego quamquam quid sit nescio, tamen hoc

---

* Supporter of Marius with Saturninus.

excellent in all else, could have brought themselves to hug to their hearts that envenomed and pestilential viper? What, I should like to know, was the bait whereby they were deceived? "It is my wish," says one and another, "that Pompeius should have his detractors at mass meetings." What! could he suffer detraction from the vilification of Clodius? It is my hope that that great man, to whom I am so deeply indebted for my restoration, may understand this in the sense in which it is said; I, at all events, shall say only what I feel. I do declare that it was when Clodius extolled Pompeius with his highest congratulations, then, so it seemed to me, he was

51 detracting from his splendid reputation. I ask you, was the fame of Gaius Marius brighter when Gaius Glaucia *a* was panegyrizing him, or when he later vented his wrath upon him in abuse? What! did that madman, who had for long been blindly rushing upon doom and retribution, show in any viler or more detestable light when he was accusing Gnaeus Pompeius than when he was abusing the senate generally? What surprises me in this is that this latter act of Clodius should not be viewed with disgust by such good patriots, since they find their indignation gratified by the former. But that excellent gentlemen may cease to feel delight at such behaviour, let them read the proceedings of that mass meeting of Clodius of which I speak, in which he compliments, or shall I rather say defames, Pompeius. At all events, he congratulates him, asserting that he is the only member of the community who is worthy of the empire's glory, intimating his own deep attachment and his reconciliation

52 with him. What may be the meaning of this I

statuo, hunc, si amicus esset Pompeio, laudaturum
illum non fuisse. Quid enim, si illi inimicissimus
esset, amplius ad eius laudem minuendam facere
potuisset? Videant ii, qui illum Pompeio inimicum
esse gaudebant ob eamque causam in tot tantisque
sceleribus conivebant et non numquam eius indomitos
atque effrenatos furores plausu etiam suo proseque-
bantur, quam se cito inverterit. Nunc enim iam
laudat illum : in eos invehitur, quibus se antea vendi-
tabat. Quid existimatis eum, si reditus ei gratiae
patuerit, esse facturum, qui tam libenter in opinionem
53 gratiae irrepat? XXV. Quas ego alias optimatium
discordias a dis immortalibus definiri putem? nam
hoc quidem verbo neque P. Clodius neque quisquam
de gregalibus eius aut de consiliariis designatur.
Habent Etrusci libri certa nomina, quae in id genus
civium cadere possint. DETERIORES, REPULSOS, quod
iam audietis, hos appellant, quorum et mentes et res
sunt perditae longeque a communi salute disiunctae.
Qua re cum di immortales monent de optimatium
discordia, de clarissimorum et optime meritorum
civium dissensione praedicunt : cum principibus
periculum caedemque portendunt, in tuto collocant

---

a With regard to the relations between Pompey and
Clodius, it should be remembered that Clodius, though
nominally the instrument of both Pompey and Caesar, had
probably been privately commissioned by the latter, now in
Gaul, to exasperate Pompey by any means in his power.
See Introduction to Speeches *Post reditum.*

b Containing the formulae on which the *haruspices* based
their interpretations.

cannot divine, but my conviction is that if Clodius
were a friend to Pompeius he would not have
congratulated him. For if he had been Pompeius'
bitterest foe, what could he have said that would
have more directly tended to impair his reputation ?
I would ask those who felt delight at Clodius' hostility
to Pompeius, and who were thereby misled into
shutting their eyes to his innumerable wickednesses,
even on some occasions hailing with their own
applause his acts of incorrigible and headstrong
recklessness, to note how rapid was his change of
face. At this present moment he is congratulating
Pompeius ; but he is bitterly attacking those whose
favour he was but now courting. If he finds the
road to reconciliation with Pompeius thrown open
to him, how do you think he will act, when he is so
glad to worm himself into a reconciliation which is
3 purely supposititious ? [a] XXV. To what other dissensions among the nobles am I to think that a pointed
allusion is being made by the immortal gods ? For,
indeed, in this particular clause there is no express
mention either of Publius Clodius nor of any of his
associates or advisers. But the Etruscan books [b]
employ certain definite terms which are peculiarly
applicable to this type of citizen. As you will
shortly hear, they apply the epithets " baser,"
" rejected " to those who are desperate both in
purpose and in purse, and are in both alienated
from the cause of the common welfare. Wherefore,
when the immortal gods warn us against the dissensions of the nobles, they are prophesying to us with
regard to quarrels which concern our most distinguished and meritorious citizens ; and when they
foreshadow danger and death to our highest, they

Clodium, qui tantum abest a principibus quantum a
54 puris, quantum ab religiosis.   Vobis, o carissimi atque
optimi cives, et vestrae saluti consulendum et pro-
spiciendum vident.   Caedes principum ostenditur :
id, quod interitum optimatium sequi necesse est,
adiungitur : ne in unius imperium res recidat, admonemur.   Ad quem metum si deorum monitis non
duceremur, tamen ipsi nostro sensu coniecturaque
raperemur.   Neque enim ullus alius discordiarum
solet esse exitus inter claros et potentes viros nisi aut
universus interitus aut victoris dominatus aut regnum.
Dissensit cum Mario, clarissimo cive, consul nobilissimus et fortissimus, L. Sulla : horum uterque ita
cecidit victus, ut victor idem regnaverit.   Cum
Octavio collega Cinna dissedit : utrique horum se-
cunda fortuna regnum est largita, adversa mortem.
Idem iterum Sulla superavit : tum sine dubio habuit
regalem potestatem, quamquam rem publicam re-
55 cuperarat.   Inest hoc tempore haud obscurum odium
atque id insitum penitus et inustum animis hominum
amplissimorum : dissident principes : captatur oc-
casio. Qui non tantum opibus valent, nescio quam
fortunam tamen ac tempus exspectant : qui sine
controversia plus possunt, ei fortasse non numquam

grant security to Clodius, who is as far removed from the highest as he is from the chaste and the scrupulous. It is upon you, O brightest and best of our citizens, that Heaven sees that the duty devolves of taking measures and provisions for your own safety. The murder of our highest is portended ; and there is a further reference to what must inevitably follow the destruction of our nobility ; we are warned, that is to say, " that the state lapse not to the rule of one." Did not a divine behest direct us to this apprehension, we should none the less be forcibly driven upon it by our own powers of perception and inference ; for indeed it is a commonplace that dissension between men of renown and authority can have no other issue save a general cataclysm, or, failing that, the despotic domination of the triumphant person. A quarrel arose between that renowned citizen Marius and that noble and gallant consul Lucius Sulla ; each of these successively fell vanquished, and yet each was no sooner the vanquisher than he became a despot. Cinna fell out with his colleague Octavius ; upon each of these prosperity bestowed a tyrant's power, adversity death. Once again Sulla prevailed ; and then beyond all doubt he wielded a king's power, albeit he had restored the republic. At the present time hatred does more than merely rankle ; it is engrained and inured in the souls of our proudest ; there is discord in high places, and there are those who are ready to clutch the opportunity. Those who are opposed by a superiority of power are yet alert to catch at the skirts of some happy chance or random conjuncture of events ; while those who enjoy an undisputed pre-eminence are as often as

consilia ac sententias inimicorum suorum extime-
scunt. Tollatur haec e civitate discordia : iam omnes
isti qui portenduntur metus exstinguentur : iam ista
serpens, quae tum hic delitiscit, tum se emergit et
fertur illuc, compressa atque illisa morietur.

XXVI. Monent enim eidem, NE OCCULTIS CONSILIIS
RES PUBLICA LAEDATUR. Quae sunt occultiora quam
eius, qui in contione ausus est dicere iustitium edici
oportere, iuris dictionem intermitti, claudi aerarium,
iudicia tolli ? nisi forte existimatis hanc tantam col-
luvionem illi tantamque eversionem civitatis in men-
tem·subito in Rostris nec cogitanti venire potuisse.
Est quidem ille plenus vini, stupri, somni plenusque
inconsideratissimae ac dementissimae temeritatis :
verum tamen nocturnis vigiliis, etiam coitione hominum, iustitium illud concoctum atque meditatum
est. Mementote, patres conscripti, verbo illo nefario
temptatas aures nostras et perniciosam viam au-
diendi consuetudine esse munitam.

56 Sequitur illud : NE DETERIORIBUS REPULSISQUE HONOS
AUGEATUR. REPULSOS videamus : nam DETERIORES
qui sint post docebo. Sed tamen in eum cadere hoc

not apprehensive of the purposes and meditations of their rivals. Let us sweep this spirit of discord from our society ; then forthwith will all these terrors which cast their shadow upon us be abolished, and then will yonder serpent, who now lurks here, and now comes forth from his lair and darts thither, be crushed and pounded to his death.

XXVI. And indeed we are warned from the same source " that the republic be not harmed by secret designs." What designs can be more secret than his, who dared to say at a mass meeting that a cessation of public business should be proclaimed, that the administration of justice should be arrested, that the treasury should be closed, and that the courts should be done away with ? What indeed, unless we are to believe that the idea of so wholesale an inundation and destruction of our society could have flashed unpremeditated upon his thoughts as he stood upon the rostra ? I grant you that wine, debauchery, slumber, and a recklessness utterly devoid of reflection and of reason, are the very stuff of his life ; but the cessation of public business which he suggests can only have been hatched and plotted in the watches of the night, and by more heads than one. Do not forget, conscript fathers, that our ears have been affronted by his outrageous words, and that it is by making us familiar with their sound that he has paved the road that is to end in our doom.

There follows the injunction, " Let not honour be increased for the baser and the rejected." Let us consider this word " rejected " ; later I will demonstrate to you who are meant by " the baser." Meanwhile, however, it may be taken for granted that

verbum maxime, qui sit unus omnium mortalium sine ulla dubitatione deterrimus, concedendum est. Qui sunt igitur repulsi ? Non, ut opinor, ii, qui aliquando honorem vitio civitatis, non suo, non sunt adsecuti. Nam id quidem multis saepe optimis civibus atque honestissimis viris accidit. Repulsi sunt ii, quos ad omnia progredientes, quos munera contra leges gladiatoria parantes, quos apertissime largientes non solum alieni, sed etiam sui vicini tribules urbani rustici reppulerunt. Hi ne honore augeantur, monent. Debet esse gratum quod praedicunt, sed tamen huic malo populus Romanus ipse nullo haru-

57 spicum admonitu sua sponte prospexit. Deteriores cavete : quorum quidem est magna natio, sed tamen eorum omnium hic dux est atque princeps. Etenim si unum hominem deterrimum poëta praestanti aliquis ingenio fictis conquisitisque vitiis deformatum vellet inducere, nullum profecto dedecus reperire posset, quod in hoc non inesset, multaque in eo penitus defixa atque haerentia praeteriret. XXVII. Parentibus et dis immortalibus et patriae nos primum natura conciliat : eodem enim tempore et suscipimur in lucem et hoc caelesti spiritu augemur et certam in

---

ᵃ Presumably by restoring Cicero from exile, and so baffling Clodius.

the word is most appropriately used of one who is beyond all rivalry and all question the basest of mortals. Who, then, are " the rejected " ? Not, surely, those whose failure to gain promotion on any occasion has been due to a flaw in their citizenship, not in their character ; for this indeed is a misfortune which has frequently happened to many citizens of undoubted excellence and uprightness. The " rejected " are rather those who are prepared to go to any lengths, who provide gladiatorial entertainments in defiance of the laws, who offer bare-faced bribes, and who on every occasion are rejected not merely by those unconnected with themselves, but by their kinsfolk, their neighbours, their tribesmen, and their fellow-citizens both in the city and in the provinces ; it is these whose honour we are warned not to increase. We must, of course, be grateful for the admonition, but nevertheless the Roman people itself has spontaneously, and independently of any warning of soothsayers, taken measures to cope with this evil.[a] It is against " the baser " that you must be on your guard ; their name is legion, but Clodius is prince and master of them all ; and indeed, if some poet of surpassing genius were desirous of presenting to us an individual defiled by all the vices that imagination and ingenuity could suggest, I am sure that he could devise no infamy that was not to be found in Clodius, and that many sins that are ineradicably embedded in his soul would be overlooked. XXVII. Our parents, the immortal gods, our fatherland,—to all these nature binds us at the hour of our birth ; for at that one time we are accepted by the first as participants in the light of day, we are endowed by the second with the breath of the heaven

sedem civitatis ac libertatis ascribimur. Iste parentum nomen, sacra, memoriam, gentem Fonteiano
nomine obruit : deorum ignes, solia, mensas, abditos
ac penetrales focos, occulta et maribus non invisa solum, sed etiam inaudita sacra inexpiabili scelere pervertit idemque earum templum inflammavit dearum,
58 quarum ope etiam aliis incendiis subvenitur. Quid
de patria loquar ? qui primum eum civem vi, ferro,
periculis urbe, omnibus patriae praesidiis depulit,
quem vos patriae conservatorem esse saepissime
iudicaritis : deinde everso senatus, ut ego semper
dixi, comite, duce, ut ille dicebat, senatum ipsum,
principem salutis mentisque publicae, vi, caede incendiisque pervertit : sustulit duas leges, Aeliam et
Fufiam, maxime rei publicae salutares : censuram
exstinxit : intercessionem removit : auspicia delevit :
consules, sceleris sui socios, aerario, provinciis, exercitu armavit : reges qui erant vendidit, qui non erant
appellavit : Cn. Pompeium ferro domum compulit :
imperatorum monumenta evertit : inimicorum domus disturbavit : vestris monumentis suum nomen
inscripsit. Infinita sunt scelera, quae ab illo in
patriam sunt edita. Quid, quae in singulos cives, quos
necavit ? socios, quos diripuit ? imperatores, quos

---

[a] We learn from *Pro Milone*, Chap. XXVII., that Clodius
burned a shrine of the nymphs ; this incident seems to
be referred to here, and probably it was a shrine of the
Naiads.

[b] Pompey.

[c] See *In senatu*, Chap. V. *n.*

[d] Q. Catulus ; see *De domo sua*, Chap. XXXVIII.

[e] See *ibid.* Chap. XXX.

above us, and we are enrolled into the citizenship and
freedom of a fixed home. Clodius by adopting the
name of Fonteius has wiped out the name, the
religion, the memory, and the clan of his parents ;
by his inexpiable crime he has trampled upon the
fires of the gods, their thrones, their tables, their
enshrined and mystic hearths, and their secret rites,
which are forbidden not merely to the gaze but
even to the hearing of males ; and he has burned
the temple of the very goddesses whose gifts are
employed to quench ordinary conflagrations.[a] And
what of his dealings with his fatherland ? In the
first place, by armed violence and by menaces he
banished from the city and from all the protection
his country could have afforded him a citizen whom
you repeatedly pronounced to be that country's preserver ; then, having worked the downfall of one [b]
whom I have always described as the senate's friend,
and whom he asserted to be its leader, he overturned
the senate itself by fire and massacre ; he abolished
two laws, the Aelian and the Fufian,[c] which were of
supreme service to the state ; he swept away the
censorship, he removed the right of veto, he annulled
the auspices, he equipped the consuls, who were his
partners in crime, with funds, provinces, and an
army ; native governors who were kings he sold, those
who were not he so entitled ; he drove Gnaeus
Pompeius to his house by force of arms, he overturned the monuments of generals,[d] he demolished
the houses of his enemies, upon your monuments he
inscribed his own name.[e] The catalogue of the
crimes which he let loose upon his country is without
end. And what of the individual citizens whom he
has done to death, of the allies whom he has sundered

59 prodidit ? exercitus, quos temptavit ? Quid vero ?
ea quanta sunt, quae in ipsum se scelera, quae in suos
edidit ? quis minus umquam pepercit hostium castris
quam ille omnibus corporis sui partibus ? quae navis
umquam in flumine publico tam vulgata omnibus
quam istius aetas fuit ? quis umquam nepos tam libere est cum scortis quam hic cum sororibus volutatus ? quam denique tam immanem Charybdim poëtae
fingendo exprimere potuerunt, quae tantos exhauriret
gurgites, quantas iste Byzantiorum Brogitarorumque
praedas exsorbuit ? aut tam eminentibus canibus
Scyllam tamque ieiunis quam quibus istum videtis,
Gelliis, Clodiis, Titiis Rostra ipsa mandentem ?

60 Qua re, id quod extremum est in haruspicum responsis, providete, NE REI PUBLICAE STATUS COMMUTE-
TUR. Etenim vix haec, si undique fulciamus, iam
labefacta, vix, inquam, nixa in omnium nostrum
humeris cohaerebunt. XXVIII. Fuit quondam ita
firma haec civitas et valens, ut negligentiam senatus
vel etiam iniurias civium ferre posset : iam non
potest. Aerarium nullum est : vectigalibus non fruuntur qui redemerunt : auctoritas principum cecidit :
consensus ordinum est divulsus : iudicia perierunt :
suffragia descripta tenentur a paucis : bonorum animus ad nutum nostri ordinis expeditus iam non erit :

---

a Sex. Clodius ; see Chap. VI.
b It is impossible to indicate the play upon the two uses
of *rostra*—(1) prows, (2) platform in forum decorated with
prows. "Scylla devoured only the men, not the ships ;
your creatures devour (*i.e.* make havoc of) not only the
sailors on the ship of state, but even the ship itself."
c The *publicani*, who bought from the state the right of
collecting the revenues in certain provinces, and made what
they could out of the deal.

from us, the generals whom he has betrayed, the armies with which he has tampered ? More than all this, how shocking are the crimes which he has committed against himself and against his own ! Who has ever used a hostile camp with less consideration than he has used to all his physical organs ? What ship that plies at the public ferry has ever been so free to common traffic as was his youth ? What debauchee ever wallowed so dissolutely with strumpets as he has with his sisters ? Finally, what Charybdis so monstrous has the imagination of poets been able to depict, or capable of gulping down such oceans as the vast booty of Byzantines and Brogitaruses which he has engulfed ? Or what Scylla in fiction was ever ringed by dogs with such craning necks and such famished jaws as those which you see him employing—creatures like Gellius, Clodius,*a* and Titius—to crunch the very prows *b* themselves ?

Act, therefore, upon the final clause in the response of the soothsayers, which bids you " change not the condition of the republic." And indeed scarcely, though we prop the tottering structure upon this side and upon that, scarcely, I say, will the support given by our united shoulders enable it to cohere. XXVIII. There was a time when the fabric of our state was so firm and sound that it could survive the scouting of the senate and even outrage done to its citizens. It cannot so survive to-day. The treasury is non-existent, those who have contracted for the revenues *c* get no profit therefrom, the prestige of our highest lies in the dust, the unity of the orders is shattered, the courts are no more, the right of voting is assigned to a selected few, the moral support of patriots will soon cease to be ever ready to answer

397

civem qui se pro patriae salute opponat invidiae
61 frustra posthac requiretis. Qua re hunc statum, qui
nunc est, qualiscumque est, nulla alia re nisi concordia
retinere possumus : nam ut meliore simus loco ne
optandum quidem est illo impunito : deteriore autem
statu ut simus, unus est inferior gradus aut interitus
aut servitutis. Quo ne trudamur, di immortales nos
admonent, quoniam iam pridem humana consilia
ceciderunt. Atque ego hanc orationem, patres conscripti, tam tristem, tam gravem, non suscepissem,
non quin hanc personam et has partes honoribus
populi Romani, vestris plurimis ornamentis mihi
tributis deberem et possem sustinere, sed tamen
facile tacentibus ceteris reticuissem, sed haec oratio
omnis fuit non auctoritatis meae, sed publicae religionis. Mea fuerunt verba fortasse plura, sententiae
quidem omnes haruspicum, ad quos aut referri
nuntiata ostenta non convenit aut eorum responsis
62 commoveri necesse est. Quod si cetera magis per-
vulgata nos saepe et leviora moverunt, vox ipsa deorum immortalium non mentes omnium permovebit ?
Nolite enim id putare accidere posse, quod in fabulis
saepe videtis fieri, ut deus aliqui delapsus de caelo
coëtus hominum adeat, versetur in terris, cum ho-

the least call of our order, and the day is at hand
when you will look in vain for a citizen who will
dare to brave hatred in his country's cause. This
being so, it is by unity of will alone that we can
maintain the present condition of the state, such as
it is. Amelioration is something that we cannot even
pray for, so long as Clodius goes unpunished ; and
in degeneration we can but descend one step—to
destruction or to slavery ; and it is to prevent our
being pushed down to this level that the immortal
gods give us this warning, since human devices have
for long now been impotent. I, indeed, should never
have undertaken to speak upon so grave and serious
a matter—not that it lay beyond my duty or my
power to sustain my present rôle and character,
honoured, as I have been, with the offices which are
at the bestowal of the Roman people, and with many
distinctions conferred by you, but in the universal
silence I might easily have kept silence myself—
had it not been that I have all this time been pleading
the cause, not of my own dignity, but of the religion
of the state. My words, perchance, have been over
many, but the opinions which those words express
are those of the soothsayers, to whom the prodigies
announced to us should not be referred at all, unless
we are to look upon it as a solemn duty to lay their
responses to heart. And if other manifestations, less
impressive, perhaps, though more widely bruited,
have not failed to move us, shall not the feelings of
all of us be stirred by the actual voice of the immortal
gods ? For you must not think that that can happen
which you often see represented upon the stage,—
that some god can float down from heaven and
mingle in the gatherings of men, walk abroad upon

minibus colloquatur. Cogitate genus sonitus eius, quem Latinienses nuntiarunt, recordamini illud etiam, quod nondum est relatum, quod eodem fere tempore factus in agro Piceno Potentiae nuntiatur terrae motus horribilis cum quibusdam multis metuendisque rebus. Haec eadem profecto quae pro-
63 spicimus impendentia pertimescetis. Etenim haec deorum immortalium vox, haec paene oratio iudicanda est, cum ipse mundus cum maria atque terrae motu quodam novo contremiscunt et inusitato aliquid sono incredibilique praedicunt. In quo constituendae nobis quidem sunt procurationes et obsecratio, quem ad modum monemur. Sed faciles sunt preces apud eos, qui ultro nobis viam salutis ostendunt : nostrae nobis sunt inter nos irae discordiaeque placandae.

the earth, and hold converse with humanity. Reflect upon the nature of the sound which the Latins reported; recall, too, the portent which has not yet been officially notified, the awful earthquake, accompanied by many strange and fearful circumstances, which is reported to have occurred at about the same time at Potentia in Picenum; then surely you will dread this menace which we see looming upon us. And indeed it is as a voice, nay, an eloquent appeal, of the immortal gods that this must be viewed, when the world with its seas and lands shudders with a weird motion, and by a sound beyond experience and beyond belief conveys to us tidings of the future. In such circumstances it is our duty to hold services of reparation and supplication, as we are bidden. But while prayers are the easy resource of those who generously point out to us the path of safety, it is for *us* to mitigate our own mutual animosities and discords.

THE SPEECH ON BEHALF OF
GNAEUS PLANCIUS

INTRODUCTION

GNAEUS PLANCIUS was quaestor in Macedonia in
58. His headquarters were at Thessalonica, and
thither Cicero came, a dejected exile, in danger of
his life from the banished associates of Catiline.[a]
The propraetor of the province was L. Apuleius
Saturninus, who had been a friend of Cicero, but
who was now afraid to show him any kindness.
Plancius, however, displayed a nobler spirit; and
from May to November he watched over Cicero
with great faithfulness at a time when the fallen
orator was suffering the torments of humiliation,
and, if we may believe hints he drops in a letter to
his brother, was even contemplating suicide.[b]

In 56 Plancius was a tribune of the plebs, and in
55 stood as a candidate for the aedileship. Something, we know not what, occurred to interfere with
the elections, and they were postponed until the
following summer, when Plancius was elected along
with A. Plotius. Among the unsuccessful candidates
was M. Juventius Laterensis, who, though a plebeian,
was a *nobilis*, inasmuch as members of his family

---

[a] Chap. XLI. [b] *Ad Q. fr.* i. 3. 1.

had held magistracies. A few weeks after the election, Laterensis, galled by his defeat at the hands of one who was merely an *eques*,[a] prosecuted Plancius on the ground that he had won his victory by illegal methods.

It is necessary, in order to understand Cicero's argument, to describe briefly the particular illegality which Plancius was alleged to have committed. The institution of annual popular election at Rome, and the practice of personal solicitation for votes, laid open many avenues for corruption, and from as early as the fourth century B.C. we find measures constantly being passed to impede the exertion of undue influence — *ambitus*, or " going about," as it was called. Moreover, as the voting was " sectional " (it was not the majority of heads but the majority of tribes or centuries that won the day), bribery was made easier for candidates, who were enabled to distribute their bounty systematically ; and the frequency of legislation against this is a measure of its prevalence.

A common and growing form of corruption in Cicero's day was that by means of *sodalicia*, translated in this speech as " associations " ; in the previous year (55) a law [b] had been actually passed (Lex Licinia de Sodaliciis) against the procuring of votes by the intrigues of such associations. They were political clubs within the tribes, whose " aim was to organize and retain in their own hands a system of bribery, so as, if possible, to divert any charge of *ambitus* from the candidate to themselves, trusting to their

---

[a] *i.e.* with property rated at over 400,000 sesterces (about £4000).

[b] Chap. XV.

numbers to afford them security " (Holden). These associations might interfere with the purity of elections in two ways : they might still further simplify bribery, as the candidate needed only to approach the leader, who would presumably exercise control over the members ; and they could exert violence and intimidation towards the unattached and unorganized voters.

Now, in his speech for the prosecution, Laterensis seems to have adduced no adequate proof that Plancius had resorted to these associations ; but rather, while bringing his charge under the Lex Licinia, to have made *ambitus* pure and simple the substance of his accusation.[a] And he had had, Cicero urges, an ulterior motive in so doing. It was because, he says, this law bore with especial hardness upon defendants, owing to the peculiar constitution of the jury in cases where its infringement was in question. Ordinarily at this time juries were chosen by lot from all the tribes, representation being equally divided between senators, *equites*, and *tribuni aerarii*[b]; and both prosecutor and defendant had equal rights of challenging them. But in cases brought under the Lex Licinia the prosecutor named four tribes, out of which the jury was to be selected ; the defendant had the right to challenge one of these tribes, and the jury was taken from the other three, the defendant having no further power of challenge. Consequently the constitution of the jury lay entirely in the hands of the prosecutor. The Lex Licinia

[a] Chap. XVII.
[b] The class next below the *equites*, whose property was rated between 400,000 and 300,000 sesterces ; see also Chap. VIII. *n.*

404

took it for granted that the tribes the prosecutor would name would be those in which the offence had been committed; but Laterensis avoided naming these, and Cicero therefore charges him with having contravened the spirit, if not the letter, of the law.

The penalty enacted was exile; but we have no information as to whether this penalty was inflicted, or whether Cicero's clever handling of the case, combined with his somewhat overstrained pathos in the peroration, succeeded in winning Plancius' acquittal. Two letters [a] which the orator addressed to him in 46 show us that he was living at Corcyra, but we can base no assertion upon this.

---

[a] *Ad fam.* iv. 14 and 15.

ORATIO
PRO CNAEO PLANCIO

1 I. Cum propter egregiam et singularem Cn.
Plancii, iudices, in mea salute custodienda fidem
tam multos et bonos viros eius honori viderem esse
fautores, capiebam animo non mediocrem volupta-
tem, quod, cuius officium mihi saluti fuisset, ei
meorum temporum memoriam suffragari videbam.
Cum autem audirem meos partim inimicos partim
invidos, huic accusationi esse fautores, eamdem-
que rem adversariam esse in iudicio Cn. Plancio,
quae in petitione fuisset adiutrix, dolebam,
iudices, et acerbe ferebam, si huius salus ob eam
ipsam causam esset infestior, quod is meam salutem
atque vitam sua benevolentia, praesidio, custodiaque
2 texisset. Nunc autem vester, iudices, conspectus
et consessus iste reficit et recreat mentem meam,
cum intueor et contemplor unumquemque vestrum.
Video enim hoc in numero neminem, cui mea salus
cara non fuerit; cuius non exstet in me summum

THE SPEECH ON BEHALF OF
GNAEUS PLANCIUS

[DELIVERED BEFORE A SPECIALLY NOMINATED JURY, 54]

I. When I saw so many patriotic gentlemen eagerly supporting the candidature of Gnaeus Plancius on account of the remarkable and exceptional loyalty he displayed towards me at a time of great personal danger, it gave me considerable pleasure to reflect that the memory of that crisis in my life was enlisted in favour of one whose services had been the means to my preservation. But when I heard that this accusation was being forwarded by those who were either enemies or detractors of myself, so that the same connexion which had aided my client in his pursuit of office was like to harm him when he was on his trial, I was grieved and bitterly disappointed, gentlemen, to think that his safety should be endangered simply and solely because my own safety, nay, my very life, had been secured by his goodwill and vigilant protection. But at the present moment, gentlemen, the sight of you assembled here bids me take fresh heart of grace ; for as I scan with careful eye each several member of the court, I see that there is no one of you who has not had my safety at heart, who has not laid me under the deepest obligations, and to whom I am not

meritum ; cui non sim obstrictus memoria beneficii
sempiterna. Itaque non extimesco ne Cn. Plancio
custodia meae salutis apud eos obsit, qui me ipsi
maxime salvum voluerunt, saepiusque, iudices,
mihi venit in mentem admirandum esse M.
Laterensem, hominem studiosissimum et dignitatis
et salutis meae, reum sibi hunc potissimum delegisse,
quam metuendum, ne vobis id ille magna ratione
3 fecisse videatur. Quamquam mihi non sumo tantum,
iudices, neque arrogo, ut Cn. Plancium suis erga me
meritis impunitatem consecutum putem. Nisi eius
integerrimam vitam, modestissimos mores, summam
fidem, continentiam, pietatem, innocentiam osten-
dero, nihil de poena recusabo. Sin omnia prae-
stitero quae sunt a bonis viris exspectanda, petam
a vobis, iudices, ut, cuius misericordia salus mea
custodita sit, ei vos vestram misericordiam, me
deprecante, tribuatis. Equidem ad reliquos labores,
quos in hac causa maiores suscipio, quam in ceteris,
etiam hanc molestiam assumo, quod mihi non
solum pro Cn. Plancio dicendum est, cuius ego
salutem non secus, ac meam, tueri debeo, sed etiam
pro me ipso, de quo accusatores plura paene quam
4 de re reoque dixerunt. II. Quamquam, iudices, si
quid est in me ipso ita reprehensum, ut id ab hoc

***

bound by the ineffaceable recollection of benefits received. I am, therefore, without any apprehension that Gnaeus Plancius' watchful care over my safety should prejudice him in the eyes of men who themselves earnestly desired my restitution, and the sentiment which haunts me is rather surprise that Marcus Laterensis, who has been so solicitous for my honour and my safety,[a] should have selected my client of all men for his attack, than fear lest you should decide that he has had cogent reasons for 3 the course he has adopted. Not, gentlemen, that I have so good a conceit of myself as to presume to fancy that my client's services to myself entitle him to exemption from all prosecution. If I fail to demonstrate to you the utter incorruptibility of his life, and the self-control that guides his actions, his unswerving devotion to honour and high principles, and the disinterested loyalty that animates all his relations, I shall take no exception to any penalty you may impose. But if I show him to be possessed of all those qualities which are to be looked for in a gentleman and a patriot, then, gentlemen, I shall ask you to bestow your clemency, at my intercession, upon one who by his own clemency shielded and succoured myself. The labours involved in my present advocacy are already greater than those of the general run of cases ; but I must go beyond these, and take upon myself the further burden of speaking, not only on behalf of Gnaeus Plancius, whose safety I am in duty bound to protect no less carefully than my own, but also on behalf of myself, for our opponents have said almost more about me 4 than about my client and his case. II. But, gentlemen, if any criticism has been passed upon myself

seiunctum sit, non me id magnopere conturbat:
non enim timeo, ne, quia perraro grati homines
reperiantur, idcirco, cum me nimium gratum illi
esse dicant, id mihi criminosum esse possit. Quae
vero ita sunt agitata ab illis, ut aut merita Cn.
Plancii erga me minora esse dicerent, quam a me
ipso praedicarentur ; aut, si essent summa, negarent
ea tamen ita magni, ut ego putarem, ponderis
apud vos esse debere. Haec mihi sunt tractanda,
iudices, et modice, ne quid ipse offendam ; et tum
denique, cum respondero criminibus, ne non tam
innocentia reus sua, quam recordatione meorum
temporum, defensus esse videatur.

5   Sed mihi in causa facili atque explicata, per-
difficilis, iudices, et lubrica defensionis ratio pro-
ponitur. Nam, si tantummodo mihi necesse esset
contra Laterensem dicere, tamen id ipsum esset
in tanto usu nostro tantaque amicitia molestum.
Vetus enim est lex illa iustae veraeque amicitiae,
quae mihi cum illo iam diu est, ut idem amici semper
velint ; neque est ullum certius amicitiae vinculum
quam consensus et societas consiliorum et volun-
tatum. Mihi autem non id est in hac re molestissi-
mum, contra illum dicere, sed multo illud magis,
quod in ea causa contra dicendum est, in qua quaedam
hominum ipsorum videtur facienda esse contentio.
410

in which he is not involved, that does not greatly trouble me. Gratitude is the rarest of human qualities, and I have no fear, therefore, lest the imputation of excessive gratitude to my client should be converted into a damaging charge against me. But there are two theories which our opponents have actively canvassed, and with which it is my duty to deal : first, that the services rendered to me by Gnaeus Plancius have been less than I made them out to be ; and second, that, were they never so great, they ought nevertheless to have no such great weight with you as I might suppose them to have. In dealing with them I must walk warily, that I may myself be void of offence ; and I must not deal with them at all until I have replied to the actual charges, that it may not appear that the case for the defence relies rather upon the recollection of my own crisis than upon my client's innocence.

5   The case, gentlemen, is simple and straightforward enough, but the lines of defence open to me are fraught with difficulties and pitfalls. If, in the first place, I were called upon merely to attack Laterensis, this course would in itself be an affront to our old associations of cordial friendship. Complete unity of aim is the traditional condition of genuine and sincere friendship, and this has been the relation in which I have for long stood towards my opponent ; and indeed there is no surer bond of friendship than the sympathetic union of thought and inclination. But although it is painful for me to choose the course of attacking my friend, it is still more painful that the case in which I am called upon to do so is one in which a comparison of individual qualities

6 seems to be inevitable. For there is one question

6 Quaerit enim Laterensis, atque hoc uno maxime
urget, qua se virtute, qua laude Plancius, qua
dignitate superarit. Ita, si cedo illius ornamentis,
quae multa et magna sunt, non solum huius
dignitatis iactura facienda est, sed etiam largitionis
recipienda suspicio est. Sin hunc illi antepono,
contumeliosa habenda est oratio, et dicendum est
id, quod ille me flagitat, Laterensem a Plancio
dignitate esse superatum. Ita aut amicissimi
hominis existimatio offendenda est, si illam accusa-
tionis conditionem sequar, aut optime de me meriti
salus deserenda.

III. Sed ego, Laterensis, caecum me et prae-
cipitem ferri confitear in causa, si te aut a Plancio,
aut ab ullo, dignitate potuisse superari dixero.
Itaque discedam ab ea contentione, ad quam tu
me vocas, et veniam ad illam, ad quam me causa
7 ipsa deducit. Quid ? tu magistratuum [1] iudicem
putas esse populum ? Fortasse nonnumquam est.
Utinam vero semper esset ! Sed est perraro, et
si quando est, in iis magistratibus est mandandis,
quibus salutem suam committi putat : his levioribus
comitiis, diligentia, et gratia petitorum honos paritur,

[1] *Holden foll. Müller* : in magistratibus *Madvig.*

---

[a] The argument of this passage may be summarized
thus : " To draw comparisons between yourself and Plancius
would be not only rash, but also irrelevant. Election to
these minor offices does not depend on the possession of
superior endowments, and therefore the fact that Plancius
was elected aedile over your head does not suggest either
that he is a better man than you, or that the people did you
an injustice."

which Laterensis propounds, and for an answer to which he presses with peculiar urgency; it is the question by what moral qualities, by what superiority in distinction or reputation, Plancius surpasses himself. Consequently, if I yield the palm to my opponent's endowments (and they are beyond question many and great), I must not merely jettison my client's honour, but I must lay myself open to the suspicion of corrupt collusion; if, on the other hand, I put the claims of my client before those of my friend, my speech must be devoted to vituperation, and I must state, since he importunes me for an answer, that the merits of Laterensis are surpassed by those of Plancius. So I am faced with the alternative of either damaging the reputation of a dear friend, if I pursue the line to which his speech has prompted me, or of betraying the cause of one to whom I am under a deep obligation.

III. But if I, Laterensis, assert that in point of reputation you may have been surpassed by Plancius, or indeed by any one, I should virtually confess myself guilty of blind precipitancy in my conduct of the case.[a] Avoiding, therefore, the comparison to which you challenge me, I shall have recourse to another, 7 which lies directly in my path. I ask you, do you consider the people to be competent critics of the merits of their magistrates? Sometimes no doubt they are. Would that they always were! But on rare occasions they are competent, and those occasions arise when they fill by their election those offices to which they consider that their safety is being entrusted. But in the less important elections, with which we are dealing now, success is won by the personal efforts and popularity of the

non iis ornamentis, quae esse in te videmus. Nam, quod ad populum pertinet, semper dignitatis iniquus iudex est, qui aut invidet, aut favet. Quamquam nihil potes in te, Laterensis, constituere, quod sit proprium laudis tuae, quin id tibi sit commune cum Plancio.

8 Sed hoc totum agetur alio loco ; nunc tantum disputo de iure populi ; qui et potest et solet nonnumquam dignos praeterire ; nec, si a populo praeteritus est, quem non oportuit, a iudicibus condemnandus est, qui praeteritus non est. Nam si ita esset, quod patres apud maiores nostros tenere non potuerunt, ut reprehensores essent comitiorum, id haberent iudices vel quod multo etiam minus est ferendum. Tum enim magistratum non gerebat is, qui ceperat, si patres auctores non erant facti : nunc postulatur a vobis, ut eius exsilio, qui creatus sit, iudicium populi Romani reprehendatis. Itaque quoniam, qua nolui, ianua sum ingressus in causam, sperare videor, tantum afuturam esse orationem meam a minima suspicione offensionis tuae, te ut potius obiurgem, quod iniquum in discrimen adducas dignitatem tuam, quam ut ego eam ulla contumelia coner attingere.

9 IV. Tu continentiam, tu industriam, tu animum

candidates, and not by the possession of those endowments which so patently belong to you. For in popular politics, he who is actuated either by prejudice or by partisanship will always be but a partial judge of merit ; not that I would admit, Laterensis, that you can lay claim to a monopoly of any distinction which Plancius does not share with you.

I shall treat of this matter in its entirety elsewhere ; for the present I am dealing solely with the right of the people, who are both empowered and frequently accustomed to pass by men of merit ; and it does not follow that if a candidate has been passed over by the people, who ought not to have been so passed over, he who has not been passed over ought to be condemned by a jury. For if this were so, our juries would virtually possess a power which in the days of our ancestors the patricians were unable to retain, the power of passing their censure upon the elections ; or they would possess a power even more intolerable, for in the old days the man who had been elected to an office did not enter upon it if the patricians withheld their assent ; whereas what is demanded of you to-day is that, by your condemnation of the people's choice, you should pass a stricture upon the people's wisdom. So, since I have entered into the case by a door by which I was reluctant to enter it, I think I have nevertheless a hope that, so far from incurring the least suspicion of wounding your susceptibilities by my speech, I shall rather take you to task for submitting your merits to an invidious ordeal than endeavour to taint them by any disparaging reference.

IV. Do you consider that when you failed to be

in rem publicam, tu virtutem, tu innocentiam, tu
fidem, tu labores tuos, quod aedilis non sis factus,
fractos esse et abiectos et repudiatos putas ? Vide
tandem, Laterensis, quantum ego a te dissentiam.
Si, medius fidius, decem soli essent in civitate viri
boni, sapientes, iusti, graves, qui te indignum
aedilitate iudicavissent, gravius de te iudicatum
putarem, quam est hoc, quod tu metuis, ne a
populo iudicatum esse videatur. Non enim comitiis
iudicat semper populus, sed movetur plerumque
gratia ; cedit precibus ; facit eos, a quibus est
maxime ambitus. Denique, etiam si iudicat, non
dilectu aliquo aut sapientia ducitur ad iudicandum,
sed impetu nonnumquam, et quadam etiam temeri-
tate. Non est enim consilium in vulgo, non ratio,
non discrimen, non diligentia : semperque sapientes
ea, quae populus fecisset, ferenda, non semper
laudanda duxerunt. Quare cum te aedilem fieri
oportuisse dicis, populi culpam, non competitoris,
accusas.

10   Ut fueris dignior, quam Plancius : (de quo ipso
ita tecum contendam paullo post, ut conservem
dignitatem tuam) sed, ut fueris dignior, non
competitor, a quo es victus, sed populus, a quo es
praeteritus, in culpa est. In quo primum illud

elected aedile, your self-control, your energy, your patriotism, your courage, your integrity, your honour, and your devotion to duty were thereby frustrated, ignored, and tossed aside with scorn ?   Mark, I pray you, Laterensis, how far I disagree with you, if such be your opinion.   I protest that, were there but ten only among our citizens who, with sound political views and endowed with wisdom, justice, and sobriety, had counted you unworthy of the aedileship, I should attach greater weight to such a pronouncement on you than to this, which you fear may seem to be a deliberate verdict passed by the people. Deliberate verdicts are not invariably arrived at in popular elections, which are often guided by partiality and swayed by prayers ; the people promotes those who court it most assiduously ; and even if after all it does give a deliberate verdict, that verdict is determined, not by a discriminating wisdom, but frequently by impulse and a spirit of headstrong caprice.   For the multitude is a stranger to deliberation, to reason, to discernment, and to patient scrutiny ; and all great thinkers have held that acquiescence, but not always approval, should be accorded to the acts of the people.   Wherefore, in saying that you ought yourself to have been appointed aedile, you lay the blame upon the people, and not upon your opponent.

10   Let us assume that your merit was greater than that of Plancius.   I shall shortly join issue with you on this very point, without any disparagement to your reputation.   However, granting this assumption, it is not the candidate who defeated you, but the people who passed you over, that is to blame. Herein you must bear in mind, first, that the elec-

debes putare, comitiis, praesertim aediliciis, studium
esse populi, non iudicium ; eblandita illa, non
enucleata esse suffragia ; eos, qui suffragium ferant,
quid cuique ipsi debeant, considerare saepius, quam,
quid cuique a re publica debeatur   Sin autem mavis
esse iudicium, non tibi id rescindendum est, sed
ferendum.   Male iudicavit populus.   At iudicavit.
Non debuit.   At potuit.   Non fero.   At multi
clarissimi et sapientissimi cives tulerunt.   Est enim
haec conditio liberorum populorum, praecipueque
huius principis populi, et omnium gentium domini
ac victoris, posse suffragiis vel dare, vel detrahere,
quod velit, cuique : nostrum est autem, nostrum,
qui in hac tempestate populi iactemur ac fluctibus,
ferre modice populi voluntates, allicere alienas,
retinere partas, placare turbatas : honores si magni
non putemus, non servire populo : sin eos expetamus,
non defatigari supplicando.

V. Venio iam ad ipsius populi partes, ut illius
contra te oratione potius, quam mea, disputem.
Qui si tecum congrediatur, et, si una voce loqui
possit, haec dicat : " Ego tibi, Laterensis, Plancium
non anteposui : sed, cum essetis aeque boni viri,
meum beneficium ad eum potius detuli, qui a me

---

a *Enucleata,* literally "stripped of the husk," hence
metaphorically, "given without the husk of bad motives."

tions, and above all those of the aediles, are the expression of the party feeling of the populace, not of their maturer judgement; their votes are wheedled out of them, rather than honestly won *a* ; the voters too often consider what they themselves owe to a particular candidate rather than what is due to him from the state. But should you prefer to consider the elections the expression of deliberate judgement, you must acquiesce in that expression, and not reverse 11 it. Its judgement was depraved, you say. Yes, but it was an undoubted judgement. It had no moral right so to judge. No, but it had a legal right. You refuse to acquiesce in it. But it has been acquiesced in in the past by many citizens of great distinction and wisdom. For it is the privilege of free peoples, and above all of this people, whose conquests have given it paramount sway over the whole world, that by its votes it can bestow or take away its offices as it likes. We too have our part to play; tossed as we are upon the stormy billows of popular favour, we must bear contentedly with the people's will, win it to ourselves when it is estranged, grapple it to us when we have won it, and pacify it when it is in turmoil. If we set no great store by its awards, we are not called upon to do it homage; but if we set our hearts upon them, we must not grow weary in courting its favour.

12 V. Let me view the matter now from the standpoint of the people itself, and argue with you through its mouth rather than my own. Could it meet and hold discourse with you now, it would say, " I have not preferred Plancius to you, Laterensis, but, since there was no choice between you as good patriots, I chose to bestow my favours upon the man who

41)

contenderat, quam ad eum, qui mihi non nimis
submisse supplicarat " : respondebis, credo, te,
splendore et vetustate familiae fretum, non valde
ambiendum putasse. At vero te ille ad sua instituta,
suorumque maiorum exempla revocabit ; semper
se dicet rogari voluisse, semper sibi supplicari ; se
M. Seium, qui ne equestrem quidem splendorem
incolumem a calamitate iudicii retinere potuisset,
homini nobilissimo, innocentissimo, eloquentissimo,
M. Pisoni, praetulisse ; praeposuisse se Q. Catulo,
summa in familia nato, sapientissimo et sanctissimo
viro, non dico C. Serranum, stultissimum hominem :
fuit enim tamen nobilis : non C. Fimbriam, novum
hominem : fuit enim et animi satis magni, et consilii :
sed Cn. Manlium, non solum ignobilem, verum sine
virtute, sine ingenio, vita etiam contempta ac
13 sordida. " Desiderarunt te, inquit, oculi mei, cum
tu esses Cyrenis. Me enim, quam socios, tua frui
virtute malebam ; et quo plus intererat, eo plus
aberat a me, quum te non videbam. Deinde sitien-
tem me virtutis tuae deseruisti ac dereliquisti.
Coeperas enim petere tribunatum plebis temporibus
iis, quae istam eloquentiam et virtutem requirebant : quam petitionem quum reliquisses, si hoc

---

^a *i.e.* Laterensis went to Cyrene as pro-quaestor, thus
keeping away from Rome at a time when his services were
needed there.
^b In 59, when Caesar and Bibulus were consuls.

importuned me for them, rather than upon the man
who would not demean himself to the homage of a
supple knee." I imagine that your answer would be
that your reliance upon an ancient and illustrious
lineage had led you to believe that an energetic
canvass was unnecessary. But the people, on the
other hand, would retort by reminding you of its
established usage and ancestral precedent ; it would
point out that it has always desired to be asked, and
to be approached in suppliant guise ; that it gave
preference to Marcus Seius, who could not protect
untarnished from the sentence of the courts the
lustre even of his equestrian position, over the noble,
incorruptible, and eloquent Marcus Piso ; that to
Quintus Catulus, in spite of his lofty birth, his great
sagacity, and his exemplary character, it preferred,
I will not say Gaius Serranus, for he, though a fool,
was yet a noble, nor Gaius Fimbria, for he, though
of a family unknown in public life, was yet endowed
with considerable force of character and prudence—
it preferred Gnaeus Manlius, who was not merely
low-born, but low-principled, a man of no parts,
whose life was degraded and despicable into the
bargain. "My eyes searched for you in vain," it
says, "when you were at Cyrene.[a] I had rather
that the benefit of your virtues should be at my
disposal than at that of my allies, and, when I saw
you not, my sense of loss was bitter in proportion to
the value to me of what I had lost ; and then, though
I was athirst for your virtues, you abandoned me
and left me to my own devices. You undertook
your candidature for the tribunate of the plebs at
a crisis [b] which called out for eloquence and honesty
such as yours ; if your abandonment of that candi-

indicasti, tanta in tempestate te gubernare non
posse, de virtute tua dubitavi : si nolle, de voluntate.
Sin, quod magis intelligo, temporibus te aliis reser-
vasti, ego quoque, inquiet populus Romanus, ad ea
te tempora revocavi, ad quae tu te ipse servaras.
Pete igitur eum magistratum, in quo mihi magnae
utilitati esse possis ; aediles quicumque erunt, iidem
mihi sunt ludi parati : tribuni plebis, permagni
interest, qui sint. Quare aut redde mihi quod
ostenderas : aut, si, quod mea minus interest, id
te magis forte delectat, reddam tibi istam aedilitatem, etiam negligenter petenti. Sed amplissimos
honores ut pro dignitate tua consequare, condiscas,
censeo, mihi paullo diligentius supplicare.''

4 VI. Haec populi oratio est ; mea vero, Laterensis,
haec : Quare victus sis, non debere iudicem quaerere,
modo ne largitione sis victus. Nam si, quotiescumque
praeteritus erit is, qui non debuerit praeteriri, toties
oportebit, eum, qui factus erit, condemnari, nihil
iam est, quod populo supplicetur ; nihil, quod
diribitio, nihil, quod renuntiatio suffragiorum ex-
spectetur ; simul ut, qui sint professi, videro, dicam :
5 hic familia consulari est, ille praetoria ; reliquos
video esse equestri loco : sunt omnes sine macula,

---

a The conduct of the public games was one of the chief
functions of the aediles.
b The praetor C. Alfius Flavus.

dature was an expression of your sense of inability to guide the helm of the state in such troubled waters, I had doubts of your capacity ; if it intimated your reluctance, I doubted of your patriotism ; but if, as I find it easier to believe, you did but reserve yourself for a later crisis, I too "—so the Roman people will say—" have recalled you to face that crisis with a view to which you had reserved yourself. Seek, then, an office wherein your services may be of great value to me ; whoever may be the aediles, the games ^{a} organized for me are the same ; but the personality of the tribunes of the plebs is a matter of paramount importance to me. Wherefore, either let me realize the hopes I once reposed in you, or, if your preference is for a course of meaner value to myself, I will bestow upon you that aedileship for which you apply so perfunctorily ; but, if you would attain to those high honours which your merit deserves, I suggest that you learn to do me a more earnest homage."

VI. This is the appeal of the people, Laterensis. But *I* would reason with you thus. It is not the duty of the president of the court ^{b} to investigate the causes of your defeat, provided that it was not compassed by bribery. For if an elected magistrate is to be condemned upon all occasions when his fellow-candidate has been undeservedly passed over, then there is no longer any reason why we should supplicate for popular favour, or why we should wait for the telling of the votes or the statement of the poll. I have but to read the list of candidates and I shall say, " This man is of consular, that man of praetorian family ; I notice that the remainder belong to the equestrian order. The records of them all are

sunt aeque boni viri atque integri ; sed servari
necesse est gradus : cedat consulari generi prae-
torium, nec contendat cum praetorio nomine equester
locus. Sublata sunt studia, exstinctae suffragationes,
nullae contentiones, nulla libertas populi in mandandis magistratibus, nulla exspectatio suffragiorum : nihil, ut plerumque evenit, praeter opinionem
accidet : nulla erit posthac varietas comitiorum. Sin
hoc persaepe accidit, ut et factos aliquos et non
factos esse miremur : si campus, atque illae undae
comitiorum, ut mare profundum et immensum, sic
effervescunt quodam quasi aestu, ut ad alios accedant,
ab aliis autem ·recedant : in tanto nos impetu
studiorum et motu temeritatis, modum aliquem, et
consilium, et rationem requiremus ?

16   Quare noli me ad contentionem vestrum vocare,
Laterensis. Etenim si populo grata est tabella,
quae frontes aperit hominum, mentes tegit, datque
eam libertatem, ut, quod velint, faciant, promittant
autem, quod rogentur, cur tu id in iudicio, ut
fiat, exprimis, quod non fit in campo ? Hic, quam
ille, dignior : perquam grave est dictu. Quomodo
igitur est aequius ? Sic credo : quod agitur ; quod
satis est iudici : hic factus est. Cur iste potius,

untarnished; all are equally good men and true, but the degrees must be maintained; so let the praetorian rank give place to the consular, and let not the equestrian order compete with the scion of a praetorian stock." Away with partisanship, have done with the hustings, let us have no more contested elections, no more freedom of the people to bestow offices, no more suspense to hear how the voting has gone; and you will find that the usual element of surprise will vanish, and the elections will lose the charm of their uncertainty. But if, on the other hand, it commonly happens that we are surprised at the election of some and the non-election of others; if, like the fathomless and infinite ocean, the troubled waters of the voting-place and the popular assemblies seethe with the impulse of inscrutable tides, so that here they lift and float a bark upon their bosom, and here strand another high and dry; shall we, amid the ebb and flow of party spirit and caprice, be disappointed that we cannot find therein system or deliberation or cool logic?

16 Do not, therefore, Laterensis, challenge me to institute a comparison between you. For if the people cherishes its privileges of voting by ballot, which allows a man to wear a smooth brow while it cloaks the secrets of his heart, and which leaves him free to act as he chooses, while he gives any promise he may be asked to give, why do you insist that the courts should determine what the hustings cannot? To say that one has greater merit than another is an exceedingly offensive way of putting it. How then may we put it more fairly? Surely thus: he was elected; this statement goes straight to the heart of the matter, and is all the judge wishes to know.

quam ego ? Vel nescio, vel non dico, vel denique, quod mihi gravissimum esset si dicerem, sed impune tamen deberem dicere : Non recte. Nam quid assequerere,[1] si illa extrema defensione uterer : Populum, quod voluisset, fecisse, non quod debuisset ?

17 VII. Quid ? si populi quoque factum defendo, Laterensis, et doceo, Cn. Plancium non obrepsisse ad honorem, sed eo venisse cursu, qui semper patuerit hominibus ortis hoc nostro equestri loco, possumne eripere orationi tuae contentionem vestrum, quae tractari sine contumelia non potest, et te ad causam aliquando crimenque deducere ? Si, quod equitis Romani filius est, inferior esse debuit : omnes tecum equitum Romanorum filii petiverunt. Nihil dico amplius. Hoc tamen miror, cur tu huic potissimum irascare, qui longissime a te afuit. Equidem, si quando, ut fit, iactor in turba, non illum accuso, qui est in summa sacra via, cum ego ad Fabium fornicem* impellor : sed eum, qui in me ipsum incurrit atque incidit. Tu neque Q. Pedio, forti viro, succenses, neque huic A. Plotio,

---

[1] *Manutius corr. for* assequerer MSS.

---

* At south-east end of Forum ; built 121.

Why the defendant rather than myself, you ask? Perhaps I do not know; perhaps I do not choose to say; or perhaps I might suggest that he was elected by corrupt means—a suggestion most damaging to my client, but which ought not to endanger his chances in this court. But supposing I were to adopt so extreme a line of defence as to urge that the act of the people was prompted by caprice rather than conscience, how, pray, would you stand to gain by this?

7 VII. But put the case that I justify even this act of the people, Laterensis, and demonstrate that Plancius, so far from insinuating himself into office, attained to it by a path which has for ever been open to those who, like myself, are born of equestrian families, can I by this means detach you from the comparison between yourself and my client which was the main topic of your speech, and which we cannot pursue without invidious personalities? Can I pin you at last to the question at issue and the charge against Plancius? If the fact that he is the son of a Roman knight ought to have put him at a disadvantage to yourself, I would point out that your fellow-candidates were to a man sons of Roman knights. I will press the point no further; but I am surprised that you should have picked out for your resentment the candidate who most of all out-distanced you in the poll. If, as may very well happen, I am jostled in a crowd, I do not, when pushed near the arch of Fabius,[a] accuse somebody standing at the top of the Sacred Way, but rather the man who violently collides against my own person. To point my moral, you do not vent your wrath upon the gallant Quintus Pedius, nor upon my accomplished

427

ornatissimo homini, familiari meo : et ab eo, qui
hos dimovit, potius, quam ab iis, qui in te ipsum
incubuerunt, te depulsum putas.

18   Sed tamen haec tibi est prima cum Plancio generis
vestri familiaeque contentio, qua abs te vincitur.
Cur enim non confitear, quod necesse est ? Sed
non hic magis, quam ego a meis competitoribus,
et alias, et in consulatus petitione vincebar. Sed
vide, ne haec ipsa, quae despicis, huic suffragata
sint. Sic enim conferamus. Est tuum nomen
utraque familia consulare. Num dubitas igitur,
quin omnes, qui favent nobilitati, qui id putant
esse pulcherrimum, qui imaginibus, qui nominibus
vestris ducuntur, te aedilem fecerint ? Equidem
non dubito. Sed, si parum multi sunt, qui nobili-
tatem ament : ' num ista est nostra culpa ?

      Etenim ad caput et ad fontem utriusque generis
19 veniamus. VIII. Tu es ex municipio antiquissimo
Tusculano, ex quo plurimae familiae sunt consulares,
in quibus est etiam Iuventia—tot e reliquis municipiis omnibus non sunt—hic est e praefectura
Atinati, non tam prisca, non tam honorata, non
tam suburbana. Quantum interesse vis ad rationem

---

      [a] Descendants of those who had held curule magistracies
had the right of displaying busts of their ancestors in their
hall (*atrium*).
      [b] 15 miles south-east of Rome.
      [c] Extreme south-east of Latium ; *praefecturae* were
governed by officers sent annually by the *praetor urbanus*.

friend Aulus Plotius ; but you choose to impute your humiliation to the man who pushed these out of his path, rather than to those who elbowed you personally.

However, the first comparison you make between yourself and Plancius is in the matter of birth and family. Here (for why should I not frankly admit what is obvious ?) you have the better of him. But you have the better of him no more than my fellow-candidates had the better of me, when I stood for the consulship and for other offices besides. And consider whether the very deficiencies which you despise in him did not help him. Let us look at it in this way. You are of consular rank both on your father's and your mother's side. Can you then hesitate to believe that your election to the aedile-ship was supported by all those who uphold the claims of birth, and who count it their chief pride that they do so, and by all those who are lured by the glamour of your ancestral busts [a] and your impressive titles ? Personally, I cannot doubt it. If, then, the lovers of birth are less numerous than you would have them, is my client to be blamed for that ?

But let us pursue this question of birth to the fountain-head. VIII. You are a native of the ancient corporate town of Tusculum,[b] which numbers among its inhabitants more families of consular rank (among them that of the Juventii) than all the other corporations put together ; while my client is from the prefecture of Atina,[c] which is neither so ancient, nor so distinguished in its sons, nor so accessible from the city. What weight as regards electoral prospects would you wish to be assigned to this

429

petendi ? Primum utrum magis favere putas Atinates,
an Tusculanos, suis ? alteri (scire enim hoc propter
vicinitatem facile possum) cum huius ornatissimi
atque optimi viri, Cn. Saturnini, patrem aedilem,
cum praetorem viderunt, quod primus ille non modo
in eam familiam, sed etiam in praefecturam illam, sellam curulem attulisset, mirandum in modum
laetati sunt ; alteros (credo, quia refertum est
municipium consularibus ; nam malevolos non esse
certo scio), numquam intellexi vehementius suorum
20 honore laetari. Habemus hoc nos : habent nostra
municipia. Quid ego de me, de fratre meo loquar ?
quorum honoribus agri, prope dicam, ipsi montesque
faverunt. Num quando vides Tusculanum aliquem
de M. Catone illo, in omni virtute principe, num de
Ti. Coruncanio, municipe suo, num de tot Fulviis
gloriari ? verbum nemo facit. At, in quemcumque
Arpinatem incideris, etiamsi nolis, erit tamen tibi,
fortasse etiam de nobis aliquid, aliquid certe de C.
Mario audiendum. Primum igitur hic habuit studia
suorum ardentia : tu tanta, quanta in hominibus
21 iam saturatis honoribus esse potuerunt. Deinde
tui municipes, sunt illi quidem splendidissimi

---

^a Offices of consul, praetor, and curule aedile.

difference ? Which, in the first place, do you think are the more ardent supporters of their fellow-townsmen—the people of Atina or those of Tusculum ? The former (as I am enabled to know from being a near neighbour of theirs) showed intense delight when they saw the father of the excellent and distinguished Gnaeus Saturninus, who is with us in the court, appointed first aedile and then praetor, because he was the first to introduce the curule *a* dignity not merely into his family, but into the prefecture ; while I have never gathered that the latter exhibit much enthusiasm over distinctions conferred upon their fellow-citizens. This, I imagine, is owing to the fact that ex-consuls elbow one another in their streets ; I am confident that it is not to be imputed to lack of generosity. Speaking for myself and my own township, I may certainly say that we exhibit these traits of public spirit. Need I refer to my own case or to that of my brother ? I might almost say that our distinctions have been acclaimed by our very fields and hills. But do you ever see a Tusculan boasting of the great Marcus Cato, prince of all virtues, or of their fellow-townsman Tiberius Coruncanius, or of all the great who have borne the name of Fulvius ? Never a word. But whenever you come across a man of Arpinum, you will have to listen, willy-nilly, to some fragment of gossip, possibly even about me, but certainly about Gaius Marius. So my client, in the first place, was backed by the ardent partisanship of his townsfolk, while yours backed you no more than was to be expected of men who are already surfeited with distinctions. In the second place, your fellow-burgesses, highly distinguished

homines, sed tamen pauci, si quidem cum Atinatibus conferantur. Huius praefectura plena virorum fortissimorum, sic ut nulla tota Italia frequentior dici possit. Quam quidem nunc multitudinem videtis, iudices, in squalore et luctu supplicem vobis. Hi tot equites Romani, tot tribuni aerarii (nam plebem a iudicio dimisimus, quae cuncta comitiis adfuit), quid roboris, quid dignitatis huius petitioni attulerunt? Non enim tribum Teretinam, de qua dicam alio loco, sed dignitatem, sed oculorum coniectum, sed solidam et robustam et assiduam frequentiam praebuerunt; nostra municipia coniunctione etiam vicinitatis vehementer moventur.

22   IX. Omnia, quae dico de Plancio, dico expertus in nobis. Sumus enim finitimi Atinatibus. Laudanda est, vel etiam amanda vicinitas, retinens veterem illum officii morem, non infuscata malevolentia, non assueta mendaciis, non fucosa, non fallax, non erudita artificio simulationis vel suburbano, vel etiam urbano. Nemo Arpinas non Plancio studuit, nemo Soranus, nemo Casinas, nemo Aquinas. Totus ille tractus celeberrimus, Venafranus, Allifanus, tota denique nostra illa aspera, et montuosa,

---

ᵃ In early times plebeian collectors of war-tax; later, a distinct order based on property qualification and ranking below *equites*.
ᵇ In which the people of Atina voted.
Cicero's birthplace.

though they undoubtedly are, are a mere handful
compared with those of Atina ; while my client's
prefecture is packed with high-hearted gentlemen,
in such numbers as cannot be demonstrably surpassed in any other in all Italy. You see them
thronging this court to-day, gentlemen of the jury ;
they have come in the garb and guise of mourners
to appeal for your mercy. Must not so many
Roman knights, so many tribunes of the treasury,[a]—
not to mention the proletariate, who were present
to a man at the election, and who have been dismissed from this court,—must not all these have
lent vast material and moral support to my client's
candidature ? They brought him not, indeed, the
Teretine [b] tribe, of which I shall speak later, but they
made him a figure of importance, the cynosure of
all eyes, and enlisted for him a compact, vigorous,
and indefatigable body of adherents. For neigh-
bourly sympathy often provokes great displays of
feeling in our municipal towns.

IX. All that I say about Plancius I say from
personal experience ; for we at Arpinum [c] are neighbours of the people of Atina. Neighbourliness is a
quality that demands our commendation, nay, our
love, for it keeps alive the old-world spirit of kindliness, it is uncoloured by the sinister hues of petty
spite, it lives in no atmosphere of falsehood, it is
tricked out by no hypocritical pretensions, it is unschooled in that studied counterfeiting of emotions
characteristic of the suburbs and even of the city.
There was no one at Arpinum, at Sora, at Casinum,
at Aquinum, but was Plancius' adherent. Thickly-
populated districts of Venafrum and Allifae, and,
in a word, all our rugged countryside, which holds

et fidelis, et simplex, et fautrix suorum regio, se
huius honore ornari, se augeri dignitate arbitrabatur.
Iisdemque nunc ex municipiis adsunt equites Romani
publice, cum testimonio : nec minore nunc sunt
sollicitudine, quam tum erant studio. Etenim est
gravius spoliari fortunis quam non augeri dignitate.
23 Ergo ut alia in te erant illustriora, Laterensis, quae
tibi maiores tui reliquerant, sic te Plancius hoc
non solum municipii, verum etiam vicinitatis genere
vincebat. Nisi forte te Labicana, aut Gabina, aut
Bovillana vicinitas adiuvabat. Quibus e municipiis
vix iam, qui carnem Latinis petant, reperiuntur.
Adiungamus, si vis, id, quod tu huic obesse etiam
putas, patrem publicanum : qui ordo quanto adiu-
mento sit in honore, quis nescit ? Flos enim equitum
Romanorum, ornamentum civitatis, firmamentum
24 rei publicae, publicanorum ordine continetur. Quis
est igitur, qui neget, ordinis eius studium fuisse in
honore Plancii singulare ? Neque iniuria ; vel quod
erat pater is, qui est princeps iam diu publicanorum ;
vel quod is ab sociis unice diligebatur ; vel quod

---

a P.'s conviction would entail banishment and a fine.
b The ancient festival of the cities of the Latin League.
c See note on *De har. resp.* Chap. XXVIII. Contrast
the tone with which the *publicani* are spoken of here
with that which was prevalent in the provinces, *e.g.* Pales-
tine (see the Gospels, *passim*), and with our own feeling
about tax-collectors. It must be remembered that *Italy* was
not taxed.

among its hills hearts loyal and unaffected and staunchly true to the bond of kinship, counted my client's distinction an honour, his promotion a compliment, to itself. Roman knights have come from these same townships and are here to-day to present their official testimony, and the suspense they feel for Plancius now is only equalled by their zeal for him then ; for indeed deprivation of property *a* is a more bitter fate than failure to win 3 promotion to public office. In those blessings which your ancestors had bequeathed to you, Laterensis, you outshone him, but, to balance this, Plancius conquered you in virtue of the loftier spirit that animated not only his township, but all the country round ; unless, indeed, we are to suppose that you were assisted by your neighbours at Labicum or Gabii or Bovillae, communities which to-day can scarcely find envoys to send for their share of the victims at the Latin Festival.*b* Let us add, if you will, to my client's advantages the fact that his father was a tax-farmer, a fact which you consider to be an actual slur upon him. Who does not know the value of the services of that profession in the pursuit of office ? For the flower of the Roman knighthood, the ornament of our society and the backbone of our political life, is to be found among 24 the body of tax-farmers.*c* Who, accordingly, will be so bold as to deny that its influence in forwarding Plancius' candidature was most marked ? It was only right that it should have been so, whether we consider the fact that his father has, for some time, been a director of a tax-farming company, or that his partners were singularly attached to him, or that he was a most indefatigable canvasser, or that it

diligentissime rogabat ; vel quia pro filio supplicabat ;
vel quia huius ipsius in illum ordinem summa officia
quaesturae tribunatusque constabant ; vel quod
illi in hoc ornando ordinem se ornare, et consulere
liberis suis arbitrabantur.

X. Aliquid praeterea,—timide dico, sed tamen
dicendum est :—non enim opibus, non invidiosa
gratia, non potentia vix ferenda, sed commemoratione
beneficii, sed misericordia, sed precibus aliquid
attulimus etiam nos. Appellavi populum tributim,
submisi me et supplicavi ; ultro mehercule se mihi
etiam offerentes, ultro pollicentes rogavi. Valuit
25 causa rogandi, non gratia. Nec, si vir amplissimus,
cui nihil est, quod roganti concedi non iure possit,
de aliquo, ut dicis, non impetravit, ego sum arrogans,
quod me valuisse dico. Nam, ut omittam illud,
quod ego pro eo laborabam, qui valebat ipse per
sese, rogatio ipsa semper est gratiosissima quae
est officio necessitudinis coniuncta maxime. Neque
enim ego sic rogabam, ut petere viderer, quia
familiaris esset meus, quia vicinus, quia huius

---

a Pompey.

b T. Ampius Balbus (trib. 63), who proposed that Pompey
should be allowed to wear triumphal insignia at the games.

was on a son's behalf that he courted the electorate, or that my client's own great services to the equestrian order during his quaestorship and tribunate were universally recognized, or that the members of that order thought that an honour paid to Plancius was an honour to their own body and a means of securing advancement for their children.

X. Some small contribution also—I mention the fact with diffidence, though mention it I must—was made even by myself, a contribution which took the form, not of material assistance or of invidious influence or of an odious personal ascendancy, but of adverting to the benefits he had conferred upon me, of awakening sympathetic interest, and of prayers in his behalf. I appealed to the people tribe by tribe ; I demeaned myself to becoming a suppliant. My suit was unnecessary, for spontaneous offers and promises were heaped upon me. It was the motive of the plea, not the personality of the pleader, that carried weight ; and if a certain gentleman *a* whose high standing entitled him to the concession of his every request failed, as you point out, to obtain his suit on behalf of one particular client,*b* it does not necessarily follow that I am presumptuous, because I say that my efforts bore fruit. For, apart from the fact that the man on whose behalf I was exerting myself was not dependent upon external assistance, the mere solicitation of a vote always creates the most favourable impression, when it is most directly actuated by the claims of friendship. And indeed my own method of solicitation was such as to suggest that I was canvassing for him, not because he was my friend or my neighbour, nor because I had been on very intimate

parente semper plurimum essem usus, sed ut
quasi parenti, et custodi salutis meae. Non potentia
mea, sed causa rogationis fuit gratiosa. Nemo
mea restitutione laetatus est, nemo iniuria doluit,
cui non huius in me misericordia grata fuerit.
26 Etenim, si ante reditum meum Cn. Plancio se vulgo
viri boni, cum hic tribunatum peteret, ultro offere-
bant : cui nomen meum absentis honori fuisset, ei
meas praesentis preces non putas profuisse ? An
Minturnenses coloni, quod C. Marium e civili ferro,
atque ex impiis manibus eripuerunt, quod tecto
receperunt, quod fessum inedia fluctibusque recrea-
runt, quod viaticum congesserunt, quod navigium
dederunt, quod eum linquentem terram eam, quam
servaverat, lacrymis, votis ominibusque [1] prosecuti
sunt, aeterna in laude versantur : Plancio, quod me
vel vi pulsum, vel ratione cedentem receperit, iuverit,
custodierit ; his, et senatui, populoque Romano,
ut haberent, quem reducerent, conservarit : honori
hanc fidem, misericordiam, virtutem fuisse miraris ?
27   XI. Vitia mehercule Cn. Plancii, res eae, de
quibus dixi, tegere potuerunt : ne tu, in ea vita, de
qua iam dicam, tot et tanta adiumenta huic honori
fuisse mirere.   Hic est enim, qui adolescentulus cum
A. Torquato profectus in Africam, sic ab illo gravis-

---

[1] votis omnibus lacrimisque *Müller*: lacrimis votisque
omnibus MSS.

---

[a] Extreme south of Latium ; in 88 Marius, driven from
Rome, took ship for Africa, but was compelled to land and
conceal himself among the marshes at the mouth of the Liris,
near Minturnae.

terms with his father, but rather because he was, in a sense, the only begetter and saviour of my life. It was no personal ascendancy, but the motive of my appeal, that won men's hearts. No one was glad at my restoration or grieved at my wrongs who did not feel gratitude to Plancius because he had shown me pity. And if before my return men of sound views came forward on all hands and spontaneously offered their services to Plancius, can you believe that my presence and prayers availed him naught, when my name, even in my absence, was a recommendation to him? The colonists of Minturnae [a] rescued Gaius Marius from those traitorous hands that lifted the sword against the state; they gave shelter and repose to his starved and storm-tossed limbs; they contributed to pay the expenses of his voyage; they provided him with a ship and, as he left the land he had preserved, they bade him farewell with tearful prayers and blessings. They enjoy an eternity of glory; and can you be surprised that Plancius is honoured for the loyal sympathy and courage wherewith, after my forcible expulsion, or discreet retirement, if you prefer to call it so, he welcomed, aided, and protected me, and wherewith he preserved me for these gentlemen, for the senate, and for the Roman people, that there might still be some one whom they might one day recall?

7 XI. Such behaviour as that upon which I have been dwelling would have been enough to cover a multitude of sins committed by Plancius; do not then, sir, be surprised that from the noble career which I shall shortly describe to you he drew so many potent aids to his promotion. It was my client who, in early youth, went to Africa in the suite of Aulus

simo, et sanctissimo, atque omni laude et honore
dignissimo viro dilectus est, ut et contubernii necessi-
tudo, et adolescentuli modestissimi pudor postulabat;
quod, si adesset, non minus ille declararet, quam hic
illius frater patruelis et socer, T. Torquatus, illi omni et
virtute et laude par : qui est quidem cum illo maximis
vinculis et propinquitatis et affinitatis coniunctus,
sed ita magnis amoris, ut illae necessitudinis causae
leves esse videantur. Fuit in Creta postea con-
tubernalis Saturnini, propinqui sui, miles huius Q.
Metelli, quibus quum fuerit probatissimus, hodieque
sit, omnibus esse se probatum debet sperare. In
ea provincia legatus fuit C. Sacerdos : qua virtute,
qua constantia vir ! L. Flaccus : qui homo ! qui
civis ! qualem hunc putent, assiduitate testimonioque
28 declarant. In Macedonia tribunus militum fuit :
in eadem provincia postea quaestor. Primum
Macedonia sic eum diligit, ut indicant hi principes
civitatum suarum : qui cum missi sint ob aliam
causam, tamen huius repentino periculo commoti,
huic assident, pro hoc laborant : huic si praesto

Torquatus, and the affection that was felt for him by that man of incorruptible character and lofty principles, who was supremely worthy of every honour and distinction, was such as naturally grew out of the intimacy of tent-fellowship with a young man of such honour and self-control. Were he here to-day, he would be as emphatic in his corroboration of what I say as Titus Torquatus here present, his cousin and son-in-law, his match in every virtue and merit, who is bound to his father-in-law by the closest ties, indeed, of relationship and affinity, but, above all, by an affection so profound as to make the relations of ordinary intimacy seem trivial by comparison. Later, while in Crete, he was the companion of his kinsman Saturninus, and served under Quintus Metellus, who is present here, and the approbation he received, and receives to-day, from these two gives him good ground for hope that he has been approved universally. You know the uprightness and strength of character of Gaius Sacerdos; you know how great Lucius Flaccus is as a man and as a citizen. Both of these were legates in that province, and vouch for the high opinion they have of my client by their constant attendance upon him and by their personal testimony. 8 In Macedonia he was military tribune, and afterwards quaestor in the same province. Chieftains of the Macedonian states are in the court to-day to testify to the affection in which that country holds him. They have come to Rome on an altogether different errand, but in sympathy for my client's unforeseen peril they have put themselves unreservedly and unwearyingly at his service, for they believe that by ranging themselves at his side they

fuerint, gratius se civitatibus suis facturos putant,
quam si legationem suam et mandata confecerint.
L. vero Apuleius hunc tanti facit, ut morem illum
maiorum, qui praescribit, in parentum loco quae-
storibus suis praetores esse oportere, officiis bene-
volentiaque superarit.   Tribunus plebis fuit, non
fortasse tam vehemens, quam isti, quos tu iure
laudas, sed certe talis, quales si omnes semper
fuissent, numquam desideratus vehemens esset
tribunus.

29   XII. Omitto illa, quae si minus in scena sunt,
at certe, cum sunt prolata, laudantur : ut vivat
cum suis ; primum cum parente (nam meo iudicio
pietas fundamentum est omnium virtutum), quem
veretur ut deum (neque enim multo secus est parens
liberis), amat vero ut sodalem, ut fratrem, ut
aequalem.   Quid dicam cum patruo ? cum affinibus ?
cum propinquis ? cum hoc C. Saturnino, ornatissimo
viro ? cuius quantam honoris huius cupiditatem fuisse
creditis, cum videtis luctus societatem ?   Quid de
me dicam ? qui mihi in huius periculo reus esse
videor ? quid de his tot viris talibus, quos videtis

will please the states they represent more than by the accomplishment of the mission upon which they have been sent. Furthermore, Lucius Apuleius Saturninus esteems him so highly that by his kindness and devotion he has even bettered the traditional maxim which enjoins that the relation between a praetor and his quaestor should be that of a father towards his son. His career as tribune of the plebs was perhaps not marked by the energy of those tribunes whom you quite rightly praise, but we may without hesitation affirm that had the line he pursued been universally adopted in the past, drastic methods on the part of tribunes would have been rendered superfluous.

XII. I will not dwell upon those scenes of his life which, although enacted off the stage of publicity, yet have praise accorded to them when they are brought into public view. I will not speak of his private relations, first with his father (for in my opinion filial affection is the basis of all virtues), whom he reveres as divine, and indeed a parent is little short of that in his children's eyes, but whom he loves as a companion, as a brother, and as a comrade of like years with himself. Need I allude to his relations with his uncle, with his kin both by blood and by marriage, and with our accomplished friend Saturninus? You see how that gentleman identifies himself with my client's grief, and can you not gather from that how fervent was his desire that he should be elected to office? Need I allude to myself, who, under the shadow which hangs over him, feel that I myself am standing in the dock? Need I allude to the numerous gentlemen of such high standing as we see present, who, as you see, have

veste mutata ? Atque haec sunt indicia solida,
iudices, et expressa ; haec signa probitatis non
fucata forensi specie, sed domesticis inusta notis
veritatis. Facilis [1] est illa occursatio et blanditia
popularis ; adspicitur, non attrectatur ; procul
apparet, non excutitur, non in manus sumitur.
30 Omnibus igitur rebus ornatum hominem, tam
externis, quam domesticis ; nonnullis rebus inferiorem, quam te, generis, dico, et nominis : superiorem
aliis, municipum, vicinorum, societatum studio,
temporum meorum memoria ; parem virtute, integritate, modestia, aedilem factum esse miraris ?

Hunc tu vitae splendorem maculis adspergis
istis ? Iacis adulteria, quae nemo non modo nomine,
sed ne suspicione quidem possit agnoscere. Bi-
maritum appellas, ut verba etiam fingas, non solum
crimina. Ductum esse ab eo in provinciam aliquem
dicis, libidinis causa : quod non crimen est, sed
impunitum in maledicto mendacium. "Raptam
esse mimulam." Quod dicitur Atinae factum a
iuventute, vetere quodam in scenicos iure maxi-
31 meque oppidano. O adolescentiam traductam ele-

---

[1] facilis *MSS.* : fragilis *B* : futtiliṣ *Holden.*

---

[a] A sign of mourning ; in the case of senators, this
was done by changing the broad-striped tunic (*laticlavia*)
for the narrow-striped, which was the official dress of the
equites.

[b] *Oppidanus* in a Roman mouth had the same touch
of contempt that "provincial" has with us. Cp. the
opposite sense of *urbanus.*

laid aside their official garb?[a]   Yes, proofs such as
these, gentlemen, are substantial and indubitable;
they are tributes to my client's integrity which
are not coloured with the hypocritical hues of
specious rhetoric, but stamped with the inalienable
characters of truth.   The compliment and the
courtesy wherewith we woo popular favour are
an easy task.   They take the eye, but they will not
bear the test of touch.   They make a brave show
from a distance, but scrutiny and close handling are
fatal to them.   Can you wonder, then, at the election
to the office of aedile of one who, though in some
respects he may be inferior to yourself, in respect, I
mean, of name and fame, is nevertheless your superior
in the support given to him by his townsfolk, his
neighbours, and his business partners, and in his
association with me in the crisis of my life, is your
equal in virtue, incorruptibility, and self-mastery, and
is adorned with every quality which lends intrinsic as
well as extrinsic worth?

And would you dim with your sullying insinuations
the lustre of that untarnished life?   You hint darkly
at acts of immorality, charges which cannot even be
suspected, far less substantiated, against him.   Not
content with inventing charges, you invent names for
your charges, and call him "bigamist."   You say
that he took with him to the province a companion
to be the instrument of his base passions; this statement is not a charge, but a reckless and libellous
falsehood.   You say that he raped a ballet-girl;
we hear that this crime was once committed at Atina
by a band of youths who took advantage of an old
privilege allowed at the scenic games, especially in
country towns.[b]   What a tribute to the propriety

ganter! cui quidem cum, quod licuerit, obiiciatur,
tamen id ipsum falsum reperiatur. "Emissus aliquis
e carcere." Et quidem emissus per imprudentiam,
emissus, ut cognostis, necessarii hominis optimique
adolescentis rogatu : idem postea praemandatis
requisitus. Atque haec, nec ulla alia, sunt coniecta
maledicta in eius vitam, de cuius vos pudore, religione,
integritate dubitetis.

XIII. Pater vero, inquit, etiam obesse filio debet.
O vocem duram atque indignam tua probitate,
Laterensis! Pater ut in iudicio capitis, pater ut
in dimicatione fortunarum, pater ut apud tales
viros obesse filio debeat ? qui si esset turpissimus,
si sordidissimus, tamen ipso nomine patrio valeret
apud clementes iudices et misericordes ; valeret,
inquam, communi sensu omnium, et dulcissima
32 commendatione naturae. Sed cum sit Cn. Plancius
is eques Romanus, ea primum vetustate equestris
nominis, ut pater, ut avus, ut maiores eius omnes
equites Romani fuerint, summum in praefectura
florentissima gradum tenuerint et dignitatis et
gratiae ; deinde, ut ipse in legionibus P. Crassi,
imperatoris, inter ornatissimos homines, equites

---

[a] See below, § 33. These "acrimonious expressions"
against the senatorial party were used by the elder Plancius
when he had taken the lead in asking, on behalf of the tax-
collecting company of which he was a member, for a reduction of the price paid for the farming of the revenues in
Asia. The country was in a turmoil, owing to the war with
Mithridates, and the *publicani* stood to lose.

of my client's youthful days. He is reproached with an act which he was permitted by privilege to commit, and yet even that reproach is found to be baseless. You say that he released a criminal from prison. True, but the release was inadvertent, as you are aware, and was ordered at the request of an excellent young man whose claims upon my client were not to be put by ; and a warrant was subsequently issued for the reapprehension of the prisoner. These, gentlemen, and these alone, are the scandals alleged against my client's life, and it is on these that you are asked to base your doubts of his scrupulous honour and integrity.

XIII. " But the son," says Laterensis, " must be made to pay for the sins of the father." [a] What an inhuman sentiment, Laterensis, and how ill it accords with your high principles ! Is it really so ? Must the sins of the father be visited upon the son in a trial where his civil status is endangered, where his worldly fortunes are at stake, and where the issue is to be decided by a jury so distinguished as the present ? Were he never so wicked and never so depraved, his father's mere name should yet carry weight with a merciful and compassionate jury ; it should carry weight through the sentiments that animate our common humanity and through the seductive appeal of nature. But since Plancius' character as a Roman knight is such, and his standing as a Roman knight of so long date, that his father, his grandfather, and all his ancestors were Roman knights, and occupied in a flourishing prefecture the highest position of prestige and social influence ; that Plancius himself was a figure of outstanding brilliance among the Roman knights who were themselves the

447

Romanos, summo splendore fuerit; ut postea princeps inter suos, plurimarum rerum sanctissimus et iustissimus iudex, maximarum societatum auctor, plurimarum magister: si non modo in eo nihil umquam reprehensum, sed laudata sunt omnia: tamen is oberit honestissimo filio pater, qui vel minus honestum et alienum tueri vel auctoritate sua, vel gratia possit?

33 "Asperius,"inquit," locutus est aliquid aliquando." Immo fortasse liberius. "At id ipsum, "inquit," non est ferendum." Ergo hi ferendi sunt, qui queruntur, libertatem equitis Romani se ferre non posse? Ubinam ille mos? ubi illa aequitas iuris? ubi illa antiqua libertas, quae malis oppressa civilibus, extollere iam caput, et aliquando recreata, se erigere debebat? Equitum ego Romanorum in homines nobilissimos maledicta, publicanorum in Q. Scaevolam, virum omnibus ingenio, iustitia, integritate praestantem, aspere, et ferociter, et libere dicta commemorem? XIV. Consuli P. Nasicae praeco Granius, medio in foro, cum ille, edicto iustitio, domum decedens rogasset Granium, quid tristis

---

^a This is not incompatible with what has been said above. See Chap. IX. end.
^b Proverbial for his caustic wit; cp. *Ad fam.* ix. 15. 2.

most gifted body to be found in the legions of the
general Publius Crassus ; and, finally, that he was
a leading character among his fellow-burgesses, a
conscientious and impartial critic of affairs, the promoter of important companies, and himself the
director of very many ; if, so far from any reproach
being whispered against him, he has been universally
commended, is he still, in spite of all this, to be
made to suffer for the sins of a father, whose moral
and social influence ^{a} would be adequate to shield one
who was far less respected, and even one who was
not connected with him by ties of blood ?

33   " But on one occasion," you say, " the elder
Plancius made use of acrimonious expressions." I
deny it, though I admit that his expressions may have
been over-frank.   " Very well," rejoins my opponent,
" but even over-frankness is intolerable."   What !
are these cavillers themselves tolerable, who suggest
that freedom of speech on the part of a Roman
knight is intolerable ? What has become of the tradition of old ?   And the equity of our legal system,
where is it ?   Where is the freedom of ancient days,
which it is now high time should be rearing her head
and proudly renewing her youth after the tyranny
of our civil calamities ?   Need I allude to the attacks
made by Roman knights upon members of our
highest nobility, or to the undaunted and outspoken
strictures passed by the tax-farmers upon Quintus
Scaevola, who knew no equal in intellect, in justice,
and in integrity ?   XIV. Publius Nasica, when
consul, had ordered a cessation of public business,
and was on his way homewards when, in the middle
of the forum, he met Granius ^{b} the auctioneer, and
asked him why he was so downcast.   Might it be

esset : an quod reiectae auctiones essent ? " Immo
vero," inquit, "quod legationes." Idem tribuno plebis,
potentissimo homini, M. Druso, sed multa in re publica
molienti, cum ille eum salutasset, ut fit, dixissetque,
" Quid agis, Grani ? " respondit. " Immo vero, tu
Druse, quid agis ? " Ille L. Crassi, ille M. Antonii
voluntatem asperioribus facetiis saepe perstrinxit
impune. Nunc usque eo oppressa nostra arrogantia
civitas est, ut, quae fuit olim praeconi in ridendo,
nunc equiti Romano in plorando non sit concessa
34 libertas. Quae enim umquam Plancii vox fuit
contumeliae potius, quam doloris ? quid est autem
umquam questus, nisi cum a sociis et a se iniuriam
propulsaret ? Cum senatus impediretur, quo minus,
id quod hostibus semper erat tributum, responsum equitibus Romanis redderetur, omnibus illa
iniuria dolori publicanis fuit, sed eum ipsum
dolorem hic tulit paullo apertius. Communis ille
sensus in aliis fortasse latuit : hic, quod cum ceteris
animo sentiebat, id magis quam ceteri et vultu
35 promptum habuit et lingua. Quamquam, iudices
(agnosco enim ex me), permulta in Plancium, quae
ab eo numquam dicta sunt, conferuntur. Ego quia

---

^a The sting lies in the implication that Scipio, as consul,
was denying foreign envoys the right of access to the senate
in order to extort a bribe from them.

^b The pun on *Quid agis?* cannot fully be brought out
in the English. In the first place it means " How do you
do ? " and in the second " What intrigues are you engaged
upon ? "

because the auctions had been postponed? "No," was the reply, "it is because the hearing of the embassies has been postponed."*a* On another occasion Granius met Marcus Drusus, the tribune of the plebs, an influential man, but absorbed in political intrigue. Drusus saluted him, and made the formal inquiry, "How are you getting on, Granius?" "No," replied Granius; "it is I who should ask *you* how *you* are getting on."*b* It was Granius too who often employed the licence granted to his brusque wit in sarcastic comments upon the political designs of Lucius Crassus or Marcus Antonius. But now this state of ours is so crushed beneath the weight of a pompous self-sufficiency that to-day a Roman knight has less freedom to raise his voice in protest than an auctioneer had once to raise it in ridicule.

4 To what expressions did the elder Plancius ever commit himself which did not breathe a spirit of indignation rather than of insult? And when did he ever raise his voice in protest, save to protect himself and his partners from wrong? When the senate was prevented from replying to a petition of the Roman knights, a privilege which had never been refused even to our enemies, the injustice was resented by all the tax-farmers, but Plancius made rather less efforts to conceal this resentment than did the others. They, no doubt, stifled within their breasts the expression of their corporate emotion; while Plancius, more than the rest, bore upon his countenance and upon his tongue, for all to see and hear, those feelings which the rest shared with him.

35 Not, gentlemen,—and here I speak from my own experience,—not but what several remarks are attributed to Plancius which never passed his lips.

CICERO

dico aliquid aliquando, non studio adductus, sed aut contentione dicendi, aut lacessitus; et quia, ut fit in multis, exit aliquando aliquid, si non perfacetum, attamen fortasse non rusticum, quod quisque dixit, me id dixisse dicunt. Ego autem, si quid est, quod mihi scitum esse videatur, et homine ingenuo dignum atque docto, non aspernor; stomachor vero, cum aliorum non me digna in me conferuntur. Nam quod primus scivit legem de publicanis, tum, cum vir amplissimus consul id illi ordini per populum dedit, quod per senatum, si licuisset, dedisset, si in eo crimen est, quia suffragium tulit, quis non tulit publicanus? si, quia primus scivit, utrum id sortis esse vis, an eius, qui illam legem ferebat? Si sortis, nullum crimen est in casu; si consulis, statuis[1] etiam hunc a summo viro principem esse ordinis iudicatum.

36   XV. Sed aliquando veniamus ad causam. In qua tu nomine legis Liciniae, quae est de sodaliciis, omnes ambitus leges complexus es. Neque enim

---

[1] statuis *Pet.*: splendor etiam Planci MSS.

---

[a] Caesar, when he enacted that the *publicani* should be remitted one-third of the sum paid for their contract. The matter was "talked out" by Cato in the Senate, so Caesar brought it before the *Comitia Tributa*. Here the presiding magistrates (in this case Caesar) had the right of deciding which tribe should open the voting. He chose Plancius' tribe (Teretina), and Plancius (the elder) was the first man to give his vote.

[b] See Introduction to this speech.

Because I may happen on some occasion to pass a remark which is not the outcome of deliberate forethought, but which is uttered in the heat of argument or under the impulse of a momentary annoyance, and because, as will happen with many men, some phrase goes abroad which I would not presume to call witty, but which perhaps is not altogether pointless, I am reported to have said what anyone has said. For my own part, if I am credited with an epigram which I think clever and worthy of a scholar and a gentleman of sense, I make no objection ; but I take umbrage when I am reputed to have uttered words which are unworthy of me and belong to others. As regards the fact that he was the first to vote for the law that dealt with the tax-farmers, on an occasion when a consul *a* of supreme distinction accorded to that body through the medium of the popular assembly a privilege which he would have accorded them through the medium of the senate had he been permitted to do so, if you say that his giving his vote is a chargeable offence, who was there among the tax-farmers who did not give his vote ? If the offence lies in the fact that he was the first to vote, do you impute this fact to chance, or to the proposer of the law ? If you impute it to chance, then you have nothing to charge *him* with ; if to the consul, then you admit that our highest accounted Plancius to be the leading man of his order.

36   XV. But it is time that I should pass on to the question at issue, wherein, though nominally conducting your prosecution under the Licinian law *b* which deals with illegal combination, you have resort to all measures bearing upon corrupt practices.

quidquam aliud in hac lege, nisi editicios iudices,
secutus es ; quod genus iudiciorum si est aequum
ulla in re nisi hac tribuaria, non intelligo quamobrem senatus hoc uno in genere tribus edi voluerit
ab accusatore neque eamdem editionem transtulerit
in ceteras causas, de ipso denique ambitu reiectionem
fieri voluerit iudicum alternorum, cumque nullum
genus acerbitatis praetermitteret, hoc tamen unum
37 praetereundum putarit. Quid ? huiusce rei tandem
obscura causa est ? an et agitata tum, cum īsta
in senatu res agebatur, et disputata hesterno die
copiosissime a Q. Hortensio, cui tum est senatus
assensus ? Hoc igitur sensimus : cuiuscumque tribus
largitor esset per hanc consensionem, quae magis
honeste quam vere sodalitas nominaretur, quam
quisque tribum turpi largitione corrumperet, eum
maxime iis hominibus, qui eius tribus essent, esse
notum.   Ita putavit senatus, cum reo tribus
ederentur eae, quas is largitione devinctas haberet,
eosdem fore testes et iudices. Acerbum omnino
genus iudicii, sed tamen, si vel sua, vel ea, quae
maxime esset cuique coniuncta, tribus ederetur, vix
recusandum.
38   XVI. Tu autem, Laterensis, quas tribus edidisti ?
Teretinam, credo. Fuit id certe aequum, et certe

ᵃ Who had opened the case for the defence.
  ᵇ *Sodalicia*, the word elsewhere translated " association,"
conveyed disgrace ; *sodalitas*, the word used here, was
the name for a perfectly legitimate club, usually social
and religious.
  ᶜ The free Roman population was divided into thirty-
five tribes, four town (*urbanae*) and thirty-one country
(*rusticae*). See Introduction, p. 403.

The only point in which you have followed the law of Licinius is the form of the nomination of the jury which it enjoins ; if this system of empanelling is fair in any respect save in this nomination of tribes, I am at a loss to account for the fact that only in cases of this nature has the senate ruled that the tribes should be nominated by the prosecutor, and has never extended this nomination to all kinds of cases ; but in cases dealing expressly with corrupt practices it has allowed prosecutor and defendant to challenge the jury alternately, and, though it has imposed every other oppressive feature, it has not thought fit to impose that of a nominated jury. But is the motive of this enactment really so hard to seek ? Was it not thrashed out when the matter was under discussion in the senate, and exhaustively demonstrated yesterday by Quintus Hortensius,[a] with whose conclusions the senate was in agreement ? Now our original feeling in the matter was that when a man had bribed any particular tribe by means of that form of combination which, in compliment rather than in accuracy, is known as an association,[b] such a man was best known to those who belonged to that tribe ; accordingly, the senate thought that, inasmuch as the tribes nominated to try a defendant would be those tribes whom he had attached to his cause by bribery, the same persons would serve at once as both jurymen and evidence. An oppressive system, gentlemen, in all conscience ; but one to which a defendant could hardly object, if the tribe named to try him were either his own, or one which circumstances had closely connected with him.

XVI. But which tribes did you nominate, Laterensis ? The Teretine,[c] I have no doubt. Such

exspectatum est, et fuit dignum constantia tua.
Cuius tu tribus venditorem, et corruptorem, et
sequestrem Plancium fuisse clamitas, eam tribum
profecto, severissimorum praesertim hominum et
gravissimorum, edere debuisti. At Voltiniam : lubet
enim tibi nescio quid etiam de illa tribu criminari,—
hanc igitur ipsam cur non edidisti ? Quid Plancio
cum Lemonia ? quid cum Ufentina ? quid cum
Crustumina ? nam Maeciam non quae iudicaret,
39 sed quae reiiceretur, esse voluisti. Dubitatis igitur,
iudices, quin vos M. Laterensis suo iudicio, non
ad sententiam legis, sed ad suam spem aliquam
de civitate delegerit ? dubitatis, quin eas tribus,
in quibus magnas necessitudines habet Plancius,
cum ille non ediderit, iudicarit officiis ab hoc
observatas, non largitione corruptas ? Quid enim
potest dicere, cur ista editio non summam habeat
acerbitatem, remota ratione illa, quam in decernendo
40 secuti sumus ? Tu deligas ex omni populo aut
amicos tuos, aut inimicos meos, aut denique eos,
quos inexorabiles, quos inhumanos, quos crudeles
existimes ? Tu, me ignaro, nec opinante, inscio notes

---

[a] *Sequester*, originally a trustee ; in C.'s time, one in
whose hands money was deposited by the bribers in trust
for the bribed.

a nomination would at any rate have been fair.
It was what we expected, and what would have
been in keeping with your high principles. You
were morally bound to nominate that tribe whose
seller, briber, and depositary[a] you cry out that
Plancius was, especially as it was composed of men
of austerity and conscientiousness. Perhaps you
nominated the Voltinian; for you are pleased to
utter vague allegations against that tribe too.
Why then did you not nominate that tribe ? What
had Plancius to do with the Lemonian tribe, or the
Ufentine, or the Crustumine ? I make no mention
of the Maecian tribe, for your idea in nominating
that was that he should challenge it, not that it
should judge him. Can you then hesitate to believe,
gentlemen, that Marcus Laterensis, in arbitrarily
picking you out of the whole body of citizens, has
consulted some private designs of his own, rather
than the spirit of the law ? Can you hesitate to
believe that, in avoiding the nomination of those
tribes with which Plancius has close bonds of relation,
my opponent has betrayed his opinion that these
tribes were not corruptly bribed by my client, but
viewed by him with the affection that springs from
obligation and service ? Can my opponent show how
his method of nomination, wherein he has ignored
the principle on which we acted when we passed the
law, can fail to bear most hardly upon my client ?
40 Is it right that you should select from the whole
people a jury which consists either of your friends
or of the enemies of the accused, or of men whose
character you judge to be without pity, deaf to all
prayers, lost to all human sympathy ? Is it right
that you should take us off our guard, unwitting and

et tuos, et tuorum necessarios, iniquos vel meos, vel
etiam defensorum meorum ? eodemque adiungas,
quos natura putes asperos, atque omnibus iniquos ?
deinde effundas repente, ut ante consessum meorum
iudicum videam, quam potuerim, qui essent futuri,
suspicari ? apud eosque me, ne quinque quidem
reiectis, quod in proximo reo de consilii sententia
constitutum est, cogas causam de fortunis omnibus
41 dicere ? Non enim, si aut Plancius ita vixit, ut
offenderet sciens neminem, aut tu ita errasti, ut eos
ederes imprudens, ut nos, invito te, tamen ad iudices,
non ad carnifices veniremus, idcirco ista editio per
se non acerba est.

XVII. An vero nuper clarissimi cives nomen
editicii iudicis non tulerunt, cum ex cxxv iudicibus,
principibus equestris ordinis, quinque et lxx reus
reiiceret, l referret, omniaque potius permiscuerunt,
quam ei legi conditionique parerent : nos neque ex
delectis iudicibus, sed ex omni populo, neque editos
ad reiiciendum, sed ab accusatore constitutos iudices
42 ita feremus, ut neminem reiiciamus ? Neque ego
nunc legis iniquitatem queror, sed factum tuum a
sententia legis doceo discrepare : et illud acerbum

unsuspecting, and ear-mark your own intimates
and those of your friends, or my ill-wishers and those
of our supporters, and add to their number men
whom you hold to be curmudgeons and misanthropes
born ? And that after that you should display them
to our gaze with such suddenness that not until
we saw our jury sitting upon the bench should we
have an inkling who they were likely to be ; and
without even challenging five individuals of them,
though this privilege was allowed to the defendant
by the president after consultation with his advisers
in the last prosecution upon this charge, we should
be forced to plead a case wherein our all is at stake ?
41 For if Plancius' life is clear of deliberate wrong to
anyone, and if, by your inadvertent error, your
nomination, in spite of yourself, was such that we
have come up before jurymen instead of executioners,
it does not therefore follow that your mode of
selection is in itself any less cruel.

XVII. Recently our most distinguished citizens
rejected the bare notion of a nominated jury, when
it was proposed that out of a panel of a hundred and
twenty-five members, the heads of the equestrian
order, the accused should have the right of refusing
seventy-five and retaining fifty, and they moved
heaven and earth sooner than tolerate the conditions
which such a measure would impose ; and shall we
be so tame-spirited as to challenge no single individual
in a jury selected not from the whole people, but
from a limited field, not nominated for us to reject,
42 but appointed by the prosecutor ? I am making no
protest at this time against the unfairness of the
law, but merely demonstrating how far your conduct
declined from its spirit ; and had you carried out

459

iudicium si, quemadmodum senatus censuit populusque iussit, ita fecisses, ut huic et suam, et ab hoc
observatas tribus ederes, non modo non quererer,
sed hunc iis iudicibus editis, qui testes iidem esse
possent, absolutum putarem; neque nunc multo
secus existimo. Cum enim has tribus edidisti,
ignotis te iudicibus uti malle quam notis indicavisti,
fugisti sententiam legis; aequitatem omnem
reiecisti; in tenebris, quam in luce, causam versari
43 maluisti. Voltinia tribus ab hoc corrupta; Teretinam habuerat venalem. Quid diceret apud Vol-
tinienses aut tribules suos iudices? immo vero
tu quid diceres? quem iudicem ex illis aut tacitum
testem haberes aut vero etiam excitares? Etenim,
si reus tribus ederet, Voltiniam fortasse Plancius
propter necessitudinem ac vicinitatem, suam vero
certe edidisset. Et, si quaesitor huic edendus
fuisset, quem tandem potius quam hunc C. Alfium,
quem habet, cui notissimus esse debet, vicinum,
tribulem, gravissimum hominem iustissimumque,
edidisset? cuius quidem aequitas et ea voluntas erga

the forms of that oppressive procedure in accordance with the decree of the senate and the will of the people, by nominating to act in his case his own tribe and those tribes with which he had cultivated relations, I should, so far from protesting, consider my client as good as acquitted, since the jury nominated to pronounce a verdict upon him would consist of men who would be witnesses as well; as it is, I set my expectation not greatly below this. For your nomination of these tribes has betrayed the fact that you prefer to meet jurymen who are strangers to my client than those who are acquainted with him, that you have evaded the spirit of the law, that you have repudiated the principles of equity, and that you choose that the atmosphere of the case should be one of obscurity rather than of light. You say that he has bribed the Voltinian tribe, that he had purchased the vote of the Teretine; and what therefore could he say before a jury composed of Voltinians, or of his own tribesmen? I retort your question upon you. What could you say? What individual from such a bench would give you the witness of his silence, or even be stirred into utterance at your cue? Indeed, if it were possible for the accused to nominate the tribes, Plancius would perhaps have nominated the Voltinian, as being his intimates and neighbours, and his own tribe, assuredly. And had it been his to nominate a president for the court, whom, pray, would he have been more likely to nominate than our actual president, Gaius Alfius, to whom he must needs be well known, who is his neighbour and his fellow-tribesman, and who is the most conscientious and upright of men? Indeed, his impartial spirit, and the hopes he fixes upon the

Cn. Plancii salutem, quam ille sine ulla cupiditatis suspicione prae se fert, facile declarat, non fuisse fugiendos tribules huic iudices, cui quaesitorem tribulem exoptandum fuisse videatis.

44 XVIII. Neque ego nunc consilium reprehendo tuum, quod non eas tribus, quibus erat hic maxime notus, edideris; sed a te doceo consilium non servatum senatus. Etenim quis te tum audiret illorum ? aut quid diceres ? sequestremne Plancium ? respuerent aures, nemo agnosceret, repudiarent. An gratiosum ? illi libenter audirent, nos non timide confiteremur. Noli enim putare, Laterensis, legibus istis, quas senatus de ambitu sancire voluerit, id esse actum, ut suffragatio, ut observantia, ut gratia tolleretur. Semper fuerunt boni viri, qui apud 45 tribules suos gratiosi esse vellent. Neque vero tam durus in plebem noster ordo fuit, ut eam coli nostra modica liberalitate noluerit, neque hoc liberis nostris interdicendum est, ne observent tribules suos, ne diligant, ne conficere necessariis suis suam tribum possint, ne par ab iis munus in sua petitione respectent. Haec enim plena sunt officii, plena ob-

acquittal of Plancius without arousing the least suspicion of partisanship, plainly prove that my client had no reason for avoiding a jury composed of his own tribesmen, when it is obvious that he could have wished nothing so much as to have a fellow-tribesman presiding over the court.

4 XVIII. I do not here criticize your policy in not having nominated the tribes with which my client was best acquainted, but I am endeavouring to show you that you have not acted up to the policy of the senate. Had you done so, what man of the jury would have listened to you? Or what would you have said? That Plancius was a corrupt agent? Every ear would reject it, not a man allow it; they would repudiate it. Or that he was popular? They would have been delighted to hear it; we should have admitted it without misgiving. For you must not think, Laterensis, that the measures dealing with corrupt practices which the senate has submitted to the will of the people had for their object the abolition of electoral rivalry, interest, and popularity; there have always been honest gentlemen who have not scrupled to desire popularity among their 45 fellow-tribesmen. Nor has our senatorial order ever been so unsympathetic towards the lower orders as to be unwilling that relations with them should be cultivated on the basis of such a measure of affability as is open to us; nor must we impose upon our children a veto which will forbid them to court the respect and affection of their fellow-tribesmen, or tell them that it is wrong for them to secure for their friends the votes of their tribe, or to look for a like service from their friends in their own elections. Such amenities as these are instinct with the spirit

servantiae, plena etiam antiquitatis. Isto in genere
et fuimus ipsi, cum ambitionis nostrae tempora
postulabant, et clarissimos viros esse vidimus et
hodie esse videmus quam plurimos gratiosos. De-
curiatio tribulium, descriptio populi, suffragia largitione devincta severitatem senatus et bonorum
omnium vim ac dolorem excitarunt. Haec doce,
haec profer, huc incumbe, Laterensis, decuriasse
Plancium, conscripsisse, sequestrem fuisse, pro-
nuntiasse, divisisse : tum mirabor te iis armis
uti, quae tibi lex dabat, noluisse. Tribulibus enim
iudicibus non modo severitatem illorum, si ista
vera sunt, sed ne vultus quidem ferre possemus.

46 Hanc tu rationem cum fugeris, cumque eos
iudices habere nolueris, quorum in huius delicto
cum scientia certissima, tum dolor gravissimus esse
debuerit, quid apud hos dices, qui abs te taciti
requirunt cur hoc sibi oneris imposueris, cur se
potissimum delegeris, cur denique se divinare
malueris quam eos, qui scirent, iudicare ?

of courtesy, kindliness, and chivalry. Such a course I have myself adopted, when it has been required by the exigencies of my own candidature; I have seen many eminent men do the like, and to-day we see very many men who enjoy popularity. It is the systematic organization of the tribes and the electorate into sections and allotments, and the restriction of the freedom of the poll by bribery, which in the past has awakened the severity of the senate and the indignant wrath of all good patriots. Bend all your powers, Laterensis, to the task of demonstrating by substantial proof that Plancius resorted to sectional canvassing, to making a register of votes of which he was secure, to being a depository of bribes, or that he made any promises or distributions of money whatsoever; and if you can prove this, I shall be surprised that you refused to avail yourself of those weapons which the law put into your hands. For were his jury to-day his tribesmen, we should find not merely their severity but even their gaze intolerable, supposing that your allegations were true. But now that you have declined such a course of action, and have refused to empanel men who, in dealing with any delinquencies of my client, would have shown a most indubitable acquaintance with the facts and a most overwhelming indignation, what can you say to the present jury, who in silent perplexity are wondering why you should have laid this burden upon them, why you should have gone out of your way to choose them to sit upon the bench, and why you should prefer their guess-work to the verdict of those who could base their judgement upon knowledge?

XIX. Ego Plancium, Laterensis, et ipsum gratiosum esse dico et habuisse in petitione multos
cupidos sui gratiosos, quos tu si sodales vocas,
officiosam amicitiam nomine inquinas criminoso.
Sin, quia gratiosi sint, accusandos putas, noli mirari
te id, quod tua dignitas postularit, repudiandis
47 gratiosorum amicitiis non esse assecutum. Nam,
ut ego doceo, gratiosum esse in sua tribu Plancium,
quod multis benigne fecerit, pro multis spoponderit,
in operas plurimos patris auctoritate et gratia
miserit, quod denique omnibus officiis per se, per
patrem, per maiores suos totam Atinatem praefecturam comprehenderit, sic tu doce sequestrem
fuisse, largitum esse, conscripsisse, tribules decuriavisse. Quid si non potes, noli tollere ex ordine
nostro liberalitatem, noli maleficium putare esse
gratiam, noli observantiam sancire poena.

Itaque haesitantem te in hoc sodalitiorum tribuario crimine ad communem ambitus causam
contulisti, in qua desinamus aliquando, si videtur,
48 vulgari et pervagata declamatione contendere. Sic
enim tecum ago. Quam tibi commodum est, unam
tribum delige tu : doce id, quod debes, per quem

XIX. I tell you, Laterensis, that not only is Plancius himself popular, but that the host of ardent supporters who backed his candidature were also popular. If you apply to these the name of "associates," you are sullying disinterested friendship with a name which is a stain; but if you think that their popularity renders them amenable to prosecution, cease to wonder that by your refusal to cultivate the friendship of popular persons you should have failed to win that distinction which your merits demanded as their due. For as I, on my side, prove that Plancius is a popular man in his tribe, and that he has become so by showing kindnesses to many, acting as security for many, and procuring official posts for several through his father's interest and popularity, and finally that by his own merits, his father's, and those of his ancestors, he has included the whole prefecture of Atina in the circle of his universal beneficence, so it lies with you to prove that he was a depositary and a bestower of bribes, and that he worked by registers and tribal allotments. If you cannot do this, do not rob our order of its free and open spirit, do not consider popularity to be a misdemeanour, or attach a penalty to the amenities of life.

Floundering, therefore, in this charge of corrupting the tribes by association, you have clutched at the general charge of bribery; and, in discussing this, let us once and for all, if you please, have done with the stale and vapid commonplaces of rhetoric. I will deal with the matter in this way. Choose any one tribe which it suits your book to choose; prove (for the burden of proof lies with you) who were

sequestrem, quo divisore corrupta sit. Ego, si id facere non potueris, quod, ut opinio mea fert, ne incipies quidem, per quem tulerit, docebo. Estne haec vera contentio ? placetne sic agi ? Num possum magis pedem conferre (ut aiunt), aut propius accedere ? Quid taces ? quid dissimulas ? quid tergiversaris ? Etiam atque etiam insto atque urgeo, insector, posco, atque adeo flagito crimen ; quamcumque tribum, inquam, delegeris, quam tulerit Plancius, tu ostendito, si poteris, vitium ; ego, qua ratione tulerit, docebo ; nec erit haec alia ratio Plancio ac tibi, Laterensis. Nam ut quas tribus tu tulisti, si iam ex te requiram, possis, quorum studio tuleris, explicare, sic ego hoc contendo, me tibi ipsi adversario, cuiuscumque tribus rationem poposceris, redditurum.

49 XX. Sed cur sic ago ? Quasi non comitiis iam superioribus sit Plancius designatus aedilis. Quae comitia primum habere coepit consul quum omnibus in rebus summa auctoritate tum harum ipsarum legum ambitus auctor ; deinde habere coepit subito, praeter opinionem omnium ; ut ne si cogitasset quidem quispiam largiri, daretur spatium com-

---

[a] Ironical; C. means Laterensis himself.
[b] M. Licinius Crassus, who had himself carried the *lex Licinia* (see Chap. XV. above).

the depositaries and who the distributors who were
the agents of its subornment ; if you show us that
you are unable to do this (and in my opinion you
will not be able even to begin to do it), I will show
you who [a] was responsible for Plancius' success in the
poll. Is this a fair method of fighting ? Does it
satisfy you ? Have I any better means of closing
and grappling with you, if I may borrow a simile ?
Why this silence, this dissembling, this reluctance ?
At every turn you are dogged, harassed, persecuted ;
I demand that you shall produce your charges ;
nay, I importune you for them. No matter what
tribe you may pick out of those whose vote Plancius
secured, I defy you to demonstrate a flaw ; I will
demonstrate the means by which he secured their
vote. And in doing so I shall apply to you, Laterensis,
the same logical process as I apply to Plancius.
For as you would be able to give a clear account,
supposing I were to demand it of you, of the personal
factors which helped you to carry the tribes whose
votes you secured, so I affirm that I am ready to
present you—yes, even you, my opponent—with
an account of the reasons and motives that swayed
the voting of any tribe you like to adduce.

49   XX. But all this argument is superfluous, for it
ignores the fact that in the previous election Plancius
had already been marked down for the aedileship.
That election was, in the first place, opened by a
consul [b] who, apart from his great general eminence,
had been the mover of the very laws concerning
corruption with which we are dealing ; and, in the
second place, it was opened so suddenly and so
unexpectedly that, even had any man contemplated
bribery, he would not have found sufficient time

parandi. Vocatae tribus ; latum suffragium ; diri-
bitae tabellae, renuntiatae ; longe plurimum valuit
Plancius. Nulla largitionis nec fuit nec esse potuit
suspicio. An tandem una centuria praerogativa
tantum habet auctoritatis ut nemo umquam prior
eam tulerit, quin renuntiatus sit aut iis ipsis comitiis
consul, aut certe in illum annum : aedilem tu
Plancium factum miraris, in quo non exigua pars
populi, sed universus populus voluntatem suam
declararit ? cuius in honore non unius tribus pars,
sed comitia tota comitiis fuerint praerogativa ?
50 Quo quidem tempore, si id, Laterensis, facere
voluisses aut si gravitatis esse putasses tuae, quod
multi nobiles saepe fecerunt, ut, cum minus va-
luissent suffragiis quam putassent, postea prolatis
comitiis prosternerent se et populo Romano fracto
animo atque humili supplicarent, non dubito quin
omnis ad te conversura fuerit multitudo. Numquam
enim fere nobilitas, integra praesertim atque inno-
cens, a populo Romano supplex repudiata fuit. Sed,
si tibi gravitas tua et magnitudo animi pluris fuit,
sicut esse debuit, quam aedilitas, noli, cum
habeas id, quod malueris, desiderare id, quod

470

for the necessary preliminaries. The tribes had been called upon, the votes taken, the tablets sorted, and the result announced. Plancius was far the most influential of the candidates, and neither was there attached to him, nor could there possibly have been, any suspicion of bribery. The century which votes first carries of itself such weight that no candidate for the consulship has ever secured its vote without being ultimately declared first consul either at that very election or at any rate for the following year ; and is it possible that you should be surprised at Plancius' election to the aedileship, when not merely a small fraction, but the whole of the electorate, has given a clear intimation of its will regarding him ? In conferring this distinction upon him, it was not a section of a single tribe that gave the lead to the rest, but it was a whole electorate giving the lead to the ensuing election. That, Laterensis, was your opportunity ; had it suited with your inclination, had you thought it consonant with your self-respect, to act as many nobles have often acted, who, realizing that their strength in votes was less than they had anticipated, have forthwith obtained an adjournment, and have supplicated the Roman people on bended knee, chagrined and humiliated, I have not the least doubt that the whole populace would have come over to your side. Rarely has it happened that the prayers of a noble, above all of a noble who is blameless and irreproachable, have been ignored by the Roman people. But if you valued a sublime and unbending temper of mind above the aedileship, as indeed you had every right to value it, then, possessing that which you esteem more highly, do not lament your loss of that which

minoris putaris. Equidem primum ut honore dignus essem, maxime semper laboravi ; secundo ut existimarer ; tertium mihi fuit illud, quod plerisque primum est, ipse honos : qui iis denique debet esse iucundus, quorum dignitati populus Romanus testimonium, non beneficium ambitioni dedit.

51 XXI. Quaeris etiam, Laterensis, quid imaginibus tuis, quid ornatissimo atque optimo viro, patri tuo, respondeas mortuo. Noli ista meditari, atque illud cave potius, ne tua ista querela dolorque nimius ab illis sapientissimis viris reprehendatur. Vidit enim pater tuus Appium Claudium, nobilissimum hominem, vivo patre suo, potentissimo et clarissimo cive, C. Claudio, aedilem non esse factum, et eumdem sine repulsa factum esse consulem ; vidit hominem sibi maxime coniunctum, egregium virum, L. Volcatium, vidit M. Pisonem in ista aedilitate offensiuncula accepta summos a populo Romano esse honores adeptos. Avus vero tuus et P. Nasicae tibi aediliciam praedicaret repulsam, quo cive neminem ego statuo in hac re publica fortiorem, et C. Marii, qui duabus aedilitatis acceptis repulsis septies consul est factus, et L. Caesaris, Cn. Octavii, M. Tullii ; quos omnes scimus

52 aedilitate praeteritos, consules esse factos. Sed quid ego aedilicias repulsas colligo ? quae saepe

you esteem less. For my own part, I have always first endeavoured to deserve honour; secondly, to be thought to deserve it; the honour itself, first in the estimation of most, has held the third place in my own, and yet it cannot fail to be a source of delight to those, and those alone, to whom it has been accorded by the Roman people as a testimony to their merits, and not as a reward for assiduity in the making of interest.

51 XXI. You ask us, moreover, Laterensis, what answer you are to make to your ancestral busts, and to that excellent and accomplished gentleman, your late father. Dwell not upon this thought, but dwell rather upon the fear lest they in their wisdom should censure the complaints of your too mortified spirit. Your father saw the failure of the noble Appius Claudius to obtain the aedileship, though his brother Gaius was the most influential and eminent citizen then living; but he also saw Appius elected consul at the first attempt. He saw his close friend, the exemplary Lucius Volcatius, and Marcus Piso too, sustain insignificant rebuffs in standing for this office by which you set so great store, before they advanced to the highest honours which it is in the power of the Roman people to bestow. Your grandfather, too, would tell you of the failure to win the aedileship of Publius Nasica, than whom I hold that the state has had no more gallant citizen, and of Gaius Marius, who, after being twice defeated for the aedileship, was seven times elected consul, and of Lucius Caesar, Gnaeus Octavius, and Marcus Tullius; all of these we know were passed over for the aedileship, and 52 were afterwards elected consuls. But why this catalogue of failures to obtain this office? They

eiusmodi habitae sunt, ut iis, qui praeteriti essent, benigne a populo factum videretur. Tribunus militum, L. Philippus, summa nobilitate et eloquentia, quaestor C. Caelius, clarissimus ac fortissimus adolescens, tribuni plebis P. Rutilius Rufus, C. Fimbria, C. Cassius, Cn. Orestes, facti non sunt : quos tamen omnes consules factos scimus esse. Quae tibi ultro pater et maiores tui non consolandi tui gratia dicent, neque vero quo te liberent aliqua culpa, quam tu vereris ne a te suscepta videatur, sed ut te ad cursum istum tenendum, quem a prima aetate suscepisti, cohortentur. Nihil est enim, mihi crede, Laterensis, de te detractum : detractum dico ? si mehercule vere, quod accidit, interpretari velis, est aliquid etiam de virtute significatum tua. XXII. Noli enim existimare non magnum quemdam motum fuisse illius petitionis tuae, de qua ne aliquid iurares destitisti. Denuntiasti, homo adolescens, quid de summa re publica sentires. Fortius tu quidem quam nonnulli defuncti honoribus, sed apertius quam vel 53 ambitionis vel aetatis tuae ratio postulabat. Quamobrem in dissentiente populo noli putare nullos fuisse, quorum animos tuus ille fortis animus offenderet ; qui te incautum fortasse nunc tuo loco demovere potuerunt, providentem ante et praecaventem numquam certe movebunt.

---

^a The aedileship was an expensive office to hold, as it involved the giving of public games.

^b Caesar's agrarian law enacted that candidates should swear not to propose any other system of land-occupation than that which it laid down ; see *Ad Att.* ii. 18. 2.

have often occurred under circumstances which have led the defeated parties to believe that they received a boon from the people.[a] That eloquent noble, Lucius Philippus, was never elected tribune of the plebs, that renowned and gallant young man Gaius Caelius was never elected quaestor, Publius Rutilius Rufus, Gaius Fimbria, Gaius Cassius, Gnaeus Orestes were never elected tribunes of the plebs, and yet, in spite of everything, all these, as we know, became consuls. Instances such as these your father and your ancestors will of themselves bring to your mind, not indeed to console you, or to clear you of any stain of reproach, which you fear you may be thought to have contracted, but rather to encourage you to persevere in that career on which you embarked in your early years. Believe me, Laterensis, you have suffered no detraction. Detraction? Nay, if you will but put a right construction upon events, your defeat is, in a sense, a recognition of your merit. XXII. Do not think that your candidature for the tribunate, when you withdrew your name to avoid taking a certain oath,[b] failed to arouse very considerable remark. By that act you intimated in early youth what were your views on vital questions of state ; you were bolder, no doubt, than many who have successful careers behind them, but nevertheless too frank to further your own youthful ambitions. In view of this, and in view of the wide divergence of popular feeling, you must not think that none were scandalized by your uncompromising attitude ; it was these, possibly, who took you off your guard, and so were able to oust you ; but, if you are forewarned and forearmed, you will assuredly never again be so ousted.

An te illa argumenta duxerunt? "Dubitatis,"
inquit, "quin coitio facta sit, cum tribus plerasque
cum Plotio tulerit Plancius?" An una fieri potuerunt, si una tribus non tulissent? "At nonnullas
punctis paene totidem." Quippe cum iam facti
prope superioribus comitiis declaratique venissent.
Quamquam ne id quidem suspicionem coitionis
habuerit. Neque enim umquam maiores nostri
sortitionem constituissent aediliciam, nisi viderent
accidere posse, ut competitores pares suffragiis
54 essent. Et ais prioribus comitiis Aniensem a Plotio
Pedio, Teretinam a Plancio tibi esse concessam:
nunc ab utroque eas avulsas, ne in angustum venirent. Quam convenit nondum cognita populi voluntate hos, quos iam tum coniunctos fuisse dicis,
iacturam suarum tribuum, quo vos adiuvaremini,
fecisse; eosdem, cum iam essent experti quid
valerent, restrictos et tenaces fuisse? Etenim
verebantur, credo, angustias, quasi res in contentionem aut in discrimen aliquod posset venire.
Sed tamen tu A. Plotium, virum ornatissimum,
in idem crimen vocando indicas eum te arripuisse,

---

^a Who stood for the aedileship with Plancius. *Coitio* is
"a combination of one candidate with another to prevent
the election of a third" (Holden), a practice not unknown
in modern politics.

^b Which had been interrupted. Laterensis alleged that
before the first election Plancius and Plotius had promised
to himself and Pedius respectively the support of those
tribes on whose votes they could rely, but that before the
second they had retracted this arrangement, and promised
this support to each other.

476

But it may be, gentlemen, that you have been influenced by reasoning such as this. "Can you doubt," asks my opponent, "that collusion was employed, seeing that Plancius and Plotius [a] together carried the votes of so many tribes?" But could they have been elected together, if they had not carried the votes of the tribes together? "Yes," he objects, "but in some of the tribes they scored an almost exactly equal number of points." Naturally, since they had both come to the poll with their election and declaration virtually accomplished at the previous election. Yet even this circumstance should not involve them in any suspicion of collusion; and indeed our ancestors would never have provided for the election of aediles by lot, had they not foreseen the possibility of two candidates receiving the 54 same number of votes. You allege, moreover, that at the former election [b] Plotius agreed to surrender the tribe of Anio to Pedius, and Plancius the Teretine tribe to yourself; but that at the latter election they both retracted their concessions, fearing a close count of the poll. A most consistent course of action, surely, that these men, who you allege were even then in close collusion, should, while the popular will was still quite uncertain, have sacrificed their own tribes to assist you, and that the same men, after having learned the extent of their power, should have become selfishly retentive. You would have us believe that in the latter election they feared a close count, and imagined that doubt and suspense would accompany the decision. Moreover, by involving the accomplished Aulus Plotius in the same charge with my client, you betray the fact that you have haled before the tribunal of justice the man

a quo non sis rogatus. Nam quod questus es plures te testes habere de Voltinia quam quot in ea tribu puncta tuleris, indicas aut eos testes te producere, qui, quia nummos acceperint, te praeterierint, aut te ne gratuita quidem eorum suffragia tulisse.

55 XXIII. Illud vero crimen de nummis, quos in circo Flaminio deprehensos esse dixisti, caluit re recenti: nunc in causa refrixit. Neque enim qui illi nummi fuerint nec quae tribus nec qui divisor, ostendis. Atque is quidem eductus ad consules, qui tum in crimen vocabatur, se inique a tuis iactatum graviter querebatur. Qui si erat divisor, praesertim eius, quem tu habebas reum, cur abs te reus non est factus? cur non eius damnatione aliquid ad hoc iudicium praeiudicii comparasti? Sed neque tu habes haec neque eis confidis. Alia te ratio, alia cogitatio ad spem huius opprimendi excitavit. Magnae sunt in te opes; late patet gratia; multi amici, multi cupidi tui, multi fautores laudis tuae. Multi huic invident; multis etiam pater, optimus vir, nimium retinens equestris iuris et libertatis

---

a Built on the Prata Flaminia, between the Capitol and the Tiber, by C. Flaminius, who was killed at the Trasimene, 217. There appears to have been no claimant for this money, and the inference was that it was intended for bribed voters.

b See note on Chap. XIII.

who did not, like the other, intercede with you in
his own behalf. I say this, because by complaining
that you have more witnesses from the Voltinian
tribe than the number of votes you got in that
tribe, you show, either that those whom you are
producing as witnesses are men who were bribed to
withhold their vote from you, or even that you made
it worth their while to vote for you.

55 XXIII. Again, that matter of the seizure of cash
in the Circus of Flaminius,[a] which you formulate into
a charge, was a nine days' wonder at the time, but
interest in it has cooled since the trial began ; for
you fail to demonstrate what the money was or for
what tribe it was intended or who was deputed to
distribute it. Indeed, the man who was brought
before the consuls on the charge of being implicated
in the affair expressed bitter indignation at the rough
handling he had received from your agents. If he
was the distributor, especially if he was employed as
such by the man whom you intended to prosecute,
why did you not prosecute him also ? Why did you
not secure by his condemnation a verdict which
might have served as a precedent for the present
trial ? But you are not supported by these facts,
nor do you rely upon their support ; other motives,
and other trains of thought, have inflamed you
with a hope that you can compass my client's ruin.
You have vast material resources and extensive social
influence ; you have hosts of friends, partisans, and
well-wishers, who are zealous for your glory. My
client, on the other hand, is the object of considerable jealousy ; many think that his excellent father
has been too tenacious of the rights and the in-
dependence of the equestrian order.[b] There is also

videtur ; multi etiam communes inimici reorum omnium, qui ita semper testimonium de ambitu dicunt, quasi aut moveant animos iudicum suis testimoniis, aut gratum populo Romano sit, aut ab eo facilius ob eam causam dignitatem, quam volunt, 56 consequantur. Quibuscum me, iudices, pugnantem meo more pristino non videbitis ; non quo mihi fas sit quidquam defugere, quod salus Plancii postulet, sed quia neque necesse est me id persequi voce, quod vos mente videatis, et quod ita de me meriti sunt illi ipsi, quos ego testes video paratos, ut eorum reprehensionem vos vestrae prudentiae assumere, meae modestiae remittere debeatis. Illud unum vos magnopere oro atque obsecro, iudices, cum huius, quem defendo, tum communis periculi causa, ne fictis auditionibus, ne disseminato dispersoque sermoni fortunas innocentium subiiciendas putetis. 57 Multi amici accusatoris, nonnulli etiam nostri iniqui, multi communes obtrectatores atque omnium invidi multa finxerunt. Nihil est autem tam volucre, quam maledictum ; nihil facilius emittitur, nihil citius excipitur, nihil latius dissipatur. Neque ego, si fontem maledicti reperietis, ut negligatis,

that large class who show an undiscriminating hostility to all who stand in the dock, and who give glib testimony in charges of corruption, imagining that by their evidence they can sway the minds of the jury, ingratiate themselves with the Roman people, or by such means pave the way for themselves towards gaining at its hands those offices on which

56 they have set their hearts. You will find, gentlemen, that I shall not use my ordinary methods in combating this class of witnesses; not that I can with honour shirk any duty imposed upon me by considerations of Plancius' safety, but because there is no need for me to use my voice to set forth that which you see with your minds, and also because the persons whom I see ready to give evidence have done such good service to myself that the task of criticizing them is one which you must impose on your own good judgement, and permit me diffidently to forgo. One thing I do most earnestly beg of you, gentlemen, in view of the peril which threatens, not my client merely, but every one of us; do not consider it right that the fate of the guiltless should lie at the mercy of fictitious rumours and idle gossip which has been sown broadcast and passed from

57 mouth to mouth. The inventions against my client have been multitudinous as their inventors; often they have been the work of the prosecutor's friends, sometimes of our own ill-wishers, often of those who make it their business to backbite and look askance upon all and sundry without respect of persons. But there is nothing which is so volatile as slander, nothing which slips abroad so readily, is caught up so greedily, or disseminated so widely. If you should trace these slanders to their source, I would not have

aut dissimuletis umquam postulabo. Sed si quid
sine capite manabit aut si quid erit eiusmodi,
ut non exstet auctor, qui audierit autem aut ita
negligens vobis esse videbitur, ut unde audierit
oblitus sit, aut ita levem habebit auctorem, ut
memoria dignum non putarit, huius illa vox vulgaris,
AUDIVI, ne quid reo innocenti noceat, oramus.

58 XXIV. Sed venio iam ad L. Cassium, familiarem
meum, cuius ex oratione ne illum quidem Iuventium
tecum expostulavi, quem ille omni et virtute et
humanitate ornatus adolescens primum de plebe
aedilem curulem factum esse dixit. In quo, Cassi,
si ita tibi respondeam, nescisse id populum Romanum,
neque fuisse qui id nobis narraret, praesertim
mortuo Congo, non, ut opinor, admirere, cum ego
ipse non abhorrens a studio antiquitatis me hic id
ex te primum audisse confitear. Et quoniam tua
fuit perelegans ac persubtilis oratio, digna equitis
Romani vel studio vel pudore, quoniamque sic ab
his es auditus, ut magnus honos et ingenio et humani-
tati tuae tribueretur, respondebo ad ea, quae
dixisti, quae pleraque de ipso me fuerunt.; in quibus
ipsi aculei, si quos habuisti in me reprehendendo,
59 tamen mihi non ingrati acciderunt. Quaesisti,
utrum mihi putarem, equitis Romani filio, faciliorem
fuisse ad adipiscendos honores viam, an futuram

---

^a Junior counsel (*subscriptor*) to Laterensis.
^b *i.e.* Laterensis, whom Cicero rallies upon his "cele-
brated " ancestor.
^c A celebrated antiquarian, spoken of as still living in
De oratore, i. 256, which was written in 55.

you esteem their author lightly, nor shelter his guilt ; but if no head-waters can be found for some trickling rumour, and if it cannot from the nature of things be brought home to anyone, and if it shall appear to you that he who heard it was so careless as to have forgotten from whom he heard it, or that it sprang from a source so insignificant that he who heard it thought it not worth his while to remember, then we do beg you not to allow the trite phrase " I heard it said," in the mouth of such a man, to be detrimental to my innocent client.

58 XXIV. But I now come to my friend Lucius Cassius,[a] and I have not yet called *you*[b] to account as regards the Juventius whom that excellent and cultivated young man mentioned in his speech as being the first plebeian to be elected curule aedile.   As to that, Cassius, if, in replying to this statement of yours, I were to assert that the Roman people were not aware of this fact, and that there has been no one to tell us of it, especially now that Congus [c] is dead, you would not, I take it, be surprised ; for indeed, though I am somewhat of an antiquarian myself, I must confess that I never heard of the fact until I heard it from you.   Your speech was a model of grace and adroitness ; it was characterized by that energy and self-restraint which we associate with the Roman knighthood, and was listened to with an attention which is a high recommendation to your culture and intelligence ; consequently, I will reply to your remarks, which dealt very largely with myself ; even your sarcastic strictures gave me matter for self-satis-

59 faction.   You asked whether I thought that official dignity had been more accessible to myself, the son of a Roman knight, than it was likely to be to

esse filio meo, qui esset familia consulari. Ego vero
quamquam illi omnia malo quam mihi, tamen
illi honorum aditus numquam faciliores optavi quam
mihi fuerunt. Quin etiam, ne forte ille sibi me potius
peperisse iam honores quam iter demonstrasse
adipiscendorum putet, haec illi soleo praecipere
(quamquam ad praecepta aetas non est gravis) quae
ille a Iove ortus suis praecipit filiis:

vigilandum est semper: multae insidiae sunt bonis;
id quod multi invideant . . .

Nostis cetera. Nonne, quae scripsit gravis ille
et ingeniosus poëta, scripsit non ut illos regios
pueros, qui iam nusquam erant, sed ut nos et nostros
liberos ad laborem et laudem excitaret.

60   Quaeris, quid potuerit amplius assequi Plancius,
si Cn. Scipionis fuisset filius. Magis aedilis fieri non
potuisset, sed hoc praestaret, quod ei minus in-
videretur. Etenim honorum gradus summis hominibus et infimis sunt pares, gloriae dispares. XXV.
Quis nostrum se dicit M'. Curio, quis C. Fabricio,
quis C. Duilio parem? quis A. Atilio Calatino? quis
Cn. et P. Scipionibus? quis Africano, Marcello,
Maximo? tamen eosdem sumus honorum gradus,
quos illi, assecuti. Etenim in virtute multi sunt
adscensus, ut is gloria maxime excellat, qui virtute
plurimum praestet. Honorum populi finis est,

---

    [a] He was now in his 12th year.
    [b] Atreus; the lines are from the tragedy of this name
by Accius (170–94).
    [c] C. here passes on to deal with an argument of Cassius
that Plancius' birth and ability did not justify his promotion.
    [d] More commonly known as Regulus.

my son, who was of consular family; and my answer is, that though I always give him the first and myself the second place in my wishes, I have never hoped that the avenues to honour would be easier for him than they were to myself. Lest he should think that rather than showing him the way to win honours in the future I have already won his honours for him, I am accustomed to give him the advice (though advice is somewhat beyond him[a] at his present years) which that king[b] who was himself sprung from Jupiter gave to his sons:

> Be wakeful aye; with snares the good are hemmed;
> For jealous hearts are rife . . .

No doubt you recall the rest of the passage. These lines were written by an earnest and gifted poet, whose object in writing them was to kindle the spirit of industry and ambition, not in those young princes who were merely the figments of his imagination, but in us and in our children.

60 What more, you ask, could Plancius have gained if he had been the son of Gnaeus Scipio?[c] He could not have been made aedile more easily, but he would have the advantage of being less an object of envy; for the steps of office are equal for the greatest and meanest of men, but in the glory they bring wholly unequal. XXV. Which of us claims to be the equal of Manius Curius, of Gaius Fabricius, of Gaius Duilius, of Aulus Atilius Calatinus,[d] of Gnaeus and Publius Scipio, of Africanus, of Marcellus, or of Fabius Maximus? Yet we have climbed the steps of office just as they did. For indeed in virtue there are many grades, and it follows that the highest glory is won by the highest virtue. Of offices, on the

consulatus, quem magistratum iam octingenti fere
consecuti sunt ; horum, si diligenter quaeres, vix
decimam partem reperies gloria dignam.   Sed
nemo umquam sic egit, ut tu : Cur iste fit consul ?
quid potuit amplius, si L. Brutus esset, qui civitatem
dominatu regio liberavit ? honore nihil amplius,
laude multum. Sic igitur Plancius nihilominus
quaestor est factus, et tribunus plebis, et aedilis,
quam si esset summo loco natus : sed haec, pari
61 loco orti, sunt innumerabiles alii consecuti. Profers
triumphos T. Didii et C. Marii, et quaeris, quid
simile in Plancio.   Quasi vero isti, quos commemoras,
propterea magistratus ceperint, quod triumpharant,
et non, quia commissi sunt iis magistratus in quibus
triumpharent, re bene gesta triumpharint.   Rogas,
quae castra viderit : qui et miles in Creta, hoc
imperatore, et tribunus in Macedonia militum fuerit,
et quaestor tantum ex re militari detraxerit temporis,
quantum in me custodiendum transferre maluerit.
62 Quaeris, num disertus ?   Immo, id quod secundum
est, ne sibi quidem videtur.   Num iurisconsultus ?
Quasi quisquam sit, qui sibi hunc falsum de iure
respondisse dicat.   Omnes enim istiusmodi artes in

ᵃ Quintus Metellus Creticus.

other hand, such as the people bestows, the crown is the consulate, which has been now gained by nearly eight hundred; and a diligent search will discover that scarce a tithe of these were worthy of glory. Yet no one ever adopts your line of reasoning and asks, " Why has that fellow been made consul ? What more could he have attained if he had been Lucius Brutus, who freed the state from the despotism of a tyrant ? " Nothing more in rank, I grant you, but much in glory. So in the same way Plancius has been elected quaestor, tribune of the plebs, and aedile, just as much as if his birth had been of the highest; but these offices have been won by countless others of no higher social grade than he. You quote the triumphs won by Titus Didius and Gaius Marius, and ask what Plancius can show to match them; as though, forsooth, those whose names you mention had received offices because they had won triumphs, and had not rather won triumphs as a result of military successes, because the offices entrusted to them gave them opportunities of winning those triumphs. You ask what active service he has seen. Well, he served in Crete under a general [a] who is in the court to-day, and he was military tribune and quaestor in Macedonia, allowing himself distraction from his military duties only for such periods as he preferred to devote to my protection. Has he eloquence, you ask ? So far from that, he does not even possess the quality which is next in value to eloquence, of thinking that he is eloquent. You ask whether he is a competent lawyer, as though complaints had been made of my client's inefficiency as a legal adviser. The absence of proficiency in

487

iis reprehenduntur, qui, cum professi sunt, satisfacere non possunt, non in iis, qui se afuisse ab istis studiis confitentur. Virtus, probitas, integritas in candidato, non linguae volubilitas, non ars, non scientia requiri solet. Ut nos in mancipiis parandis, quamvis frugi hominem, si pro fabro, aut pro tectore emimus, ferre moleste solemus, si eas artes, quas in emendo secuti sumus, forte nesciverit, sin autem emimus, quem vilicum imponeremus, quem pecori praeficeremus, nihil in eo nisi frugalitatem, laborem, vigilantiam esse curamus, sic populus Romanus deligit magistratus quasi rei publicae vilicos ; in quibus si qua praeterea est ars, facile patitur ; sin minus, virtute eorum et innocentia contentus est. Quotus enim quisque disertus ? quotus quisque iuris peritus est, ut eos numeres, qui volunt esse ? quod si praeterea nemo est honore dignus, quidnam tot optimis et ornatissimis civibus est futurum ?

63 XXVI. Iubes Plancium de vitiis Laterensis dicere. Nihil potest, nisi eum nimis in se iracundum putavisse. Idem effers Laterensem laudibus. Facile patior id te agere multis verbis, quod ad iudicium non pertineat, et id te accusantem tam diu dicere, quod ego defensor sine periculo possim confiteri,

such directions as these is only considered blame-worthy when those who profess competence fail to substantiate their own professions, and not when men admit that they have never applied themselves in those directions ; what we look for in a candidate is uprightness, honesty, incorruptibility, not a glib tongue, professional skill, a deep knowledge. In purchasing slaves, however honest a man may be, if we have bought him as a carpenter or a plasterer, we are annoyed if he turns out to be ignorant of the business we had in view when we bought him. But if we buy a slave to occupy the post of steward or shepherd, the only qualities we care about in him are frugality, industry, and vigilance. This is how the Roman people selects its magistrates, for they are, as it were, stewards of the republic. If, in addition to the necessary moral qualities, they are experts in any direction, the people is well pleased ; if not, then uprightness and integrity are quite enough for it. For how small a fraction of man-kind is eloquent or proficient in the law, even if we include those who are ambitious to be so ! And if no one apart from these is worthy of honour, what shall we do with all our best and most admirable citizens ?

XXVI. You challenge Plancius to adduce flaws in the life of Laterensis. There are no flaws to adduce, unless perhaps that he has shown too bitter a resentment against my client. At the same time you speak of Laterensis in terms of fulsome praise. I have not the least objection to your dwelling at considerable length on a theme which is irrelevant to the question before the court, or that you in your prosecution should enlarge upon a fact which I in my defence can concede without damaging my

CICERO

Atqui non modo confiteor, summa in Laterense
ornamenta esse, sed te etiam reprehendo, quod
ea non enumeres, alia quaedam inania et levia
conquiras. Praeneste fecisse ludos. Quid ? alii
quaestores nonne fecerunt ? Cyrenis liberalem in
publicanos, iustum in socios fuisse. Quis negat ?
sed ita multa Romae geruntur, ut vix ea, quae fiunt
64 in provinciis, audiantur. Non vereor, ne mihi aliquid,
iudices, videar adrogare, si de quaestura mea dixero.
Quamvis enim illa floruerit, tamen eum me postea
fuisse in maximis imperiis arbitror, ut non ita mihi
multum gloriae sit ex quaesturae laude repetendum :
sed tamen non vereor, ne quis audeat dicere, ullius
in Sicilia quaesturam aut gratiorem aut clariorem
fuisse. Vere mehercule hoc dicam : sic tum existi-
mabam, nihil homines aliud Romae nisi de quaestura
mea loqui. Frumenti in summa caritate maximum
numerum miseram ; negotiatoribus comis, merca-
toribus iustus, municipibus liberalis, sociis abstinens,
omnibus eram visus in omni officio diligentissimus.
Excogitati quidam erant a Siculis honores in me
65 inauditi. Itaque hac spe decedebam, ut mihi
populum Romanum ultro omnia delaturum putarem.

---

a 25 miles east of Rome ; now Palestrina.
b See note on Chap. IX.
c Cicero was quaestor in Sicily in 75.

case. Yet not merely do I grant that the highest endowments are to be found in Laterensis, but I would even find fault with you for being at pains to gather instances of specious and trivial qualities, instead of enumerating the solid endowments he possesses. You say that he exhibited games at Praeneste.[a] What! have other quaestors never done so? You say that at Cyrene he was generous to the tax-farmers and just to the companies.[b] Who denies the fact? But in the bustle of life at Rome it is almost impossible to attend to what goes on in the provinces. I have no fear, gentlemen, of appearing to have too good a conceit of myself, if I say a word about my own quaestorship. My tenure of that office was successful enough, but I think that the achievements of my later tenure of the highest offices have led me to look for but a modest distinction from the credit I gained in the quaestorship; still, I am not afraid that anyone should venture to assert that any Sicilian quaestor has won greater renown or popularity.[c] At that time I can say with most assured confidence that I thought that my quaestorship was the sole topic of conversation at Rome. I had dispatched an enormous quantity of corn at a time of very high prices; the universal opinion was that I was civil to the financiers, just to the merchants, liberal to the corn-contractors, never enriching myself at the expense of the allies, and that I spared no pains in all my official duties; the Sicilians had contemplated the bestowal upon me of unparalleled honours; so I retired from the province filled with the notion that the Roman people would spontaneously lay all their distinctions at my feet. It happened that on

491

At ego, cum casu diebus iis, itineris faciendi causa,
decedens e provincia, Puteolos forte venissem, cum
plurimi et lautissimi solent esse in iis locis, concidi
paene, iudices, cum ex me quidam quaesisset
quo die Roma exissem et num quidnam esset novi.
Cui cum respondissem, me e provincia decedere :
" etiam mehercule," inquit, " ut opinor, ex Africa."
XXVII. Huic ego iam stomachans fastidiose, " immo
ex Sicilia," inquam. Tum quidam, quasi qui omnia
sciret : " Quid ? tu nescis," inquit, " hunc Syracusis
quaestorem fuisse ? " Quid multa ? destiti stoma-
chari, et me unum ex iis feci, qui ad aquas venissent.

66 Sed ea res, iudices, haud scio an plus mihi pro-
fuerit, quam si mihi tum essent omnes congratulati.
Nam posteaquam sensi populo Romano aures
hebetiores, oculos autem esse acres atque acutos,
destiti quid de me audituri essent homines cogitare ;
feci, ut postea quotidie me praesentem viderent ;
habitavi in oculis ; pressi forum ; neminem a con-
gressu meo, neque ianitor meus, neque somnus
absterruit. Ecquid ego dicam de occupatis meis
temporibus, cui fuerit ne otium quidem umquam
otiosum ? Nam quas tu commemoras, Cassi, legere
te solere orationes, quum otiosus sis : has ego scripsi
ludis et feriis, ne omnino umquam essem otiosus.
Etenim M. Catonis illud, quod in principio scripsit

---

[a] Cicero had been quaestor of the other administrative
district of Sicily which had its centre at Lilybaeum.
492

my way back from the province I had arrived at
Puteoli, intending to make the journey thence by
land, just at the season when the place was thronged
with fashionable people ; and I nearly swooned,
gentlemen, when someone asked me on what day
I had left Rome, and whether there was any news.
When I replied that I was on my way back from my
province, he said, " Why, of course, you come from
Africa, do you not ? " XXVII. " No," I answered,
somewhat coolly, for I was now in high dudgeon,
" from Sicily." Hereupon another of the party
interposed, with an omniscient air, " What ! don't
you know that our friend has been quaestor at
Syracuse ª ? " To cut my story short, I dropped the
dudgeon, and made myself just one of those who
had come for the waters.

66 This experience, gentlemen, I am inclined to
think was more valuable to me than if I had been
hailed with salvoes of applause ; for having once
realized that the ears of the Roman people were
somewhat obtuse, but their eyes keen and alert,
I ceased henceforth from considering what the
world was likely to hear about me ; from that day
I took care that I should be seen personally every
day. I lived in the public eye ; I frequented the
forum ; neither my door-keeper nor sleep prevented
anyone from having audience of me. Not even
when I had nothing to do did I do nothing, and how
do you think I fared when my time was fully
occupied ? Those speeches, Cassius, which you tell
us it is your custom to read in your hours of leisure,
I have spent festivals and holidays in writing, and
consequently absolute leisure was a thing I never
knew. I have always thought that a sublime and

Originum suarum, semper magnificum et praeclarum putavi, *clarorum virorum atque magnorum non minus otii quam negotii rationem exstare oportere.* Ita, si quam habeo laudem, quae quanta sit nescio, parta Romae est, quaesita in foro, meaque privata consilia publici quoque casus comprobaverunt, ut etiam summa res publica mihi domi fuerit gerenda, 67 et urbs in urbe servanda. Eadem igitur, Cassi, via munita Laterensi est, idem virtutis cursus ad gloriam ; hoc facilior fortasse, quod ego huc, a me ortus et per me nixus, adscendi : istius egregia virtus adiuvabitur commendatione maiorum.

Sed, ut redeam ad Plancium, numquam ex urbe afuit, nisi sorte, lege, necessitate. Non valuit rebus iisdem, quibus fortasse nonnulli. At valuit assiduitate, valuit observandis amicis, valuit liberalitate ; fuit in oculis ; petivit ; ea est usus ratione vitae, qua, minima invidia, novi homines plurimi sunt eosdem honores consecuti.

68   XXVIII. Nam quod ais, Cassi, non plus me Plancio debere quam bonis omnibus, quod iis aeque mea salus cara fuerit, ego me debere bonis omnibus

---

[a] The earliest *Latin* history of Rome, written by Cato the Censor (234–149).

[b] *i.e.* the statesman must rely, not on showy achievements in the provinces, but on the steady grind of work at home.

[c] When quaestor in Macedonia.

[d] When on war service as *tribunus militum.*

noble sentiment which Marcus Cato expresses in the opening passage of his *Origins*,[a] where he says that great and eminent men should attach as much importance to their hours of relaxation as to their hours of toil. In this way, any reputation I possess, and for all I know it is but small, has been won at Rome, and earned in the forum ; my private plans have been justified by public events, so that in my home I have had to direct even the vital issues of state policy, and in the city the city has had to be preserved.[b] The same road lies open to Laterensis, Cassius ; virtue shows him the same avenue to fame as she showed to myself ; but for him perhaps in one respect the path is easier. Self-started and self-supported, I have worked my way to my present position, but his shining virtues will be reinforced by the recommendation of illustrious ancestors.

But to return to Plancius. My client never left the city, save when his absence was enforced by the lot,[c] the law,[d] or the imperious calls of business ; he had not the same qualifications as others may have had ; but qualifications he nevertheless had, the qualifications of steady application, of attentive service to his friends, of a generous heart. He lived in the public view, he stood for office, and his life generally was guided by those principles which have enabled very many, like himself without antecedents, to rise untraduced, as far as may be, to the same honours to which he has attained.

XXVIII. For with regard to your assertion, Cassius, that I am under no deeper obligation to Plancius than to all good patriots, because they all had my safety equally at heart, I do admit that all

fateor. Sed etiam ii, quibus ego debeo, boni viri,
et cives, aediliciis comitiis aliquid se meo nomine
debere Plancio dicebant. Verum fac me multis
debere, et in iis Plancio : utrum igitur me conturbare
oportet, an ceteris, quum cuiusque dies venerit,
hoc nomen, quod urget, nunc, quum petitur, dis-
solvere ? Quamquam dissimilis est pecuniae debitio
et gratiae. Nam qui pecuniam dissolvit, statim non
habet id, quod reddidit, qui autem debet, aes retinet
alienum ; gratiam autem, et qui refert, habet :
et qui habet, in eo ipso, quod habet, refert. Neque
ego nunc Plancio desinam debere, si hoc solvero :
nec minus ei redderem voluntate ipsa, si hoc molestiae
69 non accidisset. Quaeris a me, Cassi, quid pro
fratre meo, qui mihi est carissimus, quid pro meis
liberis, quibus nihil potest mihi esse iucundius,
amplius quam quod pro Plancio facio facere possim,
nec vides istorum ipsorum caritate ad huius salutem
defendendam maxime stimulari me atque excitari.
Nam neque illis huius salute, a quo meam sciunt
esse defensam, quidquam est optatius, et ego ipse
numquam illos adspicio quin, cum per hunc me iis
conservatum esse meminerim, huius meritum in me
recorder.

---

a This passage is repeated almost word for word in *Ad
Quirites*, Chap. IX. end.

patriots have me in their debt; but those very
patriots and honest citizens, whose debtor I am,
affirmed that on my account they owed to Plancius
a debt which the election of the aediles enabled
them to discharge. Let us grant, then, that I am
in debt to many, and to Plancius among them;
ought I then to declare myself to be a bankrupt?
Ought I not rather to discharge to all the rest
their several debts as each falls due, and settle the
account that presses at once, when it is demanded?
And yet a pecuniary obligation is a very different
thing from a moral obligation.[a] He who discharges
a debt in money, ceases forthwith to possess that
which he has paid; while he who remains a debtor
keeps what does not belong to him. But in a moral
debt, when I pay I keep, and when I keep, I pay by
the very act of keeping. If I discharge this debt to
Plancius, I shall not thereby cease to be his debtor,
and I should be repaying my debt to him none the
less by my good wishes, if the present unfortunate
69 situation had not occurred. You ask me, Cassius,
what I could do for my brother, whom I love deeply,
or for my children, the sweetest things that life
holds for me, more than I am doing for Plancius,
and you show by your question that you fail to
realize that it is the affection I feel for them which
more than anything else stirs and impels me to
champion my client in his hour of peril. For not
only do they hold his safety dear above all things,
since they know that by him my own was guarded,
but I myself can never look upon them without
recalling the obligation I am under to him,
remembering, as I do, that it was his efforts that
preserved me for them.

497

Opimium damnatum esse commemoras, servatorem ipsum rei publicae ; Calidium adiungis, cuius lege Q. Metellus in civitatem sit restitutus ; reprehendis meas pro Plancio preces, quod nec Opimius suo nomine liberatus sit, nec Q. Metelli Calidius. XXIX. De Calidio tibi tantum respondeo, quod ipse vidi : Q. Metellum Pium, consulem, praetoriis comitiis, petente Q. Calidio, populo Romano supplicasse, cum quidem non dubitaret et consul et homo nobilissimus patronum esse illum suum et familiae
70 nobilissimae dicere. Quo loco quaero ex te, num id in iudicio Calidii putes, quod ego in Plancii facio, aut Metellum Pium, si Romae esse potuisset, aut patrem eius, si vixisset, non fuisse facturum. Nam Opimii quidem calamitas utinam ex hominum memoria posset evelli ! Vulnus illud rei publicae, dedecus huius imperii, turpitudo populi Romani, non iudicium putandum est. Quam enim illi iudices, si iudices et non parricidae patriae nominandi sunt, graviorem potuerunt rei publicae infligere securim, quam cum illum e civitate eiecerunt, qui praetor finitimo, consul domestico bello, rem publicam
71 liberarat ? At enim nimis ego magnum beneficium Plancii facio, et, ut ais, id verbis exaggero. Quasi vero me tuo arbitratu, et non meo, gratum esse

---

^a Consul 121, and leader of attack upon C. Gracchus. He was condemned to exile in 109 for having received bribes from Jugurtha.

^b Refused to swear obedience to Saturninus' agrarian law, and went into voluntary exile, 100. Calidius, his restorer, was *trib. plebis* in 99.

^c Son of Q. Metellus above, gained his surname from this incident.

498

You remind us that even that saviour of the state, Opimius,[a] was condemned; you mention Calidius, too, on whose motion it was that Quintus Metellus [b] was restored to civil rights; and you blame my intercession on behalf of Plancius, pointing out that his own credit did not secure acquittal for Opimius, nor that of Metellus for Calidius. XXIX. In the matter of Calidius I must confine myself in my reply to incidents of which I was a witness; when Quintus Calidius was a candidate at the election of praetors, Quintus Metellus Pius,[c] who was then consul, interceded with the Roman people on his behalf, not hesitating, consul and great noble though he was, to assert that Calidius was the protector of himself and his noble family. And in this connexion I put it to you, do you think that Metellus Pius, if he could have been at Rome at the time, or his father, if he had been alive, would not have done for Calidius at his trial what I am doing for Plancius in his? As regards Opimius, would that his sad story could be erased from the memory of men! His fall must be looked upon as a death-blow to the state, a disgrace to our empire, a stain upon the name of the Roman people, rather than the verdict of a court of law. For what deadlier blow could those jurymen, if jurymen they are to be called, and not rather unnatural children of their fatherland, have inflicted upon the state, than to eject from his citizen rights the man who had liberated the state, as praetor, from war with a neighbouring people and, as consul, from civil war? You say that I exaggerate the great kindness which Plancius did me, and that I apply to it terms which it does not deserve; as though it behoved me to submit my gratitude to

oporteat. Quod istius tantum meritum, inquit? an quia te non iugulavit? immo vero, quia iugulari passus non est. Quo quidem tu loco, Cassi, etiam purgasti inimicos meos meaeque vitae nullas ab illis insidias fuisse dixisti. Posuit hoc idem Laterensis. Quamobrem de isto paullo post plura dicam : de te tantum requiro, utrum putes odium in me mediocre inimicorum fuisse? quod fuit ullorum umquam barbarorum tam immane ac tam crudele in hostem? an fuisse in iis aliquem aut famae metum, aut poenae, quorum vidisti toto illo anno ferrum in foro, flammam in delubris, vim in tota urbe versari? Nisi forte existimas, eos idcirco vitae meae pepercisse, quod de reditu meo nihil timerent. Et quemquam putas fuisse tam excordem, qui, vivis his, stante urbe et curia, rediturum me, si viverem, non putaret? Quamobrem non debes is homo et is civis praedicare vitam meam, quae fidelitate amicorum conservata sit, inimicorum molestia non esse appetitam.

72   XXX. Respondebo tibi nunc, Laterensis, minus fortasse vehementer, quam abs te sum provocatus : sed profecto nec considerate minus, nec minus amice. Nam primum illud fuit asperius, me, quae

---

ᵃ 58, when Piso and Gabinius were consuls and Clodius *trib. plebis.*

your discretion rather than my own. " What is the great service he has done you ? " asks my opponent. " Was it that he did not strangle you ? " No, I reply, it was that he did not suffer me to be strangled. Incidentally, Cassius, you even whitewashed my enemies, and denied that they laid any plot against my life. Laterensis also positively asserted as much. I will deal with your partner at greater length later. All I ask of you now is this. Can you think that the hatred my enemies bore me was an ordinary hatred ? Why, what barbarians have ever displayed such inhumanity and ruthlessness to their declared foes ? Or can you think that fear of disgrace or retribution had any weight with men whose weapons, as you saw, were paraded throughout that year *a* in the forum, whose flames licked our temples, and whose lawlessness stalked abroad through the city ? Unless, indeed, you would have us believe that the reason why those men spared my life was because they had no apprehensions that I should ever return. Was there any man, think you, so undiscerning as to think that while these gentlemen who occupy the bench still lived, and while the city and the senate-house still stood, I should not return, if there was life yet in me ? There was not ; and a person of your understanding as a man and a citizen has no business to declare that my life, which was preserved by the loyalty of my friends, was not the object of the mischievous endeavours of my foes.

72   XXX. I now proceed to reply to you, Laterensis, using less vehemence, perhaps, than you prompt me to use, but in a spirit, I dare avow, of no less consideration and friendship. It was, in the first place, somewhat unkind of you to suggest that my remarks

de Plancio dicerem, mentiri, et temporis causa
fingere. Scilicet homo sapiens excogitavi, quamobrem viderer maximis beneficii vinculis obstrictus,
cum liber essem et solutus. Quid enim ? mihi
ad defendendum Plancium parum multae, parum
iustae necessitudines erant familiaritatis, vicinitatis,
patris amicitiae ? quae si non essent, vererer,
credo, ne turpiter facerem, si hoc splendore et
hac dignitate hominem defenderem. Fingenda fuit
mihi videlicet causa peracuta, ut ei, quem mihi
debere oporteret, ego me omnia debere dicerem.
At id etiam gregarii milites faciunt inviti, ut coronam
dent civicam et se ab aliquo servatos esse fateantur :
non quo turpe sit protectum in acie ex hostium
manibus eripi (nam id accidere nisi forti viro et
pugnanti cominus non potest), sed onus beneficii
reformidant, quod permagnum est alieno debere
73 idem quod parenti. Ego, cum ceteri vera beneficia, etiam minora, dissimulent, ne obligati esse
videantur, eo me beneficio obstrictum esse ementior,
cui ne referri quidem gratia posse videatur ? An
hoc tu, Laterensis, ignoras ? qui, cum mihi esses
amicissimus, cum vel periculum vitae tuae mecum
sociare voluisses, cum me in illo tristi et acerbo
luctu atque discessu non lacrimis solum tuis, sed

---

a So called, because bestowed by one citizen upon
another, in return for the saving of his life in battle.
502

about Plancius were falsehoods and inventions of
opportunism. Your idea was that, from motives of
policy, I devised reasons for appearing to be bound
to my client by ties of the deepest obligation, whereas
I was in reality under no engagement whatever.
What ! Were the claims arising from intimacy, from
neighbourhood, and from friendship with his father,
not many enough or not urgent enough to warrant
my undertaking Plancius' defence ? Without these
claims upon me, I should, I suppose, have reason to
fear that I might be guilty of reprehensible conduct
in defending so illustrious and so influential a man.
I was, forsooth, driven to invent a subtle motive
for alleging that I owed everything to the man
who might naturally be expected to be in
debt to me. But even common soldiers show reluctance in making, by their bestowal of the civic
crown,[a] an admission that they owe their life to some
one ; not that it is humiliating to have been shielded
in the battle and rescued from the enemy's hands,
for this can only happen to a brave man who fights
in the thick of the foe, but they shrink from the
overpowering burden of being under the same
obligation to a stranger that they owe to a parent.
73 The world in general is anxious to disclaim real
obligations, even when they are trifling, because
they would not seem to be beholden to anyone ;
and is it likely that I am feigning myself to be
bound by an obligation which seems quite impossible of repayment ? Are you blind to this truth,
Laterensis ? When you were on terms of close
friendship with me, when you were ready even to
risk your life at my side, when in the bitter heart-
rending hour of my departure you had put, not

animo, corpore, copiis prosecutus esses, cum
meos liberos et uxorem me absente tuis opibus
auxilioque defendisses, sic mecum semper egisti,
te mihi remittere atque concedere, ut omne studium
meum in Cn. Plancii honorem consumerem, quod
eius in me meritum tibi etiam ipsi gratum esse
74 dicebas. Nihil autem me novi, nihil temporis causa
dicere, nonne etiam illa testis est oratio, quae est
a me prima habita in senatu? in qua cum perpaucis
nominatim egissem gratias, quod omnes enumerari
nullo modo possent, scelus autem esset quemquam
praeteriri, statuissemque eos solum nominare, qui
causae nostrae duces et quasi signiferi fuissent,
in his Plancio gratias egi. Recitetur oratio, quae
propter rei magnitudinem dicta de scripto est, in
qua ego homo astutus ei me dedebam, cui nihil
magnopere deberem, et huius tanti officii servitutem
adstringebam testimonio sempiterno. Nolo cetera,
quae a me mandata sunt litteris, recitare : praeter-
mitto, ne aut proferre videar ad tempus, aut eo
genere uti litterarum, quod meis studiis aptius quam
consuetudini iudiciorum esse videatur.

---

^a *In senatu*, Chap. XIV.
^b *e.g.* the poem " De consulatu," for which see *Ad fam.*
i. 9. 23, and Juv. x. 120-126.

merely your tears, but your powers, mental, bodily, and material, at my service, when you had protected my wife and children in my absence with your succour and your substance, in all your dealings with me you gave me to believe that you readily granted me full permission to devote all my efforts to promoting Plancius' advancement, because, as you alleged, you yourself viewed with gratitude his
74 services to me. And as a proof that I do but say what I have always said, and have not changed my tune to suit the time, have you not the speech[a] which I delivered before the senate immediately upon my return ? In that speech I alluded gratefully, though only cursorily, to a small selection of my benefactors, for it would have been impossible to mention every one, though it would have been criminal to make any omissions, and I had determined to name those only who had been leaders and standard-bearers in my cause. Among those whom I thanked on that occasion was Plancius. Let this speech be read to the court, for, in view of the importance of the occasion, it was delivered from manuscript. In it I, like the artful fellow you would have me to be, declared my devotion to one to whom I was in no particular debt, and so cemented by an undying testimony the fetters of obligation which his signal service had laid upon me. I forbear to read to you my other literary compositions[b] bearing upon my subject; I waive them, lest, in bringing them to your notice, I should lay myself open to the charge of opportunism, or of reliance upon a type of literature, which may seem to accord better with my own pursuits than with the conventional usage of these courts.

75 XXXI. Atque etiam clamitas, Laterensis : " Quousque ista dicis ? nihil in Cispio profecisti, obsoletae iam sunt preces tuae.'' De Cispio mihi igitur obiicies, quem ego de me bene meritum quia te teste cognoveram, te eodem auctore defendi ? et ei dices, " quousque," quem negas, quod pro Cispio contenderim, impetrare potuisse ? Nam istius verbi, " quousque,'' haec poterat esse invidia : datus est tibi ille ; condonatus ille ; non facis finem ; ferre non possumus. Ei quidem, qui pro uno laborarit, et ipsum id non obtinuerit, dici " quousque " irridentis magis est quam reprehendentis. Nisi forte ego unus ita me gessi in iudiciis, ita et cum his et inter hos vixi, is in causis patronus, is in re publica civis et sum et semper fui, solus ut a te constituar, qui nihil a iudicibus debeam umquam impetrare. Et **76** mihi lacrimulam Cispiani iudicii obiectas. Sic enim dixisti : " Vidi ego tuam lacrimulam.'' Vide, quam me verbi tui poeniteat. Non modo lacrimulam, sed multas lacrimas, et fletum cum singultu videre potuisti. An ego, qui meorum lacrimis me absente commotus simultates, quas mecum habebat, de-

---

^a *Trib. plebis* 57, when he supported Cicero, who later defended him on a charge of corrupt practices.
^b Note that the Latin is the contemptuous dim. *lacrimula*.

75 XXXI. Again, you hurl at me, Laterensis, this question : " For how much longer are you going to talk in this strain ? Your reference to Cispius *a* brought you no advantage ; your style of appeal is out of date." What ! will you cast my defence of Cispius in my teeth, when it was your information that brought his services to me to my notice, and at your instigation also that I championed his cause ? And, in view of the part I played, will you ask me " for how much longer "—me, whose efforts on Cispius' behalf you now say were fruitless ? The malignity of your question " for how much longer " may be brought out in plain speech as follows : " For your sake one culprit has been surrendered, another pardoned ; you are incorrigible ; we cannot stand it." That the question " for how much longer " should be put to one who, after toiling hard for one particular client, has then failed to win the object of his toil, savours rather of ridicule than of rebuke ; or is it that you would have us believe that the peculiar nature of my behaviour in the courts, of my daily life and social dealings with these gentlemen, and of my conduct as a civil advocate, warrant that you should pick me out for your special designation as one who deserved never to

76 obtain from a jury what he asks ? You reproach me with the " one poor tear " *b* I shed at the trial of Cispius. " I marked your one poor tear," say you. Mark now how short of the truth your expression seems to me to fall ; you could have seen on that occasion not merely " one poor tear," but floods of them, sighs and weeping commingled. What ! would you have me exhibit no symptoms of grief when danger threatened one who had been so

posuisset meaeque salutis non modo non oppugnator
(ut inimici mei putarant) sed etiam defensor fuisset,
huius in periculo non dolorem meum significarem ?
77 Tu autem, Laterensis, qui tum lacrimas meas gratas
esse dicebas, nunc easdem vis invidiosas videri.

XXXII. Negas tribunatum Plancii quidquam at-
tulisse adiumenti dignitati meae. Atque hoc loco
(quod verissime facere potes) L. Racilii, fortissimi
et constantissimi viri, divina in me merita commemoras. Cui quidem ego, sicut Cn. Plancio, numquam dissimulavi me plurimum debere, semper que
prae me feram. Nullas enim sibi ille neque contentiones neque inimicitias neque vitae dimicationes
nec pro re publica nec pro me defugiendas putavit.
Atque utinam, quam ego sum in illum gratus, tam
licuisset per hominum vim et iniuriam populo
Romano ei gratiam referre ! Sed si non eadem
contendit in tribunatu Plancius, existimare debes
non huic voluntatem defuisse, sed me, quum tantum
iam Plancio deberem, Racilii beneficiis fuisse con-
78 tentum. An vero putas iudices idcirco minus
mea causa facturos, quod me esse gratum crimineris ?
An, quum Patres conscripti illo senatusconsulto,
quod in monumento Marii factum est, quo mea salus
omnibus est gentibus commendata, uni Cn. Plancio

<a> *Trib. plebis* with Cispius above.
<b> The temple of " Honour and Virtue."

affected by the tears of my dear ones, when I myself was far away, that he had waived his old differences with me, and, so far from standing forth, as my enemies had anticipated, as the assailant of my well-77 being, had actually become its champion ? And you, Laterensis, who then expressed yourself as touched by my tears, now turn round and try to cast infamy upon them.

XXXII. You say that when Plancius was tribune he contributed nothing to the strength of my position, and in this connexion you urge, and are most justified in urging, the superhuman services conferred upon me by the gallant and resolute Lucius Racilius.[a] I have never concealed my deep sense of obligation to Racilius, as well as to Plancius, and I shall never cease to proclaim it ; for he always held it to be his duty to shirk no struggles or enmities or personal perils in the service of the state and of myself. Would that the Roman people had not been prevented by the lawless violence of the times from expressing to him a gratitude commensurate with my own ! You must impute the fact that Plancius did not perhaps go to the same lengths in his tribunate, not to any deficiency of goodwill on his part, but to the fact that, being already under such great obligations to Plancius, I was amply satisfied 78 with the services of Racilius. Or do you think that the jury will be less inclined to sympathize with me because of that gratitude which you make into a charge against me ? The conscript fathers, in that decree which they passed in the temple which is the memorial to Marius,[b] and in which the cause of my restoration was recommended to the whole world, expressed their thanks to Plancius alone, for he alone

gratias egerint (unus enim fuit de magistratibus
defensor salutis meae), cui senatus pro me gratias
agendas putavit, ei ego a me referendam gratiam
non putem ? Atqui haec cum vides, quo me
tandem in te animo putas esse, Laterensis ? ullum
esse tantum periculum, tantum laborem, tantam
contentionem, quam ego non modo pro salute tua,
sed etiam pro dignitate defugerim ? Quo quidem
etiam magis sum, non dicam miser (nam hoc quidem
abhorret a virtute verbum), sed certe exercitus, non
quia multis debeo (leve enim est onus beneficii
gratia) sed quia saepe concurrunt propriae [1] ali-
quorum bene de me meritorum inter ipsos contentiones, ut eodem tempore in omnes verear ne
vix possim gratus videri.

79   Sed ego hoc meis ponderibus examinabo, non
solum quid cuique debeam, sed etiam quid cuiusque
intersit, et quid a me cuiusque tempus poscat.
XXXIII. Agitur studium tuum, vel etiam, si vis,
existimatio, laus aedilitatis : at Cn. Plancii salus,
patria, fortunae. Salvum tu me esse cupisti : hic
fecit etiam, ut esse possèm. Distineor tamen et
divellor dolore, et in causa dispari offendi te a
me, doleo : sed, medius fidius, multo citius meam
salutem pro te abiecero, quam Cn. Plancii salutem

---

[1] propriae *Keil* : propter MSS.

---

[a] It was a doctrine of the Stoics that the good man could
never be unhappy.

of the magistrates had espoused my cause ; and shall I not think it my duty to show my gratitude to him, whom the senate thought it their duty to thank on my behalf ? Bearing all this in mind, Laterensis, what feelings do you think I cherish towards you ? Do you think that there is any peril, any hardship, any struggle so great that I should shrink from meeting it, if I could so further, not your welfare only, but even your mere worldly position ? For this reason I am the more—not "unhappy"—for that is a word which is not found in the dictionary of the virtuous man *a*—but at any rate perplexed, not because I have many creditors, for the obligation which a kindness imposes is but a light burden, but because the several claims upon me of my various benefactors are often mutually conflicting, and the result, I fear, is that it is impossible for me to seem grateful, at one and the same time, to all.

79 I shall now, however, proceed to weigh in the scales of my own discretion not merely my obligation to each individual, but also the interests that each has at stake, and the demands which the emergency of each makes upon me. XXXIII. *Your* stake lies in the achievement of your ambitions, or, if you prefer to put it on a higher ground, your reputation, and the credit you gain by becoming aedile ; my client, on the other hand, stakes his citizenship, his country, and his fortunes. *Your* wish was for my safety ; *he* put into my hands the power of gaining that safety. But I am torn by a painful dilemma, and in such a disparity of interests it goes to my heart to offer you an affront ; but, upon my honour, I will far more readily sacrifice my existence as a citizen in your behalf, than surrender that of Plancius

80 tradidero contentioni tuae. Etenim, iudices, cum
omnibus virtutibus me affectum esse cupio, tum
nihil est, quod malim quam me et gratum esse
et videri. Haec est enim una virtus non solum
maxima, sed etiam mater virtutum omnium reli-
quarum. Quid est pietas nisi voluntas grata in
parentes? qui sunt boni cives, qui belli, qui domi
de patria bene merentes, nisi qui patriae beneficia
meminerunt? qui sancti, qui religionum colentes,
nisi qui meritam diis immortalibus gratiam iustis
honoribus et memori mente persolvunt? Quae
potest esse iucunditas vitae sublatis amicitiis?
quae porro amicitia potest esse inter ingratos?
81 Quis est nostrum liberaliter educatus, cui non
educatores, cui non magistri sui, atque doctores,
cui non locus ipse mutus ille, ubi altus aut doctus
est, cum grata recordatione in mente versetur?
Cuius opes tantae esse possunt aut umquam fuerunt
quae sine multorum amicorum officiis stare possint?
quae certe sublata memoria et gratia nulla exstare
possunt. Equidem nihil tam proprium hominis
existimo quam non modo beneficio, sed etiam
benevolentiae significatione alligari : nihil porro tam
inhumanum, tam immane, tam ferum quam committere ut beneficio non dicam indignus, sed victus
82 esse videare.[a] Quae cum ita sint, iam succumbam,
Laterensis, isti tuo crimini, meque in eo ipso, in

---

[a] "So that one does not so much as attempt to requite
it" (Holden).

80 to your claims. For indeed, gentlemen, while I would fain have some tincture of all the virtues, there is no quality I would sooner have, and be thought to have, than gratitude. For gratitude not merely stands alone at the head of all the virtues, but is even mother of all the rest. What is filial affection, if not a benevolent gratitude to one's parents? What is patriotism, what is service to one's country in war and peace, if it is not a recollection of benefits received from that country? What is piety and religion, save a due reverence and remembrance in paying to the immortal gods the thanks that we owe? Take friendship away, and what joy can life continue to hold? More, how can friendship exist at all between those who are devoid

81 of gratitude? Who is there of us that has received an enlightened upbringing who does not constantly ponder with grateful recollection upon those who had the care of him, upon his tutors and teachers, and even upon the inanimate scenes of his rearing and schooling? Who is there, who has there ever been, so rich in material wealth as to be indeper dent of the good offices of many friends? And assuredly these good offices themselves cannot exist independently of memory and gratitude. For my part, I consider no faculty to be so essentially human as the power of recognizing the obligation not merely of a kindly act, but even of anything which betrays a kindly thought; and there is nothing which so violates our humanity, or so much lowers us to the level of the brute beasts, as to allow ourselves to give the impression of being, I will not say unworthy of,

82 but overcome by, a favour.[a] Since this is so, Laterensis, I will at once capitulate to your charge

quo nihil potest esse nimium, quoniam ita tu vis,
nimium gratum esse concedam : petamque a vobis,
iudices, ut eum beneficio complectamini, quem qui
reprehendit, in eo reprehendit, quod gratum praeter
modum dicat esse. Neque enim illud ad negligen-
dam meam gratiam debet valere, quod dixit idem,
vos nec nocentes nec litigiosos esse, quo minus me
apud vos valere oporteret. Quasi vero in amicitia
mea non haec praesidia (si quae forte sunt in me)
parata semper amicis esse maluerim quam necessaria.
Etenim ego de me tantum audeo dicere, amicitiam
meam voluptati pluribus, quam praesidio fuisse :
meque vehementer vitae meae poeniteret, si in mea
familiaritate locus esset nemini nisi litigioso aut
nocenti.

83   XXXIV. Sed hoc nescio quomodo frequenter
in me congessisti, saneque in eo creber fuisti, te
idcirco in ludos causam coniicere noluisse, ne ego,
mea consuetudine aliquid de tensis misericordiae
causa dicerem, quod in aliis aedilibus ante fecissem.
Nonnihil egisti hoc loco. Nam mihi eripuisti ornamentum orationis meae. Deridebor, si mentionem
tensarum fecero, cum tu id praedixeris. Sine

---

    a Lat. had urged that Cic. should have no influence with
the jury, because they would not be likely to need his help
as an advocate.

    b At the *Ludi Romani* the statues of gods were carried
in cars from the Forum to the Circus Maximus ; see *De har.
resp.* Chap. XI.

    c It would naturally be advantageous to an aedile that
his trial should coincide with games which he himself was
providing ; " Cic. here meets irony with irony " (Reid).

and, since you will have it so, plead guilty to excess in that wherein excess is impossible, and I will ask you, gentlemen, to bring within the scope of your kindness one whose critic only criticizes him because he has been inordinately grateful. For it ought to have no influence in inducing you to be indifferent to my gratitude, if that same critic says that *you* are neither criminals nor lovers of litigation, so that I ought not to have any influence with you.[a] As if, in the case of my friends, I would not prefer that such protection as I can afford—if I can afford any—should not rather be ready for their use than required by them. For indeed I venture to say this much about myself, that my friendship has been a source of pleasure in more cases than it has been a source of protection ; and I should indeed have cause to think my life ill spent if there were room in my intimacy for none save lovers of litigation and criminals.

XXXIV. But some inscrutable impulse has led you to ply me incessantly with this form of argument, and you have also harped persistently upon the statement that your motive in endeavouring to prevent this trial from synchronizing with the games was that I might not introduce some pathetic reference to the sacred cars,[b] as you said that I had done on previous occasions, when I was defending aediles.[c] On this occasion your efforts have certainly not been fruitless, for you have robbed me of what was to have been the leading embellishment of my speech. Now that you have predicted my use of the sacred cars, I shall have but to breathe a word of them to arouse a smile ; and, if I cannot mention the sacred cars, how shall I be able to make a speech

tensis autem quid potero dicere ? Hic etiam addidisti, me idcirco mea lege exsilio ambitum sanxisse, ut miserabiliores epilogos possem dicere. Non vobis videtur cum aliquo declamatore, non cum laboris

84 et fori discipulo disputare ? Rhodi enim, inquit, ego non fui. Me vult fuisse : sed fui, inquit (putabam in Vaccaeis dicturum) bis in Bithynia. Si locus habet reprehensionis ansam aliquam, nescio cur severiorem Nicaeam putes, quam Rhodum : si spectanda causa est, et tu in Bithynia summa cum dignitate fuisti, et ego Rhodi non minore. Nam, quod in eo me reprehendisti, quod nimium multos defenderim : utinam et tu, qui potes, et ceteri, qui defugiunt, vellent me labore hoc levare ! Sed fit vestra diligentia, qui causis ponderandis omnes fere repudiatis, ut ad nos pleraeque confluant, qui miseris

85 et laborantibus nihil negare possumus. Admonuisti etiam, quod in Creta fuisses, dictum aliquod in petitionem tuam dici potuisse : me id perdidisse. Uter igitur nostrum est cupidior dicti ? egone, qui, quod dici potuit, non dixerim : an tu, qui etiam ipse in te dixeris ? Te aiebas de tuis rebus gestis

---

a *Lex Tullia de ambitu*, 63.
b Where there was a celebrated school of oratory.
c A remote (and therefore unlettered) tribe in Spain.
d *i.e.* on military service.
e *Creta*, chalk, used for whitening garments, hence *cretatus* = *candidatus*.

at all ? You also asserted that my motive in attaching the penalty of exile to the offence of bribery in the terms of my law [a] was that in my perorations I might be able to make more harrowing appeals to pity. You would imagine, gentlemen, would you not, that his opponent was a professional ranter, instead of one who had undergone a laborious apprenticeship to the bar ? " For I," he says, " never went to Rhodes," [b] implying that I did. " But," he adds, " I have been "—I thought he was going to say " among the Vaccaei [c] "—" twice in Bithynia. [d] " If localities give any handle for censure, I cannot understand why you should think that Nicaea is a place of stricter morals than Rhodes ; if we are to consider our respective motives, the business that took me to Rhodes was just as highly respectable as the business that took you to Bithynia. And as regards the fault you find with me for being too fond of appearing as counsel for the defence, I should be only too glad if you who have the ability, and others who shirk the responsibility, would relieve me of this arduous task. It is the punctiliousness of men ·like you that is to blame ; you scrupulously weigh the merits of all the briefs submitted to you and reject nearly all, and the result is that most of them are crowded upon me, who have not the heart to say " no " to the unhappy victims of embarrassment. You reminded me also that the fact that you had been in Crete gave me an opportunity, which I let slip, of making a pun [e] upon your candidature. Which of us, pray, is the more alert for the pun ? I, who let slip the offered chance of punning, or you, who took it and turned it against yourself ? Again, you said

nullas litteras misisse, quod mihi meae, quas ad aliquem misissem, obfuissent. Quas ego mihi obfuisse non intelligo : rei publicae video prodesse potuisse.

86 XXXV. Sed sunt haec leviora : illa vero gravia atque magna, quod meum discessum, quem saepe defleras, nunc quasi reprehendere et subaccusare voluisti. Dixisti enim, non auxilium mihi, sed me auxilio defuisse. Ego vero fateor, me, quod viderim mihi auxilium non deesse, idcirco illi auxilio pepercisse. Qui enim status, quod discrimen, quae fuerit in re publica tempestas illa, quis nescit ? Tribunicius me terror, an consularis furor movit ? Decertare mihi ferro magnum fuit cum reliquiis eorum, quos ego florentes atque integros sine ferro viceram ? Consules post hominum memoriam teterrimi atque turpissimi, sicut et illa principia et hi recentes rerum exitus declararunt, quorum alter exercitum perdidit, alter vendidit, emptis provinciis a senatu, a re publica, a bonis omnibus defecerant : qui exercitu, qui armis, qui opibus plurimum poterant, cum quid sentirent nesciretur, furialis illa vox

    a The Scholiast says that this was a voluminous and arrogant letter sent by C. to Pompey in Asia, describing his achievements as consul. Pompey sent a cool reply, which mortified Cicero and afforded some merriment to his enemies. See *Pro Sulla*, § 64.
    b See Chap. XXIX. *n.*
    c Piso, in Macedonia.
    d Gabinius lent his troops to Ptolemy to win back his throne.
    e *i.e.* from Clodius, when they should have been allotted by the senate.
    f The triumvirs, Pompey, Caesar, Crassus.

that you had sent no dispatch dealing with your achievements, because the dispatch[a] which I sent to a certain person had done me more harm than good. I cannot see that the dispatch in question did me any harm, but I am well aware that it was calculated to do good to the state.

XXXV. But these are comparatively trivial points; I pass now to one of greater weight and moment, I mean the fact that although in the past you constantly expressed deep sympathy with me in my retirement, you now evince a desire to cast something like censure and aspersion upon me because of it. You have done this by alleging that it was not helpers who failed me, but I who failed my helpers. I, on my side, frankly admit that I made no use of proffered assistance, but it was because I saw that I did not need it. For who can be unaware of the critical and stormy nature of the period through which the state was at that time passing? Was it dread of the tribunes or the madness of the consuls which determined my course? Would it have been a difficult matter for me finally to crush with the sword the remnant of those whom without the sword I had conquered in the heyday of their unimpaired might? Of the consuls of that year,[b] the vilest and most degraded in human memory, as is proved not only by their earliest acts, but also by subsequent events of which we have been witnesses, one lost his army,[c] the other sold it,[d] and by purchasing their provinces[e] they had proved traitors to the senate, to the state, and to all good patriots. When nothing could be known concerning the public sentiments of those[f] whose possession of troops, arms, and money made them the chief forces in the state, there was

nefariis stupris, religiosis altaribus effeminata, secum et illos et consules facere acerbissime personabat. Egentes in locupletes, perditi in bonos, servi in 87 dominos armabantur. At erat mecum senatus, et quidem veste mutata, quod pro me uno post hominum memoriam publico consilio susceptum est. Sed recordare qui tum fuerint consulum nomine hostes, qui soli in hac urbe senatum senatui parere non siverint, edictoque suo non luctum patribus conscriptis, sed luctus indicia ademerint. At erat mecum cunctus equester ordo : quem quidem in contionibus saltator ille Catilinae consul proscriptionis denuntiatione terrebat. At tota Italia convenerat : cui quidem belli intestini et vastitatis metus inferebatur.

XXXVI. Hisce ego auxiliis studentibus atque incitatis uti me, Laterensis, potuisse confiteor ; sed erat non iure, non legibus, non disceptando decertandum ; nam profecto, praesertim tam bona in causa, numquam, quo ceteri saepe abundarunt, id mihi ipsi auxilium meum defuisset ; armis fuit, armis, inquam, fuit dimicandum ; quibus a servis atque a servorum ducibus caedem fieri senatus et bonorum

---

a Clodius, who took part in the mysteries of the Bona Dea.

b Gabinius, of whom Macrobius speaks as one of the most skilful dancers of his day.

one [a] who, having doffed his manhood in unhallowed debaucheries at hallowed altars, raised his infatuate voice to din into our ears the mortifying announcement that his designs were supported not only by them, but by the two consuls ; the poor were being armed against the rich, traitors against patriots, slaves against their masters. You say the senate was on my side. It was ; the senate in the garb of mourning, too, which had been officially assumed by it for no one save myself in the memory of man. But remember what enemies moved among us then in the guise of consuls, enemies who, alone in the city's history, would not permit the senate to obey the senate, and who by their edict forbade to the conscript fathers not merely the sentiment, but the very manifestation of grief. You say the whole equestrian order was on my side. Yes, but it was an order whom threats of proscription publicly uttered by Catiline's pet dancer,[b] the consul, were cowing into submission. All Italy, you say, was solid for me. Yes, but it was an Italy that shuddered at the prospect of civil war and its attendant desolation.

XXXVI. Of these helpers, Laterensis, so zealous and so enthusiastic, I admit that I might have availed myself. But the struggle was to be decided, not by equity, not by law, not by argument ; otherwise there is no doubt that, especially in so good a cause, my own resources, by which others have so often and so amply profited, would never have failed me. No ; arms and arms alone were to be the umpires, and it would have been calamitous to the commonwealth that they should have been used by slaves and the leaders of slaves for the

521

88 rei publicae exitiosum fuisset. Vinci autem improbos a bonis fateor fuisse praeclarum, si finem tum vincendi viderem : quem profecto non videbam. Ubi enim praesto fuissent mihi aut tam fortes consules, quam L. Opimius ? quam C. Marius ? quam L. Flaccus ? quibus ducibus improbos cives res publica vicit armatis : aut, si minus fortes, attamen tam iusti, quam P. Mucius, qui arma, quae privatus P. Scipio sumpserat, ea, Ti. Graccho interempto, iure optimo sumpta esse defendit ? Esset igitur pugnandum cum consulibus. Nihil amplius dico, nisi illud, victoriae nostrae graves adversarios paratos, interitus 89 nullos ultores esse videbam. Hisce ego auxiliis salutis meae si idcirco defui, quia nolui dimicare, fatebor, id quod vis, non mihi auxilium, sed me auxilio defuisse. Sin autem, quo maiora studia in me bonorum fuerunt, hoc iis magis consulendum et parcendum putavi, tu id in me reprehendis, quod Q. Metello laudi datum est, hodieque est, et semper erit maximae gloriae ? quem, ut potes ex multis audire, qui tum affuerunt, constat invitissimis viris bonis cessisse, nec fuisse dubium quin contentione et armis superior posset esse. Ergo ille

---

a Consul 100, helped to quell Saturninus.

b P. Mucius Scaevola, the great jurist, consul in 133, when Tib. Gracchus was slain.

c Numidicus, one of C.'s stock parallels to his own case. He retired from the city (100) when Saturninus and Glaucia brought in their legislation, to which all senators were required to swear allegiance.

522

88 massacre of the senate and good patriots. I grant
you that it would have been a grand thing
for traitors to be conquered by patriots, if only I
could have made an end of conquest there; but of
this I saw no prospect. For where could I have
found at hand to help me consuls as brave as Lucius
Opimius, Gaius Marius, or Lucius Flaccus,[a] under
whose armed leadership the republic quelled her
traitorous citizens, or, if brave men were lacking,
consuls so upright as Publius Mucius,[b] who proved
that Publius Scipio, though a private citizen, was
amply justified in his resort to arms by his destruction of Tiberius Gracchus? We should have had,
then, to contend with the consuls. I will say but
one thing more on this matter: I realized that, if
we won, formidable adversaries would be set in
array against us; but that, if we fell, there would
89 be none to avenge us. If I say that my motive in
refusing to avail myself of the help of those who
were ready to strike for my safety was a reluctance to
fight, I shall make the confession you desire, that it
was not my helpers who failed me, but I my helpers.
But if I say that the more earnest good patriots
showed themselves in my cause, the more careful
of their interests and sparing of their efforts I thought
it my duty to be, can you impute blame to me for
that which in the case of Quintus Metellus[c] has been
counted to his credit, and to-day is, and ever will be,
the fairest jewel in his reputation? It is a generally
known fact, the truth of which you can ascertain
from many eyewitnesses, that his retirement was
attended by the deep regrets of men of sound views,
and yet that he could indubitably have prevailed
had he resorted to the arbitrament of arms. He

cum suum, non cum senatus factum defenderet,
cum perseverantiam sententiae suae, non salutem
rei publicae retinuisset, tamen ob illam causam
quod illud voluntarium vulnus accepit, iustissimos
omnium Metellorum et clarissimos triumphos gloria
et laude superavit, quod et illos ipsos improbissimos
cives interfici noluit, et ne quis bonus interiret in
eadem caede providit : ego tantis periculis pro-
positis cum, si victus essem, interitus rei publicae,
si vicissem, infinita dimicatio pararetur, committerem
ut idem perditor rei publicae nominarer, qui servator
fuissem ?

90 XXXVII. Mortem me timuisse dicis. Ego vero
ne immortalitatem quidem contra rem publicam
accipiendam putarem, nedum emori cum pernicie
rei publicae vellem. Nam, qui pro re publica vitam
ediderunt (licet me desipere dicatis), numquam
mehercule eos mortem potius, quam immortalitatem
assecutos putavi. Ego vero, si tum illorum impiorum
ferro ac manu concidissem, in perpetuum res publica
civile praesidium salutis suae perdidisset. Quin
etiam, si me vis aliqua morbi, aut natura ipsa con-
sumpsisset, tamen auxilia posteritatis essent im-
minuta, quod peremptum esset mea morte id
exemplum, qualis futurus in me restituendo fuisset
senatus populusque Romanus. An si umquam in
me vitae cupiditas fuisset, ego mense Decembri mei

was acting in defence of his own conduct, not that
of the senate; it was the tenor of his own convictions, not the welfare of the state, that he had
refused to abandon; and yet merely for the reason
that the blow he sustained was one that he might
have avoided, the fame and renown of his triumph
has outshone that of the most eminent men who
have borne his name, inasmuch as he not only
opposed the execution of those villainous traitors,
but also took measures to prevent that any good
patriot should be involved in the doom they suffered;
and, in face of such grave peril, and the prospect of
the downfall of the state should I fail, and an
endless series of struggles should I prevail, was I,
who had once been the saviour of the republic, now
to gain for myself the name of its destroyer?

XXXVII. You say that I was afraid of death.
But the truth is, that I could not look upon even
immortality as desirable, if it was to be achieved at
my country's cost; far less could I choose to die, and
carry my country with me to perdition. For I have
always thought—call me a fool if you will—that those
who have sacrificed their lives for the state have not
died so much as achieved immortality. In my own
case, had I fallen by the armed violence of those
enemies of their country, the country would have
lost for ever the guardian of her civil well-being;
nay more, even had the assaults of disease or the
processes of nature carried me off, the welfare of
posterity would even then have been impaired, inasmuch as by my death the world would have been
deprived of the spectacle of the efforts of the senate
and the Roman people for my restoration. Had I
ever been in love with my life, should I, in the

525

consulatus omnium parricidarum tela commossem?
quae, si viginti quiessem dies, in aliorum vigiliam
consulum recidissent. Quamobrem, si vitae cupiditas
contra rem publicam est turpis, certe multo mortis
cupiditas mea turpior fuisset cum pernicie civitatis.

91   Nam quod te in re publica liberum esse gloriatus
es, id ego et fateor et laetor et tibi etiam in hoc
gratulor : quod me autem negasti, in eo neque te
neque quemquam diutius patiar errare. XXXVIII.
Nam, si quis idcirco aliquid de libertate mea deminu-
tum putat, quod non ab omnibus eisdem, a quibus
antea solitus sum dissentire, dissentiam, primum,
si bene de me meritis gratum me praebeo, non
debeo [1] incurrere in crimen hominis nimium memoris,
nimiumque grati ? sin autem sine ullo rei publicae
detrimento respicio etiam aliquando salutem tum
meam, tum meorum, certe non modo non sum
reprehendendus, sed etiam, si ruere vellem, boni
92 viri me, ut id ne facerem, rogarent. Res vero ipsa
publica, si loqui posset, ageret mecum, ut, quoniam
sibi servissem semper, numquam mihi, fructus
autem ex sese non, ut oportuisset, laetos et uberes,

---

[1] *So Lambinus for* desino *of* MSS.

---

a 63; the reference is, of course, to the conspiracy of
Catiline.
b An allusion to C.'s "recantation" of opposition to the
triumvirate of Caesar, Pompey, and Crassus after the
conference at Luca in 56.

December of the year of my consulship,[a] have roused into activity the weapons of all who had forsworn their country ? Had I remained quiet for twenty days, it would have fallen to other consuls to keep guard against them. If, then, it is disgraceful to cling to life against the interests of the state, much more would it have been disgraceful for me to seek death, when by so doing I should have wrought the ruin of the community.

You have boasted of the perfect freedom of action which you enjoy in politics ; I am delighted to grant you your boast, and would even go so far as to congratulate you on your possession of it ; but when you deny the possession of it to me, I can no longer allow either you or anyone else to remain under a delusion in the matter. XXXVIII. For if anyone thinks that my liberty of action has been curtailed because I am no longer at variance with all those with whom I was once at variance, I would remind him in the first place that if I display gratitude for benefits received, I ought not therefore to incur the charge of having too retentive a memory or cherishing an excessive gratitude.[b] But if on occasions my consideration for the safety of myself and those who belong to me involves no harm to the state, I am sure that, so far from being blameworthy for entertaining those considerations, men of sound views would ask me to desist, if they saw me inclined to run upon destruction. Nay, the state herself, could she speak, would plead with me thus : " Since," she would say, " you have always served me, and never yourself, and since the wage you have won from that service has been, not joy and wealth, as it should

527

sed magna acerbitate permixtos tulissem, ut iam
mihi servirem, consulerem meis : se non modo satis
habere a me, sed etiam vereri, ne parum mihi pro
93 eo, quantum a me haberet, reddidisset. Quid, si
horum ego nihil cogito, et idem sum in re publica,
qui fui semper ? tamenne libertatem requires meam ?
quam tu ponis in eo, si semper cum iis, quibuscum
aliquando contendimus, depugnemus. Quod est
longe secus. Stare enim omnes debemus tamquam
in orbe aliquo rei publicae, qui quoniam versatur,
eam deligere partem, ad quam nos illius utilitas
salusque converterit.

XXXIX. Ego autem Cn. Pompeium, non dico
auctorem, ducem, defensorem salutis meae (nam
haec privatim fortasse officiorum memoriam quaerunt,
et gratiam, sed dico hoc, quod ad salutem rei publicae
pertinet), ego eum non tuear, quem omnes in re
publica principem esse concedunt ? ego C. Caesaris
laudibus desim, quas primum populi Romani, nunc
etiam senatus, cui me semper addixi, plurimis
atque amplissimis iudiciis videam esse celebratas ?
Tum hercule me confitear non iudicium aliquod
habuisse de rei publicae utilitate, sed hominibus
94 amicum aut inimicum fuisse. An, cum videam

---

[a] e.g. by lex Vatinia (59) C. was given government of
Gaul for five years.

[b] And in 57 the senate, on motion of Cic., decreed him
a public thanksgiving.

have been, but a cup of bitter grief, serve yourself now for once, and think of your dear ones ; my
fear is, not that your services to me have been
insufficient, but rather that the return I have made
to you has been scanty and out of all measure with
the extent of your service." Furthermore, if none
of these considerations moves me, and if my politics
are the same as they have always been, will you
even then affirm that I enjoy no liberty of action ?—
a liberty which you assume to consist in the maintenance of a relentless hostility towards those with
whom one has been once at variance. But this is
very far from the truth ; for we should look upon
political life as a wheel, and since that wheel is
always turning, we should make choice of that
party to which we are directed by the interest and
well-being of the state.

XXXIX. But with regard to my relations with
Pompeius—whom I will not describe as the author,
promoter, and champion of my restoration, for these
are personal terms, and imply a grateful remembrance
of benefits received ; I prefer to describe him in
respect of his relation to the welfare of the state at
large,—would you have me pay no regard to one who
is universally admitted to be the chief man in the
state ? Would you have me fail in due appreciation
of the merits of Gaius Caesar, seeing, as I do, that
those merits have received repeated recognition in
the form of laudatory resolutions of the Roman
people,[a] in the first instance, and latterly of the
senate also,[b] whose adherent I have always been ?
Were I to fail in this, I should certainly admit thereby
that my standard was not the public interest, but
rather my own personal predilections and dislikes.

navem secundis ventis cursum tenentem suum, si
non eum petat portum, quem ego aliquando probavi,
sed alium non minus tutum atque tranquillum, cum
tempestate pugnem periculose potius quam illi
salute praesertim proposita obtemperem et paream ?
Ego vero haec didici, haec vidi, haec scripta legi ;
haec de sapientissimis et clarissimis vitis et in hac
re publica et in aliis civitatibus monumenta nobis et
literae prodiderunt, non semper easdem sententias
ab iisdem, sed, quascumque rei publicae status,
inclinatio temporum, ratio concordiae postularet,
esse defensas. Quod ego et facio, Laterensis, et
semper faciam, libertatemque, quam tu in me
requiris, quam ego neque dimisi umquam, neque
dimittam, non in pertinacia, sed in quadam modera-
tione positam putabo.

95   XL. Nunc venio ad illud extremum, quod dixisti,
dum Plancii in me meritum verbis extollerem,
me arcum[1] facere ex cloaca, lapidemque e sepulchro
venerari pro deo. Neque enim mihi insidiarum
periculum ullum, neque mortis fuisse. Cuius ego
temporis rationem explicabo brevi neque invitus.
Nihil enim ex meis est temporibus, quod minus
pervagatum, quodque minus aut mea commemoratione celebratum sit, aut hominibus auditum atque

---

[1] arcum *emended by Cobet for* arcem *of* MSS.

---

[a] Proverb = " to make a mountain of a mole-hill " ; the
MSS. have *arcem*, " fortress."

530

94 Or, supposing that I am a passenger on a ship wafted on its course before a favouring breeze, and supposing that, instead of making for the harbour which I at some time or other may have chosen, she bears for another just as safe and calm as that, shall I fight with the elements to my own hazard, or shall I not rather yield myself submissively to their leading, especially when they point the way to safety? All my knowledge, all my experience, all my reading, all the testimony that the records of literature give us concerning men of wisdom and eminence in this and in other states, goes to prove, not that men have held the same unvarying convictions till their death, but rather that they have adapted them to political circumstances, to the tendency of the times, and to considerations of public tranquillity. This is, and this will continue to be, Laterensis, my principle of action, and I shall always believe that that liberty of action, which you fail to find in me, but upon which I have never lost my hold, nor ever will, consists, not in an immovable tenacity of opinion, but in a sweet reasonableness.

95 XL. I come now to the closing passage in your speech, wherein you said that, by bestowing fulsome phrases upon Plancius' services to myself, I was making a triumphal arch out of a sewer,[a] and giving divine honours to a piece of sepulchral masonry; for, as you allege, I had no reason to apprehend either conspiracy or murder. I shall now proceed to give a brief outline of the course of events in question, and I shall do so without reluctance; for there is no aspect of that critical period of my life which has had less publicity accorded to it, to which I have made less reference, and which is less a subject of

notum. Ego enim, Laterensis, ex illo incendio
legum, iuris, senatus, bonorum omnium cedens,
cum mea domus ardore suo deflagrationem urbi
atque Italiae toti minaretur, nisi quievissem,
Siciliam petivi animo, quae et ipsa erat mihi, sicut
domus una coniuncta et obtinebatur a C. Vergilio,
quocum me uno vel maxime quum vetustas tum
amicitia, cum mei fratris collegia tum rei publicae
96 causa sociarat. Vide nunc caliginem temporum
illorum. Cum ipsa paene insula mihi sese obviam
ferre vellet, praetor ille, eiusdem tribuni plebis
contionibus propter eamdem rei publicae causam
saepe vexatus, nihil amplius dico nisi me in
Siciliam venire noluit. Quid dicam ? C. Vergilio,
tali civi et viro, benevolentiam in me, memoriam
communium temporum, pietatem, humanitatem,
fidem defuisse ? Nihil, iudices, est eorum : sed,
quam tempestatem nos vobiscum non tulissemus,
metuit, ut eam ipse posset opibus suis sustinere. Tum
consilio repente mutato a Vibone Brundisium terra
petere contendi ; nam maritimos cursus prae-
97 cludebat hiemis magnitudo. XLI. Cum omnia illa
municipia, quae sunt a Vibone Brundisium, in fide

---

popular rumour or knowledge. When,[a] Laterensis, I turned from the holocaust wherein law, equity, senate, and all who loved their country were consumed, and left the scene of action, and when the blazing ruins of my home threatened to involve in their flames the city and the whole of Italy, unless I submitted tamely, my thoughts turned to Sicily, which, besides the fact that from old associations it was a second home to me, was then governed by Gaius Vergilius, with whom I had peculiarly close connexions, not only from our ancient and intimate friendship, but also because he had been my brother's colleague, and because we shared the same political 96 views. Judge now of the gloom that enwrapt us in those days ; just when the island itself seemed to be stretching out its arms in welcome to me, my friend the praetor, who, from his adherence to the same political tenets as myself, had so often been assailed by the harangues of the same tribune of the plebs, refused (I state the fact without further comment) to permit me to set foot in Sicily. What construction am I to put upon this ? Am I to think that a citizen and a gentleman like Gaius Vergilius was deficient in kindly feeling towards myself, in a recollection of our association in those critical times, in a sense of duty, humanity, and honour ? Far from it, gentlemen, but he doubted his ability to hold out, alone and unaided, against the storm which I had failed to weather with you at my side. Then, forced suddenly to change my plans, I started on the overland journey to Brundisium ; for the severity of the weather put a sea-voyage out of the question. 97 XLI. All the corporate towns lying between Vibo[b] and Brundisium, gentlemen, were loyal to my cause,

mea, iudices, essent, iter mihi tutum multis
minitantibus magno cum suo metu praestiterunt.
Brundisium veni, vel potius ad moenia accessi.
Urbem unam mihi amicissimam declinavi, quae se
vel potius exscindi quam e suo complexu ut eriperer
facile pateretur. In hortos me M. Laenii Flacci
contuli, cui cum omnis metus, publicatio bonorum,
exsilium, mors proponeretur, haec perpeti, si
acciderent, maluit quam custodiam mei capitis
dimittere. Huius ego et parentis eius, prudentissimi
atque optimi senis, et fratris et utriusque filiorum
manibus in navi tuta ac fideli collocatus eorumque
preces et vota de meo reditu exaudiens Dyrrhachium,
98 quod erat in fide mea, petere contendi. Quo cum
venissem, cognovi, id quod audieram, refertam esse
Graeciam sceleratissimorum hominum ac nefariorum,
quorum impium ferrum ignesque pestiferos meus ille
consulatus e manibus extorserat : qui antequam
de meo adventu audire potuissent, cum tamen
abessent aliquot dierum viam, in Macedoniam ad
Planciumque perrexi. Hic vero simul atque me
mare transisse cognovit (audi, audi, atque attende,
Laterensis, ut scias, quid ego Plancio debeam,
confitearreque aliquando me, quod faciam, et grate
et pie facere : huic quae pro salute mea fecerit, si
minus profutura sint, obesse certe non oportere).
Nam, simulac me Dyrrhachium attigisse audivit,

---

and, in spite of many threats from without and great fears from within, they guaranteed the security of my passage. I came to Brundisium, or rather approached the walls ; it was deeply attached to me, but I turned aside from it, though it declared that it would rather be razed to the ground than acquiesce in my being torn from its embrace. I made my way to the gardens of Laenius Flaccus, who, though denounced with every kind of threat, with the confiscation of his property, with exile, and with death, said that he would endure all these, if they should come upon him, rather than forgo the office of protecting my person. He, with his aged father, the wisest and the best of men, with his brother and both his sons, personally set me on board a safe and trustworthy vessel, and, with the murmur of their prayers and vows for my return in my ears, I made for Dyrrhachium,[a] because I had reason to hope for 98 protection there. Having arrived, I ascertained, what had already been rumoured, that Greece teemed with vile and impious criminals, from whose hands I, in that year when I was consul, had wrested their traitorous swords and incendiary torches ; although they were several days' journey distant, I set out at once to join Plancius in Macedonia, not allowing them time to learn of my arrival. He, as soon as he learnt that I had made the passage (hear me, Laterensis, hear and mark what I say, that you may know what I owe to Plancius, and may at length confess that what I am doing I do from a grateful and a dutiful heart, and that what he did for my protection, though it may not help, should assuredly at least not harm him),—as I was saying, as soon as he heard that I had touched at Dyrrhachium, he

statim ad me lictoribus dimissis, insignibus abiectis,
90 veste mutata profectus est. O acerbam mihi, iudices,
memoriam temporis illius et loci, cum hic in me
incidit, cum complexus est conspersitque lacrimis
nec loqui prae maerore potuit! o rem tum auditu
crudelem tum visu nefariam! o reliquos omnes dies
noctesque eas, quibus iste a me non recedens
Thessalonicam me in quaestoriumque perduxit!
Hic ego nunc de praetore Macedoniae nihil dicam
amplius, nisi eum et civem optimum semper et
mihi amicum fuisse, sed eadem timuisse quae
ceteros. Cn. Plancium fuisse unum, non qui minus
timeret, sed, si acciderent ea, quae timerentur,
100 mecum ea subire et perpeti vellet. Qui, cum ad
me L. Tubero, meus necessarius, qui fratri meo
legatus fuisset, decedens ex Asia venisset easque
insidias, quas mihi paratas ab exsulibus coniuratis
audierat, animo amicissimo detulisset, in Asiam
me ire propter eius provinciae mecum et cum meo
fratre necessitudinem comparantem non est passus:
vi me, vi, inquam, Plancius et complexu suo retinuit,
multosque menses a capite meo non discessit abiecta
quaestoria persona, comitisque sumpta.

101   XLII. O excubias tuas, Cn. Planci, miseras!
o flebiles vigilias! o noctes acerbas! o custodiam
etiam mei capitis infelicem! si quidem ego tibi

---

a Q. Cicero was propraetor in Asia 61.

immediately dismissed his lictors, discarded his official
insignia, doffed his official robes, and set out to meet
99 me. How bitter to me, gentlemen, is the memory
of that time and that place, when he fell upon my
neck, embraced me, bedewed me with his tears, and
was dumb for very grief! It is a pitiful story, but
the reality was heart-breaking. Figure to yourselves all the days and nights that followed, when
my client, never letting me out of his sight, saw me
safely to Thessalonica, where he lodged me in the
quaestor's official residence. I shall not allude here
to the praetor of Macedonia, save to remark that he
had always been an unimpeachable patriot, and on
good terms with myself, but the universal fears were
also his; Gnaeus Plancius alone, though he feared
no less than did the rest, was ready to face at my
side and endure to the bitter end the realization of
100 those fears. When my friend Lucius Tubero, who
had been legate to my brother, visited us on his
return from Asia, and reported to me in a spirit of
true friendliness the plots which he heard had been
laid against my life by exiled conspirators, I was just
preparing to cross into Asia, whither I had been
prompted to go by the close intimacy that bound
that province to my brother[a] and myself; but
Plancius would not suffer me to go. Yes, it was by
the sheer physical restraint of his embrace that he
kept me back, and for many months afterwards, doffing
the character of a quaestor and assuming that of a
comrade, he accompanied me wherever I went.

101 XLII. O the misery of your lonely watches,
Plancius! O the dreariness and the torment of
those sleepless nights! My death might perchance
have stood you in good stead, and now, what pitiful

vivus non prosum, qui fortasse mortuus profuissem.
Memini enim, memini, neque umquam obliviscar
noctis illius, cum tibi vigilanti, assidenti, maerenti,
vana quaedam miser atque inania falsa spe inductus
pollicebar ; me, si essem in patriam restitutus,
praesentem tibi gratiam relaturum ; sin aut vitam
mihi fors ademisset, aut vis aliqua maior reditum
peremisset, hos, hos (quos enim ego tum alios
animo intuebar ?) omnia tibi illorum laborum praemia
pro me persoluturos. Quid me adspectas ? quid mea
promissa repetis ? quid meam fidem imploras ?
Nihil tibi ego tum de meis opibus pollicebar, sed de
horum erga me benevolentia promittebam ; hos
pro me lugere, hos gemere, hos decertare pro meo
capite vel vitae periculo velle videbam ; de horum
desiderio, luctu, querelis quotidie aliquid tecum
simul audiebam ; nunc timeo ne nihil tibi praeter
lacrimas queam reddere, quas tu in meis acerbi-
102 tatibus plurimas effudisti. Quid enim possum aliud,
nisi maerere ? nisi flere ? nisi te cum salute mea
complecti ? Salutem tibi iidem dare possunt, qui
mihi reddiderunt. Te tamen—exsurge, quaeso—
retinebo et complectar : nec me solum deprecatorem
fortunarum tuarum, sed comitem sociumque pro-
fitebor : atque (ut spero) nemo erit tam crudeli animo

irony is it that the life you so vigilantly preserved should be helpless to aid you! Never, never, while I live, shall I forget that night! You took no rest; you never left my side; and all I could do in return for your sympathetic grief was to make you a few promises, promises that were false and fantastic as my own miserable fool's paradise. I swore that if ever I should be restored to my country, my gratitude should be deputed to none for expression; but, should fate deprive me of life, or any force beyond my control make my return impossible, I engaged that these gentlemen—for who else at that time had any place in my thoughts?—should repay you to the full for your efforts in my behalf. Why do you gaze upon me so? Why do you appeal to me to be true to my word, and to fulfil my promises? I had no warrant for the promises I then made to you; I did but draw upon the credit of the good feelings of these gentlemen towards me. Their tears, their sighs were for me, as I knew; they were ready to fight to the bitter end for my life, even at the peril of their own. When I was with you, not a day passed but word came of their yearning, their sorrow, their indignation; and now my heart misgives me that the tears you shed so plentifully for me in my dark hours are all I have where-

102 with to pay your account. For what can I do save weep and lament, and link my fortunes with your own? Only those who gave life back to me can give life to you. Come what may,—stand up, I beg, that all may look on you,—my arms shall hold you to me, and I shall avow myself to be not merely the interceder for your fortunes, but your partner and your comrade; and none, I trust, will be so

tamque inhumano nec tam immemor non dicam
meorum in bonos meritorum, sed bonorum in me,
qui a me mei servatorem capitis divellat ac distrahat.
Non ego meis ornatum beneficiis a vobis deprecor,
iudices, sed custodem salutis meae ; non opibus
contendo, non auctoritate, non gratia ; sed precibus,
sed lacrimis, sed misericordia : mecumque vos simul
hic miserrimus et optimus obtestatur parens et
103 pro uno filio duo patres deprecamur. Nolite,
iudices, per vos, per fortunas, per liberos vestros,
inimicis meis, iis praesertim, quos ego pro vestra
salute suscepi, dare laetitiam gloriantibus vos iam
oblitos mei salutis eius, a quo mea salus conservata
est, hostes exstitisse. Nolite animum meum debilitare tum luctu tum etiam metu commutatae vestrae
voluntatis erga me : sinite me, quod vobis fretus
104 huic saepe promisi, id a vobis ei persolvere. Teque,
C. Flave, oro et obtestor, qui meorum consiliorum in
consulatu socius, periculorum particeps, rerum, quas
gessi, adiutor fuisti, meque non modo salvum semper,
sed etiam ornatum florentemque esse voluisti, ut
mihi per hos conserves eum, per quem me tibi et
his conservatum vides. Plura ne dicam, tuae me
etiam lacrimae impediunt vestraeque, iudices, non

heartless or so insensible, so forgetful. I will not
say of my services to the patriotic party, but of their
services to me, as to tear from my side the saviour
of my person, and bid me live henceforth without
him. I cry your mercy for him, gentlemen, not as for
one whom my services have advanced, but as for
one who has watched over my welfare ; the ground
of my appeal is not wealth, not prestige, not social
influence, but prayers, tears, and your own compassionate hearts. With my own adjuration is
united that of his excellent but unhappy parent ;
yes, two fathers appeal to you for a single son. I
103 conjure you by your fortunes and by your children,
gentlemen, do not vouchsafe to my foes, those above
all whose hostility I incurred by my championship of
you, the triumph of being able to boast that, so soon
forgetful of my claims upon you, you are the declared enemies of the life of him to whom I owe the
preservation of my own. Forbear to shatter my
spirit not with grief alone, but with the apprehension
that your goodwill has been alienated from me ;
and permit me to discharge by a draft upon you those
repeated promises to my client which my reliance
upon you induced me to make to him. And I do
104 most earnestly, Gaius Flavus, beg and implore you,
who were associated with my policy when I was
consul, who have shared my dangers and furthered my
achievements, and who have ever been solicitous
not merely for my personal safety, but for my
honour and success, to do me the favour of using
this jury as an instrument in saving one by whose
instrumentality I, as you well know, was saved to
serve you and them. I am prevented from adding
more by your tears, and by yours, gentlemen,

solum meae : quibus ego magno in metu meo subito inducor in spem, vos eosdem in hoc conservando futuros, qui fueritis in me, quoniam istis vestris lacrimis de illis recordor, quas pro me saepe et multum profudistis.

besides my own—tears which, in the midst of my
grave apprehensions, awake in me a sudden hope
that you will exhibit the same qualities in the rescue
of my client from ignominy as you exhibited towards
myself in a similar situation ; for those tears which
you are shedding now recall to my mind those
which so often and so copiously you have outpoured
for me

INDEX OF PROPER NAMES

(The references throughout are to the chapters)

544

INDEX OF PROPER NAMES

545

INDEX OF PROPER NAMES

INDEX OF PROPER NAMES

INDEX OF PROPER NAMES

INDEX OF PROPER NAMES

550

INDEX OF PROPER NAMES

Printed in Great Britain by R. & R. Clark, Limited, *Edinburgh*

THE LOEB CLASSICAL LIBRARY

VOLUMES ALREADY PUBLISHED

LATIN AUTHORS

THE LOEB CLASSICAL LIBRARY

THE LOEB CLASSICAL LIBRARY

NEMESIANUS, AVIANUS, with "Aetna," "Phoenix" and other poems. J. Wight Duff and Arnold M. Duff.

OVID : THE ART OF LOVE AND OTHER POEMS. J. H. Mozley. Revised by G. P. Goold.

OVID : FASTI. Sir James G. Frazer. [by G. P. Goold.

OVID : HEROIDES AND AMORES. Grant Showerman. Revised

OVID : METAMORPHOSES. F. J. Miller. 2 Vols. Vol. I revised by G. P. Goold.

OVID : TRISTIA AND EX PONTO. A. L. Wheeler.

PETRONIUS. M. Heseltine ; SENECA : APOCOLOCYNTOSIS. W. H. D. Rouse. Revised by E. H. Warmington.

PHAEDRUS AND BABRIUS (Greek). B. E. Perry.

PLAUTUS. Paul Nixon. 5 Vols.

PLINY : LETTERS, PANEGYRICUS. B. Radice. 2 Vols.

PLINY : NATURAL HISTORY. 10 Vols. Vols. I-V. H. Rackham. Vols. VI-VIII. W. H. S. Jones. Vol. IX. H. Rackham. Vol. X. D. E. Eichholz.

PROPERTIUS. H. E. Butler.

PRUDENTIUS. H. J. Thomson. 2 Vols.

QUINTILIAN. H. E. Butler. 4 Vols.

REMAINS OF OLD LATIN. E. H. Warmington. 4 Vols. Vol. I (Ennius and Caecilius). Vol. II (Livius, Naevius, Pacuvius, Accius). Vol. III (Lucilius, Laws of the XII Tables). Vol. IV (Archaic Inscriptions).

SALLUST. J. C. Rolfe.

SCRIPTORES HISTORIAE AUGUSTAE. D. Magie. 3 Vols.

SENECA : APOCOLOCYNTOSIS. Cf. PETRONIUS.

SENECA : EPISTULAE MORALES. R. M. Gummere. 3 Vols.

SENECA : MORAL ESSAYS. J. W. Basore. 3 Vols.

SENECA : NATURALES QUAESTIONES. T. H. Corcoran. 2 Vols.

SENECA : TRAGEDIES. F. J. Miller. 2 Vols.

SENECA THE ELDER. M. Winterbottom. 2 Vols.

SIDONIUS : POEMS AND LETTERS. W. B. Anderson. 2 Vols.

SILIUS ITALICUS. J. D. Duff. 2 Vols.

STATIUS. J. H. Mozley. 2 Vols.

SUETONIUS. J. C. Rolfe. 2 Vols.

TACITUS : AGRICOLA AND GERMANIA. M. Hutton ; DIALOGUS. Sir Wm. Peterson. Revised by R. M. Ogilvie, E. H. Warmington, M. Winterbottom.

TACITUS : HISTORIES AND ANNALS. C. H. Moore and J. Jackson. 4 Vols.

TERENCE. John Sargeaunt. 2 Vols.

TERTULLIAN : APOLOGIA AND DE SPECTACULIS. T. R. Glover ; MINUCIUS FELIX. G. H. Rendall.

VALERIUS FLACCUS. J. H. Mozley.

THE LOEB CLASSICAL LIBRARY

Varro : De Lingua Latina. R. G. Kent. 2 Vols.
Velleius Paterculus and Res Gestae Divi Augusti.
F. W. Shipley.
Virgil. H. R. Fairclough. 2 Vols.
Vitruvius : De Architectura. F. Granger. 2 Vols.

GREEK AUTHORS

Achilles Tatius. S. Gaselee.
Aelian : On the Nature of Animals. A. F. Scholfield.
3 Vols.
Aeneas Tacticus, Asclepiodotus and Onasander. The
Illinois Greek Club.
Aeschines. C. D. Adams.
Aeschylus. H. Weir Smyth. 2 Vols.
Alciphron, Aelian and Philostratus : Letters. A. R.
Benner and F. H. Fobes.
Apollodorus. Sir James G. Frazer. 2 Vols.
Apollonius Rhodius. R. C. Seaton.
The Apostolic Fathers. Kirsopp Lake. 2 Vols.
Appian : Roman History. Horace White. 4 Vols.
Aratus. Cf. Callimachus : Hymns and Epigrams.
Aristides. C. A. Behr. 4 Vols. Vol. I.
Aristophanes. Benjamin Bickley Rogers. 3 Vols. Verse
trans.
Aristotle : Art of Rhetoric. J. H. Freese.
Aristotle : Athenian Constitution, Eudemian Ethics.
Virtues and Vices. H. Rackham.
Aristotle : The Categories. On Interpretation. H. P.
Cooke ; Prior Analytics. H. Tredennick.
Aristotle : Generation of Animals. A. L. Peck.
Aristotle : Historia Animalium. A. L. Peck. 3 Vols.
Vols. I and II.
Aristotle : Metaphysics. H. Tredennick. 2 Vols.
Aristotle : Meteorologica. H. D. P. Lee.
Aristotle : Minor Works. W. S. Hett. " On Colours,"
" On Things Heard," " Physiognomics," " On Plants,"
" On Marvellous Things Heard," " Mechanical Prob-
lems," " On Invisible Lines," " Situations and Names of
Winds," " On Melissus, Xenophanes, and Gorgias."
Aristotle : Nicomachean Ethics. H. Rackham.
Aristotle : Oeconomica and Magna Moralia. G. C.
Armstrong. (With Metaphysics, Vol. II.)
Aristotle : On the Heavens. W. K. C. Guthrie.

4

THE LOEB CLASSICAL LIBRARY

ARISTOTLE: ON THE SOUL, PARVA NATURALIA, ON BREATH.
W. S. Hett.

ARISTOTLE: PARTS OF ANIMALS. A. L. Peck: MOVEMENT
AND PROGRESSION OF ANIMALS. E. S. Forster.

ARISTOTLE: PHYSICS. Rev. P. Wicksteed and F. M. Corn-
ford. 2 Vols.

ARISTOTLE: POETICS; LONGINUS ON THE SUBLIME. W. Ham-
ilton Fyfe; DEMETRIUS ON STYLE. W. Rhys Roberts.

ARISTOTLE: POLITICS. H. Rackham.

ARISTOTLE: POSTERIOR ANALYTICS. H. Tredennick; TOPICS.
E. S. Forster.

ARISTOTLE: PROBLEMS. W. S. Hett. 2 Vols.

ARISTOTLE: RHETORICA AD ALEXANDRUM. H. Rackham.
(With PROBLEMS, Vol. II.)

ARISTOTLE: SOPHISTICAL REFUTATIONS. COMING-TO-BE AND
PASSING-AWAY. E. S. Forster; ON THE COSMOS. D. J.
Furley.

ARRIAN: HISTORY OF ALEXANDER AND INDICA. 2 Vols.
Vol. I. P. Brunt. Vol. II. Rev. E. Iliffe Robson.

ATHENAEUS: DEIPNOSOPHISTAE. C. B. Gulick. 7 Vols.

BABRIUS AND PHAEDRUS (Latin). B. E. Perry.

ST. BASIL: LETTERS. R. J. Deferrari. 4 Vols.

CALLIMACHUS: FRAGMENTS. C. A. Trypanis; MUSAEUS:
HERO AND LEANDER. T. Gelzer and C. Whitman.

CALLIMACHUS: HYMNS AND EPIGRAMS, AND LYCOPHRON.
A. W. Mair; ARATUS. G. R. Mair.

CLEMENT OF ALEXANDRIA. Rev. G. W. Butterworth.

COLLUTHUS. Cf. OPPIAN.

DAPHNIS AND CHLOE. Cf. LONGUS.

DEMOSTHENES I: OLYNTHIACS, PHILIPPICS AND MINOR
ORATIONS: I-XVII AND XX. J. H. Vince.

DEMOSTHENES II: DE CORONA AND DE FALSA LEGATIONE.
C. A. and J. H. Vince.

DEMOSTHENES III: MEIDIAS, ANDROTION, ARISTOCRATES,
TIMOCRATES, ARISTOGEITON. J. H. Vince.

DEMOSTHENES IV-VI: PRIVATE ORATIONS AND IN NEAERAM.
A. T. Murray.

DEMOSTHENES VII: FUNERAL SPEECH, EROTIC ESSAY, EX-
ORDIA AND LETTERS. N. W. and N. J. DeWitt.

DIO CASSIUS: ROMAN HISTORY. E. Cary. 9 Vols.

DIO CHRYSOSTOM. 5 Vols. Vols. I and II. J. W. Cohoon.
Vol. III. J. W. Cohoon and H. Lamar Crosby. Vols IV
and V. H. Lamar Crosby.

DIODORUS SICULUS. 12 Vols. Vols. I-VI. C. H. Oldfather.
Vol. VII. C. L. Sherman. Vol. VIII. C. B. Welles. Vols.

5

IX and X. Russel M. Geer. Vols. XI and XII. F. R. Walton. General Index. Russel M. Geer.

DIOGENES LAERTIUS. R. D. Hicks. 2 Vols. New Introduction by H. S. Long.

DIONYSIUS OF HALICARNASSUS : CRITICAL ESSAYS. S. Usher. 2 Vols.

DIONYSIUS OF HALICARNASSUS : ROMAN ANTIQUITIES. Spelman's translation revised by E. Cary. 7 Vols.

EPICTETUS. W. A. Oldfather. 2 Vols.

EURIPIDES. A. S. Way. 4 Vols. Verse trans.

EUSEBIUS : ECCLESIASTICAL HISTORY. Kirsopp Lake and J. E. L. Oulton. 2 Vols.

GALEN : ON THE NATURAL FACULTIES. A. J. Brock.

THE GREEK ANTHOLOGY. W. R. Paton. 5 Vols.

THE GREEK BUCOLIC POETS (THEOCRITUS, BION, MOSCHUS). J. M. Edmonds.

GREEK ELEGY AND IAMBUS WITH THE ANACREONTEA. J. M. Edmonds. 2 Vols.

GREEK MATHEMATICAL WORKS. Ivor Thomas. 2 Vols.

HERODES. Cf. THEOPHRASTUS : CHARACTERS.

HERODIAN. C. R. Whittaker. 2 Vols.

HERODOTUS. A. D. Godley. 4 Vols.

HESIOD AND THE HOMERIC HYMNS. H. G. Evelyn White.

HIPPOCRATES AND THE FRAGMENTS OF HERACLEITUS. W. H. S. Jones and E. T. Withington. 4 Vols.

HOMER : ILIAD. A. T. Murray. 2 Vols.

HOMER : ODYSSEY. A. T. Murray. 2 Vols.

ISAEUS. E. S. Forster.

ISOCRATES. George Norlin and LaRue Van Hook. 3 Vols.

[ST. JOHN DAMASCENE]: BARLAAM AND IOASAPH. Rev. G. R. Woodward, Harold Mattingly and D. M. Lang.

JOSEPHUS. 9 Vols. Vols. I-IV. H. St. J. Thackeray. Vol. V. H. St. J. Thackeray and Ralph Marcus. Vols. VI and VII. Ralph Marcus. Vol. VIII. Ralph Marcus and Allen Wikgren. Vol. IX. L. H. Feldman.

JULIAN. Wilmer Cave Wright. 3 Vols.

LIBANIUS : SELECTED WORKS. A. F. Norman. 3 Vols. Vols. I and II.

LONGUS : DAPHNIS AND CHLOE. Thornley's translation revised by J. M. Edmonds ; and PARTHENIUS. S. Gaselee.

LUCIAN. 8 Vols. Vols. I-V. A. M. Harmon. Vol. VI. K. Kilburn. Vols. VII and VIII. M. D. Macleod.

LYCOPHRON. Cf. CALLIMACHUS : HYMNS AND EPIGRAMS.

LYRA GRAECA. J. M. Edmonds. 3 Vols.

LYSIAS. W. R. M. Lamb.

THE LOEB CLASSICAL LIBRARY

Manetho. W. G. Waddell; Ptolemy: Tetrabiblos. F. E. Robbins.

Marcus Aurelius. C. R. Haines.

Menander I. New edition by W. G. Arnott.

Minor Attic Orators. 2 Vols. K. J. Maidment and J. O. Burtt.

Musaeus: Hero and Leander. *Cf.* Callimachus: Fragments.

Nonnos: Dionysiaca. W. H. D. Rouse. 3 Vols.

Oppian, Colluthus, Tryphiodorus. A. W. Mair.

Papyri. Non-Literary Selections. A. S. Hunt and C. C. Edgar. 2 Vols. Literary Selections (Poetry). D. L. Page.

Parthenius. *Cf.* Longus.

Pausanias: Description of Greece. W. H. S. Jones. 4 Vols. and Companion Vol. arranged by R. E. Wycherley.

Philo. 10 Vols. Vols. I-V. F. H. Colson and Rev. G. H. Whitaker. Vols. VI-X. F. H. Colson. General Index. Rev. J. W. Earp.

Two Supplementary Vols. Translation only from an Armenian Text. Ralph Marcus.

Philostratus: The Life of Apollonius of Tyana. F. C. Conybeare. 2 Vols.

Philostratus: Imagines; Callistratus: Descriptions. A. Fairbanks.

Philostratus and Eunapius: Lives of the Sophists. Wilmer Cave Wright.

Pindar. Sir J. E. Sandys.

Plato: Charmides, Alcibiades, Hipparchus, The Lovers, Theages, Minos and Epinomis. W. R. M. Lamb.

Plato: Cratylus, Parmenides, Greater Hippias, Lesser Hippias. H. N. Fowler.

Plato: Euthyphro, Apology, Crito, Phaedo, Phaedrus. H. N. Fowler.

Plato: Laches, Protagoras, Meno, Euthydemus. W. R. M. Lamb.

Plato: Laws. Rev. R. G. Bury. 2 Vols.

Plato: Lysis, Symposium, Gorgias. W. R. M. Lamb.

Plato: Republic. Paul Shorey. 2 Vols.

Plato: Statesman, Philebus. H. N. Fowler; Ion. W. R. M. Lamb.

Plato: Theaetetus and Sophist. H. N. Fowler.

Plato: Timaeus, Critias, Clitopho, Menexenus, Epistulae. Rev. R. G. Bury.

Plotinus. A. H. Armstrong. 6 Vols. Vols. I-III.

THE LOEB CLASSICAL LIBRARY

DESCRIPTIVE PROSPECTUS ON APPLICATION

CAMBRIDGE, MASS.	LONDON
HARVARD UNIV. PRESS	WILLIAM HEINEMANN LTD